Life without Parole

DATE DUE

D1291107

THE CHARLES HAMILTON HOUSTON INSTITUTE
SERIES ON RACE AND JUSTICE

The Charles Hamilton Houston Institute for Race and Justice at Harvard Law School seeks to further the vision of racial justice and equality through research, policy analysis, litigation, and scholarship, and will place a special emphasis on the issues of voting rights, the future of affirmative action, the criminal justice system, and related areas.

Life without Parole

America's New Death Penalty?

Edited by
Charles J. Ogletree, Jr., and Austin Sarat

NEW YORK UNIVERSITY PRESS
New York and London

NEW YORK UNIVERSITY PRESS
New York and London
www.nyupress.org

References to Internet websites (URLs) were accurate at the time of writing.
Neither the author nor New York University Press is responsible for URLs that
may have expired or changed since the manuscript was prepared.

Library of Congress Cataloging-in-Publication Data
Life without parole : America›s new death penalty? / [edited by] Charles J. Ogletree, Jr.,
Austin Sarat.
    p. cm.
Includes bibliographical references and index.
ISBN 978-0-8147-6247-9 (hardback)
ISBN 978-0-8147-6248-6 (pb)
ISBN 978-0-8147-6249-3 (ebook)
1. Parole — United States. 2. Life imprisonment — United States.
3. Capital punishment — United States. I. Ogletree, Charles J. II. Sarat, Austin.
KF9750.L54   2012
364.6'5 — dc23   2012005678

New York University Press books are printed on acid-free paper,
and their binding materials are chosen for strength and durability.
We strive to use environmentally responsible suppliers and materials
to the greatest extent possible in publishing our books.

Manufactured in the United States of America

c 10 9 8 7 6 5 4 3 2 1
p 10 9 8 7 6 5 4 3 2 1

Contents

Acknowledgments

The work contained in this book was first presented at a conference at Amherst College on December 3–4, 2010. We are grateful to our contributors for their fine work and commitment to our project and to Matthew Brewster and Heather Richard for their skilled research assistance. The December 2010 conference initiated an annual series of meetings jointly sponsored by Amherst College's Charles Hamilton Houston Forum on Law and Social Justice and Harvard Law School's Charles Hamilton Houston Institute for Race and Justice. We are grateful for the opportunity to honor Houston for his singular contributions to America's continuing quest for justice and equality.

Introduction

Lives on the Line: From Capital Punishment to Life without Parole

—————— CHARLES J. OGLETREE, JR., AND AUSTIN SARAT ——————

Death, in its finality, differs more from life imprisonment than a 100-year prison term differs from one of only a year or two.

> —Justice Stewart, *Woodson v. North Carolina*

Life without parole is a very strange sentence when you think about it. The punishment seems either too much or too little. If a sadistic or extraordinarily cold, callous killer deserves to die, then why not kill him? But if we are going to keep the killer alive when we could otherwise execute him, why strip him of all hope?

> —Robert Blecker, quoted in Adam Liptak, "Serving Life with No Chance of Redemption," *New York Times*, October 5, 2005

Writing in October 2005, *New York Times* reporter Adam Liptak observed that "in just the last 30 years, the United States has created something never before seen in its history and unheard of around the globe: a booming population of prisoners whose only way out of prison is likely to be inside a coffin. . . . Driven by tougher laws and political pressure on governors and parole boards, thousands of lifers are going into prisons each year, and in many states only a few are ever coming out, even in cases where judges and prosecutors did not intend to put them away forever."[1] In fact, in every decade over the last third of the 20th century, at least eight states joined the list of those authorizing sentences of life without parole (LWOP) as part of their criminal code (see figure I.1).

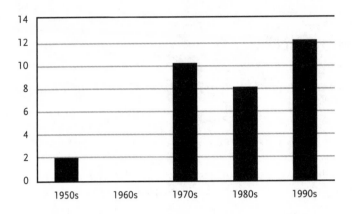

Fig. I.1. State enactment of LWOP statutes in the United States over time. *Source*: Steven Mulroy, "Avoiding 'Death by Default': Does the Constitution Require a 'Life without Parole' Alternative to the Death Penalty?," 79 *Tulane Law Review* (2005): 45on. 32.

As a result of these legislative changes, LWOP sentences increased exponentially.[2] Between 1992 and 2008, the LWOP population in the United States increased 230%,[3] so that today more prisoners are serving life terms than ever before (see figure I.2).[4]

Yet life sentences in general, and LWOP in particular, are by no means new to the American experience. LWOP has been a feature of American penal practice for almost a century. Some of its earliest uses are found in habitual criminal statutes, today known as "three-strike laws." For example, Ohio's 1929 habitual criminal statute provided that those sentenced "serve a term of his or her natural life."[5] Such statutes have been a significant source of the recent growth in the LWOP population. Thus, "Alabama's habitual offender statute caused the 'life without possibility of parole' population to increase by an average of 277 persons per year between 1981 and 1986."[6] Table I.1 summarizes current three-strike laws, the felonies they include, and the number of people sentenced to LWOP under them. Only states with three-strike laws that mandate LWOP are represented.

In addition to LWOP's early, and continuing, association with habitual criminal statutes, it has, since the middle of the 20th century, been used regularly as a sentence in murder cases.[7] Indeed one of the most conspicuous factors in the growth of LWOP as a sentence in those cases has been an alliance of death penalty abolitionists and conservative, tough-on-crime politicians. For abolitionists, life without parole, as James Liebman notes,

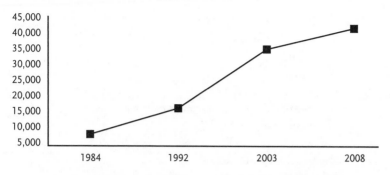

Fig. I.2. Growth in LWOP population in the United States, 1984–2008. *Sources*: Figures from 1984: Donald Macdonald and Leonard Morgenbersser, "Life without Parole Statutes in the United States," NYS Department of Correctional Services, Division of Program Planning, Research, and Evaluation, 1984; figures from 1992: Kathleen McGuire and Ann L. Pastore, eds., *Sourcebook of Criminal Justice Statistics 1992*, Bureau of Justice Statistics, 1993; figures from 2003: Marc Mauer, Ryan S. King, and Malcolm C. Young, "The Meaning of 'Life': Long Prison Sentences in Context," Sentencing Project, May 2004; figures from 2008: Ashley Nellis and Ryan King, "No Exit: The Expanding Use of Life Sentences in America," Sentencing Project, 2009.

"has been absolutely crucial to whatever progress has been made against the death penalty. The drop in death sentences [from 320 in 1996 to 125 in 2004] would not have happened without LWOP."[8] Or, as Liptak writes, the growth of LWOP "is in some ways an artifact of the death penalty. Opponents of capital punishment have promoted life sentences as an alternative to execution. And as the nation's enthusiasm for the death penalty wanes amid restrictive Supreme Court rulings and a spate of death row exonerations, more states are turning to life sentences."[9]

For some advocates of LWOP, it is a milder alternative to the unique harshness of capital punishment. As one oft-repeated phrase puts it, "death is different." For death penalty abolitionists, the availability of LWOP as an alternative sanction for serious crimes can be a powerful tool in arguing against morally fraught state killing. A recent poll found that 70% of Californians are in favor of the death penalty.[10] Offered LWOP as an alternative, however, only 41% favored the death penalty for first-degree murder.[11] Strong majoritarian support for capital punishment, this seems to suggest, can be undermined effectively by upholding LWOP as a viable alternative.

For strict retributivists, on the other hand, precisely because "death is different," capital punishment is the sole appropriate response to certain crimes, such as murder.[12] However, while justice sometimes requires death, it also

TABLE I.1

State Three-Strike Laws Requiring Mandatory LWOP

State	"Strike Zone"	Number of Strikes	Number Sentenced
Georgia	Murder, armed robbery, kidnapping, rape, aggravated child molesting, aggravated sodomy, aggravated sexual battery	Two	
	Any felony*	Four	7,631**
Indiana	Murder, rape, sexual battery with a weapon, child molesting, arson, robbery, burglary with a weapon or resulting in serious injury, drug dealing	Three	38
Louisiana	Murder, attempted murder, manslaughter, rape, armed robbery, kidnapping, serious drug offenses, serious felony offenses,	Three	N/A
	Any four felony convictions with at least one on the above list	Four	
Maryland	Murder, rape, robbery, first- or second-degree sexual offense, arson, burglary, kidnapping, carjacking, manslaughter, use of firearm in felony, assault with intent to murder, rape, rob, or commit sexual offense; separate prison terms required for each offense	Four	330
Montana	Deliberate homicide, aggravated kidnapping, sexual intercourse without consent, ritual abuse of a minor	Two	0
	Mitigated deliberate homicide, aggravated assault, kidnapping, robbery	Three	
New Jersey	Murder, robbery, carjacking	Three	10
North Carolina	47 violent felonies; separate indictment and finding that offender is "violent habitual offender"	Three	22
South Carolina	Murder, voluntary manslaughter, homicide by child abuse, rape, kidnapping, armed robbery, drug trafficking, embezzlement, bribery, certain accessory and attempted offenses	Two	14
Tennessee	Murder, aggravated kidnapping, robbery, arson, rape, rape of child; prior prison term required	Two	14
	Same as above, plus rape, aggravated sexual battery; separate prison terms required	Three	
Utah	Any first- or second-degree felony	Three	N/A

State	"Strike Zone"	Number of Strikes	Number Sentenced
Virginia	Murder, kidnapping, robbery, carjacking, sexual assault, conspiracy with these crimes	Three	328
Washington	Murder, manslaughter, rape, child molestation, robbery, aggravated assault, explosion with threat to humans, extortion, kidnapping, vehicular assault, arson, attempted arson, burglary, any felony with deadly weapon, treason, prompting prostitution, leading organized crime	Three	209
Wisconsin	Murder, manslaughter, vehicular homicide, aggravated battery, abuse of children, robbery, sexual assault, taking hostages, kidnapping, arson, burglary	Three	9
Federal government	Murder, voluntary manslaughter, assault with intent to commit murder or rape, robbery, aggravated sexual abuse, abusive sexual contact, kidnapping, aircraft piracy, carjacking, extortion, arson, firearms use, serious drug crimes	Three	35

* In Georgia, any four felonies mandate a maximum sentence, not necessarily LWOP.

** This statistic includes all those sentences in the scheme described just above; thus, the true LWOP is not known for certain. All sentence statistics as of 2004.

Source: Jennifer Walsh, *Three Strikes Laws* (Westport, CT: Greenwood, 2007), 120.

demands gradations of punishment. "If we more nearly matched crime with punishment," argues noted retributivist Robert Blecker, "we would design a pain-free death for those who killed their victims painlessly, while reserving a painful death for those who sadistically tortured their victims."[13] Collapsing these fine gradations of punishment into a single punishment, either death or life without parole, would, in this line of thinking, be a betrayal of justice.

While conservative support for LWOP seems consistent with a tough-on-crime politics,[14] support for LWOP among abolitionists requires some explanation. Part of their rationale for advocating LWOP rested on public opinion polls that showed support for capital punishment to be based, in part, on worries about the premature parole of violent felons. And what is true for the general public also seems to be true for jurors. John Blume et al., reporting on their research on capital juries, note that "future dangerousness is on the minds of most capital jurors, and is thus 'at issue' in virtually all capital trials, no matter what the prosecution says or does not say."[15] Between 53% and 66% of jurors surveyed stated that the deliberations focused a "fair amount" on the issue of future dangerousness. Additionally, among those surveyed from cases in which the prosecution did not put future dangerousness at issue, 77% reported that personal concern that the defendant might again be a harm to society was important in how they voted.[16]

Abolitionists support LWOP to allay those worries. Some abolitionists have even gone so far as to argue that not allowing juries to consider LWOP in the sentencing phase of capital trials is unconstitutional.[17] They claim that "the absence of an LWOP option causes the death penalty to be imposed as an expedient rather than as the product of a reasoned judgment that death is the appropriate punishment."[18] They believe that without an LWOP option jurors are offered a forced choice, a choice with a bias toward death. This forced choice is of particular concern since it seems incompatible with the heightened standards of reliability required in capital sentencing by the Supreme Court's *Furman* and *Gregg* decisions.

Nonetheless, some recent research raises questions about the wisdom of the abolitionist embrace of LWOP. It reveals that "the enactment of life-without-parole statutes is correlated with a small decrease in the number of death sentences handed down, but it has not led to a significant reduction in execution."[19] Additional evidence suggests that "the patterns of death sentences in different states mirror each other, regardless of whether or when those states pass life-without-parole statutes."[20] Moreover, "from 1992 to 2003, the number of prisoners incarcerated for life without parole jumped from 12,453 to 33,633. Over the same period, the number of Americans on death row increased from 2575 to 3374. In other words, while the death row population grew by 31%, the population of those incarcerated for LWOP grew 170%."[21]

Reflecting on the abolitionist embrace of LWOP, Julian Wright argues that "instead of saving lives, the sanction toughens the sentences of criminals who would not have received the death penalty under the sentencing structure" beforehand.[22] In his view, the most important result of the adoption of LWOP has been to spur life sentences for *noncapital crimes*. "Death penalty abolitionists," he says, "have a responsibility to consider carefully the effects of such laws on noncapital defendants before they engineer or encourage their passage."[23]

In spite of such concerns, abolitionists continue to provide support necessary to enact LWOP legislation. For example, in 2004, the Kansas legislature, controlled by Republicans, passed an LWOP statute authored by death penalty advocates. The bill was signed into law, however, by Kathleen Sebelius, Kansas's anti-death-penalty governor.[24]

Despite LWOP's popularity among abolitionists and tough-on-crime politicians,[25] controversy surrounding it remains intense. While some maintain that LWOP is an appropriate sanction because of its deterrent and retributive functions, and defend it by arguing that its use has been partially responsible for America's declining crime rates,[26] others claim that "the movement toward reduced discretion in such cases [as LWOP] has resulted in lengthier periods of incarceration than are necessary to achieve public safety goals."[27]

Critics also highlight issues of cost. As more inmates are sentenced to life, the overall cost of imprisonment increases dramatically. Not only will it cost more to incarcerate a larger population, they suggest, but it will also become increasingly costly to house aging prisoners. Resulting in large part from the increase in life and LWOP sentences, "from 1979 through 2002, the average inmate age increased from 28.7 to 34.7 years, and this growth rate is expected to continue until 2010 when it is projected to accelerate. . . . And while prisoners over the age of fifty make up only 6% of the prison population in Georgia currently, this 6% currently consumes 12% of the prison healthcare resources."[28] The Sentencing Project estimates that it costs approximately $1 million to house a prisoner from age forty to age seventy.[29]

Moreover, incarcerating criminals until death may not be necessary to serve public safety goals. Mauer et al. survey several studies on recidivism and find that

> lifers have very low rates of recidivism, including for violent crimes. For example, in Michigan, 175 persons convicted of murder were paroled between 1937 and 1961; none committed another homicide and only four were returned to prison for other offenses. In Canada, between 1920 and 1967, 119 persons originally sentenced to death for murder had their sentences commuted to life and were eventually released on parole; one was convicted of another homicide. From 1959 to 1967, an additional 32 persons were released and by 1967 only one had been convicted of a new offense (not a murder).[30]

Studies such as these strongly suggest that LWOP sentences are excessive from a deterrence and public safety perspective.

There is also evidence that, as is the case with capital punishment, LWOP is riddled with racial disparity. "Racial and ethnic minorities," Ashley Nellis and Ryan King observe, "serve a disproportionate share of life sentences.

Two-thirds of people with life sentences (66.4%) are nonwhite, reaching as high as 83.7% of the life sentenced population in the state of New York."[31] Additionally, in 2008, the United Nations Committee on the Elimination of Racial Discrimination (CERD) expressed concern over "stark racial disparities" in the American criminal justice system, noting further that "young offenders belonging to racial, ethnic and national minorities, including children, constitute a disproportionate number of those sentenced to life imprisonment without parole."[32]

Evidence of race effects on the adult LWOP population is also troubling. Nellis and King found that "while 45% of the parole-eligible population is African American, blacks comprise 56.4% of the LWOP population."[33] Not only are blacks overrepresented initially within the life-sentenced population, this statistic indicates that blacks are deemed parole ineligible disproportionately as well. These findings of racial disparities are hardly surprising: discriminatory sentencing drives the demographics of prison populations from death row down to the county jail.

However, sociologist Bruce Western argues that incarceration is not merely a symptom of social inequality but that it *creates* and *exacerbates* inequality by undermining families and further separating poor communities of color from the American mainstream.[34] Western demonstrates that incarceration is a collection of policy responses that exact their own long-term, negative effects on communities. Such policies, he argues, not only fail to protect communities from crime but also widen the inequality gap and the psychological distance between people of color who live in distressed communities and everyone else.

LWOP, more than any other form of incarceration, imposes a *permanent* disruption on marginal and minority communities. It permanently hardens the psychological degradation of distressed minority communities by conveying the message that offenders from these communities are distinctly *irredeemable*: they must be locked up forever because they could never change.

For law and order advocates, LWOP's promise of permanent containment is precisely what recommends it. Homicidal home invaders, serial rapists, terrorists, and other serious offenders are seen as so dangerous to society that community safety can be assured only by punishment that both permanently incapacitates the offender and serves as a strong deterrent to would-be criminals.[35]

For critics of LWOP, it is its mechanical and final quality that raises concerns. They contend that all mandatory LWOP sentences should be invalidated just as mandatory death penalty sentences have been. As Andrew Mun puts it, "capital punishment and mandatory life sentences without parole share one important characteristic: the offender never regains freedom. Both punishments assume that the offender exhibits an incapacity for reform and rehabilitation."[36] Leon Sheleff argues that the U.S. Supreme Court should "consider whether life imprisonment is not in violation of the 'cruel and unusual' provision not just because it is disproportional to the crime, nor because the due process provision of the Fourteenth Amendment have been violated, but because, in and of itself, a life sentence constitutes cruelty."[37] Sheleff notes that "the Court could consider 'evolving standards of decency' and examine the evidence, admittedly limited, yet nevertheless growing, on the nature of confinement when there is no, or only little, hope of release."[38]

Until recently, such arguments seemed quite futile. Almost forty years ago, the Supreme Court ruled in *Schick v. Reed* that President Eisenhower's commutation of the defendant's death sentence to LWOP was constitutionally valid. The Court held that the "without parole" stipulation was not an abuse of discretion as the defendant charged.[39] While the Court's discussion of parole was not extensive, the ruling nonetheless provided impetus for legislatures in passing further LWOP statutes.

Five years later, in *Government of the Virgin Islands v. Gereau*, the defendant in an LWOP case argued that "the sentence's sheer length precluded any opportunity for parole and thus eliminated any incentive for rehabilitation."[40] He alleged that his sentence was cruel and unusual punishment. The Third Circuit Court of Appeals did not agree. Deferring to state legislatures, it cited *Schick* as establishing that LWOP did not violate the Eighth Amendment.

In 1985, in *U.S. v. O'Driscoll*, the Tenth Circuit ruled that LWOP was not disproportionate punishment under the Eighth Amendment when imposed on a notorious kidnapper. The precedential significance of *O'Driscoll* was the Court's ruling that the "vicious propensities of the defendant and his lack of ... respect for human life" permitted the sentence.[41] The Court held that "retribution and rehabilitation are equally permissible goals of rehabilitation," thus invalidating the proportionality claim against LWOP.[42] In *Harmelin v. Michigan* and *Ewing v. California*, the Supreme Court continued this trend of upholding LWOP sentences.[43] Reflecting on this line of cases, Wright notes that "at the federal level [the] issue [of LWOP's constitutionality] may never have been argued thoroughly, but it has been decided definitively."[44]

Yet recent developments suggest that LWOP's constitutional status is not unshakably stable. The Supreme Court's decision in *Graham v. Florida* illustrates this fact.[45] The Court in *Graham* held that LWOP is an unconstitutionally cruel and unusual punishment when imposed on juveniles for *nonho-*

micide offenses. As the Court noted, "when compared to an adult murderer, a juvenile offender who did not kill or intend to kill has a twice diminished moral culpability."[46] For all those whose culpability is *not* "twice diminished," the opinion's logic suggests, LWOP retains its moral and legal validity.

That said, perhaps *Graham* opens up new ground to contest harsh punishments. As Justice Thomas put it in his dissent, "'Death is different' no longer. The Court now claims not only the power categorically to reserve the 'most severe punishment' for those the Court thinks are 'the most deserving of execution,' . . . but also to declare that 'less culpable' persons are categorically exempt from the 'second most severe penalty.'"[47]

And, as Thomas further points out, the Court presents no coherent theory of juvenile cognition that meaningfully distinguishes the juvenile rapist and the juvenile murderer.[48] So perhaps—to Justice Thomas's horror, no doubt—categorical bars on harsh punishment might continue to expand. Unlike capital punishment, the distinction between LWOP and slightly shorter prison sentences is a fragile one. So where the meaning and morality of LWOP are up for grabs, so too might be the viability of many lesser sentences.

Although LWOP has become both a more prominent and controversial part of the carceral state, scholars have done little to unearth its meaning and significance in American society, politics, and law. While a substantial body of scholarship focuses on efforts to explain the late 20th-century incarceration boom in the United States,[49] little attention has been focused specifically on LWOP. When it has been talked about, LWOP has generally been folded into broad theories seeking to explain America's penchant for incarceration. *Life without Parole: America's New Death Penalty?* looks inside the dramatic and well-documented growth of incarceration to focus specifically on LWOP.

This book is divided into two parts. In part 1, the contributors consider LWOP in light of broader developments in the history and modern practice of punishment. Chapters in part 2 examine social, political, and legal factors that shape efforts to reform or eliminate LWOP sentences.

Part 1 begins with a chapter by Josh Bowers, who examines LWOP in light of the history and current practices of capital punishment. His chapter focuses specifically on the presence and absence of reasoned deliberation over equitable blameworthiness, or "equitable discretion," in LWOP and death cases. From this angle, Bowers suggests that contemporary LWOP sentences, because they are often mandatory, bear a resemblance to the historical death penalty. "LWOP is not so much the new death penalty," he argues, "as the old one."

As Bowers sees it, today's LWOP sentencing resembles the English criminal justice system from the early 17th to early 19th centuries—during the period of the so-called Bloody Code. The Bloody Code combined mandatory death sentencing with "unofficial" opportunities for discretionary intervention. Juries and other legal authorities had significant discretion to circumvent the mandates of the Bloody Code. The jury acted as a quasi-legislative body, structuring "the substantive law to meet the equitable demands of the particular case." While the Bloody Code was "clearly harsh in its penalty," it was "positively lenient in its administration."

When it comes to modern American sentencing practices (which now tend to be mandatory and determinate), the death penalty is an anomaly. The Supreme Court has resisted the application of mandatory sentencing rules to capital sentencing. The Court refuses to let the states "swing the pendulum from unfettered capital-sentencing discretion to unbending determinacy." Two principal mechanisms have been established to ensure particularized sentencing in the administration of the death penalty: (1) proportionality review and (2) the bifurcated trial structure. While the Bloody Code allowed for an enormous amount of deadly error, the guided discretion of modern capital-sentencing procedure resets the default to moderation.

In contrast, LWOP sentencing and other noncapital-sentencing procedures in the United States have been practically stripped of meaningful equitable discretionary practices. In this way, LWOP statutes come to look more like the Bloody Code than the contemporary death penalty. Yet today, juries, judges, and other officials are no longer able to soften the ostensibly mandatory and draconian nature of criminal codes. The risk of arbitrary harshness is, Bowers contends, even greater under LWOP than under the historical death penalty of the Bloody Code. Bowers does not envision a return to the unchecked equitable discretion of early England but recommends a middle course somewhere between wholly "mechanistic" and wholly "evaluative" approaches.

He argues that modern capital-sentencing procedures should be applied to LWOP sentencing. As he sees it, LWOP is no less final than capital punishment. Nor is it any less severe. Bowers proposes "leveling the equitable playing field between life and death." LWOP, in his view, should not be imposed without equitable discretion.

Jessica S. Henry continues the exploration of the meaning of LWOP by focusing on the need to broaden the context within which LWOP is generally discussed. She suggests that it is part of, and exemplifies, larger phenomena in the American penal system. In her view, life imprisonment should be seen as an ultimate punishment: severe, often irrevocable, and, in the case of LWOP sentences, certain to end in death. And, beyond LWOP, there are other so-called death-in-prison (DIP) sentences, such as life imprisonment with the theoretical, but not actual, possibility of release because of jurisdictional parole practices, determinate sentences that far exceed an offender's life expectancy, and indefinite civil confinement. These DIP sentences could also be described as "ultimate." Yet virtually no attention has been paid to this broader category of DIP sentences.

In Henry's view, DIP sentences are closer to capital punishment than they are to any other sanction. Both are "severe and degrading," "arbitrarily imposed," and "condemned" internationally. And yet DIP sentencing procedures lack the heightened protections and judicial scrutiny afforded to capital cases. These sentences, which surpass an individual's life span, are, in her view, designed to send a powerful message of banishment.

DIP sentences, more often than not, are as irrevocable as capital sentences, if not more so. Henry argues that DIP sentences are "by their nature" worse than death sentences. And, like the contributions to this book by Sharon Dolovich and Jonathan Simon, Henry recognizes that DIP sentences deny the humanity of those on whom they are imposed.

Henry notes that both DIP sentences and capital punishment have been condemned by other contemporary societies as violations of human rights. As Simon argues in his later chapter, many nations in Europe reject LWOP on the basis that it is inconsistent with human dignity. In other words, "no human being should be regarded as beyond improvement and therefore should always have the prospect for release."[50] Finally, Henry interprets the Court's decision in *Graham v. Florida* as an indication of its recognition that LWOP is, at least to some degree, uniquely severe.

DIP sentences, in spite of their similarity to capital punishment, remain largely underscrutinized. As I. Bennett Capers does in his later chapter, Henry believes there is a complete disconnect between the harshness of DIP sentences and the scrutiny provided to them. Henry argues that, because of the severity of DIP sentences, they should be reserved for only the worst of the worst. Arbitrariness in DIP sentencing is easily found in the context of habitual offender statutes, drug offenses, and the imposition of lengthy sentences. Still, it goes largely unnoticed and wholly unregulated. This is a situation that Henry, like Bowers, believes should be remedied by extending the procedural protections traditionally afforded in death penalty cases to all DIP sentences.

The next chapter, by Sharon Dolovich, sees LWOP as emblematic, as exemplifying the purpose and function of imprisonment more generally. As she puts it, LWOP "most effectively captures the central motivating aim of the contemporary American carceral system." Dolovich, following Henry, believes that LWOP represents a promise of "permanent exclusion" and ensures "wholesale banishment."

Dolovich's chapter describes two starkly different attitudes toward imprisonment, one she labels "reintegrationist," the other "exclusionary." She argues that, in recent years, the American penal system has come to fully embrace exclusion. The criminal justice system has become a human "sorting mechanism" in which convicts become officially branded as "noncitizens." In this system, LWOP is one of many strategies employed to maintain the "boundary between inmates and the broader society."

Dolovich outlines the emergence of the "exclusionary ideal" in the United States. Throughout most of the 20th century, she reminds us, indeterminate sentencing and parole release were the norm in what was a penal system oriented toward reintegration. The principle of rehabilitation dominated the American criminal justice system; correctional practices were aimed at inmate reform, not isolation. As Dolovich puts it, "the rehabilitative ideal at least signaled a recognition . . . that penal subjects were fellow human beings." Nevertheless, the 1970s saw a dramatic turn in penological priorities away from rehabilitation toward more punitive principles. A shift to mandatory sentencing signaled this larger move in the direction of the exclusionary ideal. "Any understanding of prisoners as people," Dolovich writes, "drops out of the picture."

Dolovich argues that the virtual disappearance of parole is also entirely consistent with the exclusionary project. "LWOP," she says, "is the perfect exclusionary strategy": irrevocable exile. Moreover, even where the possibility of parole is formally maintained, it is now rarely granted. In California, for example, during the last decade, the Board of Parole Hearings has denied 98% of petitions. This fact exemplifies an "affirmative hostility to the prospect of any reintegration" and a "relentless impulse to exclude."

Dolovich believes that LWOP, as the emblematic exclusionary penalty, is markedly similar to capital punishment. Both punishments announce the irredeemability of the prisoner. However, Dolovich suggests that LWOP may be even more severe in the sense that it is a sentence of "finality *in spite of the possibility of change.*"

Dolovich concludes by arguing that penal reform should be redirected not only from capital punishment to LWOP sentences but to the exclusionary ideal it embodies. For Dolovich it is important not to let the inescapable fact that "death is different" distract from the considerable damage the criminal justice system does even to those it chooses not to execute.

The last chapter in part 1, by Paul H. Robinson, situates LWOP in a discussion of the animating purposes of modern punishment: deterrence, incapacitation, retribution. It is against these purposes, Robinson contends, that the legitimacy of LWOP sentencing needs to be assessed. In the end, Robinson claims that none of these rationales is sufficient to support current LWOP practice.

Robinson first deals with what he sees as the flaws of instrumentalist principles: deterrence and incapacitation. While general deterrence has many obvious potential benefits, in his view it rarely fulfills its alleged crime-control potential. This failing is primarily due to the fact that deterrence is only effective when intended targets, future criminals, are aware of the presence of a penal rule. In regard to LWOP sentences, few potential offenders will actually know their own state's specific practices. Second, a deterrent effect only results if targets have the ability and inclination to rationally calculate their best interests. Again, Robinson claims that this is not often the case. Potential criminals are hardly ever inclined toward rational calculation. In fact, they are often the kind of people suffering from "distortions in rational calculations" and clouded reasoning.

General deterrence, Robinson notes, also is only effective when targets conclude that the costs of committing a crime outweigh any anticipated benefits. Once again, this is rarely the case. Even a "rational calculator" may come to the conclusion that the relatively "distant risk of receiving a LWOP sentence is not sufficiently serious as to justify passing up the immediate benefit of committing the offense."

Robinson next discusses the problems of incapacitation as a rationale in the context of LWOP. He argues that while incapacitation, unlike deterrence, is indisputably effective as a distributive principle, its use is difficult to justify both generally and specifically in the application of LWOP sentences. The kind of preventive detention that LWOP represents can be efficient and fair only when administered in an open civil-commitment system. In our current system, the dangerousness of offenders is determined based on prior criminal records. Under this practice, "false positives" commonly exceed "true positives," and people are restrained unnecessarily. Robinson argues that "a preventive detention system hidden behind the cloak of criminal justice not only fails to protect the community efficiently but also fails to deal fairly with those who are being preventively detained."

Robinson next takes up arguments about desert. An offender may simply deserve an extreme sentence. The traditional conception of desert, "deontological" or moral desert, views justice as a value in and of itself and focuses on an offender's "moral blameworthiness." On the other hand, "empirical desert" focuses on the potential utility of desert from a crime-control perspective. By reflecting community views of justice, empirical desert increases the moral credibility of the criminal law and thereby increases its crime-control effectiveness.

For Robinson, neither account of desert justifies LWOP sentences. First, LWOP practices, as they currently stand, fail to recognize the "ordinal ranking demands" of desert. Such sentencing "fails to take account," Robinson writes, "of the sometimes dramatic differences in moral blameworthiness among serious offenses." Second, Robinson further argues that LWOP sentences, in ignoring ordinal ranking, also conflict with community views of justice—thus undermining the moral credibility of the criminal law.

Robinson suggests that we need to seriously limit the use of life-imprisonment sentences. He argues that "if we value doing justice, fighting crime, and having safe and productive correctional facilities, we should prefer a sentencing system that rarely, if ever, imposes sentences of LWOP." Determinate life-imprisonment sentences should be reserved for only the most heinous crimes imaginable.

Part 2 begins with a chapter by I. Bennett Capers, who argues that we need to think about LWOP as the alternative to capital punishment, as that other death within the American criminal justice system. He claims that death penalty abolitionists, in their efforts to eradicate capital punishment, have overlooked the evils of life imprisonment without parole. Thus, the now well-recognized problems associated with capital punishment and race are hidden by the underscrutinized application of LWOP. Race is rendered largely and dangerously invisible. For Capers, the growth of LWOP in the United States is a symptom of a set of broader problems in our entire system of punishment, and reform strategies need to be broadly, not narrowly, focused.

Drawing on his experiences as a federal prosecutor, Capers discusses what he calls "our obsession with death." In this context, he describes what it meant for him to prosecute death cases and for his office to go into "death penalty mode," which invariably required an explicit focus on the presence (or irrelevance) of race in each particular case. Capers details the long, somewhat complex, process of seeking death in the American criminal justice system. He remembers losing sleep over the death-eligible cases he prosecuted. In contrast, his "other defendants" (many facing LWOP) were rendered invisible beneath the mantra "death is different." As a former member of the legal and judicial "cult of death," Capers acknowledges that he never considered his responsibility in life-without-parole cases.

Like Bowers, Capers explores the history of the "symbiotic relationship" between the death penalty and LWOP. After the Supreme Court's decision in *Furman v. Georgia*, LWOP began to appear on the criminal justice scene as the next best thing. And once the death penalty had been reinvigorated after *Gregg v. Georgia* in 1976, abolitionists looked to LWOP as a primary weapon in their fight against state killing.

Death penalty abolitionists, like most Americans, harbor a peculiar fascination with death. For them, "state-imposed death is all that matters." As a result, we have become a nation that is "willing to play the odds and risk life," while we remain wholly "unwilling to play the odds and risk death." Life without parole is seen as a triumph for defense lawyers in capital cases. But lifers become faceless. Their state-mandated deaths in prison are met not with "collective hand-wringing" but with general indifference.

As a society, Capers contends, we fail to imagine life behind bars. LWOP has become "the new normal." It strips inmates of hope and produces a chronic state of apathy, depression, and despair in a thoroughly dehumanizing environment. Thus, LWOP and capital punishment share characteristics to which no other sentences can lay claim. Echoing Dolovich, Capers writes that both LWOP and the death penalty are forms of banishment from human society.

Capers urges us to move beyond the question of what it means when the state kills. Reformers need to ask, What does it mean when the state creates prisons that act as "banishment zones," invisible, racialized cities? "The challenge," Capers says, "is not only to rethink the death penalty or LWOP but also to rethink our entire system of punishment."

Following Capers, Rachel E. Barkow's chapter also questions the consequences of the heightened scrutiny given to death penalty cases and the consequences of isolating LWOP for reform. Barkow, like Capers and Dolovich, regards LWOP as a symptom of a more profound problem of disproportionate sentencing within the American criminal justice system. As a result, Barkow is not optimistic that reforms will meaningfully affect LWOP anytime soon.

Barkow also shares Capers's belief that the death penalty abolition movement is a significant obstacle facing LWOP reform efforts. In fact, as we noted earlier, death penalty abolitionists have become ardent champions of LWOP. The acceptance and promotion of LWOP by abolitionists may foster the belief that it is not inhumane or inappropriately harsh.

Barkow does not see much prospect that LWOP sentences will get the same procedural protections as capital cases. She again brings up the entrenched belief that "death is different." Whereas one can rather easily formulate abolitionist arguments that the state should never kill a citizen, "it is harder to argue credibly that the state should never be permitted to lock someone away for the rest of his or her life."

Nevertheless, Barkow suggests that those who seek the abolition of LWOP need to focus not on the "life-imprisonment" aspect of the sentence but on the possibility of instituting a "second look." In her view, the fate of LWOP is necessarily tied to the fate of parole. Reforming LWOP sentencing will require not only a renewed faith in the ability of convicts to change but also a belief in the ability of experts to identify truly rehabilitated offenders. Abolition of LWOP would require both the rejection of retribution and the rehabilitation of rehabilitation. In other words, Barkow asserts, "The case for abolition of LWOP would thus require wholesale rethinking of the American system of punishment."

While Barkow believes that abolition of LWOP is unlikely, she explores two mechanisms for limiting its application. First, the decision in *Graham v. Florida* highlights the possibility for categorical limits. Juveniles convicted of nonviolent felonies may not be sentenced to life in prison without parole. However, Barkow does not see much benefit from such extremely narrow categorical reforms. The second path for reform involves increasing currently nonexistent procedural protections or judicial oversight of LWOP. But she sees little possibility of meaningful change coming from legislatures or a Supreme Court concerned with the slippery slope of penal reform.

Barkow worries that an obsessive focus on reforming LWOP could undermine deeper reforms of noncapital sentencing more generally. In this way, a new obsession with "life" could be just as detrimental as what Capers describes as our cultural obsession with death. Moreover, unlike Robinson, Henry, and Capers, Barkow sees the focus on the deprivation of hope that accompanies LWOP as a distraction from a more significant problem. She writes, "The real problem with LWOP is not what makes it unique from other sentences but the danger it shares with all sentences: it is in some cases a disproportionate sentence, just as life with the availability of parole is disproportionate in some cases and terms of years are disproportionate in others." LWOP, Barkow notes, "is the starkest manifestation of that problem, but the disease is far more widespread."

In the next chapter Marie Gottschalk also warns readers about the difficulties of reforming or abolishing LWOP. The financial crisis, coupled with the election of Barack Obama, she suggests, raised expectations that the United States would begin to empty its jails and prisons because it can no longer afford to keep so many people locked up. Indeed, states have already implemented reforms aimed at shrinking their incarcerated populations. These efforts, Gottschalk notes, are likely to reduce the prison population somewhat, but they may have negative consequences for people serving lengthy prison sentences, including lifers.

The thrust of the latest penal reform movement has been directed at so-called nonviolent offenders. Reformers have called for loosening penalties for nonviolent offenders as a quid pro quo for stiffening the penalties for other offenses. This reinforces the misconception that the war on drugs was the main engine of mass incarceration in the United States and that the country has been too easy on other offenders. Mass incarceration was fueled by several factors, including ratcheting up the penalties for many nondrug offenses, so much so that the United States today is far more punitive than are other advanced industrialized countries. As a result, the focus needs to shift away from the shortcomings of the war on drugs toward the "plight of people serving lengthy sentences."

Following the recent turn toward longer and less forgiving sentencing patterns, today, governors and other public officials are fundamentally opposed to releasing serious offenders, no matter the circumstances. Fear invades and paralyzes the political process. And the popularity of retributive theory is, in Gottschalk's view, a substantial obstacle to the rethinking of LWOP.

Gottschalk joins Capers and Barkow in suggesting that death penalty abolitionists have also contributed to the proliferation of LWOP and life sentences in the United States. Death penalty abolitionists have helped "normalize" a sanction that should be considered entirely opposed to any modern notion of human rights. Gottschalk specifically criticizes the abolitionist focus of the Innocence Project. Its emphasis on the innocent death-row population has overshadowed the "wider question of what constitutes justice" for both guilty death-row inmates and lifers.

Because the life-sentenced population is vastly heterogeneous in terms of the offenses that led to life sentences, some people advocate reform based on degrees of culpability and relative fairness. Gottschalk worries that such strategies may come at the cost of undermining "more universalistic arguments about redemption, rehabilitation, mercy, and aging out of crime." She describes the dangers of focusing on three specific categories of lifers: people convicted of felony murder, juveniles sentenced to LWOP, and people sent away for life under "three-strikes" laws. In all three cases, "one lifer appears more deserving of release by highlighting how less deserving other lifers are."

In her view, we must rethink how best to challenge the entire structure of mass imprisonment in the United States.

The book concludes with Jonathan Simon's chapter, which suggests that the absence of a strong "dignity tradition" today stands as the primary barrier to reform of LWOP sentences. According to Simon, the absence of a strong dignity tradition largely accounts for the harshness of American punishments, especially when compared to punishment regimes across Europe. Citing James Whitman, he argues that the difference between the American and European punishment systems is due to the respective prevalent or absent role of dignity in law and policy. Simon writes, "The reason America lacks dignitarian values in its legal system is largely an accident of its historical circumstances." That is, in contrast to Europe, colonial America never developed a recognized aristocracy. In America, there was never a "noble grade of punishment" that could be extended to all citizens. Moreover, the prolonged existence of slavery meant "the persistence of a tolerance for degradation" in the U.S. In explaining LWOP and other harsh punishments in the U.S., the absence of dignity goes along with the embrace of a "fear-based version of incapacitation" as a penal rationale.

Simon views the war on crime (and the politicization of crime that resulted) as central to the shaping of contemporary American law and policy. At the end of the 20th century, incapacitation emerged as a penal rationale in its own right largely in response to the "rise of risk management as the primary narrative of criminal justice." Using California as an example, Simon defines "total incapacitation" in terms of actual imprisonment practices, parole practices, and the prevalence of LWOP. The commitment to total incapacitation in California and throughout the country developed as politicians came to recognize a new middle-class consensus that the risks of a hyperviolent criminal class required an uncompromising commitment to prison as a permanent barrier between potential victims and the dangerous.

Nonetheless, Simon is markedly more optimistic than many of the other contributors about prospects for reform. For Simon, struggles for dignity as a value around which legal controversies can be reframed have the potential to achieve real gains in reconceptualizing, if not entirely resolving, such controversies. Although Simon admits that moving the United States away from total incapacitation will require more than a strengthening of dignity within the law, this "cultural struggle" will be most effective when "risk and dignity are being reconfigured to place fear under a stronger value of dignity." Much of Simon's chapter is devoted to discussing three areas in American social and legal culture in which dignity has begun to take hold. He reviews dignity arguments in end-of-life care, in the involuntary treatment of the mentally ill, and in the struggle for the legalization of same-sex marriage. He writes, "None of these other examples lies particularly close in a policy sense to punishment (let alone LWOP), but all of them suggest ways to reconstruct penal practices toward the end of conserving dignity." All three areas represent the generally successful strengthening of dignitarian values against a background of fear. According to Simon, the same needs to occur in the penal realm. In his view, signs of a dignity tradition emerging in several sectors outside the penal field suggest that the effort to abolish LWOP need not take a lifetime.

So, in the end, why does LWOP matter? Why is it worth dedicating an entire volume to the subject? The answer, we believe, is because punishment is at the heart of current institutional thinking about crime, and in that context LWOP belongs at (or near) the top of the punitive pecking order.[51] In our world, all too often we ignore the long series of events—many of them influenced by governmental institutions—that lead up to a sentence of life without parole. Present thinking, in its backwardness, treats the final event as if it were what mattered most. Research shows otherwise: public dollars spent on education and prevention are far more effective in, for example, stemming violence and discouraging gang affiliation than are broadening prosecutorial powers or stiffening criminal penalties for young people accused of gang-related crimes.

Yet over the past five years, Congress initially slashed and then completely eliminated funding for the Department of Education's dropout-prevention program (though funding was restored in 2010, it is at risk of being eliminated again as a "Congressional Mandate" to reduce government spending).[52] Meanwhile, as part of the 2009 economic recovery plan, the federal government spent $1 billion to hire additional police officers around the country.[53] This represents a perverse investment: each additional arrest that these new police officers make comes at the expense of efforts to eliminate behavior that results in arrest. With the circularity of the proverbial snake eating its own tail, the investment in more policing and punishment drives the need to invest in more policing and punishment.

The chapters that follow amply document these phenomena and demonstrate the richness of LWOP as an object of principle and policy debate. They ably demonstrate why LWOP is important—is worth fighting about—and that its significance, its moral and political meaning, is up for grabs. And just as much as with capital punishment, people's lives are at stake.

LWOP forces us to ask whether death really is different—or at least whether a slow death sentence is much different than a swift one.[54] Perhaps LWOP is just a lethal injection in sheep's clothing, replicating capital punishment's insidious patterns of racial application and rendering the gains from death penalty abolition all but illusory. Seen in this light, LWOP may well be the new capital punishment, with all of its baggage—but none of its process. So whether LWOP is the head of the snake or its tail, there has never been a greater need to grapple with this crucial subject. To ignore it is to be silent about the new death penalty lurking in the shadows.

NOTES

1. Adam Liptak, "To More Inmates, Life Term Means Dying behind Bars," *New York Times*, October 2, 2005, http://www.nytimes.com/2005/10/02/national/02life.web.html?scp=5&sq=liptak+&st=nyt.

2. Julian Wright, "Life-without-Parole: An Alternative to Death or Not Much of a Life at All?," 43 *Vanderbilt Law Review* (1990): 529, 534 (elaborating on the upward trend in LWOP statutes in the 1970s); see also Catherine Appleton and Bent Grøver, "The Pros and Cons of Life without Parole," 47 *British Journal of Criminology* (2007): 597 (Appleton and Grøver state that "the ratio of LWOP population to the US prison population has increased to such an extent that it is currently a hundred times greater than it was 30 years ago," thus confirming the large substantial growth since the mid-1970s).

3. Marc Mauer, Ryan S. King, and Malcolm C. Young, "The Meaning of 'Life': Long Prison Sentences in Context," Sentencing Project, May 2004, 11, http://www.sentencing-project.org/detail/publication.cfm?publication_id=27.

4. Id. See also Derral Cheatwood, "The Life-without-Parole Sanction: Its Current Status and a Research Agenda," 34 *Crime and Delinquency* (1988): 43–59.

5. Thomas Goots, "'A Thug in Prison Cannot Shoot Your Sister': Ohio Appears Ready to Resurrect the Habitual Criminal Statue—Will It Withstand an Eighth Amendment Challenge?," 28 *Akron Law Review* (1995): 253, 277.

6. Id.

7. Delaware and Maryland both adopted LWOP statutes in the 1950s, the former in 1953 and the latter in 1957. *Del. Code Ann.*, tit. II, § 4209(a); *Md. Code Ann.*, Crim. Law, § 2-303(j)(4).

8. Quoted in Adam Liptak, "Serving Life, with No Chance of Redemption," *New York Times*, October 5, 2005, http://realcostofprisons.org/blog/archives/2005/10/ny_times_servin.html.

9. Id.

10. Mark DiCamillo and Mervin Field, "Seven in Ten Californians Continue to Favor Capital Punishment," Field Research Corporation, July 22, 2010, available at http://www.field.com/fieldpollonline/subscribers/Rls2351.pdf.

11. Id. at 4. "In this context, 42% opt for life in prison and 41% for the death penalty, while 13% say it would depend on the circumstances of the case. Another 4% have no opinion."

12. See Jeanice Dagher-Margosian, "Life Means Life: Parole Rarely Granted on Non-mandatory Life Terms," 73 *Michigan Bar Journal* (1994): 1184.

13. Robert Blecker, "Killing Them Softly: Meditations on a Painful Penalty of Death," 35 *Fordham Urban Law Journal* (2008): 969, 996–997.

14. Wright, "Life-without-Parole," 529, 531.

15. John Blume, Stephen P. Garvey, and Sheri Lynn Johnson, "Future Dangerousness in Capital Cases: Always 'at Issue,'" 86 *Cornell Law Review* (2002): 397, 398–399.

16. Id. at 407.

17. Mark Lane, "Is There Life without Parole? A Capital Defendant's Right to a Mean-ingful Alternative Sentence," 26 *Loyola of Los Angeles Law Review* (1993): 327.

18. Steven Mulroy, "Avoiding 'Death by Default': Does the Constitution Require a 'Life without Parole' Alternative to the Death Penalty?," 79 *Tulane Law Review* (2004): 401, 406.

19. "A Matter of Life and Death: The Effect of Life-without-Parole Statutes on Capital Punishment," 119 *Harvard Law Review* (2006): 1838, 1850.

20. Id. at 1848.

21. Id. at 1852.

22. Wright, "Life-without-Parole," 553.

23. Id.

24. See "A Matter of Life and Death," 1854.

25. See Ashley Nellis and Ryan King, "No Exit: The Expanding Use of Life Sentences in America," Sentencing Project, July 2009, 6: "Sentencing statutes, prosecutorial practices, and parole policies have evolved in a more punitive direction. . . . In particular, support for the expansion of LWOP sentences grew out of the same mistrust of the judicial process that birthed sentencing guidelines, mandatory minimums, and 'truth-in-sentencing' laws to restrict parole eligibility."

26. See, for example, Charles Stimson and Andrew Grossman, "Adult Time for Adult Crimes: Life without Parole for Juvenile Killers and Violent Teens," Heritage Foundation, 2009, http://www.heritage.org/Research/Reports/2009/08/Adult-Time-for-Adult-Crimes-Life-Without-Parole-for-Juvenile-Killers-and-Violent-Teens.

27. Mauer, King, and Young, "The Meaning of 'Life,'" 4.

28. Amelia Inman and Millard Ramsey, "Putting Parole Back on the Table: An Effi-ciency Approach to Georgia's Aging Prison Population," 1 *John Marshall Law Journal* (2008): 239, 243. Inman and Ramsey suggest returning to parole. Their proposal allows for the return of parole eligibility for LWOP inmates under one of two conditions. When the inmate has either served 70% of his or her sentence or reached the age of 65, he or she would become parole eligible under their proposal. They purport that this would "preserve the incapacitation benefits of the longer sentences while allowing the system some flexibility to discharge inmates at the point where it is most expensive to continue to housing them." Id. at 242.

29. Mauer, King, and Young, "The Meaning of 'Life,'" 25.

30. Id. at 23.

31. Nellis and King, "No Exit," 3.

32. UN CERD, "Report of the Committee on the Elimination of Racial Discrimina-tion," 2008, available at http://tb.ohchr.org/default.aspx?ConvType=17&docType=36. The juvenile waiver process, by which juveniles are transferred to adult criminal court, is one source of racial disparity. Barry Feld states that "for decades, studies have consistently

reported racial disparities in waiver decisions and that recent 'get tough' reforms have exacerbated racial disparities." Feld cites a study that found that in 1978, 39% of all youths transferred to adult courts were black. This translates directly into discriminate LWOP sentencing. Feld reports that "judges impose LWOP sentences on black juveniles at a rate about ten times greater than they do white youths, and blacks comprise the substantial majority of all youths serving LWOP sentences." Juvenile race effects such as these are significant because of their relative reliability. The disproportionate rate of transfer avoids the circularity of the argument that blacks are overrepresented in the criminal justice system because they commit a disproportionate share of crimes. It is quite clear that "the LWOP disparity is a culmination of the effects of every discretionary decision in the juvenile and criminal justice systems that treat black youths more harshly. . . . In Michigan, more than two-thirds (69%) of all juveniles serving LWOP sentences are black, despite comprising only 15% of the youth population." Barry Feld, "A Slower Form of Death: Implications of *Roper v. Simmons* for Juveniles Sentenced to Life without Parole," 22 *Notre Dame Journal of Law Ethics and Public Policy* (2008): 15. See also Nellis and King, "No Exit," 20: "Transfer to the adult system is the stage at which these disparities are most severe; African American youth represent 35% of judicial waivers to criminal court and 58% of youth sent to adult prisons," 55.

33. Nellis and King, "No Exit," 13.

34. Bruce Western, *Punishment and Inequality in America* (New York: Russell Sage Foundation, 2006).

35. "Prosecutors Using New Life without Parole Option," ONNtv.com, June 22, 2008, http://www.10tv.com/live/content/onnnews/stories/2008/06/22/Life_WO_Parole. html?sid=102.

36. Andrew H. Mun, "Mandatory Life Sentence without Parole Found Constitutionally Permissible for Cocaine Possession." 67 *Washington Law Review* (1991): 713, 723.

37. Leon Sheleff, "The Mandatory Life Sentence—A Comparative Study of the Law in Israel, Great Britain, the United States and West Germany," 5 *Tel Aviv University Studies in Law* (1982): 115, 139. Sheleff is referring to LWOP statutes, not simply life sentences.

38. Id. at 139.

39. *Shick v. Reed*, 419 U.S. 256 (1974). The Court stated that the no-parole condition on the commutation of Schick's death sentence is similar to sanctions such as mandatory minimum sentences or statutes precluding parole.

40. *Government of the Virgin Islands v. Gereau*, 592 F.2d 192, 195 (1978).

41. *U.S. v. O'Driscoll*, 761 F.2d 589, 594 (1985).

42. Id. at 592. Several appellate jurisdictions have also upheld LWOP for rape, adding to the list of acceptable crimes to which the sanction could be applied, presumably proportionally: *Moore v. Cowan*, 560 F.2d 1298 (6th Cir. 1977); *Briton v. Rogers*, 631 F.2d 572 (8th Cir. 1980). Wright, in "Life-without-Parole," notes in the *Moore* decision that "the court even acknowledged that the precise question whether LWOP is cruel and unusual in violation of the eighth amendment was not addressed in *Schick*, but applied the precedent anyway" (536n. 33). In *Briton*, the Court deferred to the state legislatures, stating that states were permitted discretion in sentencing. See Elizabeth M. Mills, "Eight Amendment—Cruel and Unusual Punishment: Habitual Offender's Life Sentence without Parole Is Disproportionate," 74 *Journal of Criminal Law and Criminology* (1983): 1372.

43. *Harmelin v. Michigan*, 501 U.S. 957 (1991); *Ewing v. California*, 538 U.S. 11 (2003).

44. Wright, "Life-without-Parole," 538.

45. *Graham v. Florida*, 130 S. Ct. 2011 (2010).

46. Id. at 2026 (internal quotations and citations omitted).

47. Id. at 2046 (Thomas, J., dissenting).

48. Id. at 2055 (Thomas, J., dissenting). "In the end, the Court does not even believe its pronouncements about the juvenile mind. If it did, the categorical rule it announces today would be most peculiar because it leaves intact state and federal laws that permit life-without-parole sentences for juveniles who commit homicides."

49. See, for example, James Q. Whitman, *Harsh Justice: Criminal Punishment and the Widening Divide between America and Europe* (New York: Oxford University Press, 2003); and Jonathan Simon, *Governing through Crime: How the War on Crime Transformed American Democracy and Created a Culture of Fear* (New York: Oxford University Press, 2007).

50. Dirk van Zyl Smit, "Outlawing Irreducible Life Sentences: Europe on the Brink?," *Federal Sentencing Reporter* 23:1 (2010): 40.

51. Catherine Appleton and Bent Grøver, "The Pros and Cons of Life without Parole" 47 *British Journal of Criminology* (2007): 600–601, http://bjc.oxfordjournals.org/content/47/4/597.full.pdf?ijkey=l2UfWbFnl1ZzziA&keytype=ref.

52. U.S. Department of Education, "High School Graduation Initiative Also Known as School Dropout Prevention Program Funding Status (2004–2010)," http://www2.ed.gov/programs/dropout/funding.html (last modified April 27, 2010).

53. Neil Lewis, "Stimulus Plan Has $1 Billion to Hire More Local Police," *New York Times*, February 5, 2009, http://www.nytimes.com/2009/02/06/us/politics/06cops.html.

54. This issue is taken up by Robert Johnson and Sandra McGunigall-Smith, "Life without Parole, America's Other Death Penalty: Notes on Life under Sentence of Death by Incarceration," 88 *Prison Journal* (2008): 328. See also Alfred Villaume, "'Life without Parole' and 'Virtual Life Sentences': Death Sentences by Any Other Name," 8 *Contemporary Justice Review* (2005): 265.

1

Mandatory Life and the Death of Equitable Discretion

―――― JOSH BOWERS ――――――――――――――――――――――――――――

The common refrain is that the death penalty is different, but one of the most underappreciated differences between capital and noncapital punishment is the degree to which the death penalty expressly admits—indeed requires—an equitable determination before imposition. Specifically, the conviction and sentencing phases of a capital trial are bifurcated, and, although the conviction phase is limited to a legalistic determination of whether the elements of a statutory crime are met, the sentencing phase demands a normative evaluation of blameworthiness, based not only on the particulars of the criminal incident but also on the social and psychological circumstances of the defendant. In short, capital punishment provides an *express* lever for mercy that is operated by a collective—a body of laypersons charged with doing that which members of the public do well: exercising practical wisdom based on everyday experience to reach commonsense determinations about the advisability of a particular type of punishment in a particular case for a particular defendant.

By contrast, life without parole (LWOP) is frequently a *mandatory* punishment over which juries have no say and typically no knowledge. By way of background, under prevailing sentencing statutes, a mandatory LWOP sentence may result from either of two scenarios. First, the sentence may be the only alternative penalty to a discretionary death sentence. Second, the sentence may be the only available penalty for a given crime. In either event, a mandatory LWOP sentence is no product of reasoned deliberation over equitable blameworthiness. It is the required course.

In this way, the administration of mandatory LWOP is strikingly different from the administration of contemporary capital punishment. The sentencing process that results in a mandatory LWOP penalty lacks the lever for mercy that typifies death sentencing. If we are to draw an analogy, the better comparison is to the administration of the historical death penalty. Specifically, under the so-called Bloody Code, which existed in England from the seventeenth until the nineteenth century, the death penalty was the *mandatory* sentence for a host of felony convictions—just as LWOP is often the mandatory sentence today. Put simply, LWOP is not so much the new death penalty as the old one.

But the analogy is imperfect between mandatory capital punishment and mandatory LWOP. Significantly, the Bloody Code was never quite as uniformly bloody as it purported to be: lay jurors and legal authorities commonly employed a variety of mechanisms to circumvent the ultimate penalty. In short, under the Bloody Code, the sentencing law was unyielding, but law enforcement and adjudication were somewhat less formal and more flexible. Comparatively, modern mandatory LWOP—either as a backstop to discretionary death or as a stand-alone punishment—exists in a more substantively and procedurally rigid and formalized criminal justice system that lacks the commonly invoked equitable safety valves that tempered application of the Bloody Code.

To the extent an opportunity for equitable discretion remains in mandatory LWOP regimes, it rests wholly with the professional prosecutor, who controls the charging decision, but who concurrently has an institutional incentive to charge high in order to maximize bargaining power and thereby extract favorable and expeditious guilty pleas. In such circumstances, the prime determinate of whether defendants receive an LWOP sentence is not their just desserts but their willingness to bargain for a reduced charge. As such, mandatory LWOP admits no adequate adjudicative equitable screen—just faith in prosecutors to exercise their unfettered charging authority in normatively appropriate ways, notwithstanding their significant (and often contrary) instrumental reasons to forgo measured discretion.

History is not hagiography, however. For good reason, the contemporary criminal justice system has abandoned the informal opportunities for equitable intervention that were so common under the Bloody Code (but that were likewise so prone to arbitrary abuse). Unfortunately, modern criminal justice has sought no suitable alternative equitable mechanism, opting instead to shelve equitable discretion in favor of mandatory sentencing. It is, however, a false choice between unfettered equitable discretion and statutory uniformity. A viable middle path is a robust, structured, and public equitable screen—a path already charted in the capital context. My recommendation, then, is to use the capital sentencing model as a template to reconfigure LWOP sentencing.

This, of course, invites the question, Why stop at LWOP? Perhaps we should not, but, to my thinking, it would seem to be a particularly appropriate place to start.

Mandatory Capital Punishment and the Bloody Code

In common-law England, capital punishment was imposed frequently. Indeed, as many as seventy-two thousand persons were executed during the reign of Henry VIII.[1] Even against this historical backdrop, however, the period from the early seventeenth to early nineteenth century—the period of the so-called Bloody Code—stands out for the sheer number of crimes punishable by mandatory death.[2] Specifically, there were approximately 50 crimes that carried a required capital sentence in 1688. By 1820, that figure had risen to over 220 offenses.[3] Crimes as trivial as counterfeiting a stamp, stealing a rabbit, and even unlawfully felling a tree were sufficient to expose a defendant to the ultimate sanction.[4] At the same time, Parliament sought to eliminate (or at least radically limit) the availability of benefit of the clergy— a traditional mechanism to permit equitable exception from otherwise mandatory death.[5]

Individuation, however, is not so easily eradicated from criminal justice. Mandatory sentencing law is only as rigid as the human constructs and institutional arrangements put in place to apply it.[6] In the case of the Bloody Code, the system adapted to the "unmitigated severity" of the formal law with alternative means to circumvent its dictates. For instance, the king and his ministers used the pardon power frequently to avoid mandatory imposition of capital sentences.[7] And, by the sixteenth century, prosecutors had developed the unreviewable power to decline prosecution in equitably appropriate cases (and in regrettably inappropriate cases, as well).[8] Finally, and perhaps most significantly, at the trial phase, judges and juries discovered creative ways to acquit defendants of capital charges. By way of example, judges would invoke strategically doctrines such as strict construction of criminal statutes in what Livingston Hall called "a veritable conspiracy" to reject normatively problematic capital prosecutions.[9]

And, significantly, premodern juries would manipulate trial verdicts to advance the same normative end. For two reasons, these historical juries had substantially more discretion to acquit sympathetic defendants than their contemporary counterparts do. First, historical juries were arbiters of both law and fact. They were considered to be "good judges of the common law of the land" and were thus often instructed only to credit their "own consciences" or to "do justice between the parties not by any quirks of law . . . but by common sense as between man and man."[10] Second, historical juries had ample opportunity to align law to the dictates of moral intuition, because the common (and even statutory) law of the time was, itself, comparatively formless. In particular, the culpability concepts found in statutes of the era had not yet crystallized into the refined terms of art that they are today. Instead, a given amorphous *mens rea* term typically operated as little more than an "arbitrary symbol" into which decision-makers could pour the meaning they felt appropriate for the case at hand.[11] Concretely, the measure of guilt was "general moral blameworthiness"—a remarkably malleable concept even in less pluralistic times and a concept that, in any event, was not categorically implicated by technical violation of death-eligible statutes.[12] For example, even with respect to the grave crime of murder, the "loose" *mens rea* term "malice" came to be—in James Fitzjames Stephen's words—no more than a signifier of "the propriety of hanging particular people."[13]

As compared to the modern jury's verdict (which focuses principally on a mechanistic determination of act and intent), the premodern jury's verdict turned on a retributive evaluation of motive and character.[14] And code language (where it existed) provided no more than the pretext for normative judgment. Consequently, the informal and unstructured nature of the era's liability rules left significant room for the exercise of equitable discretion. In this way, the premodern jury was considered to be more than just an adjudicative body. Like a legislature, it would structure the substantive law to meet the equitable demands of the particular case by locating equitable defenses (or, alternatively, grounds for conviction) in capacious legal terms.[15]

And, significantly, when the premodern jury engaged in such normative evaluation, it was not unlawfully nullifying criminal law; rather, it was bending law according to the applicable procedural standards of the day.[16] In short, it was the jury's *duty* to *declare* the law's meaning, and, when the jury shaped the law according to a particularistic moral evaluation, the jury was just doing its job.[17] And, of course, once the jury declared the law in the immediate case, its announcement was inviolable.[18] It was not until much later that this robust and legitimate exercise of jury power was recast as unlawful nullification.[19]

However, it does not follow that the power and legal authority of the premodern jury was without limit. Its ability to intervene equitably was relegated almost exclusively to the adjudicatory phase and not at all to the sentencing phase. This highlights an important but underappreciated insight: criminal justice may be mandatory or discretionary along any of several dimensions.[20]

According to James Q. Whitman, "Systems that are harsh in one way will often *systematically mitigate* by showing mildness in another."[21] Roughly, a system may permit or forbid flexibility in enforcement, adjudication, sentencing, or the administration of punishment. Specifically, Whitman has segregated harshness according to (i) the substantive breadth of criminalized conduct, (ii) the level of enforcement, (iii) the flexibility of liability rules and affirmative defenses, (iv) the types of punishments prescribed, and (v) the certainty of administration.[22] Under this taxonomy, the Bloody Code was only clearly harsh in its penalty, while it was positively lenient in its administration (based on both the flexibility of its liability rules and the frequent executive grants of pardons). Put simply, the sentencing law was rigid, but the rest of the legal system was not.

Contemporary Capital Punishment and The Bloody Code

Skip across to the New World and ahead to the twentieth century. By the end of the progressive era, mandatory punishment—capital or otherwise—had become something of a relic.[23] Typically, judges could select from wide ranges of available sentences, and parole boards had broad discretion to determine when prison terms should end.[24] Indeed, as of 1970, every state and the federal system had adopted indeterminate sentencing for all but select crimes.[25] However, over the latter quarter of the century, determinate punishments came roaring back.[26] And, by 1996, all states and the federal government had enacted at least some kinds of determinate sentencing laws.[27]

Significantly, determinate sentencing laws come in a variety of forms that are more or less responsive to the particulars of criminal incident and offender. For example, mandatory-minimum statutes are the least context sensitive. By contrast, sentencing guidelines typically take account of at least some individual offense and offender characteristics. But, critically, even the most flexible sentencing guidelines still rely substantially on quantitative rubrics. And mathematical formulae can take us only so far since retributive worth is ultimately a qualitative measure. In any event, the vagaries of life outstrip "sentencing math" that tends to count *most* that which can be counted *most easily*—such as drug weight and monetary loss, as opposed to moral blameworthiness.[28] Thus, guidelines' determinations of desert are about as probing as the drunk who looks for his keys under the lamppost. Unsurprisingly, then, the federal guidelines have been criticized as "a sentencing process that has been drained of its humanity,"[29] a "mechanistic process."[30] In short, even guidelines are much more determinate than discretionary sentencing.

No definitive explanation accounts for the ascension of contemporary determinate sentencing, and a complete exploration of the reasons for the rise are beyond the scope of this chapter. What is striking, however, is the degree to which opposing interest groups and political factions were able to find common ground in support of the laws—at least early on.[31] Left-liberals saw determinate sentencing to be an antidote to racial and economic inequalities in discretionary sentencing.[32] Law-and-order conservatives saw determinate sentencing to be an antidote to lenient liberal judges.[33] Prosecutors, for their part, welcomed determinate sentencing as a cudgel to help fight the burgeoning war on drugs and to extract guilty pleas in a criminal justice system that had come to rely on plea bargaining as its principal mode of disposition.[34] Finally, legislators exploited determinate sentencing for political gain.[35]

Notably, in the capital sentencing context, the Supreme Court credited left-liberal concerns about unfettered discretion. Specifically, in *Furman v. Georgia*, the Court imposed a *de facto* moratorium on discretionary capital punishment that "created a substantial risk that [the penalty] would be inflicted in an arbitrary and capricious manner."[36] But, notably, the Court blocked all legislative efforts to fix this problem by making the death penalty mandatory. Specifically, ten states tried to pass mandatory capital statutes intended to address the constitutional infirmities identified in *Furman*, but the Court refused to let these states swing the pendulum from unfettered capital sentencing discretion to unbending determinacy.[37] Instead, it held that mandatory capital sentencing statutes were *per se* "unduly harsh and unworkably rigid" and thus violated the Eighth Amendment.[38] For the Court, then, particularization was a value too important to be sacrificed to a categorical imperative. In the Court's words, "[Mandatory capital punishment] treats all people convicted of a designated offense not as uniquely individual human beings, but as members of a faceless, undifferentiated mass to be subjected to the blind infliction of the penalty of death."[39]

Over time, the Court came to endorse two principal mechanisms to guarantee individualized capital sentencing determinations. First, the Court adopted a robust doctrine of proportionality review that demands an examination not only of whether the punishment is disproportionate to the crime in the abstract but of whether—all things considered—capital punishment is a disproportionately harsh response to the particular criminal incident and offender. Thus, an equitable evaluation of "moral guilt" became a critical part of the appellate court's determination of whether a defendant's death sentence is proportional.[40] Second, and more importantly, the Court provided a bifurcated capital sentencing proceeding that requires a jury to consider not just the circumstances of the criminal incident but also "the character and propensities of the offender."[41]

Significantly, however, the sentencing jury's discretion is not unfettered. In the first instance, the Court has held that a capital sentence is only constitutionally available for a narrow class of offenses[42] and offenders[43] and that a jury may not sentence a defendant to death without finding at least one legislatively enumerated (and sufficiently precise) aggravating factor.[44] But, notably, the Court has done far less to keep a capital sentencing jury from exercising mercy. Although the Court has approved of jury instructions that prohibit the jury from relying upon sympathy in reaching its capital determination,[45] the Court requires no such instructions, and, in any event, the Court otherwise has entitled the defendant to frame mitigation in "the most expansive terms."[46] Specifically, it has authorized the sentencing jury to consider "any aspect of a defendant's character or record and any of the circumstances of the offense that the defendant proffers as a basis for a sentence less than death."[47] In like fashion, the Court has held that legislatures may not even delineate an exhaustive list of relevant mitigating factors.[48]

No doubt, this creates something of an imbalance between the comparatively more rule-bound determination of whether a defendant qualifies for death and the equitable determination of whether to forgo the penalty.[49] But that is as it should be. Equity and mercy go hand in hand. According to Martha Nussbaum, there is a "close connection between equitable judgment—judgment that attends to the particulars—and mercy," because equity is "a temper of mind that refuses to demand retribution without understanding the whole story."[50]

To the extent a discretionary sentencing body will inevitably make mistakes, errors of mercy are preferable to errors of severity. Arbitrary and capricious harshness is worse than arbitrary and capricious compassion, just as the conviction of the innocent is worse than the acquittal of the guilty.[51] Put simply, justice is more offended by Type I than Type II errors.

This is not just a philosophical claim; it is a core constitutional principle. Typically, the principle is invoked only in the context of the question of *legal* guilt or innocence. For instance, the constitutional concern for erroneous convictions animates the rule that defendants are free to appeal convictions, while the government must accept even obviously legally erroneous acquittals.[52] But, critically, this constitutional principle has deeper roots that run to the *equitable* question of just deserts. Thus, as Akhil Amar has put it, "Cruel and unusual punishments are expressly prohibited by the Constitution; merciful and unusual punishments are not."[53] And, by the same logic, capital defendants have the constitutional right to appeal expressly to the equitable temperament of the sentencing body to mitigate the risk of an erroneously harsh punishment.

Comparatively, a principal problem with the Bloody Code was that it made errors of severity just too easy. The default was death. To exercise mercy or otherwise to consider the equities, the jury had to *work* to reshape the law—a task the jury could not be expected to perform consistently enough. Moreover, the jury could not provide equitable mitigation except at a high societal price: complete acquittal of an actually guilty and probably somewhat blameworthy defendant. Put differently, because juries could influence verdict but not penalty, they lacked the power to calibrate normative culpability to consequent sentence. The result was often an unattractive all-or-nothing proposition: the injustice of unwarranted exculpation or the injustice of unwarranted condemnation.[54] Thus, the Bloody Code produced frequent instances of chance windfalls *and* excessive harshness. In some instances, children as young as seven were put to death for mere theft.[55] And, in others, "the worst doers of wickedness [were] . . . thrown back upon society, again to commit crime."[56]

Mandatory LWOP and the Bloody Code

Mandatory LWOP penalties come in two principal forms. In certain settings, the sentence is the only option to a discretionary death penalty.[57] Specifically, in well over half of the states that retain the death penalty, LWOP is the required alternative.[58] In other settings, it is the only available sentence for a given crime or subcategory of crime.[59] In either event, equitable valuation is almost entirely irrelevant to the sentencing decision.[60]

Ostensibly, the Supreme Court has retained a version of proportionality review even in LWOP and other noncapital cases, but it is a weak version stripped of its equitable component—a "narrow" and formalistic conception of proportionality whereby *legal* guilt constitutes presumptive constitutionality.[61] Specifically, to raise an Eighth Amendment challenge to a noncapital penalty, a defendant must establish "an inference of gross disproportionality" based on a "threshold comparison of the crime committed and the sentence imposed."[62] Thus, a defendant must demonstrate that the crime is *categorically* disproportionate—that is to say that it is disproportionate in the abstract and not as individually applied.[63] Applying this anemic brand of proportionality review, courts have tended to declare constitutional whatever noncapital penalties democratically accountable legislatures prescribe.[64] By way of example, in *Harmelin v. Michigan*, the Supreme Court held constitutional a state statute that mandated an LWOP sentence for first-time possession of more than 650 grams of cocaine.[65] And decisions such as *Harmelin* tend to be self-reinforcing, not only by foreclosing the immediate challenge but also by setting proportionality "benchmark[s]" that insulate from proportionality review analogous statutes.[66]

Thus, noncapital mandatory sentencing has provided opportunities for neither front-end equitable intervention in the form of contextualized sentencing nor back-end equitable intervention in the form of case-specific proportionality review.[67] The length and mandatory character of punishment has become "purely a matter of legislative prerogative."[68] And mandatory penalties, in turn, have proliferated like the kudzu vine. By contrast, "humane and sensible" punishment decisions that are calibrated to "the uniqueness of the individual" have remained constitutionally reserved for only the isolated capital case.[69]

In such circumstances, contemporary LWOP statutes have come to resemble the Bloody Code more than they do the contemporary death penalty. Like historical capital crimes, contemporary LWOP statutes often prescribe mandatory sanctions. And, like the historical death penalty, the sanction is authorized for a wide variety of substantive offenses. Of course, the penalty does not reach as far as the Bloody Code. No modern jurisdiction, for instance, would require or even permit LWOP for chopping down a neighbor's tree.[70] But, significantly, almost ten percent of inmates serving LWOP—well over three thousand inmates nationwide—were convicted of only drug, property, or other nonviolent offenses.[71] Indeed, as Jessica Henry observes in her illuminating contribution to this volume, almost two-fifths of federal defendants sentenced to whole-life sentences were convicted of only drug crimes, including a first offender who pled guilty to only marijuana-related offenses.[72] Comparatively, contemporary capital punishment is constitutionally permitted only for certain types of murder and certain very serious crimes against the state, such as espionage or treason.[73]

The analogy to the Bloody Code carries only so far, however. As indicated, the common-law jury had significantly greater discretionary power to reach a trial verdict that tempered the reach of mandatory sentencing statutes. Because the early jury was aware that the wages of conviction were death, it could make the rough normative choice for acquittal over condemnation in instances when it believed that death was unwarranted. The contemporary jury has no comparable authority to recraft law to meet the equities of the case. Instead, it is legally required to take the judge's instructions as fixed and immutable commands and is permitted to find only facts and to apply those facts mechanically to prefabricated law. And the prefabricated law is, in turn, comparatively rigid and precise in its meaning. In particular, historical *mens rea* inquiries into general moral blameworthiness and evil design have yielded to element-specific inquiries into intent.[74] Accordingly, the modern jury's capacity to uncover equitable defenses in the language of vague statutes has largely disappeared in circumstances in which, put simply, the statutes are no longer vague.[75] Nor does a defendant retain much practical hope for an *ex post* fix: postconviction exercises of executive pardon or commutation powers—once so prevalent—have largely vanished, particularly in violent felony cases.[76]

Recall the five dimensions of James Q. Whitman's taxonomy of harshness: the breadth of substantive criminal law, the level of enforcement, the inflexibility of liability rules and defenses, the draconian nature of penalties, and the degree of administrative certainty. Modern mandatory punishments are harsh along all measures. Commenting on the trend in modern criminal justice generally, Whitman observed, "Against all of these movements toward harshness, it is very difficult to point to any mitigating move toward mildness."[77] In the specific context of mandatory punishments, we find that the underlying liability rules are mechanistic and the affirmative defenses narrowly defined and few; the enforcement levels are typically high, because—as will be discussed—prosecutors who may select from broad charging menus are motivated to file the most serious cognizable charges to facilitate bargaining; and, finally, the mandatory penalties are, by their nature, inflexible, and the governing substantive criminal codes are expansive, as the literature on overcriminalization reveals.[78]

At common law, the trial jury might reconstitute the law to the defendant's favor, or the king or his ministers might reset a harsh sentence after the fact. In the modern era, the jury is bound to return a verdict of guilt once the prosecutor has introduced evidence establishing the structured legal elements of the offense, and thereafter the judge is required to impose a mandatory-minimum sentence or, at best, work out a guidelines' score according to calculations that are almost as legalistic and formulaic as the determination of the underlying verdict.[79]

However, we ought not turn back the clock. Persuasive rule-of-law arguments militate against a return to the broad discretionary power exercised by the premodern trial jury. As indicated, historical application of mandatory capital punishment was haphazard or even invidious. The common-law jury might have convicted one sympathetic defendant but acquitted a culpable other, or—worse still—it might have based its determinations on such regressive considerations as reputation, affluence, social status, or race. On balance, then, legality doctrines and professionalized processes have been positive developments. But, as prevailing capital sentencing doctrine illuminates, such desirable doctrines of legality need not be synonymous with rigidity. The law can seek to find middle ground between mechanistic and evaluative approaches—between the capricious and the categorical. As Martha Nussbaum and Dan Kahan have observed, such a balance is especially desirable in the context of serious penalties, such as LWOP:

> [There should be] a place for the narrative history—*especially when the penalty that may be fixed is a severe one,* and especially where the defendant's background shows some prima facie evidence of unusual hardship or inequality. In such a case, we want to look into things more deeply, to see whether we may have missed some unusual impediment that deformed the process of character formation. At this point, a long moral and legal tradition holds that we owe it to the dignity and humanity of the defendant to let the entire history appear, in case some aspect might inspire a merciful response.[80]

Of course, the risk of abuse of equitable discretion is endemic—as is the risk of abuse across human endeavors. But it does not translate that we ought to abandon the equitable endeavor just because equitable discretion paradoxically may empower decision-makers to behave inequitably by, for example, exacerbating the oppressive treatment of historically subjugated groups.[81] The risk of abuse merely underscores the need for conscientious institutional and legal design intended to express and cabin equitable discretion optimally.[82]

Mandatory LWOP and Executive Discretion

Notably, the modern criminal justice system has not wholly stripped equitable discretion from adjudication and sentencing and has not, therefore, even fulfilled its ostensible promise of eliminating the risk of abuse. Specifically, prosecutors retain practically plenary power over the addition and subtraction of legally cognizable charges.[83] The prosecutor thereby controls the critical decision whether the defendant faces a mandatory-minimum charge in the first instance (and whether the defendant may bargain out of it).[84] Put simply, there is no mandate that a prosecutor seek a mandatory penalty. Thus, mandatory sentencing rests on a hollow premise of determinacy. In fact, the use and abuse of discretion have just been driven underground and, almost exclusively, into the hands of the professional executive, who controls the relatively invisible and informal charge and bargain determinations.[85]

Nontransparency is its own problem, but the bigger challenge is that the professional prosecutor cannot be expected to exercise equitable power consistently or appropriately.[86] Critically, I do not mean by this claim to denigrate prosecutors or their enterprise. I wish only to highlight certain extant institutional incentives and cognitive biases that may affect prosecutorial good-faith efforts to individualize charging and bargaining decisions.

First, a bit of background: the criminal justice system has seen fit to entrust the charging decision to prosecutors, because they are considered most competent to assess the evidentiary merits of cases and the practical capacities of their offices.[87] Put simply, prosecutors are best suited to exercise *legal* and *administrative* discretion.[88] This much is unobjectionable. But, significantly, discretion involves more than just legal and administrative considerations; it requires equitable considerations, as well.[89] And it is less clear that prosecutors have any like superior claim to equitable perspective.[90] In fact, I have argued elsewhere that prosecutors may have inferior claim—that the system's faith in the equitable decision-making of prosecutors is misplaced. Specifically, I raised a number of reasons to believe that prosecutors' expertise on matters legal and administrative may work against their abilities to exercise equitable discretion appropriately.

Some of the reasons are cognitive. First, prosecutors are trained professionals, and trained professionals typically develop heuristics that may frustrate adequate contextualization.[91] In this way, "mechanistic, impersonal, lawyerized criminal justice" may interfere with what some scholars have identified as an intuitive "deep human need" to humanize and particularize retributive questions.[92] Second, prosecutors are *interested*. As former Assistant U.S. Attorney I. Bennett Capers makes plain in his eye-opening chapter in this volume, the prosecutor's adversarial perspective may too readily slip into a win-at-all-costs mentality that is antithetical to individualization.[93]

A third reason is institutional—particularly, an institutional preference for expeditious guilty pleas. Here, the problem is not that prosecutors are callous but that they are motivated to disregard the equities, because the more serious a prosecutor's initial charge, the more likely it is that the defendant will agree to plea.[94] Of course, this is something of a caricature of prosecutors. Not all (or even most) prosecutors do, in fact, succumb to such institutional pressures. (Indeed, some offices have even made deliberative charge screening an institutional priority.)[95] My intention is not to describe prevailing prosecutorial charging practices but only to highlight that rational prosecutors do experience these pressures and may find them compelling.

Significantly, a prosecutor who succumbs to such pressures often has ample charging options to exploit, because the Constitution has set surprisingly few limits on the creation of substantive noncapital offenses, and legislatures have responded by enacting expansive criminal codes that proscribe "far more conduct than any jurisdiction could possibly punish."[96] As William Stuntz has observed, the effect has been a significant transfer of policymaking authority from the legislator to the prosecutor when it comes to determinations of which criminals and what conduct will or will not result in LWOP sentences.[97] And, just as the Supreme Court has done little to constrain the legislative expansion of substantive criminal codes, so too it has done little to check the prosecutor's bargaining power.[98]

For instance, in *Bordenkircher v. Hayes*, the Court held that prosecutors may use the threat of any lawful sentence to extract a guilty plea.[99] Specifically, in *Bordenkircher*, the defendant declined a five-year plea offer on an eighty-dollar forged-check charge and was recharged as a habitual offender, subject to a mandatory LWOP sentence.[100] Put simply, the prosecutor offered the defendant an equitable and individualized disposition of a few years, but only at the price of pleading guilty. When the defendant turned down this offer, the prosecutor took the equitable disposition off the table, and the defendant received a mandatory LWOP sentence. The Court held that the prosecutorial decision to elevate the charge fell well within the constitutional "give-and-take" of plea bargaining.[101] The case highlights several critical insights: the temptation for prosecutors to use habitual offender laws to threaten mandatory life in prison for relatively insignificant felonies; the temptation for defendants to take pleas in exchange for equitable sentences; and the disparate outcomes that flow from convictions for conduct ostensibly covered by mandatory sentencing laws.

There are, of course, open empirical questions as to how often defendants are pleading out of mandatory LWOP charges and into terms of years or out of capital charges and into LWOP sentences. And I do not seek to provide hard answers to these empirical questions, but only to draw attention to the analytically undeniable fact that mandatory sentencing statutes tend to provide prosecutors with effective bargaining weapons that may prove hard to resist—a point Capers makes plain in his contribution to this volume, in which he recalls the practice of his office to reflexively leverage high charges.[102] Specifically, Capers confesses, "We prosecuted our LWOP defendants as if they were . . . on an assembly line. . . . Even now, . . . I have trouble remembering even one of my LWOP defendants."[103]

To further understand the point, consider the example of Clarence Aaron, a college student who received three mandatory LWOP sentences for facilitating a drug deal in exchange for $1,500.[104] Aaron had a number of co-defendants who, unlike Aaron, cooperated and received lenient sentences—an average of eight years in prison.[105] Significantly, even the assigned U.S. Attorney conceded that the co-defendants were more culpable and equitably deserved harsher treatment than Aaron did, but Aaron was punished for refusing to play ball (or for lacking the information with which to play). Concretely, he lost his shot at an equitably appropriate sentence once he elected to take his case to trial. According to the U.S. Attorney,

> He thought he was going to win and he was given every opportunity to help himself early on and he didn't want to do it. . . . These other people were perhaps guiltier or more culpable [but] they got less because they helped solve a case. . . . And the one person . . . that didn't [help] . . . suffered . . . *the consequences of the arrogance of thinking that you're going to beat this*, that *I'm too good to take a deal*.[106]

As the Aaron case illustrates, mandatory LWOP may come to be the sentence not for the defendant who retributively deserves the punishment but for the perceived "arrogant" (but perhaps less guilty or even actually innocent) defendant who exercises constitutional rights. In this way, legislators have prescribed a punishment that only interested prosecutors can temper but that prosecutors have the least interest in tempering for reasons of equitable justice alone. The defendant must either bargain for an individualized sentence or forfeit equitable evaluation in exchange for the exercise of trial rights (putting to one side, of course, rare exercises of jury nullification, pardon, or commutation).

In the words of one prosecutor, the defendant has to "pick which horse they want to ride": litigation or cooperation.[107] And it is not much of an option. The defendant finds him- or herself facing a Morton's fork (a choice between two equally unpleasant alternatives) or even a Hobson's choice (a choice that offers only one option). That is, the defendant must submit to whatever sentence the prosecutor deems equitably (or otherwise) appropriate or face a trial process stripped free of equitable discretion.[108]

The Advantages of Lay Sentencing Discretion

But can we expect lay arbiters to better exercise equitable discretion? As I argue elsewhere, we can.[109] There are plausible reasons to believe that lay bodies contextualize the retributive inquiry better than legal technicians do.[110] More than the professional, the layperson has the capacity and inclination to cut through the thicket of legal and institutional norms (that are not the layperson's stock in trade) to the equitable question of blameworthiness that is and ought to be central to the sentencing determination.[111] As Justice Rehnquist once observed, the lay juror's "very inexperience is an asset because it secures a fresh perception of each trial, avoiding the stereotypes said to infect the judicial eye."[112]

This is a theme to which lower courts have returned repeatedly: that lay jurors are "not likely to get into the habit of disregarding any circumstances of fact, or of forcing cases into rigid forms and arbitrary classes";[113] that "the good sense of a jury . . . that take[s] a common-sense view of every question" is sometimes to be preferred to the judgment of the legal professional who "generalizes and reduces everything to an artificial system formed by study."[114] These courts have recognized an Aristotelian insight: that evaluation of just deserts is not mechanistic and technical but, instead, draws on practical wisdom about "the common concerns of life"[115]—an intuitive kind of wisdom that the layperson consults naturally.[116]

Finally, the lay jury has the advantage of size. It draws on the diverse retributive perspectives of a collective as opposed to "a lone employee of the State."[117] At least when it comes to incorporating different normative viewpoints, we ought to expect a collective to do better work than an individual.[118] Significantly, this is more than just an argument for the "wisdom of crowds."[119] A criminal justice system that equitably empowers lay bodies "fosters democratic visibility," facilitates democratic participation, and provides voice to traditionally underrepresented and subordinated groups, thereby potentially softening racial and economic sentencing disparities.[120] The Supreme Court itself seems to have implicitly understood and appreciated this reading in *Duncan v. Louisiana* when it held that a defendant is constitutionally entitled to appeal to "the common-sense judgment of a jury" over "the more tutored but perhaps less sympathetic reaction of the single judge."[121]

To some extent, recognition of these advantages sounds in "popular constitutionalism."[122] A jury with equitable power provides the people with a check on the professional prosecutor's exercise of state sovereignty.[123] Done well, such a popular screen is not synonymous with lawlessness; it is harmonious with the rule of law and with *complete* justice, which Aristotle conceptualized as legal justice tempered by equity.[124] An equitable jury has the capacity to function as a minilegislature that individualizes punishment according to local norms that keep police and prosecutors accountable and that may do better—in William Stuntz's words—to honor values of "moderation and equality" by placing equitable power "in the hands of residents of those neighborhoods where the most criminals and victims live."[125] According to Stuntz, "When prosecutors have enormous discretionary power, giving other decisionmakers discretion promotes consistency, not arbitrariness. . . . [I]nstitutional competition curbs excess and abuse."[126]

By contrast, the concentration of equitable power in the professional actor—here, the prosecutor—may, in fact, *heighten* concerns about the misuse and outright abuse of equitable discretion because professional prosecutors are comparatively hamstrung along two dimensions: first, they crave the kinds of "established rules and fixed precepts" that, in the words of Blackstone, risk "destroying [equity's] very essence, and reducing it to positive law";[127] and, second, they are likelier to act alone in reaching retributive determinations.

Finally, facilitating visibility and local participation has an added advantage: a criminal justice system that equitably empowers lay bodies is likelier to be seen as legitimate and morally credible.[128] Specifically, individuals tend to perceive lay decision-making to be more procedurally fair than professional decision-making.[129] And individuals tend to reject punishment decisions that fail to reflect communal perceptions of just deserts.[130]

Such rejection may take either of two forms—both unhealthy. Individuals may grow demoralized and apathetic toward a system of justice that fails to vest in them the responsibility to reach normative determinations.[131] Conversely, individuals may rebel. As Paul Robinson and John Darley have explained, "A system that is perceived as unjust is in danger of being subverted and ignored. On the one hand, it risks jury nullification and martyrdom that rallies resistance to its commands. On the other, it risks vigilantism."[132] Paul Robinson explores this insight further in his contribution to this volume, concluding, "[T]he empirical evidence suggests that the doctrines that produce LWOP sentences regularly and seriously conflict with the community's shared intuitions of justice. That conflict . . . undermines the criminal law's moral credibility with the community it governs and thereby undermines the law's crime-control effectiveness."[133]

Thus, mandatory LWOP statutes may prove self-defeating: efforts to strip a given institution of equitable discretion not only liberate other institutions to use and abuse discretion unchecked but may also provoke backlash and lawless subversion from the disempowered institution—a danger vividly illustrated by the unwillingness of juries and judges to enforce the Bloody Code.[134] Indeed, it was this very concern (among others) that motivated the Supreme Court to reject mandatory capital sentencing: "[A] mandatory scheme may well exacerbate the problem [of arbitrary and capricious result] . . . by resting the penalty determination on the particular jury's willingness to act lawlessly."[135]

If nothing else, mandatory sentencing regimes put jurors in tight spots: jurors are instructed to convict legally guilty defendants, but they have no control over (or even awareness of) the mandated (and perhaps equitably inappropriate) sentences. Again, the Clarence Aaron case provides a dramatic example. Years after the guilty verdict, one of the jurors was informed of Aaron's sentence during an interview for a documentary. The juror responded with shock and some apparent dismay: "I'm surprised by that, that harsh a sentence. He seemed to be a pretty promising boy. Why did he get such a high sentence, I wonder? I wish I didn't know now that they'd got life."[136] It would seem that the juror's systemic faith had been shaken by the administration of a sentence that he was legally obligated to trigger but had no authority to temper.

Allocating Sentencing Discretion

This is not to say that the system ought to shut professional prosecutors out of the sentencing determination. There are costs to abdicating discretion wholesale to lay bodies, just as there are costs to leaving it exclusively to professionals. The problem with mandatory sentencing law is not that prosecutors possess equitable discretion but that they possess it alone.

It is no simple task to determine how to optimally allocate sentencing discretion, but it is clearer that the answer ought not to be an exclusive grant of decision-making authority to the least transparent and most interested actor. Instead, the objective ought to be a *sharing* of power.[137] Different institutional actors possess different proficiencies, and the criminal justice system ought to allocate discretion to tap respective competencies.[138] As indicated, there is strong reason to believe that a lay jury is especially good at reaching intuitive determinations of blameworthiness. But, comparatively, professional prosecutors are especially good at evaluating considerations of institutional priority and administrative capacity.[139] And judges are especially good at accommodating nonretributive principles of punishment, such as deterrence, incapacitation, and rehabilitation.[140] Ideally, then, the sentencing decision ought to be influenced by *both* lay and professional bodies. Within limits, all parties have constructive roles to play. In this way, the best approach may be one in which "[d]iscretion limits discretion."[141]

The capital sentencing model provides a practical model. First, discretionary power is limited structurally by providing opportunities for each institutional actor to screen the others. The capital sentencing jury retains authority to accept or reject a capital sentence, and its decision to decline a capital sentence is final.[142] The judge retains authority to override a jury's normatively problematic decision to impose a capital sentence.[143] And the prosecutor retains equitable, legal, and administrative discretion to select and file (and thereafter bargain away from) capital charges.[144] Second, discretionary power is limited substantively by the requirement that the jury must find an enumerated aggravating factor before it may impose a capital sentence.[145] The jury is even guided in its decision to mitigate. Specifically, although a legislature may not statutorily constrain arguments for mercy, it may and typically does prescribe a set of nonexclusive enumerated mitigating factors.[146] Additionally, the judge may exclude mitigating evidence "not bearing on the defendant's character, prior record, or the circumstances of [his or her] offense."[147] In this way, the judge retains authority to channel equitable arguments for mitigation to the categories of considerations that bear most directly on normative blameworthiness and away from categories of considerations that are tangential or unrelated to individualized evaluation (for instance, abstract arguments about the morality or efficacy of capital punishment).

This would seem to be a desirable approach for a system that seeks to minimize the risk of arbitrary and capricious result but to maximize "particularized consideration of relevant aspects of the character and record of each convicted defendant before the imposition on him of a sentence of death."[148] My argument is not that the capital sentencing process is nonproblematic or even that the substantive offense is justifiable on any terms. My argument is simply that the prevailing capital sentencing structure provides a workable outline for a system that values equitable expression but not its abuse.

The Myth of Death's Difference

Perhaps the most frequently invoked argument for limiting equitable discretion to the capital context is the undertheorized, often-repeated, and almost tautological maxim that "death is different."[149] Indeed, the Supreme Court has relied on just this rationale in holding that equitable sentencing is no "constitutional imperative" in the noncapital context (even though, it is, per the Court, a matter of "enlightened policy").[150] But, as Rachel Barkow makes plain in her chapter in this volume, capital cases have no monopoly on morally salient differences. Legally alike noncapital cases also may be equitably distinct from each other.[151] Put differently, the need for equitable discretion does not evaporate once death is taken off the table. In fact, the importance of equitable evaluation may grow in noncapital cases (though the stakes, admittedly, shrink). Specifically, when it comes to the kinds of heinous criminal conduct that are punishable by death, the equities would seem relatively less likely to overweight the offender's bad act. Comparatively, when it comes to normatively more ambiguous nonviolent criminal conduct (particularly *mala prohibita* conduct), the equities are likelier to be persuasive. Ironically, then, under prevailing sentencing practices, the power to individualize fades for the very types of crime that are less intuitively blameworthy and that ought, therefore, to be more sensitive to equitable differences.

The counterargument, echoed by the Supreme Court, is that the "severity and irrevocability" of the death penalty make it a punishment different in kind, not degree.[152] But, once we scratch below the surface, it becomes less clear that LWOP is definitively milder along either dimension.[153] On the question of finality, even a short term of years may be considered as final as death in the narrow sense that the inmate cannot recover lost time.[154] But, even under a more robust reading, LWOP and death are comparable because in both contexts the defendant is scheduled to die behind bars.

Admittedly, this claim is open to an objection—that is, the question of whether the condemned person will, in fact, die within prison walls. Specifically, the finality of any death-in-prison sentence is not absolute because approaches to punishment are historically contingent.[155] Concretely, it is to some degree academic to talk *right now* about what a sentence will mean in a future *then*. For instance, in previous generations, defendants who received life sentences believed that if they lived long enough and behaved appropriately, they would one day be granted parole. But perspectives on punishment changed over time, and, consequently, the possibility of parole came to mean very little in many jurisdictions (at least with respect to violent crimes). Thus, many defendants sentenced to life *with* the possibility of parole a quarter century ago have found their past hopes for release to have been ephemeral. Perhaps the tides may turn again. Perhaps defendants sentenced to LWOP today will enjoy a rosier future, and LWOP sentences will be commuted or otherwise revisited.

This objection to the finality point is valid, but it feels a bit cheap. As with most wait-and-see arguments, the objection functions as an unproductive conversation stopper that may serve to distract from a pressing public-policy debate. In any event, we may choose, instead, to evaluate LWOP based on what the state intends by it today, rather than what the penalty may come to mean in the future. More to the point, the objection to the finality argument applies with almost equal force to the capital context. That is, approaches to capital punishment are similarly elastic (though, admittedly, the temporal window for legal change is likely to be smaller). Take Charles Manson, for instance. He may have had little hope of evading execution at the time he was sentenced to death, but then the California Supreme Court abolished the state's death penalty and Manson's sentence was commuted to life.[156] Likewise, many of Illinois's death-row inmates faced similarly grim prospects at the time they were condemned, but then Governor George Ryan declared a moratorium on capital punishment.[157] In a sense, then, no sentence is final—not even death.

Even on the question of severity, death is not definitively different. The question is to some degree subjective, as illustrated by the not uncommon phenomenon of "death-row volunteers"—those who prefer death to permanent incapacitation in what John Stuart Mill called a "living tomb."[158] Indeed, as Capers observes in his contribution to this volume, one study found that an equal plurality of "lifers" preferred death over life to life over death.[159] And, even from an external—or societal—perspective, death is not necessarily more severe. Capital punishment may satiate a retributive hunger,[160] but it concurrently provides offenders with a quicker way out. By contrast, a death-in-prison term forces bad actors to live with themselves and their transgression.[161] Paradoxically, then, to make offenders "feel guilty unto death,"[162] society must spare their lives.[163]

Ultimately, then, the conventional justification that "death is different" is almost certainly overplayed (even if it is not quite a canard). And, significantly, it is a justification that is overplayed not just by courts and law-and-order proponents. Specifically, some death penalty opponents have emphasized perceived differences between capital punishment and LWOP in an effort to provide jurors with a palatable alternative to death.[164] Thus, a cohort of criminal justice reformers have tolerated or even welcomed the turn to mandatory LWOP, calculating that a hands-off approach for tens of thousands of mandatory LWOP sentences may be a necessary evil to keep political and constitutional hands on several hundred death sentences.[165] In the process, LWOP has been granted something of a free pass even—or in fact especially—in its mandatory form.[166] But, if death is not, in fact, definitively different, then it is less than apparent why it should be subject to lay equitable evaluation while LWOP should not.

Leveling the Equitable Playing Field between Life and Death

Which brings me to my proposal: the criminal justice system ought to incorporate a lay equitable check similar to the capital sentencing model. Once again, this is not to say that the prevailing capital sentencing model is perfect. Far from it. Some degree of arbitrary lenience and harshness continues to infect the process. Worse still, social scientists have documented systemic racial and economic disparities in capital charging and sentencing.[167] And, regrettably, the Supreme Court has demonstrated an unwillingness to aggressively correct for invidious skews, even in the face of such hard empirical findings of disparate impact.[168] However, my purpose is not to linger on the extant flaws of the capital sentencing regime but instead to celebrate its chief (and perhaps only) virtue—the fact that it demands a good reason prior to the imposition of a sentence of death and that it provides a defendant with almost every opportunity to offer contrary reasons.

Again, it may be that there is never a persuasive reason for a sentence of death. Capital punishment demands its own justification and may well lack it. On this reading, arguments in favor of the prevailing capital sentencing procedure may serve to mask its substantive shortcomings. Likewise, arguments in favor of importing the capital sentencing procedure into the LWOP context may be criticized fairly as—to co-opt Justice Blackmun's famous framing—no more than an effort to "tinker with the machinery" of life without asking the more fundamental question of whether LWOP is an appropriate punishment in the first instance.[169] But, to my thinking, as long as the institution exists, it ought to be administered as fairly as possible. We ought not want to continue to impose a normatively questionable punishment in a particularly problematic form.

Thus, the turn toward LWOP has presented scholars with a choice: concentrate on the substantive question of whether LWOP is justified or the procedural question of how it ought to be administered. I do not doubt the importance of the substantive question, but I leave it to others to ask and answer it. That said, I can offer one rough-and-ready response to the objection that procedural reform may serve to provide a potentially indefensible substantive punishment with a patina of legitimacy: that is, an equitable sentencing jury not only provides a democratic check on the prosecutor; it forces the jury to take *responsibility* for its punishment decision.[170] It calls on laypersons to consider the potential punishment in light of a specific case, and—upon doing so—members of the sentencing jury are shaped and educated by that punishment decision going forward. Pithily, what they take away from the jury box, they may bring to the ballot box.

Under the proposed reforms, we might see a somewhat more dynamic relationship between the politics and punishment of crime. The jury's equitable decision might serve to bridge the divide between abstract legislation and specific incidents of crime. The concrete retributive question would be put to the people—not what punishment ought to be prescribed for which crime but what *this* punishment ought to be in *this* context for *this* offender.[171] As Paul Robinson discusses in his chapter in this volume, to the extent we think people's intuitions of justice matter, we ought to favor procedures that permit such fine-grained analysis.[172]

Enough with the preliminaries. What might such sentencing reforms look like in the LWOP context? A narrow proposal would be only to offer the capital sentencing jury an additional choice—life *with* the possibility of parole.[173] The reach of such a reform would obviously be limited: it would apply only to circumstances in which LWOP is the mandatory backstop to a discretionary death sentence. But an advantage of the narrow proposal is that it would present no added resource burden, because the court already must submit the capital sentencing decision to an equitable sentencing jury. Conceivably, some additional number of capital defendants who otherwise would have pled guilty might now submit their fate to the normative valuation of the jury, but, even if that would entail an investment of resources, it would seem to be money well spent. It is all to the good to redirect equitable discretion—at least a bit—from the prosecutor's exclusive bargaining domain to the jury and judge's shared sentencing domain. And, significantly, the proposal would do little to undermine a perceived benefit of mandatory LWOP. Specifically, juries are more willing to reject the death penalty when the alternative is LWOP, signaling that they find LWOP to be an attractive option.[174] Under the immediate proposal, it would remain an option, but that is all that it would and should be—a choice but not a backstop, *an* alternative but not the only alternative.

A more aggressive proposal would be to adopt capital-style jury sentencing for all cases in which the potential exists for an LWOP sentence or, more broadly, for any almost certain death-in-prison sentence. Critics have expressed the concern that the extension of capital sentencing procedures to LWOP could present something of a slippery slope. In Judge Alex Kozinski's words, "[I]f we put mandatory life imprisonment without parole into a unique constitutional category, we'll be hard pressed to distinguish mandatory life; the latter is nearly indistinguishable from a very long, mandatory term of years; and that, in turn, is hard to distinguish from shorter terms."[175] But, to my thinking, the concern is overblown. It is easy enough to draw a sensible bright line that approximates LWOP. For instance, a system might require sentencing by equitable jury for any potential term of more than seventy-five years or (only slightly more complicated) for any potential term of twenty-five years longer than the defendant's actuarial life. The line would be to some degree artificial, of course, but the criminal justice system draws artificial lines all the time: a defendant has a fundamental right to a jury trial for any crime punishable by 181 days, but not for a crime punishable by 180;[176] a defendant has a fundamental right to counsel when a misdemeanor conviction is punished by one-day jail, but not when the same conviction is punished by community service.[177]

Of course, the question remains: Why stop at LWOP or its functional equivalent? After all, many of my normative claims would seem to apply with almost equal force to determinate sentencing more broadly. I grant the point and come clean: my not-so-hidden (or original)[178] agenda is to call mandatory sentencing regimes into general question and to rehabilitate substantially equitable sentencing over which laypersons exercise some (but not exclusive) influence. Nevertheless, there are valid reasons to proceed cautiously.

First, and most obviously, the stakes of mandatory LWOP are higher than the stakes of conventional mandatory sentencing, and therefore the attendant problem of disregarding equitable differences across LWOP cases is comparatively greater.[179]

Second, and more critically, incremental reform would minimize the risk of overcorrection. Specifically, the immediate proposals would operate along not one but two dimensions: they would partially dismantle mandatory sentencing, *and* they would empower juries to participate equitably. As indicated, there are dangers to unfettered lay discretion, just as there are dangers to unfettered prosecutorial or judicial discretion.[180] The right balance between lay and professional equitable influence is a matter of trial and error, and, in such uncertain circumstances, modest experimentation is preferable to aggressive change. Accordingly, the immediate proposals would not abandon mandatory sentencing; they would soften it in one context only. Precisely, an equitable exception from LWOP would still result in a *mandatory* sentence of life with the possibility of parole.

Third, in the near term, it would be neither administratively nor politically feasible to roll back conventional noncapital mandatory sentencing statutes. Of course, it is no easy feat to dismantle mandatory LWOP sentences either, but it is at least practical. Under prevailing constitutional doctrine, it is unlikely that such reform would come from the Supreme Court. Accordingly, I direct the immediate proposals principally to legislators and not justices. Nevertheless, two recent jurisprudential developments hint that the Court may be moving slightly, but perceptibly, in the direction of lay equitable evaluation outside the capital sentencing context.

First, over the past decade, the Court has issued a string of decisions—beginning with *Apprendi v. New Jersey*—that entitle a defendant to submit to a jury any fact determination that enhances a penalty beyond the prescribed statutory maximum.[181] Although *Apprendi* and its lineage have focused exclusively on factual determinations, a number of commentators have observed that the logic of the decisions extends also to the "moral . . . decision-making that underlies sentencing."[182] For instance, the Court recently endorsed a vision of the jury as a "circuitbreaker" in "the State's machinery of justice."[183] And the need for such a circuitbreaker would seem to be as great—if not greater—in the equitable context.[184]

Second, in *Graham v. Florida*, the Court applied a robust vision of proportionality review to hold cruel and unusual life without parole for juvenile offenders in nonhomicide cases.[185] The case marks the first instance since *Solem v. Helm* in which the Court has deemed a mere term of incarceration to be unconstitutionally disproportionate.[186] Specifically, more than a quarter century ago, the *Solem* Court vacated a mandatory LWOP sentence for a recidivist defendant convicted of uttering a forged check.[187] But, in the decades following *Solem*, the Court repeatedly affirmed life sentences for seemingly inconsequential felonies. Over the years, *Solem* had come to be seen as an outlier.[188] Against that backdrop, *Graham* is something of a surprise and may represent a small but firm step away from the almost categorical position that a legislatively valid prison sentence cannot be cruel and unusual and toward the constitutional requirement of an individualized proportionality determination in noncapital cases.[189]

Indeed, the significance of *Graham* has not escaped academic attention. Several reformers have read into the decision an auspicious sign that the Court may soon come to endorse a more vigorous conception of proportionality review in noncapital cases.[190] I hope they are right. Even so, such a move would not be enough, because equitable justice is underserved by proportionality review alone. Proportionality review is desirable, but, in isolation, it shortchanges necessary normative evaluation by individualizing at the appellate level only. And appellate courts pay deference to trial judges. Specifically, to get relief, the defendant must establish that the trial court's sentence was constitutionally disproportionate under an abuse of discretion standard.[191] Such deference means that somewhat (but not grossly) disproportionate mandatory sentences will be left undisturbed. By contrast, a guided lay sentencing body pays deference to no prior sentencing determination because it acts *first*, and it brings to its decision a locally representative perspective on relative blameworthiness. Put simply, individualized sentencing individualizes immediately and directly.[192] Proportionality review remains one step removed.

Conclusion

When it comes to the procedural law of capital punishment, there has been something of an inversion from historical form. At common law, an equitable determination of wickedness was central to the conviction phase but was legally irrelevant to the sentencing phase. Today, the equitable determination is central to the sentencing phase but is legally irrelevant to the conviction phase. But when it comes to determinate sentencing, the transformation is incomplete or, more precisely, half formed. Lawful equitable intervention is foreclosed at both the conviction and sentencing phases. What remains is too little space for individualized retributive judgment—much less the kind of robust, public, and structured equitable screen supplied by the modern capital sentencing jury.

This is an especial concern in the context of mandatory LWOP. Such a severe penalty should not be imposed without an appropriate proportionality assessment that relies on particularized reasoned deliberation and normative evaluation. Of course, mandatory LWOP fails to meet this mark. As a backstop to a discretionary death sentence, mandatory LWOP provides no option to give the defendant *less* than natural life—even in circumstances in which the jury and the judge agree that a lesser sentence is normatively appropriate. As a stand-alone punishment, mandatory LWOP commands the penultimate penalty for a broad swath of criminal conduct—even for some types of nonviolent drug possession.[193]

In the rush to find an alternative to death, some traditional criminal justice reformers have lost sight of the normative question of whether the system *ought* to incarcerate a defendant for natural life and the procedural questions of who ought to make the call and under what circumstances. The answer cannot be blind faith in the unfettered discretion of prosecutors to do the right thing in the right case. It is simply too much to expect rational prosecutors to do so adequately and consistently. Instead, the system ought to confront the particularized retributive question on its own terms, uncoupled from the prosecutorial-dominated charge and bargain processes and the necessarily more mechanistic guilt determination.[194] The sentencing hearing is the appropriate setting for equitable evaluation of this kind. And the lay jury is a uniquely capable body to reach a guided and appropriately constrained commonsense determination of what constitutes proportional punishment for a particular offender in a particular context.[195] Prevailing capital sentencing procedure provides a model of just such an express, formal, and lay equitable screen.

This book asks the question of whether LWOP is the new death penalty. This chapter answers "not yet." But, at least along the equitable dimension, we ought to make it so.

NOTES

I received helpful insights and feedback on earlier drafts from Charles Barzun, Risa Goluboff, Marie Gottschalk, Charles Ogletree, Austin Sarat, Fred Schauer, and many of the participants at the Amherst conference where the chapters in this book were first presented. I would also like to thank Mark McBride, Stephanie Moore, Matt Schwee, and Dan Sharpe for phenomenal research assistance.

1. John Laurence, *A History of Capital Punishment* (New York: Citadel, 1960), 4–9.

2. Ibid.

3. Ibid., 9–14; Jim Hornby, *In the Shadow of the Gallows: Criminal Law and Capital Punishment in Prince Edward Island, 1769–1941* (Charlottetown: University of Prince Edward Island, 1998), 6.

4. Laurence, *A History of Capital Punishment*, 9–14; Victor A. C. Gatrell, *The Hanging Tree: Execution and the English People, 1770–1868* (New York: Oxford University Press, 1994), 7–8.

5. Livingston Hall, "Strict or Liberal Construction of Penal Statutes," *Harvard Law Review* 48 (March 1935): 749–51 (discussing the resistance of "courts, juries, and even prosecutors" to legislative efforts to "oust[] . . . benefit of the clergy . . . in various forms of fraud, embezzlement, and aggravated larceny" during the first half of the eighteenth century); Roscoe Pound, "Discretion, Dispensation and Mitigation: The Problem of the Individual Special Case," *New York University Law Review* 35 (April 1960): 930–31 (indicating that "dispensation as a means of individualized application of law [became] odious" and was abandoned in 1688 because of the perceived propensity of royal and papal agents to abuse the power).

6. Michael Tonry, *Sentencing Matters* (New York: Oxford University Press, 1996), 147; Josh Bowers, "Contraindicated Drug Courts," *UCLA Law Review* 55 (April 2008): 796–97.

7. James Q. Whitman, *Harsh Justice: Criminal Punishment and the Widening Divide between America and Europe* (New York: Oxford University Press, 2003), 36 ("[T]he

facial harshness of the eighteenth-century English Bloody Code . . . was mitigated by an extensive pardoning practice. While many were condemned to death, many of those were pardoned."); Thomas A. Green, *Verdict According to Conscience: Perspectives on the English Criminal Trial Jury, 1200–1800* (Chicago: University of Chicago Press, 1985), 145 (describing an extensive postconviction system of pardon and commutation); Peter King, *Crime, Justice, and Discretion in England, 1740–1820* (New York: Oxford University Press, 2000), 310.

8. Austin Sarat and Conor Clarke, "Beyond Discretion: Prosecution, the Logic of Sovereignty, and the Limits of Law," *Law & Social Inquiry* 33 (Spring 2008): 401.

9. Hall, "Strict or Liberal Construction," 749–51 (referring to "absurd" interpretations of statutes); see also John C. Jeffries, "Legality, Vagueness, and the Construction of Penal Statutes, and Vagueness," *Virginia Law Review* 71 (March 1985): 198 (referring to strict construction as a "makeweight" that permits a court to reach what it deems to be the right result).

10. William E. Nelson, "The 18th Century Background of Marshall's Constitutional Jurisprudence," *Michigan Law Review* 76 (May 1978): 910 (quoting jury instruction and letter from James Sullivan to Elbridge Gerry (Dec. 25, 1779)); see also Ronald Jay Allen, Joseph L. Hoffmann, Debra A. Livingston, and William J. Stuntz, *Comprehensive Criminal Procedure* (New York: Aspen, 2005), 78 ("Criminal law, the body of rules that define the elements of crimes, had little meaning, since juries could decide what the law was on an ad hoc basis."); Akhil Reed Amar, *America's Unwritten Constitution* (New York: Basic Books, forthcoming 2012) (unpublished manuscript on file with author).

11. Richard J. Bonnie, Anne M. Coughlin, John C. Jeffries, Jr., and Peter W. Low, *Criminal Law*, 3rd ed. (New York: Foundation, 2010), 856, 856n. b (quoting James Fitzjames Stephen and noting that courts adopted no fixed meaning for terms such as "malice aforethought" but instead that "judges allocated criminal homicides between murder and manslaughter . . . according to which offenders deserved to be hanged"). At common law, murder was conventionally defined along the following lines: "When a man of sound memory and of the age of discretion unlawfully kills any reasonable creature in being and under the King's peace, with malice aforethought, either express or implied by the law, the death taking place within a year and a day." Ibid., 856–57n. c.

12. Francis Bowes Sayre, "Mens Rea," *Harvard Law Review* 45 (April 1932): 1025 (observing that "[n]o two judges have the same standards of morals" and that if *mens rea* is not "carefully defined," it will be applied capriciously according to "individual, internal standards" of conscience); Green, *Verdict According to Conscience*, 56, 98, 269.

13. Bonnie et al., *Criminal Law*, 856n. b. Thomas Andrew Green observed in his seminal exploration of the early English trial jury that "somewhere in between the deserved and undeserved acquittals lay the presumably large number of acquittals based on jury repudiation of the death sanction." Green, *Verdict According to Conscience*, 28–29. Philip Mackey noted a similar phenomenon in the United States, where early American juries refused to convict defendants of crimes that carried mandatory death sentences. Philip English Mackey, "The Inutility of Mandatory Capital Punishment: An Historical Note," *Boston University Law Review* 54 (1974): 32–33 (observing that "[v]irtually all capital laws in the United States were mandatory in the colonial and early national periods").

14. King, *Crime, Justice, and Discretion in England*, 256, 299; Green, *Verdict According to Conscience*, 98, 105; Sayre, "Mens Rea," 1019.

15. Jeffrey Abramson, *We the Jury: The Jury System and the Ideal of Democracy* (New York: Basic Books, 1994), 31 ("[J]urors generally had effective power to control the content of the province's substantive law."); Green, *Verdict According to Conscience*, 56 (describing how the jury "reflected the interests of the local community as opposed to those of central authorities"); cf. William Stuntz, "Unequal Justice," *Harvard Law Review* 121 (June 2008): 1974 (advocating vague criminal statutes as a means to permit local juries to craft appropriate equitable defenses); Paul H. Robinson and John M. Darley, *Justice, Liability, and Blame: Community Views and the Criminal Law* (Boulder, CO: Westview, 1995), 213 (observing that early juries employed expansive conceptions of self-defense even when the acts did not meet the "stringent requirements" of the law).

16. Admittedly, the point is somewhat debatable. Compare Hall, "Strict or Liberal Construction," 749–51 (arguing that efforts to circumvent mandatory strict construction amounted to "administrative nullification"), with Stuntz, "Unequal Justice" (arguing that comparatively vague statutes permit juries to lawfully discover equitable defenses); Amar, *America's Unwritten Constitution*.

17. Stuntz, "Unequal Justice"; Allen et al., *Comprehensive Criminal Procedure*, 78 ("[T]he body of rules that define[d] the elements of crimes [] had little meaning," and the premodern jury, therefore, was free to "decide what the law was.").

18. Bushell's Case (1670), 124 Eng. Rep. 1006 (C.P.) (holding a criminal jury's verdict inviolable).

19. Sparf v. United States, 156 U.S. 51 (1895) ("[I]t is the duty of juries in criminal cases to take the law from the court and apply that law to the facts as they find them to be from the evidence. Upon the court rests the responsibility of declaring the law; upon the jury, the responsibility of applying the law so declared. . . . Under any other system, . . . government will cease to be a government of law, and become a government of men."); see also Amar, *America's Unwritten Constitution* (observing that jury decisions that are deemed to be nullification today were historically considered to be within the jury's legitimate authority).

20. Josh Bowers, "Grassroots Plea Bargaining," *Marquette Law Review* 91 (September 2007): 99 (explaining that a justice system may institute zero-tolerance policies along several dimensions: arrest, charge, bargain, or punishment).

21. Whitman, *Harsh Justice*, 36.

22. Ibid., 36–39.

23. Thomas A. Green, "Freedom and Criminal Responsibility in the Age of Pound: An Essay on Criminal Justice," *Michigan Law Review* 93 (June 1995): 1949–2007 (discussing the rise of discretionary sentencing); see also Woodson v. North Carolina, 428 U.S. 280, 291–92 (1976) ("[B]y the end of World War I, all but eight States . . . had adopted discretionary death penalty schemes or abolished the death penalty altogether. By 1963, all of these remaining jurisdictions had replaced their automatic death penalty statutes with discretionary jury sentencing."); Rachel E. Barkow, "The Court of Life and Death: The Two Tracks of Constitutional Sentencing Law and the Case for Uniformity," *Michigan Law Review* 107 (May 2009): 1177n. 188.

24. Adriaan Lanni, Note, "Jury Sentencing in Noncapital Cases: An Idea Whose Time Has Come (Again)?," *Yale Law Journal* 108 (May 1999): 1778.

25. Tonry, *Sentencing Matters*, 3–6.

26. Barkow, "The Court of Life and Death," 1177.

27. Tonry, *Sentencing Matters*, 6.

28. Douglas A. Berman, "The Virtues of Offense/Offender Distinctions," in *Criminal Law Conversations*, ed. Paul H. Robinson, Stephen Garvey, and Kimberly Kessler Ferzan (New York: Oxford University Press, 2009), 615–19.

29. Ibid., 615; see also Nancy Gertner, "What Has *Harris* Wrought?," *Federal Sentencing Reporter* 15 (December 2002): 85.

30. United States v. Justice, 877 F.2d 664, 666 (8th Cir. 1989); see also Jack B. Weinstein, "A Trial Judge's Second Impression of the Federal Sentencing Guidelines," *Southern California Law Review* 66 (November 1992): 364.

31. Tonry, *Sentencing Matters*, 6.

32. Ibid., 9, 147.

33. Ibid.; Bowers, "Contraindicated Drug Courts," 825 ("Stakeholders of varied political stripes came together to counteract what some saw as racist inequities in sentencing and what others saw as overly lenient discretionary sentencing.").

34. Ronald S. Safer and Matthew C. Crowl, "Substantial Assistance Departures: Valuable Tool or Dangerous Weapon?," *Federal Sentencing Reporter* 12 (August 1999): 41 (describing prosecutorial use of determinate sentencing laws to effectively fight the war on drugs); Rachel E. Barkow, "Institutional Design and Policing of Prosecutors: Lessons from Administrative Law," *Stanford Law Review* 61 (February 2009): 877 ("With the prevalence of mandatory minimum laws, a prosecutor's decision to bring or not bring charges can dictate whether a defendant receives a mandatory five-, ten-, or twenty-year term, or whether he or she is sentenced far below that floor."); David Bjerk, "Making the Crime Fit the Penalty: The Role of Prosecutorial Discretion under Mandatory Minimum Sentencing," *Journal of Law & Economics* 48 (October 2005): 593–95; Tonry, *Sentencing Matters*, 141, 150; William J. Stuntz, "Plea Bargaining and Criminal Law's Disappearing Shadow," *Harvard Law Review* 117 (June 2004): 2564; Richard A. Oppel, Jr., "Sentencing Shift Gives New Clout to Prosecutors," *New York Times*, Sept. 25, 2011 ("After decades of new laws to toughen sentencing for criminals, prosecutors have gained greater leverage to extract guilty pleas from defendants and reduce the number of cases that go to trial, often by using the threat of more serious charges with mandatory sentences or other harsher penalties."). By casting crisp shadows over the bargaining process, determinate sentencing laws could serve effectively to induce rational defendants to plead guilty. Stuntz, "Disappearing Shadow," 2556–58, 2568; Oppel, "Sentencing Shift Gives New Clout to Prosecutors."

35. William J. Stuntz, "The Pathological Politics of Criminal Law," *Michigan Law Review* 100 (December 2001): 505; Tonry, *Sentencing Matters*, 146–48; Stuntz, "Disappearing Shadow," 2548 (offering reasons why legislators pass unwise or even unjust mandatory-minimums statutes); Barkow, "The Court of Life and Death," 1193.

36. Gregg v. Georgia, 428 U.S. 153, 188 (1976) (describing the holding of *Furman v. Georgia*, 408 U.S. 238 (1972)).

37. Barkow, "The Court of Life and Death," 1177.

38. *Woodson*, 428 U.S. at 292; see generally John W. Poulos, "The Supreme Court, Capital Punishment and the Substantive Criminal Law: The Rise and Fall of Mandatory Capital Punishment," *Arizona Law Review* 28 (1986): 143.

39. *Woodson*, 428 U.S. at 304.

40. Enmund v. Florida, 458 U.S. 782, 801 (1982) ("[P]unishment must be tailored to his personal responsibility and moral guilt.").

41. *Woodson*, 428 U.S. at 304 (quoting *Pennsylvania ex rel. Sullivan v. Ashe*, 301 U.S. 51, 55 (1937)); Ring v. Arizona, 536 U.S. 584 (2002) (requiring a jury to find aggravating factors necessary to impose death sentence); see also California v. Brown, 479 U.S. 538, 545 (1987) (O'Connor, J., concurring) ("[E]vidence about the defendant's background and character is relevant because of the belief, long held by this society, that defendants who commit criminal acts that are attributable to a disadvantaged background, or to emotional or mental problems, may be less culpable than defendants who have no such excuse."); Thompson v. Oklahoma, 487 U.S. 815, 853 (1988) (O'Connor, J., concurring).

42. Coker v. Georgia, 433 U.S. 584 (1977) (holding unconstitutional capital punishment for rape without killing); *Enmund*, 458 U.S. 782 (holding unconstitutional capital punishment for felony murder); Kennedy v. Louisiana, 554 U.S. 407 (2008) (holding unconstitutional capital punishment for child rape).

43. Roper v. Simmons, 543 U.S. 551 (2005) (holding unconstitutional execution of juveniles); Atkins v. Virginia, 536 U.S. 304 (2002) (holding unconstitutional execution of the mentally retarded).

44. *Gregg*, 428 U.S. at 162–64; Profitt v. Florida, 428 U.S. 242, 247–50 (1976); Lowenfield v. Phelps, 484 U.S. 231, 244 (1988); see also Raoul G. Cantero and Robert M. Kline, "Death Is Different: The Need for Jury Unanimity in Death Penalty Cases," *St. Thomas Law Review* 22 (September 2009): 10 (noting that all but one of the thirty-five states that have retained the death penalty require unanimous agreement on the existence of an aggravating factor underlying a sentence of death). The Court has forbidden imposition of capital punishment based on the kind of amorphous judgment of general wickedness that undergirded the common-law guilt determination. Specifically, the Court has specified that an aggravating factor must consist of more than a mere requirement that a particular offense is "outrageously or wantonly vile, horrible and inhuman." Godfrey v. Georgia, 446 U.S. 420 (1980).

45. Saffle v. Parks, 494 U.S. 484 (1990).

46. Tennard v. Dretke, 542 U.S. 274, 284 (2004); see also Spaziano v. Florida, 454 U.S. 1037 (1981) (indicating that it is "desirable for the [capital sentencing] jury to have as much information as possible when it makes the sentencing decision"); Dan M. Kahan and Martha C. Nussbaum, "Two Conceptions of Emotion in Criminal Law," *Columbia Law Review* 96 (March 1996): 369–70n. 437 (noting that the Court has held uniformly that "appeals to mercy" are an appropriate part of capital sentencing).

47. Lockett v. Ohio, 438 U.S. 586 (1978) (holding that the sentencer is entitled to consider "as a mitigating factor, any aspect of a defendant's character or record and any of the circumstances of the offense that the defendant proffers as a basis for a sentence less than death"); see also Eddings v. Oklahoma, 455 U.S. 104 (1982) ("[T]he sentencer may determine the weight to be given relevant mitigating evidence. But they may not give it no weight by excluding such evidence from their consideration."); Payne v. Tennessee, 501 U.S. 808, 822 (1991) ("[V]irtually no limits are placed on the relevant mitigating evidence a capital defendant may introduce concerning his own circumstances."); see generally Scott Sundby, "The Lockett Paradox: Reconciling Guided Discretion and Unguided Mitigation in Capital Sentencing," *UCLA Law Review* 38 (June 1991): 1147; Stephen P. Garvey, "Aggravation and Mitigation in Capital Cases: What Do Jurors Think?," *Columbia Law Review* 98 (October 1998): 1559–61; Theodore Eisenberg, Stephen P. Garvey, and Martin

T. Wells, "But Was He Sorry? The Role of Remorse in Capital Sentencing," *Cornell Law Review* 83 (September 1998): 1632–37.

48. *Lockett*, 438 U.S. at 608.

49. Bonnie et al., *Criminal Law*, 1128 ("[D]iscretion to *take* life and discretion to *spare* life are not constitutionally equivalent" (emphasis in original)); see also *Gregg*, 428 U.S. at 199 ("Nothing in any of the cases suggests that the decision to afford an individual defendant mercy violates the Constitution.").

50. Martha C. Nussbaum, "Equity and Mercy," *Philosophy and Public Affairs* 22 (Spring 1993): 85–86, 92.

51. 4 William Blackstone, *Commentaries* *358 ("Better that ten guilty persons escape than that one innocent suffer.").

52. Fong Foo v. United States, 369 U.S. 141 (1962).

53. Amar, *America's Unwritten Constitution*.

54. Mackey, "The Inutility of Mandatory Capital Punishment," 32–33 ("[U]npunished criminals were walking the streets because juries would not convict them of capital crimes.").

55. See B. E. F. Knell, "Capital Punishment: Its Administration in Relation to Juvenile Offenders in the Nineteenth Century and Its Possible Administration in the Eighteenth," *British Journal of Criminology* 5 (1965): 198–207 (noting the execution of brother and sister, Michael and Anne Hammond, ages seven and eleven).

56. Mackey, "The Inutility of Mandatory Capital Punishment," 33 (quoting Walt Whitman, commenting on the American experience with mandatory capital punishment).

57. See, e.g., Fla. Stat. § 775.082(1) ("A person who has been convicted of a capital felony shall be punished by death . . . , otherwise such person shall be punished by life imprisonment and shall be ineligible for parole.").

58. Specifically, twenty of thirty-four death penalty states require imposition of LWOP as the alternative to death. Ala. Code § 13A-5-45; Ark. Code. Ann. § 5-10-101; Cal. Penal Code § 190.3; Conn. Gen. Stat. § 53a-46a; Del. Code Ann. Tit. 11 § 4209; Fla. Stat. §§ 775.082, 921.141; Idaho Code Ann. § 18-4004; 730 Ill. Comp. Stat. 5/5-8-1; Ind. Code Ann. § 35-50-2-9; Kan. Stat. Ann. § 21-4624; La. Rev. Stat. Ann. § 14:30; Mo. Rev. Stat. § 565.020; Neb. Rev. Stat. § 29-2520; N.H. Rev. Stat. Ann. § 630:5; N.C. Gen. Stat. § 14-17; Or. Rev. Stat. § 163.105; S.C. Code Ann. § 16-3-20; S.D. Codified Laws §§ 23A-27A-4, 24-15-4; Tex. Penal Code § 12.31; Wash. Rev. Code § 10.95.030; see also William J. Bowers and Benjamin D. Steiner, "Death by Default: An Empirical Demonstration of False and Forced Choices in Capital Sentencing," *Texas Law Review* 77 (February 1999): 707 ("Most states with the death penalty provide LWOP as a sentencing option.").

59. See, e.g., W. Va. Code § 61-2-2 (mandatory LWOP for first-degree murder in state with no death penalty); Minn. Stat. § 609.185 (same); Iowa Code § 902.1 (2010) (mandatory LWOP for all class-A felonies, including sexual abuse in the first degree and kidnapping in the first degree); Mass. Gen. Law ch. 265, § 2 (2010) (mandatory LWOP for second-degree murder); Fla. Stat. § 893.135(1)(c)(2) (mandatory LWOP for possession, sale, purchase, or transfer of thirty kilograms of certain enumerated controlled substances).

60. Harmelin v. Michigan, 501 U.S. 957, 994–95 (1991) ("There can be no serious contention . . . that a sentence which is not otherwise cruel and unusual becomes so simply because it is mandatory.").

61. *Harmelin*, 501 U.S. at 959 (Kennedy, J., concurring); Wayne A. Logan, "Proportionality and Punishment: Imposing Life without Parole on Juveniles," *Wake Forest Law Review* 33 (1998): 700–03 ("'Crime' is now typically conceived solely in terms of relative seriousness of a given offense, to the exclusion of offender culpability.").

62. *Harmelin*, 501 U.S. at 960.

63. State v. DePiano, 926 P.2d 494, 497 (Ariz. 1996) (interpreting *Harmelin* to require, as a threshold matter for proportionality review, that the court measure only the nature of the offense generally, not specifically).

64. Logan, "Proportionality and Punishment," 703 (referring to the inquiry as "circular" for this reason). But see Graham v. Florida 130 S. Ct. 2011 (2010).

65. *Harmelin*, 501 U.S. 957; cf. *Lockyer v. Andrade*, 538 U.S. 63, 66 (2003) (holding constitutional a life sentence for a recidivist thief); Rummel v. Estelle, 445 U.S. 263 (1980) (same); Ewing v. California, 538 U.S. 11, 30 (2003) (same).

66. Logan, "Proportionality and Punishment," 703n. 109 (quoting United States v. Gonzales, 121 F.3d 928, 943 (5th Cir. 1997).

67. Youngjae Lee, "The Constitutional Right against Excessive Punishment," *Virginia Law Review* 91 (May 2005): 695 (observing that "proportionality has become virtually meaningless as a constitutional principle" in noncapital cases); Barkow, "The Court of Life and Death," 1149–50 ("In nondeath cases, by contrast, the Court has made no effort . . . to require attention to individual circumstances.").

68. *Rummel*, 445 U.S. at 274 (holding constitutional a life sentence for a recidivist thief); Logan, "Proportionality and Punishment," 706 ("[S]tate and federal legislatures can exercise virtually unfettered discretion in their formulation of sentences.").

69. *Eddings*, 455 U.S. at 110; see also Barkow, "The Court of Life and Death," 1155 ("In noncapital cases . . . the Court has found no constitutional problems with even the most extreme mandatory penalties."). This divergent approach is what Rachel Barkow has referred to as the "two tracks" of constitutional sentencing law: "The Court has focused on the tiny percent of cases it views as the most sympathetic and created a special jurisprudence for them. With those cases off the table as a cause for concern, the Court can—and has—ignored the rest." Ibid., 1146–48. The tendency of courts and commentators to prioritize exceptional cases over the commonplace is no isolated phenomenon. For instance, some commentators worry that the recent hyperfocus on DNA innocence has diluted reform efforts intended to address failures that affect innocent and guilty defendants alike. As David Dow explained in the capital context, "For too many years now, . . . death penalty opponents have seized on the nightmare of executing an innocent man as a tactic to erode support for capital punishment in America. Innocence is a distraction. . . . [M]ost people on death row did what the state said they did. But that does not mean they should be executed." David R. Dow, "The End of Innocence," *New York Times*, June 16, 2006.

70. Nevertheless, many recidivist defendants have received life sentences for relatively trivial offenses. See, e.g., *Andrade*, 538 U.S. 63; *Ewing*, 538 U.S. 11; *Rummel*, 445 U.S. 263.

71. Marc Mauer, Ryan S. King, and Malcolm C. Young, *The Meaning of "Life": Long Prison Sentences in Context* (Washington, DC: Sentencing Project, 2004), 11, 13; see also *Harmelin*, 501 U.S. 957.

72. Jessica S. Henry, "Death-in-Prison Sentences: Overutilized and Underscrutinized," this volume, 66–95 (collecting cases). As Henry observes, federal life terms are techni-

cally sentences to life without parole, because there is no parole in the federal system. Henry also spotlights recidivist state defendants who have been sentenced to LWOP for seemingly trivial felonies such as forgery, larceny, distribution of less than half a gram of cocaine, and participation in a twenty-dollar marijuana sale.

73. *Kennedy*, 554 U.S. 407 (holding capital punishment unconstitutional for child rape and barring capital punishment for all nonhomicide offenses, except crimes against the state); *Enmund*, 458 U.S. 782 (effectively barring capital punishment for felony murder).

74. Sayre, "Mens Rea," 994, 1019.

75. Stuntz, "Unequal Justice"; Whitman, *Harsh Justice*, 35–36 (noting that "flexible doctrines of liability, permitting defendants to plead excuse or justification—extenuating circumstances, broadly"—permit greater space for "a form of authority to exercise mercy").

76. Mauer, King, and Young, *The Meaning of "Life,"* 4; cf. Whitman, *Harsh Justice*, 37 (describing modern American trend toward harshness in terms of enforcement practices, punishment practices, and parole and pardon (non)practices).

77. Whitman, *Harsh Justice*, 37.

78. *Infra* notes 96–98 and accompanying text.

79. Berman, "The Virtues of Offense/Offender Distinctions," 616; Gertner "What Has *Harris* Wrought?," 85.

80. Kahan and Nussbaum, "Two Conceptions of Emotion," 368–69 (describing the distinct functions of mechanistic guilt determinations and evaluative sentencing).

81. Green, *Verdict According to Conscience*, 17, 62, 105, 281; Gatrell, *The Hanging Tree*, 8 ("Although wealthy murderers and forgers were hanged occasionally, most of those hanged were the "poor and marginalized."); cf. Nancy J. King, "How Different Is Death? Jury Sentencing in Capital and Non-capital Cases Compared," *Ohio State Journal of Criminal Law* 2 (Fall 2004): 196 (discussing the capriciousness of unguided jury sentencing); see generally John Beattie, "Crime and Inequality in Eighteenth-Century London," in *Crime and Inequality*, ed. John Hagan and Ruth D. Peterson (Stanford: Stanford University Press, 1995): 116–39.

82. Stephanos Bibas, "Forgiveness in Criminal Procedure," *Ohio State Journal of Criminal Law* 4 (Spring 2007): 347 ("[A]ll of these concerns are legitimate but far from fatal. Discrimination, arbitrariness, and variations in temperament, eloquence, and attractiveness are endemic problems in criminal justice. Remorse, apology, and forgiveness are at least neutral metrics and criteria to structure and guide discretion."); cf. Kenneth Culp Davis, *Discretionary Justice: A Preliminary Inquiry* (Urbana: University of Illinois Press, 1971), 21 ("[T]he conception of equity that discretion is needed as an escape from rigid rules are a far cry from the proposition that where law ends tyranny begins.").

83. Bordenkircher v. Hayes, 434 U.S. 357, 364 (1978) ("[S]o long as the prosecutor has probable cause to believe that the accused committed an offense defined by statute, the decision whether or not to prosecute, and what charge to file or bring before a grand jury, generally rests entirely in his discretion."); see also United States v. Goodwin, 457 U.S. 368 (1982) (noting that "the prosecutor should remain free before trial to exercise the broad discretion" to select charges).

84. Logan, "Proportionality and Punishment," 706; Inmates of Attica Correctional Facility v. Rockefeller, 477 F.2d 375 (2d Cir. 1973) ("[T]he courts are not to interfere with the free exercise of the discretionary powers of the attorneys of the United States in their control over criminal prosecutions."); Barkow, "Institutional Design," 869; Josh Bowers,

"Legal Guilt, Normative Innocence, and the Equitable Decision Not to Prosecute," *Columbia Law Review* 110 (November 2010): 1657–60, 1664–66.

85. Barkow, "The Court of Life and Death," 1153, 1166 (observing that prosecutorial charging discretion "adds to the likelihood of discriminatory application of [determinate] sentencing in noncapital cases"); Barkow, "Institutional Design," 883; Stuntz, "Disappearing Shadow," 2556–58; Kahan and Nussbaum, "Two Conceptions of Emotion," 363 ("[M]echanistic doctrines will not stop . . . inappropriate . . . motivations. They only drive those assessments underground.").

86. Bowers, "Legal Guilt, Normative Innocence."

87. Ibid.

88. Ibid.

89. Ibid.

90. Ibid.

91. Ibid.; Stephanos Bibas, "Transparency and Participation in Criminal Procedure," *New York University Law Review* 81 (June 2006): 931 (noting that professional criminal justice "insiders may take too narrow a view when evaluating what factors matter to outsiders"); Hamilton v. People, 29 Mich. 173 (1874) (contrasting "the good sense of a jury . . . that take[s] a common-sense view of every question" with the legal professional, who "generalizes and reduces everything to an artificial system formed by study").

92. Bibas, "Forgiveness in Criminal Procedure," 348.

93. I. Bennett Capers, "Defending Life," chap. 5 in this volume; see also Josh Bowers, "Punishing the Innocent," *University of Pennsylvania Law Review* 156 (May 2008): 1128 (discussing prosecutors' conviction mentality).

94. Bowers, "Legal Guilt, Normative Innocence"; Coolidge v. New Hampshire, 403 U.S. 443 (1971) (observing that prosecutors are too involved with the "competitive enterprise of ferreting out crime" to analyze cases objectively); Oppel, "Sentencing Shift Gives New Clout to Prosecutors."

95. Ronald Wright and Marc Miller, "The Screening/Bargaining Tradeoff," *Stanford Law Review* 30 (October 2002): 58–84. Of course, state-specific sentencing law constrains the degree to which any given prosecution office may use charging discretion to supplement bargaining strength.

96. Stuntz, "The Pathological Politics of Criminal Law," 507; cf. Oppel, "Sentencing Shift Gives New Clout to Prosecutors" ("There have been so many laws passed in the various states that . . . [prosecutors can] use[] as leverage in negotiations.") (quoting Scott Burns, executive director of the National District Attorney's Association).

97. Stuntz, "The Pathological Politics of Criminal Law," 507; Oppel, "Sentencing Shift Gives New Clout to Prosecutors" ("With mandatory minimums and other sentencing enhancements out there, prosecutors can often dictate the sentence that will be imposed.") (quoting Professor Paul Cassell).

98. Capers, "Defending Life"; cf. John H. Langbein, "Torture and Plea Bargaining," *University of Chicago Law Review* 46 (Autumn 1978): 18 ("Plea bargaining concentrates effective control of criminal procedure in the hands of a single officer. . . . Plea bargaining merges the[] accusatory, determinative, and sanctional phases of the procedure in the hands of the prosecutor.").

99. *Bordenkircher*, 434 U.S. 357; Brady v. United States, 397 U.S. 742 (1970).

100. *Bordenkircher*, 434 U.S. 357.

101. Ibid.

102. Capers, "Defending Life," 167–89 ("[W]e would literally consult actuarial life-expectancy tables to provide us a floor for plea negotiations, the goal being to achieve the equivalent of life without parole.")

103. Ibid., 167–89.

104. "Snitch," *Frontline*, season 17, episode 9, directed by Ofra Bikel, aired January 12, 1999, PBS; Jennifer Lawinski, "Locked Up for Life, Part One: The Case of Clarence Aaron," *Fox News*, December 4, 2008, http://www.foxnews.com/story/0,2933,461747,00.html.

105. Lawinski, "Locked Up for Life".

106. "Snitch" at 1:18:54 (emphasis added).

107. Ibid. at 32:01.

108. Stuntz, "Disappearing Shadow," 2563 ("Prosecutors can credibly threaten . . . punishments in order to induce plea bargains at the customary price . . . fixed by the prosecutors themselves.").

109. Bowers, "Legal Guilt, Normative Innocence."

110. Ibid.; Josh Bowers, "Outsourcing Equitable Discretion" (manuscript in progress); see also Bibas, "Forgiveness in Criminal Procedure," 348.

111. Bibas, "Transparency," 914 ("On average . . . [professional] insiders are more concerned with and informed about practical constraints. . . . [Lay] outsiders, knowing and caring less about practical obstacles and insiders' interests, focus on . . . offenders' just desserts. . . . [They] care about a much wider array of justice concerns than do lawyers, including . . . blameworthiness, and apologies."); Jenia I. Turner, "Implementing *Blakely*," *Federal Sentencing Reporter* 17 (December 2004): 111 ("Greater jury involvement in sentencing ensures that sentences do not stray too far from popular understandings of blameworthiness and fairness."); Colleen P. Murphy, "Integrating the Constitutional Authority of Civil and Criminal Juries," *George Washington Law Review* 61 (1993): 734 (observing that the jury is a "one-time actor in the justice system" and thus "is not susceptible to the cynicism that may beset" professionals); Bowers, "Legal Guilt, Normative Innocence."

112. Parklane Hosiery Co. v. Shore, 439 U.S. 322, 355 (1979) (Rehnquist, J., dissenting) (quoting Harry Kalven, Jr., and Hans Zeisel, *The American Jury* (Boston: Little, Brown, 1966), 8).

113. Hamilton v. People, 29 Mich. 173, 190 (1874).

114. State v. Williams, 47 N.C. (2 Jones) 257, 269 (1855); see also Edward. R. Wilder, "Trial of Issues of Fact—Jury v. Judges," *Western Jurist* (1879): 395 (emphasizing the "downright common sense [of the jury], unsophisticated by too much learning").

115. State v. Schoenwald, 31 Mo. 147, 155 (1860); cf. David Garland, *Punishment and Modern Society: A Study in Social Theory* (Chicago: University of Chicago Press, 1990), 1 (noting that punishment falls short of societal expectations because "we have tried to convert a deeply social issue into a technical task for specialist institutions").

116. Paul H. Robinson, "Reply," in *Criminal Law Conversations*, 62 ("[L]ay judgments about core wrongdoing are intuitional.").

117. Blakely v. Washington, 542 U.S. 296 (2004); Douglas G. Smith, "Structural and Functional Aspects of the Jury: Comparative Analysis and Proposals for Reform," *Alabama Law Review* 48 (Winter 1997): 485 ("The jury may be a superior institution to fill the

factfinding role if for no other reason than that is a group decisionmaking body rather than a single individual."); Laura I. Appleman, "The Plea Jury," *Indiana Law Journal* 85 (2010): 753 ("There is an undeniable advantage [to] having a group, instead of a single actor . . . since the breadth of a group's experience is necessarily much wider than just one, no matter how expert.").

118. As the Supreme Court noted in *Williams v. Florida*, the value of the jury "lies in the interposition between the accused and his accuser of the commonsense judgment of a *group* of laymen." Williams v. Florida, 399 U.S. 78, 100 (1970) (emphasis added).

119. James Surowiecki, *The Wisdom of Crowds* (New York: Doubleday, 2004).

120. Heather K. Gerken, "Second-Order Diversity," *Harvard Law Review* 118 (February 2005): 1122, 1143–44; see also Heather K. Gerken, "Dissent by Deciding," *Stanford Law Review* 57 (May 2005): 1745 (advocating disaggregated democratic institutions—like juries—that provide decision-making authority to conventionally powerless political minorities).

121. Duncan v. Louisiana, 391 U.S. 145, 155–56 (1968).

122. Cf. Larry D. Kramer, *The People Themselves: Popular Constitutionalism and Judicial Review* (New York: Oxford University Press, 2004).

123. Sarat and Clarke, "Beyond Discretion," 391–92 (describing the charge decision as an exercise of state sovereignty); see generally Gerken, "Second-Order Diversity," 1122, 1143–44; see also Gerken, "Dissent by Deciding."

124. Nussbaum, "Equity and Mercy," 109 (arguing that complete justice requires legal justice tempered by equity); see also Blackstone, *Commentaries*, *61 (noting that law without equity is "hard and disagreeable").

125. Stuntz, "Unequal Justice," 1995, 2031–33 (noting that "in th[e] sphere of governance, equality and local democracy go hand in hand"); see also Kahan and Nussbaum, "Two Conceptions of Emotion," 373–74 ("It's when the law falsely denies its evaluative underpinnings that it is most likely to be incoherent and inconsistent."); Allen et al., *Comprehensive Criminal Procedure*, 99. For arguments in favor of jury sentencing, see Morris B. Hoffmann, "The Case for Jury Sentencing," *Duke Law Journal* 52 (March 2003): 951–1010; Lanni, "Jury Sentencing in Noncapital Cases," 1775–1803; Jenia Iontcheva, "Jury Sentencing as Democratic Practice," *Virginia Law Review* 89 (April 2003): 311–83.

126. Stuntz, "Unequal Justice," 2039; see also Margareth Etienne, "In Need of a Theory of Mitigation," in *Criminal Law Conversations*, 631 (observing that "to leave these hard [equitable sentencing] questions in the hand of any one institutional actor—the judge, jury (or commonly, the prosecutor)—is to leave that group susceptible to accusations of caprice and lawlessness").

127. Blackstone, *Commentaries*, *61.

128. Dan M. Kahan, David A. Hoffman, and Donald Braman, "Whose Eyes Are You Going to Believe? *Scott v. Harris* and the Perils of Cognitive Illiberalism," *Harvard Law Review* 122 (January 2009): 884–85 ("By affording a factfinding role to citizens from diverse subcommunities, whose understandings of reality reflect experiences and social influences peculiar to those subcommunities, the jury contributes to the law's legitimacy."); Kahan and Nussbaum, "Two Conceptions of Emotion," 274 ("[Evaluations of equitable blameworthiness] are better because they are brutally and uncompromisingly honest. Mechanistic doctrines, by contrast, tend to disguise contentious moral issues."); Paul H. Robinson and Josh Bowers, "Perceptions of Fairness and Justice: The Shared Aims and Occasional Conflicts of Legitimacy and Moral Credibility," Scholarship at Penn. Law

Paper 365, University of Pennsylvania Law School, Philadelphia, 2011, http://lsr.nellco.org/upenn_wps/365 (work in progress).

129. Robert J. MacCoun and Tom R. Tyler, "The Basis of Citizens' Perceptions of the Criminal Jury: Procedural Fairness, Accuracy, and Efficiency," *Law and Human Behavior* 12 (September 1988): 333 ("Citizens tend to see lay decisionmaking as more fair and procedurally legitimate than professionalized decisionmaking."); Tom R. Tyler, *Why People Obey the Law* (Princeton: Princeton University Press, 2006), 31, 36–37.

130. Paul H. Robinson, "Why Does the Criminal Law Care What the Layperson Thinks Is Just? Coercive versus Normative Crime Control," *Virginia Law Review* 86 (November 2000): 1839.

131. Kahan and Nussbaum, "Two Conceptions of Emotion," 373–74 ("[I]t is when the law refuses to take responsibility for its most contentious choices that its decisionmakers are spared the need to be principled, and the public the opportunity to see correctable injustice."); see also Robinson and Bowers, "Perceptions of Fairness"; Josh Bowers, "Black Power in the Charging Decision," in *Criminal Law Conversations*, 578–79; Amar, *America's Unwritten Constitution*.

132. Robinson and Darley, *Justice, Liability, and Blame*, 6, 202 ("Each time the system is seen to convict in cases in which no community condemnation is appropriate, the system weakens the underlying force of the moral sanction. . . . If the criminal law is seen as unjust in one instance, its moral credibility and its concomitant compliance power are, accordingly, incrementally reduced.").

133. Paul H. Robinson, "Life without Parole under Modern Theories of Punishment," this volume, 000.

134. *Woodson*, 428 U.S. at 303; Mackey, "The Inutility of Mandatory Capital Punishment," 32–33.

135. *Woodson*, 428 U.S. at 303.

136. "Snitch" at 1:22:17.

137. Stuntz, "Unequal Justice," 2039; Josh Bowers, "Outsourcing Equitable Discretion"; Douglas A. Berman, "Conceptualizing *Blakely*," *Federal Sentencing Reporter* 17 (December 2004): 89.

138. Bowers, "Outsourcing Equitable Discretion."

139. Ibid.; Bowers, "Legal Guilt, Normative Innocence."

140. Bowers, "Legal Guilt, Normative Innocence."

141. Stuntz, "Unequal Justice," 2039; Davis, *Discretionary Justice?*, 26 ("Let us not oppose discretionary justice that is properly confined, structured, and checked; let us oppose discretionary justice that is improperly unconfined, unstructured, and unchecked.").

142. Ring v. Arizona, 536 U.S. 584 (2002).

143. Bonnie et al., *Criminal Law*, 1006 (interpreting the case law to stand for the proposition "that the court has residual discretion to impose a life sentence").

144. United States v. Armstrong, 517 U.S. 456 (1996).

145. See *supra* note 46 and accompanying text.

146. Lockett v. Ohio, 438 U.S. 586 (1978).

147. Ibid. at 604n. 12

148. *Woodson*, 428 U.S. at 280.

149. *Spaziano*, 454 U.S. 1037; *Woodson*, 428 U.S. at 303–04 ("[T]he penalty of death is qualitatively different from a sentence of imprisonment, however long. Death, in its

finality, differs more from life imprisonment than a 100-year prison term differs from one of only a year or two. Because of that qualitative difference, there is a corresponding difference in the need for reliability in the determination that death is the appropriate punishment in a specific case.").

150. *Woodson*, 428 U.S. at 304.

151. Rachel E. Barkow, "Life without Parole and the Hope for Real Sentencing Reform," chap. 6 in this volume; see also Barkow, "The Court of Life and Death," 1176 ("The Court's competing concern with discretion—that there be an opportunity for individualization—is likewise just as applicable in noncapital cases as in capital cases."); Logan, "Proportionality and Punishment," 703n. 108 ("All defendants are not alike, just as all crimes, even if given the same label, are not identical."); see also Bowers, "Legal Guilt, Normative Innocence."

152. *Coker*, 433 U.S. at 598; *Gregg*, 428 U.S. at 188 ("[T]he penalty of death is different in kind from any other punishment imposed under our system of criminal justice.").

153. Bowers and Steiner, "Death by Default," 707 ("LWOP and death are essentially equivalent for incapacitative purposes."); Charles Ogletree, "Supreme Court Should Apply Roper Reasoning to Upcoming Juvenile Life-without-Parole Cases," ACS (blog), October 29, 2009, http://www.acslaw.org/node/14555 (highlighting fact that, like capital punishment, LWOP is a "final and irreversible judgment"); Adam Liptak, "To More Inmates, Life Term Means Dying behind Bars," *New York Times*, October 2, 2005, http://www.nytimes.com/2005/10/02/national/02life.web.html (observing that the "only way out of prison is likely to be inside a coffin"). In the words of one man sentenced to three LWOP sentences for his participation in a drug deal, "Where in the world am I supposed to start doing three life sentences at, . . . the middle, the end? "Snitch" at 1:18.

154. Barkow, "Life without Parole and the Hope for Real Sentencing Reform"; Barkow, "The Court of Life and Death," 1174; Sherry F. Colb, "High Court Rejects Life without Parole for All Juvenile, Non-homicide Crimes," FindLaw, last modified May 26, 2010, http://writ.news.findlaw.com/colb/20100526.html ("[T]he death penalty seems distinct from prison sentences. Yet it is not really all that different."); Cf. Michael Massoglia and Christopher Uggen, "Settling Down and Aging Out: Toward an Interactionist Theory of Desistance and the Transition to Adulthood," *American Journal of Sociology* 116 (July 2010): 551 (discussing missed maturity markers among offenders and concluding that "[b]oth delinquency and official sanctions . . . can disrupt adult role transitions").

155. See generally Henry, "Death-in-Prison Sentences," for an extensive discussion of death-in-prison sentences.

156. California v. Anderson, 493 P.2d 880 (Cal. 1972).

157. Dirk Johnson, "No Executions in Illinois until System Is Repaired," *New York Times*, May 21, 2000.

158. Barkow, "The Court of Life and Death," 1169 (quoting Mill's description of a life sentence as condemning the defendant to "a living tomb, . . . cut off from all earthly hope") ("[S]ome individuals with death sentences have waived their appeals because of their view that a life sentence without parole would be worse. They preferred capital punishment to the 'slow death' of prison."); Gideon v. Wainwright, 372 U.S. 335, 349 (1963) (Clark, J., concurring) (observing that the notion "that deprival of liberty [is] less onerous than deprival of life [is] a value judgment not universally accepted"); Richard W. Garnett, "Sectarian Reflections on Lawyers' Ethics and Death Row Volunteers," *Notre Dame Law*

Review 77 (March 2002): 795; Welsh S. White, "Defendants Who Elect Execution," *University of Pittsburgh Law Review* 48 (Spring 1987): 855–61.

159. Capers, "Defending Life."

160. See Walter Berns, *For Capital Punishment: Crime and the Morality of the Death Penalty* (New York: Basic Books, 1979) (arguing that justice demands public administration of the death penalty).

161. Dan Markel, "State, Be Not Proud: A Retributivist Defense of the Commutation of Death Row and the Abolition of the Death Penalty," *Harvard Civil Rights–Civil Liberties Law Review* 40 (Summer 2005): 407–80 (opposing capital punishment on retributive grounds).

162. Michael S. Moore, "The Moral Worth of Retribution," in *Responsibility, Character, and the Emotions,* ed. Ferdinand Schoeman (New York: Cambridge University Press, 1987): 179, 212–15 (arguing that retribution gives the criminal "the benefit each of us gives himself or herself"—that we would "feel guilty unto death" and would "want to die[] . . . if we did the[se] kinds of acts").

163. Markel, "State, Be Not Proud."

164. Barkow, "The Court of Life and Death," 1148 ("[D]eath penalty abolitionists frequently tout life without parole as a viable sentencing option, even though noncapital sentencing reformers have highlighted that life without parole itself raises fundamental questions of justice."); Note, "A Matter of Life and Death: The Effect of Life-without-Parole Statutes on Capital Punishment," *Harvard Law Review* 119 (April 2006): 1838 (describing the "strange pairing of death penalty abolitionists with pro-incarceration activists"). The abolitionists' belief that LWOP is an attractive alternative to capital punishment is borne out by the data: when people are given the choice between life without parole and death, support for capital punishment drops precipitously. Mauer, King, and Young, *The Meaning of "Life."*

165. Mauer, King, and Young, *The Meaning of "Life,"* 3 (finding that, as of 2002, almost three percent of the nation's inmates—over thirty-three thousand individuals in all—were serving LWOP sentences).

166. Liptak, "Dying behind Bars" ("Opponents of capital punishment have promoted life sentences as an alternative to execution."); Barkow, "The Court of Life and Death," 1166 ("[L]egislatures continue to pass [mandatory sentencing provisions] with little thought or debate. . . . [T]he political process fails to take noncapital sentencing seriously, and the result is host of arbitrary, disproportionate punishments that fail to take into account an individual's circumstances.").

167. David C. Baldus, George G. Woodworth, and Charles A. Pulaski, Jr., *Equal Justice and the Death Penalty: A Legal and Empirical Analysis* (Boston: Northeastern University Press, 1990).

168. Lockhart v. McCree, 476 U.S. 162 (1986); McCleskey v. Kemp, 481 U.S. 279 (1987).

169. Callins v. Collins, 510 U.S. 1141, 1145 (1994) (Blackmun, J., dissenting).

170. Josh Bowers, "Accuracy and Legitimacy," in *Criminal Law Conversations*; Amar, *America's Unwritten Constitution* ("[M]odern officialdom all too often instrumentalizes and infantilizes jurors by disrespecting or derailing their moral judgment.").

171. Andrew E. Taslitz, "Empirical Desert: The Yin and Yang of Criminal Justice," in *Criminal Law Conversations,* 57 ("It is easy to speak in broad generalities, harder to choose when faced with a specific situation.").

172. Robinson, "Life without Parole under Modern Theories of Punishment"; see also Robinson and Bowers, "Perceptions of Fairness."

173. Currently, Arizona has adopted almost such a structure. At the capital sentencing phase, the jury decides whether to sentence a defendant to life or death, but then the judge makes the decision between LWOP and life with the possibility of parole. Ariz. Rev. Stat. § 13-752.

174. *Supra* note 164–65 and accompanying text.

175. Harris v. Wright, 93 F.3d 581, 584–85 (9th Cir. 1996).

176. Baldwin v. New York, 399 U.S. 66, 68 (1970); *Duncan*, 391 U.S. 145.

177. Argersinger v. Hamlin 407 U.S. 25 (1972); Scott v. Illinois, 440 U.S. 367 (1979).

178. See, e.g., Tonry, *Sentencing Matters*.

179. *Supra* note 82 and accompanying text.

180. King, "How Different Is Death?," 196 (discussing problems of unchecked jury sentencing).

181. United States v. Booker, 543 U.S. 220 (2005); *Blakely*, 542 U.S. 296; Apprendi v. New Jersey, 530 U.S. 466 (2000).

182. See, e.g., Turner, "Implementing *Blakely*," 111.

183. *Blakely*, 542 U.S. at 306.

184. Turner, "Implementing *Blakely*" ("*Blakely* does not explain . . . why the jury's role as a 'circuitbreaker' should be confined to factfinding. The history of the jury includes a limited power to make legal and moral judgments related to sentencing."); Berman, "Conceptualizing *Blakely*," 92–93 ("There is broad language in parts of the *Blakely* decision which suggests juries must now be involved in *all* punishment-enhancing sentencing determinations.").

185. *Graham*, 130 S. Ct. 2011.

186. Solem v. Helm, 463 U.S. 277 (1983); Colb, "High Court Rejects Life without Parole" ("[P]roportionality analysis—though theoretically available for all punishments—had in fact been . . . largely limited to capital punishment.").

187. *Solem*, 463 U.S. 277.

188. *Andrade*, 538 U.S. 63; *Rummel*, 445 U.S. 263; *Harmelin*, 501 U.S. 957; *Ewing*, 538 U.S. 11.

189. Colb, "High Court Rejects Life without Parole" ("There are thus currently at least five votes on the Court for the proposition that *Harmelin* and cases like it are on life support. . . . [T]he Court may now be more willing to entertain Eighth Amendment challenges to lengthy prison sentences than it has been in the past."); see also *Graham*, 130 S. Ct. at 2046 (Thomas, J., dissenting) (arguing that the majority had abandoned its death-is-different jurisprudence).

190. John F. Stinneford, "Rethinking Proportionality under the Cruel and Unusual Punishments Clause," *Virginia Law Review* 97 (2011): 899–978; William W. Berry III, "More Different Than Life, Less Different Than Death," *Ohio State Law Journal* 71, no. 6 (2010): 1109.

191. See, e.g., United States v. Simpson, 8 F.3d 546, 550 (7th Cir. 1992); see also *Solem*, 463 U.S. at 290 (noting that trial court sentencing decisions are owed substantial deference).

192. Logan, "Proportionality and Punishment," 724.

193. *Harmelin*, 501 U.S. 957.

194. Kahan and Nussbaum, "Two Conceptions of Emotion," 367 ("In determining an offender's guilt or innocence, . . . [the decision-maker] is ordinarily unconcerned with how the defendant came to be the way she is. But during the sentencing process, the law has traditionally permitted the story of the defendant's character-formation to come before the judge or jury in all its narrative complexity, in such a way as to . . . give rise to sympathetic assessment and to a merciful mitigation of punishment.").

195. Nussbaum, "Equity and Mercy," 94 ("[T]he equitable person is characterized by a sympathetic understanding of 'human things.'"); Kahan and Nussbaum, "Two Conceptions of Emotion," 287 (observing that an Aristotelian conception of appropriate conduct in a particular context requires "asking what a person of practical wisdom would do and feel in the situation," not by asking mechanistically what the law commands).

2

Death-in-Prison Sentences

Overutilized and Underscrutinized

JESSICA S. HENRY

Over 41,000 people in the United States are serving a sentence of life without the possibility of parole (LWOP).[1] In total, more than 140,600 people are serving some form of life imprisonment.[2] The data do not include the unknown number of people sentenced to prison terms that exceed their natural life expectancy. Even as a conservative estimate, the data paint a stark picture of a prison population rife with individuals serving sentences which will end only upon their death. These sentences have been described variously as "a living death sentence,"[3] "death by incarceration,"[4] a "virtual death sentence,"[5] a "prolonged death penalty,"[6] a "delayed death penalty,"[7] "a death sentence without an execution date,"[8] and the "other death penalty."[9] Each phrase attempts to capture the reality that many noncapital sentences, regardless of their formal title, are in fact "death-in-prison" (DIP) sentences.

This chapter deliberately does not limit consideration of DIP sentences to offenders serving a formal sentence of LWOP. As experience has shown, narrow definitions can have serious and unintended consequences. In recent years, for instance, the effort to eliminate capital punishment may have increased the legitimacy of other severe sanctions. Some death penalty abolitionists, capitalizing on public opinion which showed a preference for LWOP over capital punishment, argued that the severity and certainty of LWOP rendered it a more humane and palatable alternative to death. They joined forces with tough-on-crime policymakers to severely restrict capital punishment in jurisdictions such as Maryland and to entirely eliminate capital punishment in jurisdictions such as New Jersey and New Mexico.[10] As death sentences declined, LWOP sentences increased, but not in perfect substitution. LWOP sentences were not simply meted out in what would formerly have been death cases. Rather, LWOP also became a legitimate form of punishment for a host of offenses that were never death eligible in the first place.[11] In turn, other DIP sentences were perceived as less severe in comparison to formal LWOP. In this way, the concerted and well-intended effort of some abolitionists, scholars, and policymakers to avoid the execution of the few may have resulted in increased DIP sentences for the many.[12]

DIP sentences have been virtually ignored by scholars, courts, and policymakers. While capital punishment has been the subject of intense scrutiny, other severe sanctions, such as LWOP, life imprisonment, or those in which an offender is sentenced to a lengthy term of years, have lingered quietly on the sidelines. Capital cases receive heightened scrutiny because they involve the ultimate sanction of death. Yet the placement of capital punishment at the peak of the punishment hierarchy has meant that other severe sanctions, including those which end only in death, have received far less attention and scrutiny than their capital counterparts.[13] In terms of actual impact, however, literally tens of thousands of people are serving DIP sentences, while a fraction of that—3,260 as of April 2010—are serving an actual capital sentence.[14] Given the extent and breadth of DIP sentences, a robust and thoughtful discussion about their scope, application, and justification is long past due.

DIP sentences are closer on the sentencing continuum to capital sentences than other punishment because, like capital sentences, DIP sentences are severe and degrading, are arbitrarily imposed, and have been condemned by members of the international community. While DIP sentences are not the *same* as capital punishment, they are sufficiently severe in their own right to warrant the same heightened scrutiny and legal protections afforded to capital cases. Part I of this chapter defines DIP sentences. As the title of this book suggests, LWOP can certainly be described as the United States' "new death penalty." This chapter, however, urges the consideration of all sentences that result in the incarceration of individuals beyond their natural life. While the formal sentence of LWOP ensures that an individual will die in prison, so do other severe sentences, such as life imprisonment in certain jurisdictions and extremely lengthy prison terms. As will be discussed, the latter sentences pose more complex definitional challenges than LWOP does, but they nonetheless warrant inclusion into any discussion of severe sentences. Part II of this chapter examines the proposition that DIP sentences, in fact, are closer to capital punishment on the sentencing continuum than other punishments are and cites three factors in support of this relative comparison. Part II(a) demonstrates that, like capital punishment, DIP sentences are severe and degrading. The severity of DIP sentences reflects (i) the nature of the punishment itself, (ii) the denial of human dignity, and (iii) their arbitrary application. Part II(b) demonstrates that, as in the case of capital punishment, contemporary societies throughout the world have condemned DIP sentences as incompatible with human dignity and human rights. Part II(c) considers the recent U.S. Supreme Court decision in *Graham v. Florida*, in which the Court itself recognized that LWOP sentences share significant qualities with capital cases. Yet, although DIP sentences share many traits with capital sentences, they receive disparate legal treatment. Part III of this chapter compares the robust legal standards that apply in capital cases with those that are utilized in DIP cases and suggests that the difference in standards has resulted in an unjustified and almost commonplace imposition of DIP sentences. Part IV briefly explores the future prospects of DIP sentences and encourages debate on whether DIP sentences are necessary as a punishment option.

I. Death-in-Prison Sentences: Contours and Definitions

DIP sentences are varied and complex. Some sentences, such as LWOP or lengthy prison terms, offer the offender no possibility of release. Other sentences, such as life imprisonment, provide the offender with the theoretical *possibility* of release, but in practice often result in the offender's death in prison. While there are differences between the definitions of LWOP, life imprisonment, and lengthy prison terms, individuals serving those sentences share a common trait: with very few exceptions, they will remain behind bars until the expiration of their natural life.

a. LWOP and Life Imprisonment

A sentence of LWOP means that an individual is perpetually confined in prison until death, with no hope of redemption, save the remote possibility of executive clemency.[15] Its message is one of enduring renunciation: the offenders, by their criminal actions, have forever forfeited their right to exist in society. An LWOP sentence, by its very definition, can only be fulfilled by the death of the offender. It is a sentence of permanent, continual, and complete incapacitation. For the over 41,000 individuals serving an LWOP sentence, there is no possibility, absent executive intervention, that they will ever be released.

In jurisdictions that have abolished parole, life imprisonment is the functional equivalent of LWOP. Florida, Illinois, Iowa, Louisiana, Maine, Pennsylvania, South Dakota, and the federal system have eliminated parole and, as such, a sentence of life offers no possibility of release. This has had significant consequences. In Louisiana, one in nine inmates (or 10.9%) of people in prison are serving an irrevocable life sentence. Pennsylvania is close behind, with 9.4% of its prison population permanently incarcerated.[16]

In still other jurisdictions, a sentence of life imprisonment *with* the possibility of parole means simply that an individual retains the potential for release, without any guarantee that such release will occur. Offenders serving a life sentence must often wait a significant period of time before they can even petition for parole release. In Tennessee, an offender must serve a minimum of 51 years before he or she is eligible for parole.[17] In Kansas, the minimum prison term before parole eligibility is 50 years, while in Colorado the minimum term is 40 years. A 2004 report by the Sentencing Project estimated that individuals sentenced to life can expect on average to serve nearly three decades in prison before they are released on parole.[18] It is not hyperbole, then, to say that some incarcerated individuals will not survive until their first parole-eligibility date.

Even when they do, there is no guarantee that parole will be granted. Although 71% of all persons serving a life sentence retain the possibility of parole, the actual granting of parole to individuals serving a life sentence is increasingly rare.[19] As the Georgia State Board of Pardons and Parole once boasted, "There's a popular misconception that life in prison doesn't mean all of one's natural life. In just the last year, there are 21 Georgia lifers who are no longer around to tell you otherwise. If they could, they'd let you know that parole for a life sentence is a rare commodity."[20] In California, approximately 30,000 inmates are serving life sentences with the possibility of parole. Although nearly 4,000 "lifers" apply for release each year, the Board of Parole Hearings recommends parole only 2–5% of the time, and those recommendations are often rejected by the governor's office. Former governor Gray Davis reviewed 371 parole recommendations and approved parole only nine times, while former governor Arnold Schwarzenegger, who took a slightly more generous approach to parole, reviewed 830 parole recommendations as of mid-2008 and approved release 192 times. In California, then, only a minuscule fraction of all initial parole applications result in release.[21]

Parole releases for life sentences are increasingly rare because parole decisions have become increasingly politicized.[22] No politician ever lost an election because he or she denied a parole application. The inverse, of course, is not true. Former Massachusetts governor Michael Dukakis's presidential campaign was devastated after a man named Willie Horton, who was serving a life sentence for murder, escaped a Massachusetts weekend-furlough program and went on to commit a string of violent crimes. Dukakis was portrayed by his opponent, George H. W. Bush, as soft on crime and went on to lose the presidential race. Several years later, in Pennsylvania, then-lieutenant governor Mark Singel's gubernatorial aspirations were derailed after an offender whose sentence had been commuted by his office committed a murder and rape.[23] The consequences of "bad" parole decisions have led politicians to engage in a political calculus that weighs heavily against release. As a result, politically appointed parole boards and elected executive officers routinely deny parole release to eligible individuals, leaving them instead to remain incarcerated until death. A life sentence with parole that is never granted thus adds a cruel twist: the raised hope and crushing disappointment of the illusory prospect of release, dangling like the fruit above Tantalus against the backdrop of a never-ending prison term.

This is not to say, of course, that offenders serving a life sentence are never paroled. But as the California data illustrate, that release is rare and difficult to predict, rendering somewhat murky the definition of a life sentence. As the noted English jurist Lord Mustill wrote in an opinion about mandatory life imprisonment in England,

> The sentence of life imprisonment is . . . unique in that the words, which the judge is required to pronounce, do not mean what they say. Whilst in a very small minority of cases the prisoner is in the end confined for the rest of his natural life, this is not the usual or intended effect of a sentence of life imprisonment. . . . *But although everyone knows what the words do not mean, nobody knows what they do mean, since the duration of the prisoner's detention depends on a series of recommendations . . . and executive decisions.*[24]

While a small percentage of offenders serving life are eventually released from prison, the significant majority will die while serving out their sentence. In this way, LWOP and life imprisonment are both DIP sentences.

b. Lengthy Prison Terms

The term "virtual" lifers refers to men and women serving long sentences or consecutive sentences that outlast a person's natural life expectancy.[25] Lengthy prison terms that exceed an individual's life span are designed to send the very public message that the offender will never be released. In one high-profile case, Willie Clark, convicted of killing Darrent Williams of the Denver Broncos during a drive-by shooting, was sentenced after trial to LWOP, plus 1,152 years in prison.[26] In another high-profile case, Mark Rathbun, in California, was convicted of a series of horrific rapes and residential burglaries. The trial judge sentenced Rathbun to 1,030 years, plus 10 life terms.[27] These extreme sentences are not limited to violent crimes. Sholam Weiss, for instance, was sentenced to 845 years in prison for a money-laundering and fraud scheme against National Heritage Life Insurance, while his co-defendant, Keith Pound, received a sentence of 740 years in prison. Norman Schmidt received a 330-year sentence for orchestrating a fraudulent high-yield investment scheme. And, perhaps most notoriously, Bernard Madoff, at the age of 71, was sentenced to 150 years in prison.[28]

Whether a lengthy sentence constitutes a death-in-prison sentence depends on a number of factors such as the age of the offender, the actual term imposed, and the jurisdiction in which the offender is sentenced. While a 50-year sentence for a 20-year-old may provide an opportunity for release, that same sentence for a 40-year-old will likely result in death. Even that equation is somewhat jurisdictionally dependent. In all jurisdictions, offenders serving a lengthy sentence are ineligible for release until, at minimum, they complete a certain percentage of their sentence. But these practices vary considerably: 40 states have enacted truth-in-sentencing laws requiring violent offenders to serve at least 50% of their sentences in prison; 27 of those 40 states and the District of Columbia require violent offenders to serve at least 85% of their sentences in prison.[29] The sentencing landscape is further complicated by jurisdictional variations in the availability of good-time credit, under which a sentence is reduced by a certain proportion for every day served in prison. Thus, an offender sentenced to 100 years in one jurisdiction may serve only a proportion of that sentence and potentially gain release, while an offender in another jurisdiction will serve 85% of that sentence and likely die in prison.

Admittedly, life sentences and lengthy prison terms present definitional ambiguities that are absent from LWOP sentences. In thinking about the United States' "new death penalty," it would be far more analytically precise to limit the focus and scrutiny to LWOP. But that would be a mistake. Sentences that extend beyond an offender's natural life are severe and often *de facto* irrevocable. The illusion or possibility of release, turning often on idiosyncratic laws and political whims of elected officials or appointed parole boards within a particular jurisdiction, should not be permitted to obscure the reality that thousands of offenders are now serving DIP sentences that have received little scrutiny but that will nonetheless end only in death.

II. Death-in-Prison Sentences Are Closer on the Sentencing Continuum to Capital Punishment Than Are Other Punishments

In the federal justice system, and in the 34 states that retain the death penalty, capital punishment is "the ultimate sanction."[30] "Ultimate," as used by the U.S. Supreme Court, means the most severe and unique sanction available: "The penalty of death differs from all other forms of criminal punishment, not in degree but in kind. It is unique in its total irrevocability. It is unique in its rejection of rehabilitation of the convict as a basic purpose of criminal justice. And it is unique, finally, in its absolute renunciation of all that is embodied in our concept of humanity."[31]

DIP sentences are also uniquely severe in their own right. Israeli criminologist Leon Sheleff has argued that the death penalty, life imprisonment, and other severe penalties are not as distinct as we have made them out to be:

> What is it that makes for the singularity of the death penalty? It is irreversible, but so is mutilation; it is a severe punishment, but so is the torture of a life sentence. It involves the denial of dignity, but so, for all intents and purposes, does a life sentence: a human life involves not just existence and survival but the unique development of a personality, creativity, liberty, unfettered social intercourse. When these are denied, can those, who in the name of civil rights, are in the forefront of the struggle against the death penalty ignore the ultimate implications of a life sentence?[32]

The point Sheleff makes is an important one: like capital punishment, DIP sentences extinguish not only the physical life of offenders but also their human dignity and the possibility for redemption. As such, capital punishment and DIP sentences share significant characteristics, which can be broken into three primary categories. First, DIP sentences are uniquely severe and degrading punishments because of the nature of the punishment itself, because they deny human dignity, and because they are *de facto* irrevocable. Second, DIP sentences, like capital sentences, have been rejected by contemporary societies around the world. Third, the Supreme Court itself in *Graham v. Florida* (2010) recognized the unique qualities shared between capital and LWOP sentences. These categories illustrate that DIP sentences are more like capital punishment than any other form of punishment and, accordingly, that DIP sentences warrant additional care and scrutiny.

a. Death-in-Prison Sentences Are Unusually Severe and Degrading

i. Perpetual Life Imprisonment May Be a Fate Worse Than Death

DIP sentences, to some observers, are by their nature worse than capital sentences. Cesare Beccaria, an Italian death penalty abolitionist who argued for penal reform during the Enlightenment period, offered LWOP as a preferred and more miserable alternative to the death penalty:

> A great many men contemplate death with a steady, tranquil gaze; some out of fanaticism, some out of vanity, which attends us again and again to the very edge of the grave, some out of a last desperate effort to free themselves from life and misery; but neither fanaticism nor vanity can subsist among the fetters and the chains, under the rod, or under the yoke or in the iron cage, where the desperate man rather begins than ends his misery.[33]

Beccaria embraced LWOP as a mechanism to deter potential offenders, which, he argued, would make a "much stronger impression" than would the threat of death.[34] John Stuart Mill perceived life imprisonment as "living in a tomb, there to linger out what may be a long life . . . without any of its alleviation or rewards—debarred from all pleasant sights and sounds, and cut off from earthly hope."[35] Even Socrates apparently preferred death over exile from Athens, an indication that perhaps he too believed death was a kinder fate than the alternatives put before him.

Prisons are dangerous and violent, with few comforts and little variations in routine. Inmates are lonely and isolated and experience suffocating repetition and regimentation.[36] Whole-life terms may be considered worse than death because they allow for "greater suffering, or at least a longer time period for suffering."[37] Indeed, some tough-on-crime policymakers have embraced DIP sentences as a meaner and more severe punishment than the death penalty. Former New Mexico governor Bill Richardson struggled mightily over whether to repeal the death penalty. The turning point for him was when he went to see the prison cells in which prisoners serving life without parole would be held for 23 hours per day. He determined that "[t]hose cells are worse than death" and subsequently authorized the abolition of capital punishment in his state.[38] In another instance, a prosecutor in a capital case who oversaw a plea agreement to LWOP declared, "I'm glad he's not going to breathe another free breath. He'll spend the rest of his life in prison, and he'll lead a miserable existence."[39]

Many death penalty abolitionists also have embraced LWOP as a palatable alternative to capital punishment. Seizing on public opinion polls that show support for the death penalty drops when LWOP is offered as an alternative, some abolitionists have touted LWOP as a "stronger, fairer, and more reliable" sentence than capital punishment.[40] The Northern California ACLU, which opposes capital punishment, argues that LWOP is worse than capital sentences and offers none of the "comfort" or "celebrity" of death row:

> Spending even a small amount of time in California's overcrowded, dangerous prisons is not pleasant. Spending thirty years there, growing sick and old, and dying there, is a horrible experience. This is especially true given the unconstitutional failure to provide adequate health care to California's prisoners.
>
> Prisoners condemned to die in prison are not given any special treatment and, in fact, have less access to programs than other prisoners. They are housed in high security facilities with few privileges, far away from any relatives, and in crowded group cells. Ironically, people on death row are provided much more comfortable single cells and sometimes gain celebrity and attention just by being there.[41]

The strategy of promoting LWOP as an alternative to death has been largely successful.[42] James Liebman, professor of law at Columbia University, explains: "[L]ife without parole has been absolutely crucial to whatever progress has been made against the death penalty. The drop in death sentences would not have happened without LWOP."[43]

Defense attorneys in capital cases also have cited the severity of LWOP to avoid a death sentence for their clients. In Tennessee, for instance, a capital defense lawyer urged a jury to spare his client, Letalvis Cobbins, from the death penalty: "Make him suffer for every day of the rest of his life for what he did. . . . Say, 'Mr. Cobbins, you can sit there and rot.'"[44] The jury agreed and sentenced Cobbins to LWOP. Similarly, during the trial of Zacarias Moussaoui for conspiring to kill Americans on September 11, 2001, prison expert James Aiken testified that if Moussaoui were not sentenced to death, Moussaoui would "rot" for the rest of his life in a supermax, 23-hour-per-day lockdown facility. The jury opted to sentence Moussaoui to LWOP.[45] Despite the inherent severity of an LWOP sentence, a nondeath jury decision represents a hard-fought legal victory for lawyers representing capital defendants.

Yet some of those who are best positioned to know, such as correctional officials and offenders themselves, have suggested that DIP sentences are worse than death sentences. The former warden of Sing Sing prison, Lewis E. Lawes, compared capital punishment to the severity of life imprisonment: "Death fades into insignificance when compared with life imprisonment. To spend each night in jail, day after day, year after year, gazing at the bars and longing for freedom, is indeed expiation."[46] Another corrections officer commented, "I think that [LWOP] is harder to face than the death penalty in the sense that they know they are going to live the rest of their lives in this environment. . . . I think that's a little harder—they just go on day after day wondering when they are going to die."[47]

Some offenders, too, have opined that life in prison is worse than death. Death-row inmates who voluntarily drop their legal appeals in an effort to hasten their execution may perceive LWOP as a worse alternative than death: 133 death-row inmates, or nearly 9% of the 1,229 people executed since 1976, voluntarily dropped their appeals and were executed.[48] Joseph Parsons, a Utah death-row prisoner who declined to pursue his appeals, explained that he could no longer stand life in prison: "[T]he situation I'm in right now is horrible. To me, I can't think of anything worse than this [being in prison]."[49] Randy Arroyo, an offender whose death sentence was commuted to LWOP after the Supreme Court abolished capital punishment for juveniles, said, "I wish I still had the death sentence. . . . Really, death has never been my fear. What do people believe? That being alive in prison is a good life? This is slavery."[50] Death-row inmate Thomas J. Grasso issued a statement hours before his execution: "Life without parole is much worse than the death penalty. . . . All jurors should remember this. Attica and Oklahoma State Penitentiary are living hells."[51]

Not all inmates facing a life sentence prefer death, nor do all scholars perceive life to be worse than death. But it must be recognized that prisons in the United States are overcrowded and stark, full of violence, long-term isolation, abusive guards, disease, inadequate health care, and other dehumanizing conditions.[52] The endless monotony alone ensures that time passes painfully and slowly. While there may not be universal agreement that DIP sentences are *worse* than death, it is clear that DIP sentences are uniquely severe and degrading in their own right.

ii. DIP Sentences Deny the Humanity of the Offender

DIP sentences are severe and degrading not simply because the offender will live, and ultimately die, in prison. An offender serving a six-month sentence who dies in prison due to age, accident, illness, or violence cannot be said to have served a severe sentence simply because it ended in death.

Rather, DIP sentences are severe and degrading because, like capital sentences, they fail to recognize the intrinsic worth of the incarcerated person. The absence of all redemptive possibility denies human dignity. It is this quality that makes DIP sentences closer in severity to capital punishment than all other sentences.

DIP sentences are those from which the offender has no actual possibility of release, save the remote possibility of executive clemency or, in the case of a life sentence, the rare granting of parole. DIP sentences communicate to offenders that they have forfeited their right to ever walk again among society. They have been forever banished. No act by the incarcerated individual can change that assessment—neither the number of degrees attained, books written, or prison programs developed nor the model behavior demonstrated can impact the inevitable outcome of death in prison. Even in the face of great internal and genuine transformation, these offenders will be left to literally molder in prison until death. Whether they survive 10 years or 40 years behind bars matters not at all, except as administrative and economic concerns. As in the capital context, a penal policy that locks people up and permanently discards the key, in essence, discards the inviolate and innate humanity of the individual.

iii. Death-in-Prison Sentences Are Often Irrevocable

Irrevocability refers to that which cannot be recalled or undone. For instance, a capital sentence, once implemented, is irrevocable. Upon execution, offenders who have been put to death cannot be revived. If an error is uncovered, they cannot be given back their life. They cannot be compensated or provided with the means to start over. A person who is executed is gone for all eternity. Once death is imposed, it is permanent, and uniquely so.

The same does not automatically follow regarding DIP prison sentences. No prison sentence is irrevocable, in the sense that incarceration is not inherently a permanent state. A wrongly incarcerated person can be released. Compensation can be provided. Pardons can be issued. Freedom can be restored. The irrevocable costs of time spent in prison are more amorphous: missed celebrations, deaths and births, frayed or severed family ties that result from years of separation, lost wages and opportunities to advance in employment. Time spent in prison is irrevocable because it cannot be restored. Yet this reality is not unique to DIP sentences. Rather, it applies to any prison term of whatever duration, be it one year or an entire life.

But DIP sentence are often uniquely irrevocable in a practical sense. These sentences receive no heightened judicial attention or scrutiny, which leads to a reduced likelihood that they will reversed. Ninth Circuit Court of Appeals Judge Alex Kozinski once noted that innocent defendants in California are better off with a capital sentence because they will be provided with "a whole panoply of rights of appeal and review that you don't get in other cases."[53] Recent data suggest that roughly 80% of federal criminal appeals are resolved against the defendant, and, in general, scholars estimate the reversal rate for noncapital cases to be 10–20%, far below the capital reversal rate of roughly 68%.[54] As recognized in a 1990 report prepared for the American Bar Association in the context of habeas corpus relief,

> The rate of success for appeals from denial of habeas corpus relief in non-capital cases typically is estimated at 7% or less. The comparable rates for capital cases is startlingly different. Between 1976, for instance, when the Supreme Court restored the death penalty in Gregg v. Georgia, and 1983, the federal courts of appeals—when they reached the merits of the petition on habeas review—had decided according to one study more than 73% of the capital cases in favor the death sentenced prisoner.[55]

DIP sentences, therefore, are likely to remain intact relative to their capital counterparts.

If appellate intervention is unusual in noncapital cases, so is executive clemency. Although the granting of clemency is extremely rare in all cases,[56] in noncapital cases, executive clemency "has become essentially unavailable to imprisoned offenders in almost every American jurisdiction."[57] As the Supreme Court recently recognized, "the remote possibility of [executive clemency] does not mitigate the harshness of the sentence [of LWOP]."[58] While it continues to be *possible* for offenders to receive clemency, the granting of clemency is indeed a rare event.[59]

It is true that DIP sentences are not permanent, in that all incarcerated individuals, in theory, can be released. And DIP sentences are not uniquely irrevocable, in the sense that all offenders who wrongfully spend time in prison cannot be returned the intangible loss of all that was missed. Yet DIP sentences may be *de facto* irrevocable in that errors are rarely uncovered and clemency rarely invoked. The majority of offenders sentenced to die in prison will do just that. In that sense, DIP sentences are irrevocable.

b. Other Contemporary Societies Condemn DIP Sentences as Violations of Human Rights

Within the international community, many nations have recognized that both capital punishment and DIP sentences are inconsistent with human rights and human dignity. In stark contrast with the United States, for instance, capital punishment has been abolished in law or practice in 139 countries worldwide.[60] Indeed, in Europe, abolition of capital punishment is a condition precedent to admission to the European Union. International condemnation of capital punishment has been extended to other severe sanctions.

Nations around the world have begun questioning whether life imprisonment in *any* form is a legitimate punishment. In Europe, LWOP is unavailable as a sanction for all juvenile offenders, regardless of the offense, and in many European countries, *any* form of life sentence is prohibited for child offenders. Indeed, in Europe, the discussion has shifted to the acceptability of life imprisonment for *adult* offenders.[61] An official memorandum at the Council of Europe level holds that "it is inhuman to imprison a person for life without the hope of release" and adds that LWOP is "compatible neither with the modern principles on the treatment of prisoners . . . nor with the idea of the reintegration of offenders into society."[62] In Germany, France, and Italy, LWOP has been declared unconstitutional. In Portugal, Norway, and Spain, LWOP has been outlawed, as has any other form of a life sentence.

Still other European countries retain life imprisonment as a potential sentence but have a mandated term of years after which that life sentence must be reviewed. In Belgium, for instance, an offender serving a life sentence will be considered for release after 10 years. In Austria, Germany, Luxemburg, and Switzerland, an offender will be considered for release after 15 years. At the crux of these sentencing policies is the belief that "no human being should be regarded as beyond improvement and therefore should always have the prospect for release."[63]

To be sure, not every country in Europe has rejected whole-life sentences. LWOP is permitted in the Netherlands, although it is rarely imposed. In England and Wales, most life sentences are reviewed after a minimum time period, but there is a small subcategory of sentences that do not specify a minimum term for review and, in theory, could result in whole-life confinement. In France, the rule is similar, although offenders who are sentenced to life with no minimum period may still apply for release after a 30-year period.

And the European Court of Human Rights has not explicitly ruled on the question of whether LWOP for adults violates international conventions.[64]

Europe is not alone in its debate over life imprisonment. Brazil, Costa Rica, Colombia, El Salvador, Peru, and Mexico, for instance, do not permit *any* form of life imprisonment because it has been deemed inconsistent with human rights.[65] The decision to prohibit life imprisonment rests, in part, on the idea that prison has a reeducative function and that any whole-life sentence is incompatible with that function.[66]

Lengthy prison terms such as those found in the United States are unusual in Europe and elsewhere. Two recent cases illustrate the fundamental differences in approach to punishment. A man in Austria who was convicted of kidnapping and sexual assault against his 13-year-old niece was sentenced to six years in prison.[67] That same year, in Las Vegas, Nevada, a man convicted of kidnapping and sexual assault against a 13-year-old girl was sentenced to multiple life terms.[68] In Austria, the offender will have an opportunity to reintegrate into society. In the United States, the 27-year-old offender will first be eligible for parole in 80 years from the date of sentence, when he is 107 years old. Austria recognizes the potential reformation of the offender, while the United States surely does not.

Contemporary societies have rejected both capital and DIP sentences as inconsistent with human dignity and violative of human rights. Because of the severity of DIP sentences, they share with capital sentences the condemnation of the international community.

c. The Supreme Court Recently Recognized the Unique Severity of LWOP

The U.S. Supreme Court, for the first time in decades, held that a noncapital sentence was unconstitutionally severe. In *Graham v. Florida* (2010), the Supreme Court categorically struck down the use of LWOP for juvenile offenders convicted of nonhomicidal offenses. At the age of 16, Terrance Graham committed an armed burglary and was sentenced to probation. When he violated the terms of his probation, the trial judge sentenced Graham to life for that burglary. Because Florida abolished parole, Graham's life sentence meant that he would die in prison without ever being eligible for release. Graham argued, *inter alia*, that sentencing a juvenile to LWOP violated the Eighth Amendment's prohibition against cruel and unusual punishment. The Court agreed. Recognizing that LWOP is "the *second* most severe penalty permitted by law," the Court opined that life without parole sentences share some characteristics with death sentences that are shared by no other sentences. The State does not execute the offender sentenced to life without parole, but the sentence alters the offender's life by a forfeiture that is irrevocable. It deprives the convict of the most basic liberties without giving hope of restoration, except perhaps by executive clemency—the remote possibility of which does not mitigate the harshness of the sentence.[69]

Yet, despite the Court's recognition of the qualities shared between capital and LWOP sentences, the *Graham* majority went to great pains to uphold the continued viability of LWOP as a sentence for adult offenders and even for juvenile offenders in homicide cases. As Chief Justice Roberts in his concurring opinion was quick to point out, "it is perfectly legitimate for a juvenile to receive a sentence of life without parole for committing murder. This means that there is nothing *inherently* unconstitutional about imposing sentences of life without parole on juvenile offenders; rather the constitutionality of the sentence turns of the particular crimes for which they are imposed."[70] The Court's tenacious commitment to LWOP as a valid sentence for adults, regardless of the offense for which it is imposed, may mean that *Graham* is truly limited to its particular facts. Or perhaps *Graham* signals a new willingness by the Court to review severe sentences. In either scenario, members of the *Graham* Court identified the core severity of LWOP and relied on the shared characteristics between LWOP and death sentences in reaching its decision.

DIP sentences are uniquely severe and degrading, *de facto* irrevocable, condemned by members of the international community, and represent an inalterable forfeiture of the offender's life. These qualities are also present in capital cases. Yet, unlike in capital cases, DIP sentences do not receive heightened scrutiny, which results in their arbitrary and unfair application.

III. Although DIP Sentences Share Significant Characteristics with Capital Sentences, DIP Sentences Do Not Receive Heightened Legal Protections, Which Results in Their Arbitrary Imposition

Although DIP sentences are closer in severity to capital sentences than to any other form of punishment, only capital cases receive heightened legal protections. In this section, the legal protections afforded to capital cases are considered and contrasted with the legal treatment of DIP cases. This section suggests that the absence of robust protections results in the arbitrary application of DIP sentences.

a. The U.S. Supreme Court Established Different Standards in Capital and Noncapital Cases

i. Capital Cases Receive Heightened Legal Protections

Because death has long been considered different, capital cases receive heightened judicial scrutiny. Indeed, an entire and separate jurisprudence has evolved in death cases, with a unique set of constitutional and procedural safeguards at trial and sentencing designed to produce a less arbitrary and capricious capital system.[71] The Supreme Court has employed a robust proportionality review, in which it has limited the types of crimes and offenders that are eligible for capital cases. As the Court recently opined, "resort to the death penalty must be reserved for the worst of crimes, and limited in its instances of application."[72] The death penalty has been declared disproportionate for the crimes of rape,[73] child rape,[74] and felony murder when the offender did not participate in the killing.[75] The Court has thus narrowed the applicability of capital punishment to the most severe offenses.

The Supreme Court also has limited the use of capital punishment on the basis of offender characteristics. In 1986, the Court declared that capital punishment could no longer be employed against the mentally insane.[76] In 2002, the Court prohibited the use of capital punishment against the mentally retarded.[77] More recently, in 2005, the Court prohibited the application of capital punishment to offenders under the age of 18 at the time of the offense.[78] By narrowing the class of offenders, the Court has sought to limit capital punishment's application to only those who are most culpable for their actions.

In addition, the Court has approved a wide range of substantive protections designed to promote a fair and uniform system of adjudication in capital cases. Jury selection, known as *voir dire*, is a highly complex process requiring the "death qualification" of the jury. Under this system, all jurors who either are entirely opposed to capital punishment or would vote for the death penalty in every case are excluded from service. Capital trials also are bifurcated into a guilt phase and a penalty phase. Only if the jury finds the defendant guilty of capital murder does the case proceed to a penalty phase, in which aggravating and mitigating evidence is presented. Jurors are provided with "guided discretion" in evaluating the appropriateness of death, to "make rationally reviewable the process for imposing a sentence of death."[79] Moreover, mandatory death sentences are no longer available for any crime. Instead, jurors must be given the discretion to review each case and determine whether death is the appropriate penalty. As then Chief Justice Burger opined, "the need for treating each individual in a capital case with that degree of respect due the uniqueness of the individual is far more important than in non-capital cases."[80]

ii. Noncapital Cases Do Not Receive Similar Protections

The Supreme Court has been far less protective of noncapital cases. Unlike in capital cases, DIP sentences are available for categories of offenders that have been excluded from the death penalty because of reduced culpability, such as the mentally incapacitated and juveniles (with the exception of LWOP in nonhomicide cases). In addition, DIP sentences can be mandatory upon conviction of certain offenses, such as mandatory life sentences for habitual offenders. And with rare exception, the Supreme Court has employed a weak proportionality review in noncapital cases.

In 1980, in *Rummel v. Estelle*, the Supreme Court was presented with a challenge to the application of a Texas recidivist statute against a nonviolent offender with three felony fraud convictions. Although the total fraud from all three cases totaled $230, the Supreme Court rejected Rummel's challenge to his life sentence. In doing so, the *Rummel* majority opined that the length of a noncapital defendant's sentence is "purely a matter of legislative prerogative."[81] By deferring to the legislature, the Court admonished that "successful challenges to the proportionality of sentences should be exceedingly rare."[82]

Rummel set the stage for what has continued to be a parsimonious use of proportionality review in noncapital cases. In 1982, in *Hutto v. Davis*, the Court upheld a 40-year sentence for the possession and distribution of a relatively minor amount of marijuana.[83] In 1991, in *Harmelin v. Michigan*, the Court again rejected a strict proportionality analysis and upheld the sentence of LWOP for a first offender convicted of possessing a large quantity of cocaine.[84] In 2003, the Court upheld in companion cases the imposition of life sentences under California's three-strikes laws. In the first case, Gary Ewing was convicted of a third strike for stealing golf clubs valued at approximately $1,200.[85] In the second case, Leandro Andrade's second and third strikes were for stealing children's videos, which were valued in total at less than $160.[86] Both men were sentenced to life in prison, and the Court deemed both sentences to be within constitutional boundaries.

Indeed, in the 30 years leading up to the Court's 2010 decision in *Graham v. Florida*, the Court invalidated only a *single* noncapital sentence on the grounds that it was disproportionate to the crime. In 1983, in *Solem v. Helm*, the Supreme Court rejected, in a 5–4 decision, the application of LWOP to a defendant who was convicted of his seventh nonviolent felony conviction.[87]

The *Solem* majority distinguished the case from *Rummel* on the basis that there was no provision for parole release and that it was highly unlikely that his conviction would be commuted. Given the Court's consistent approval of severe noncapital sentences for even relatively minor offenses, *Solem* has proven to be the exception and, indeed, has been described by members of the Court and scholars as an "outlier."[88]

b. The Absence of Heightened Scrutiny Contributes to the Frequent and Arbitrary Imposition of DIP Sentences

Because DIP sentences are so severe, these sentences should be reserved for the worst offenders. As the Supreme Court itself recognized,

> a mandatory sentence of life imprisonment without the possibility of parole . . . share[s] one important characteristic of a death sentence: The offender will never regain his freedom. Because such a sentence does not even purport to serve a rehabilitative function, the sentence must rest on a rational determination that the punished "criminal conduct is so atrocious that society's interest in deterrence and retribution wholly outweighs any considerations of reform or rehabilitation of the perpetrator."[89]

It is true that many individuals serving DIP sentences have been convicted of serious offenses, including murder. Yet data from the Sentencing Project demonstrates that many individuals sentenced to life in prison are incarcerated for offenses other than homicide.[90] Who is sentenced to a life behind bars is not determined by a consistently applied jurisprudence across jurisdictions. Rather, random factors such as geography, race, prosecutorial discretion, and victim or offender characteristics lead to the all too frequent and haphazard application of DIP sentences. Numerous individuals serving DIP sentences are not the "worst of the worst" offenders, nor are they guilty of "atrocious" crimes. In this sense, DIP sentences are highly arbitrary.

i. LWOP for "Habitual Offenders"

Many offenders serving an LWOP sentence are doing so under their respective jurisdiction's habitual offender statute. States such as Alabama, California, Florida, Georgia, Louisiana, South Carolina, Virginia, and Washington mandate LWOP for habitual offenders.[91] The triggering offense for a habitual offender statute need not involve homicide or even serious bodily injury; indeed, the triggering offense itself may be nonviolent, and there may be ample available mitigation about the offender or the circumstances of the third-strike offense. Yet, once a prosecutor elects to charge a defendant under the applicable habitual offender statutes, judges are *required* to impose an LWOP sentence upon an individual's conviction.

LWOP is often a disproportionate punishment for the triggering crime. In September 2001, 47-year-old Sylvester Mead was found guilty of "public intimidation," based on his drunken threat in 2000 to a police officer. Mead previously had been convicted of aggravated battery and simple burglary. Under the version of Louisiana's third-felony-offender law applicable to his offense, Mead met the statutory criteria for a habitual offender because two of his three prior convictions were violent. Before the court sentenced Mead, it noted the ample mitigation present in the case. The court found that Mead was "able to attain certain goals similar to many other individuals, such as getting married, raising a family, and purchasing a home."[92] The trial court also recognized that Mead had substance and alcohol problems, which may have contributed to the public-intimidation conviction, and that the third conviction "did not involve physical violence, but rather the use of words, which were perceived by the police officer as threatening."[93] Finally, the trial court recognized that the defendant had a medical condition that would require ongoing treatment and that the defendant had successfully completed various programs in prison. Yet, because the court did not have the authority to depart from the habitual offender statutes, it was required to sentence Mead to LWOP. The Louisiana appellate courts affirmed Mead's LWOP sentence.[94]

Stories like Mead's abound. In Mississippi, Hershel Miles was sentenced as a recidivist to LWOP for forgery and petit larceny.[95] In South Carolina, Onrae Williams was sentenced to LWOP based on his conviction for the distribution of less than half a gram of cocaine in a case in which at least one of his prior qualifying convictions was for an offense that he committed as a juvenile.[96] In Louisiana, Dale Green was sentenced to LWOP in a case in which his third strike was based on his role as a middleman in a twenty-dollar marijuana sale, and his prior convictions stemmed from guilty pleas to attempted possession of cocaine and simple robbery.[97] In Florida, a 22-year-old man was sentenced to LWOP for robbing a sandwich shop, having previously been convicted of a drug offense.[98] And, of course, in California, Andrade and Ewing continue to serve their life sentences for their third nonviolent theft offenses.

In each of these cases, the defendant committed an offense in a jurisdiction with a habitual offender law. The prosecutor in each case made the decision to bring charges under that law.[99] But for these factors—which are incidental to the actual offenses—the above mentioned cases could have been resolved by probation or minimal prison terms. Instead, these individuals, even those with relatively minor criminal histories, received DIP sentences for relatively minor crimes. This is surely the height of arbitrariness.

ii. DIP for Nonviolent Drug Offenses

Habitual offenders are not the only individuals who face the prospect of a DIP sentence for a nonhomicidal offense. In 2004, 39% of all individuals sentenced to life terms in the federal system were convicted of drug offenses.[100] This is significant because parole was abolished in the federal system, and, thus, a life sentence is now a whole-life sentence. George Martorano, for instance, was a first offender charged with conspiracy and marijuana distribution. Because he had no prior convictions and was charged with a nonviolent offense, his lawyer recommended that Martorano plead guilty, assuming that Martorano would receive, at most, a 10-year sentence. The federal sentencing board recommended Martorano be sentenced to 40–52 months in prison. The federal judge overseeing his case, however, sentenced him to life.[101] Mark Young is another offender convicted in the federal system of participating in the sale of marijuana. Although Young was not a first offender, he had never previously spent a single day in prison. He too was sentenced to life in prison.[102] Clarence Aaron, a first offender and college student, was sentenced to three life sentences in federal prison for his role in a cocaine transaction.[103]

Still other offenders, including first offenders, received actual LWOP sentences for their drug crimes. Teresa Wilson was a 31-year-old mother of two when she sold prescription drugs to an undercover officer. Although this was her first offense and although the offense was nonviolent, Wilson was sentenced to LWOP.[104] Danielle Metz was sentenced to three life sentences plus 20 years for her role in helping her husband distribute narcotics.[105] None of these men and women committed violent crimes, and many were first offenders. Absent executive clemency or a change in federal law reinstating parole, these individuals will die in prison.

iii. Lengthy Terms-of-Year Sentences That End in Death

Arbitrariness can also be found in the imposition of lengthy sentences. Take the case of Noel Dauzart. Dauzart was a mentally disabled man who served as an unarmed getaway driver. He waited outside while his co-defendant held a gun to a bank teller and demanded money from the bank till. A silent alarm was activated, and both men were apprehended after the robbery, following a brief police chase. No one was injured in the course of the robbery, except Dauzart himself, who was beaten by the police upon his arrest and sustained permanent hearing loss in one ear. Dauzart received a 100-year prison term in Louisiana for armed robbery as a second felony offender. This sentence must be served "without benefit of parole, probation, or suspension of sentence," which means that Dauzart is ineligible for good-time credit or other early release.[106] He will, therefore, die in prison before coming close to the completion of his sentence.

On appeal, Dauzart raised numerous mitigating factors that he claimed should have been considered by the trial court, including the fact that he suffered from mental disorders, received psychiatric treatment as a child and while in prison, and was a special education student. After an extremely protracted appellate history (which included allegations of prosecutorial vindictiveness based on the prosecutor's decision to charge Dauzart as a habitual offender only after his original conviction and sentence of 60 years was reversed on appeal), an intermediate appellate court upheld his 100-year sentence. The court did not challenge the validity of the medical evidence offered on appeal but rather ruled that it was unable to consider that evidence in mitigation because it was not contained in the trial record. In affirming Dauzart's sentence, the court noted that since Dauzart could have been sentenced to a maximum of 198 years as a second-felony offender, the resulting 100-year sentence was not excessive. This is so even though Dauzart's co-defendant, who wielded the gun and entered the bank, pled guilty and received a 50-year sentence in exchange for his testimony against Dauzart.

Dauzart's case is compelling for many reasons. Dauzart received an extremely severe sentence—100 years without eligibility for early release, parole, or good time—for an armed robbery in which no one was injured and no money lost, in which his participation was less than that of his co-defendant, who received considerably lesser punishment, and in which significant questions exist about his mental status and his culpability. But outside of the specific facts of the Dauzart's case, perhaps a larger question should be raised: why is 100 years or, as the court noted, a potential maximum of 198 years *ever* an appropriate prison sentence for an armed robbery? Or stated another way, why are DIP sentences being handed out in cases that, while serious, do not involve the worst offenses or the most culpable offenders?

LWOP, life imprisonment, and lengthy terms-of-year sentences each result in the death of the offender in prison. These DIP sentences are meted out for crimes ranging from homicide to petty theft or public intimidation.

The sentences are arbitrary and often are based not on the offense or even the offender per se but rather on jurisdictional differences, prosecutorial charging decisions, and judicial biases. But while this arbitrariness has rightfully been condemned in the context of capital cases, it has long gone unrecognized in the context of DIP sentences.

IV. Wrestling with DIP Sentences: Practical and Theoretical Implications

DIP sentences can be criticized for their arbitrariness, the absence of proportionality, and the question of whether they are necessary to achieve legitimate objectives of the criminal justice system. Potential responses to DIP sentences, however, are mired in complex practical and theoretical questions. This final section begins to identify the challenges that arise in addressing DIP sentences. It also invites future discussion about whether DIP sentences are necessary in the American legal system.

a. Judicial and Legislative Reform of DIP Sentences?

Reform for DIP sentences can come either from the courts or from the legislature. In theory, courts are well placed to address the arbitrary and disproportionate application of DIP sentences. As discussed earlier in this chapter, there is certainly precedent for them to do so. In the capital context, the U.S. Supreme Court generated reform by severely limiting death eligibility by offender and offense characteristics, and by increasing substantive and procedural protections in all capital cases. Since DIP sentences share unique characteristics with capital cases, courts could, in theory, reduce arbitrary and disproportionate punishment by extending capital protections to DIP sentences.

Court intervention of that magnitude seems unlikely. As described by Rachel Barkow in this volume, if the Court were to engage in a more robust procedural and substantive analysis of all DIP sentences, the legal, financial, and practical consequences could be staggering.[107] Indeed, if the Court considered DIP sentences in their myriad forms, then the scope and resolution of any challenge may be unpalatably broad, since the number of offenders serving DIP sentences is more (and likely considerably so) than 43 times greater than the number of offenders on death row.[108] And while the Court could theoretically narrow its consideration to actual LWOP sentences only and not the broader category of DIP sentences, this chapter has shown that there is little principled basis to do so. Yet there is scant evidence that the Court would extend additional protections derived from capital jurisprudence, or in any other modified form, to all DIP sentences, in part, due to the fear of endless litigation.

Alternatively, the legislature could address proportionality and arbitrariness through legislative reform of sentencing laws.[109] Legislators, however, are rewarded for being tough on crime, not for reducing punishment. And, unlike in the case of capital punishment, there is no large-scale advocacy group challenging the use and application of DIP sentences. Indeed, other than isolated advocacy efforts organized around a specific issue, there is virtually no anti-DIP movement at all.[110] In California, for instance, the public has twice (in 2000 and again in 2006) voted to include additional "strike" offenses, expanding the reach of its three-strikes laws, while repeal efforts have gained little traction.[111] This trend holds throughout the country, although state fiscal crises in some jurisdictions have prompted reconsideration of tough-on-crime punishment policies.[112]

b. A Nascent Debate: The Need for DIP Sentences

The very existence of DIP sentences rests on the premise that there are offenders who cannot ever be released, either because the crime is so truly heinous or because the offender is so irrefutably dangerous. But that premise deserves additional scrutiny. Must the United States so fully embrace the existence of a punishment that determines *at the time of sentencing* that the offender will forever be beyond redemption and that provides no opportunity for revisiting that determination? Is it even possible to envision a system in which lesser offenders are never permanently incarcerated and in which even the most serious offenders retain the prospect of release?

Rachel Barkow and Paul Robinson in this volume both argue that retributive principles justify LWOP for at least the most serious of offenses and that certain offenders indeed should never be released. Still others argue that permanent incapacitation for the worst offenders must guide penal policy because we have not mastered the ability to distinguish between those who have been reformed and those who will reoffend: until the calculus for offenders' future dangerousness is perfected, violent offenders should not be released to potentially harm innocent others.[113] But should the *possibility* of reoffending justify the wholesale elimination of the redemptive possibility? Has retribution become so embedded in our cultural mind-set that we cannot imagine a less punitive punishment structure? Are we so committed to severe punishment (and the more severe the better) as the best available response to serious (and sometimes less serious) offending that we cannot envision an alternative?[114]

Perhaps the very nature of prison today eliminates the redemptive possibility. But what if prisons stopped reinforcing violence, alienation, separation, and indifference, as persuasively detailed in this volume by Sharon Dolovich, and instead became institutions not solely of punishment and incapacitation but also of reformation, reeducation, and, ultimately, transformation?[115] What if the twin possibilities of reform and release were taken seriously? What if there was automatic review of every offender's sentence after 10 years, or 20 years, or 25 years of incarceration, even for the most serious of offenses? What if that review were not merely perfunctory, as many parole hearings are today, but was a comprehensive and robust evaluation of the offender, not solely as the person who once committed an offense but also as the person he or she has become at the time of review? What if, upon an offender's release, we increased supportive reentry services or gave teeth to parole supervision? What if we accepted the possibility that people, at least some people, can—and do—change?

The vision of a criminal justice system that emphasizes restoration would require a wholesale transformation of penal philosophy. Prisons would be required to become positive forces of change. Reentry programs, including parole, would have to be ramped up in unprecedented ways.[116] An overarching shift from punitiveness would need to occur. Yet, in today's political and fiscal climate, it seems extremely unlikely that politicians and the public would support either a large-scale retraction of punitive policies or a significant shift in funding toward prison reform and offenders. Without meaningful holistic prison and reentry reform, prisons will continue to breed isolation and violence. In that context, it seems unwise, and perhaps even dangerous, to advocate for the complete abolition of DIP sentences.

DIP sentences are severe and degrading, arbitrarily imposed, inconsistent with international norms, and often irrevocable. In this sense, DIP sentences are closer on the sentencing continuum to capital cases than are other punishments. Courts nonetheless have created a bright-line distinction between capital cases and DIP sentences, providing heightened protection for the former while virtually ignoring the latter. Thousands of people will die in prison, some for nonviolent offenses, with no heightened judicial scrutiny or additional public attention. As debate about the United States' "new death penalty" begins to emerge, we need to carefully consider the consequences of a system that condemns so many people to death in prison.

1. Ashley Nellis and Ryan King, "No Exit: The Expanding Use of Life Sentences in America," Sentencing Project, 2009, at 5, http://sentencingproject.org/doc/publications/publications/inc_noexitseptember2009.pdf.

2. *Id.*

3. Alexander Cockburn, "Worse Than Death," *Nation*, April 20, 2009, at 10.

4. Robert Johnson and Sandra McGunigall-Smith, "Life without Parole, America's Other Death Penalty: Notes on Life under Sentence of Death by Incarceration," *Prison Journal* 88 (2008): 328–46.

5. Alfred C. Villaume, "'Life without Parole' and 'Virtual Life Sentences': Death Sentences by Any Other Name," *Contemporary Justice Review* 8 (2005): 265–77.

6. Hugh Adam Bedau, "Imprisonment vs. Death: Does Avoiding Schwarzschild's Paradox Lead to Sheleff's Dilemma?," *Albany Law Review* 54 (1990): 481–95.

7. Leon Sheleff, *Ultimate Penalties: Capital Punishment, Life Imprisonment, Physical Torture* (Columbus: Ohio State University Press, 1987), 131.

8. William W. Berry III, "More Different Than Life, Less Different Than Death," *Ohio State Law Journal* (2010): 71.

9. Johnson and McGunigall-Smith, "Life without Parole," at 328.

10. Jessica S. Henry, "New Jersey's Road to Abolition," *Justice Systems Journal* 29 (2008): 408.

11. Ashley Nellis, "Throwing Away the Key: The Expansion of Life without Parole Sentences in the United States," *Federal Sentencing Reporter* 23 (2010): 27–32. *See also* Note, "A Matter of Life and Death: The Effect of Life-without-Parole Statues on Capital Punishment," *Harvard Law Review* 119 (2006): 1838.

12. Carol S. Steiker and Jordan M. Steiker, "Opening a Window or Building a Wall? The Effect of Eighth Amendment Death Penalty Law and Advocacy on Criminal Justice More Broadly," *University of Pennsylvania Journal of Constitutional Law* 11 (2008): 155.

13. For an insightful discussion of the United States' continued commitment to capital punishment, see David Garland, *Peculiar Institution: America's Death Penalty in an Age of Abolition* (Cambridge: Harvard University Press, 2010).

14. NAACP Legal Defense and Educational Fund, "Death Row USA," Spring 2010, http://naacpldf.org/files/publications/DRUSA_Spring_2010.pdf.

15. Grants of executive clemency are rare. In Massachusetts, for instance, the governor did not commute a single sentence between 1997 and 2009. In the 10 preceding years, there were only seven commutations. Michael Blanding, "The Long Shadow of Willie Horton," *Boston Globe*, October 18, 2009, http://www.boston.com/bostonglobe/magazine/articles/2009/10/18/the_long_shadow_of_willie_horton?mode=PF.

16. Nellis, "Throwing Away the Key," at 28.

17. Marc Mauer, Ryan S. King, and Malcolm Young, "The Meaning of 'Life': Long Prison Sentences in Context," Sentencing Project, May 2004, at 7.

18. *Id.* at 12.

19. Nellis and King, "No Exit," at 28.

20. Georgia State Board of Pardons and Paroles, "More Violent-Crime Lifers Die in Prison Than Are Paroled," news release, June 1, 1998.

21. Blaire Russell, "*In re Lawrence and Hayward v. Marshall*: Reexamining the Due Process Protections of California Lifers Seeking Parole," *Berkley Journal of Criminal Law* 14 (Spring 2009): 251.

22. Current state experiments with parole reform typically target nonviolent offenses. West Virginia, however, recently passed a bill that would allow annual parole review for eligible offenders serving life sentences. *See* Peggy McGarry, "The Continuing Fiscal Crisis in Corrections: Setting a New Course," Vera Institute of Justice, October 2010, at 19, http://www.vera.org/download?file=3072/The-continuing-fiscal-crisis-in-corrections-10-2010-updated.pdf.

23. Blanding, "The Long Shadow of Willie Horton."

24. Quoted in Dirk van Zyl Smit, "Recent Issues in National and International Law," *International Journal Law and Psychiatry* 29 (2006): 405 (emphasis added).

25. Mauer et al., "The Meaning of 'Life,'" at 11.

26. Felisa Cardona, "Clark Sentenced to Life in Prison, with Additional 1,152 Years, for Darrent Williams' Murder," *Denver Post*, May 1, 2010, http://www.denverpost.com/news/frontpage/ci_14995716.

27. "Belmont Shore Rapist Is Sentenced," *Los Angeles Times*, September 16, 2004, http://articles.latimes.com/2004/sep/16/local/me-belmont16.

28. Liz Moyer, "It Could Have Been Worse for Madoff," *Forbes*, June 29, 2009, http://www.forbes.com/2009/06/24/bernie-madoff-prison-sentence-business-beltway-madoff.html.

29. Jeremy Travis and Joan Petersilia, "Reentry Reconsidered: A New Look at an Old Question," *Crime and Delinquency* 47 (2001): 291, 294–95.

30. *Furman v. Georgia*, 408 U.S. 238, 286–90 (1972) (Brennan, J., concurring).

31. *Id.* at 306 (Stewart, J., concurring).

32. Sheleff, *Ultimate Penalties*, at 138.

33. Cesare Beccaria, *On Crimes and Punishment* (1764), at 47.

34. *Id.* at 51.

35. John Stuart Mill, "Parliamentary Debate on Capital Punishment within Prisons Bill" (April 21, 1868), reprinted in *Philosophical Perspectives on Punishment*, ed. Gertrude Ezorsky, 271–80 (Albany: SUNY Press, 1972).

36. Johnson and McGunigall-Smith, "Life without Parole," at 337–38.

37. Berry, "More Different Than Life."

38. Trip Jennings, "Bill Richardson Admits Doubt about Death Penalty Decision," *New Mexico Independent*, March 19, 2009, http://newmexicoindependent.com/22574/bill-richardson-admits-doubt-about-death-penalty-decision.

39. P. A. Mudd, "Plea Deal: Life without Parole, Prosecutors Unwilling to Risk Conviction on Lesser Charge," *Richmond Times-Dispatch*, September 20, 2006, at A1.

40. New Jerseyans for Alternatives to the Death Penalty (Trenton, New Jersey), "The Death Penalty: Questions and Answers," http://www.njadp.org/gdabout&what=faqs. *See also* Henry, "New Jersey's Road to Abolition."

41. ACLU of Northern California, "The Truth about Life without Parole: Condemned to Die in Prison," http://www.aclunc.org/issues/criminal_justice/death_penalty/the_truth_about_life_without_parole_condemned_to_die_in_prison.shtml. Of course, death-row inmates do not live in comfortable cells. Many death-row inmates are housed in single cells within supermax prisons under severe lockdown conditions. These death-row

inmates are confined to their cells with virtually no recreational time or other "privileges" typically available to the general prison population.

42. Steiker and Steiker, "Opening a Window or Building a Wall?"

43. Adam Liptak, "Serving Life, with No Chance of Redemption," *New York Times*, October 5, 2005, http://www.nytimes.com/2005/10/05/national/05lifer.html.

44. Jamie Satterfield, "Life without Parole: Jury Rejects Death Penalty for Letalvis Cobbins," *Knox News*, August 27, 2009, from http://www.knoxnews.com/news/2009/aug/27/life-without-parole-jury-rejects-death-penalty-let/.

45. Richard A. Serrano, "The Slow Rot at Supermax," *Los Angeles Times*, May 5, 2006, http://articles.latimes.com/2006/may/05/nation/na-supermax5.

46. Lewis E. Lawes, "Why I Changed My Mind," in *Voices against Death: American Opposition to Capital Punishment, 1787–1975*, ed. Philip Mackey (New York: Burt Franklin, 1976), at 191, 194.

47. Johnson and McGunigall-Smith, "Life without Parole," at 340.

48. Death Penalty Information Center, "Information on Defendants Who Were Executed since 1976 and Designated as 'Volunteers,'" October 30, 2009, http://www.deathpenaltyinfo.org/information-defendants-who-were-executed-1976-and-designated-volunteers.

49. Johnson and McGunigall-Smith, "Life without Parole," at 353.

50. Liptak, "Serving Life," at 4.

51. John Kifner, "Grasso's Farewell: Life without Parole Worse Than Death," *New York Times*, March 21, 1995, http://www.nytimes.com/1995/03/21/nyregion/grasso-s-farewell-life-without-parole-worse-than-death.html.

52. As Sharon Dolovich argues in her chapter in this volume, these prison conditions reflect a policy of permanent exclusion, in which dire prison conditions cause inmates to embrace antisocial norms and violence. In this way, prison itself becomes an institution that reinforces the need for permanent incapacitation. *See* Dolovich, "Creating the Perfect Prisoner," chap. 3 in this volume.

53. Alex Kozinski and Steven Bright, "The Modern View of Capital Punishment," *American Criminal Law Review* 34 (1997): 1353, 1360–61. *See also* "A Matter of Life and Death," at 1853 ("Unlike death sentences, which merit a heightened level of appellate review, life without parole sentences receive no special consideration from appellate tribunals.")

54. Michael Heise, "Federal Criminal Appeals: A Brief Empirical Perspective," *Marquette Law Review* 93 (2009): 832. *See also* Marc M. Arkin, "Rethinking the Constitutional Right to a Criminal Appeal," *U.C.L.A. Law Review* 39 (1992): 503, 516 (reviewing California cases and estimating that "approximately one criminal conviction in five was modified by the appellate process"); James S. Liebman, "The Overproduction of Death," *Columbia Law Review* 100 (2000): 2053n. 90 (estimating that noncapital reversal rate is "probably far less than ten percent").

55. "Background Report on Death Penalty Habeas Corpus Issues Prepared for the American Bar Association Criminal Justice Section's Task Force on Death Penalty Habeas Corpus," *American University Law Review* 40 (1990): 53, 109 (internal citations omitted).

56. Austin Sarat, "Memorializing Miscarriages of Justice: Clemency Petitions in the Killing States," *Law and Society Review* 42 (2008): 183, 187–88.

57. ABA Justice Kennedy Commission, "Reports with Recommendations to the ABA House of Delegates," 2004, at 72, http://www.abanet.org/crimjust/kennedy/JusticeKennedyCommissionReportsFinal.pdf.

58. *Graham v. Florida*, No. 08-7412, slip op. (May 17, 2010).

59. Austin Sarat and Naaser Hussain, "On Lawful Lawlessness: George Ryan, Executive Clemency and the Rhetoric of Sparing Life," *Stanford Law Review* 56 (2004): 1307, 1310.

60. Death Penalty Information Center, "Abolitionist and Retentionist Countries," 2010, http://www.deathpenaltyinfo.org/abolitionist-and-retentionist-countries.

61. Dirk van Zyl Smit, "Outlawing Irreducible Life Sentences: Europe on the Brink?," *Federal Sentencing Reporter* 23:1 (2010): 39–48.

62. *Id.* at 43, citing Eur. Comm. of Ministers, Draft General Report on the Treatment of Long-Term Prisoners, Doc. No. CM(75)143add3 (1975).

63. Van Zyl Smit, "Outlawing Irreducible Life Sentences," at 40.

64. *Id.*

65. Dirk van Zyl Smit, "Life Imprisonment: Recent Issues in National and International Law," *International Journal of Law and Psychiatry* 29 (2006): 405, 410–11.

66. *Id.*

67. "Man Jailed in Austria for Kidnapping Niece, Abusing Her for 18 Months," *AFP*, March 19, 2010, http://www.smh.com.au/world/man-jailed-in-austria-for-kidnapping-niece-abusing-her-for-18-months-20100319-qisy.html.

68. Cara McCoy, "Man Gets Life Sentences in Girl's Kidnapping, Assault," *Las Vegas Sun*, January 13, 2010, http://www.lasvegassun.com/news/2010/jan/13/man-gets-life-sentences-girls-kidnapping-assault/.

69. *Graham*, No. 08-7412, slip op. at 19 (internal citations omitted) (emphasis added).

70. *Id.* (Roberts, J., concurring) (emphasis in the original).

71. Rachel E. Barkow, "The Court of Life and Death: The Two Tracks of Constitutional Sentencing Law and the Case for Uniformity," *Michigan Law Review* 107 (2009): 1145.

72. *Kennedy v. Louisiana*, 554 U.S. 407, 447 (2008).

73. *Coker v. Georgia*, 433 U.S. 534 (1977).

74. *Kennedy*, 554 U.S. 407.

75. *Enmund v. Florida*, 458 U.S. 782 (1982).

76. *Ford v. Wainwright*, 477 U.S. 399 (1986).

77. *Atkins v. Virginia*, 536 U.S. 304 (2002).

78. *Roper v. Simmons*, 543 U.S. 551 (2005).

79. *Godfrey v. Georgia*, 446 U.S. 420, 428 (1980) (plurality opinion) (footnotes omitted).

80. *Lockett v. Ohio*, 438 U.S. 586, 605 (1978).

81. *Rummel v. Estelle*, 445 U.S. 263, 274 (1980).

82. *Id.* at 272.

83. *Hutto v. Davis*, 545 U.S. 370 (1982).

84. *Harmelin v. Michigan*, 501 U.S. 957 (1991).

85. *Ewing v. California*, 538 U.S. 11 (2003).

86. *Lockyer v. Andrade*, 538 U.S. 63 (2003).

87. *Solem v. Helm*, 563 U.S. 277 (1983).

88. *Graham v. Florida*, 130 S. Ct. 2011, 2047 (2010) (Thomas, J., dissenting); Barkow, "The Court of Life and Death," at 1160.

89. *Harmelin*, 501 U.S. at 1028 (quoting *Furman*, 408 U.S. at 30).

90. Mauer et al., "The Meaning of 'Life,'" at 13.

91. Nellis, "Throwing Away the Key."

92. *State v. Mead*, 988 So. 2d 740 (La. App. 2d Cir. 2008).

93. *Id.* at 749.

94. *State v. Mead*, 16 So. 3d 470, 472 (La. App. 2d Cir. 2009).

95. *Miles v. State*, 864 So. 2d 963 (Miss. App. 2003).

96. *State v. Williams*, 669 S.E.2d 640 (S.C. App. 2008).

97. *State v. Green*, 839 So. 2d 970 (La. App. 2d Cir. 2003).

98. Nellis, "Throwing Away the Key."

99. I. Bennett Capers, in "Defending Life," chapter 5 in this volume, describes the "assembly line" way in which defendants facing "only" LWOP were prosecuted. Capers reflects on the indifference with which those "life" cases were handled, with an eye only to convictions for the alleged crime and little analysis into whether that was the best, or appropriate, sentence.

100. Mauer et al., "The Meaning of 'Life,'" at 19.

101. November Coalition, "The Wall: George Martorano," http://www.november.org/thewall/cases/martorano-g/martorano-g.html.

102. Eric Schlosser, "Marijuana and the Law," *Atlantic Monthly* 274:3 (September 1994).

103. November Coalition, "The Wall: Clarence Aaron," http://www.november.org/thewall/cases/aaron-c/aaron-c.html.

104. "First Time Drug Offender Serving Life without Parole," *Gadsden Times*, December 1, 1999, http://news.google.com/newspapers?nid=1891&dat=19991201&id=7cAfAAAAIBAJ&sjid=cNgEAAAAIBAJ&pg=1109,152728.

105. November Coalition, "The Wall: Danielle Metz," http://www.november.org/thewall/cases/metz-d/metz-d.html.

106. *State v. Dauzart*, 960 So. 2d 1079 (La. App. 5th Cir. 2007).

107. Rachel E. Barkow, "Life without Parole and the Hope for Real Sentencing Reform," chap. 6 in this volume.

108. This number is based on 3,261 death-row inmates in comparison with the 140,000 inmates serving a life or LWOP sentence. Because the latter number does not include lengthy terms-of-year sentences, the ratio is significantly larger.

109. Paul Robinson argues under a desert punishment rationale that LWOP sentences (and presumably those sentences that function as their equivalent) should be reserved for the most egregious of offenders and offenses. Robinson's ordinal system of punishment would restrict LWOP sentences only to those offenders with the highest degree of blameworthiness. Although Robinson does not directly address the mechanism under which LWOP would be restricted, some form of legislative or judicial intervention would be required to scale back the offenses and offenders eligible for such punishment. *See* Paul H. Robinson, "Life without Parole under Modern Theories of Punishment," chap. 4 in this volume.

110. In the case of extreme sentences for nonviolent drug offenders, there has been some limited organized success. The 2009 repeal of the New York Rockefeller drug laws reflected combined advocacy efforts of, *inter alia*, prison reform groups, defendants' families, and legal services agencies.

111. As Franklin Zimring, Gordon Hawkins, and Sam Kamin carefully document, California's three-strikes laws are firmly entrenched, favored by the public and politicians alike, with limited, and not particularly successful, organized opposition. Given public support for these laws, it is unlikely that a supermajority of the voters would vote for repeal. This is true even though the economic and social consequences of the three-strikes

law have been staggering. *See* Franklin E. Zimring, Gordon Hawkins, and Sam Kamin, *Punishment and Democracy: Three Strikes and You're Out in California* (New York: Oxford University Press, 2001).

112. Fiscal crisis may provide an opportunity for penal reform. The Pew Center has partnered with 15 states throughout the country, including Alabama, Arkansas, Illinois, Indiana, Michigan, North Carolina, Ohio, Kentucky, Texas, and Washington, in an effort to create cost-effective responses to crime and to reform sentencing policies. The Pew Center estimates that states spend approximately $50 billion per year on correctional costs, an increase of nearly 350% between 1987 and 2008. *But see* Marie Gottschalk, "Dismantling the Carceral State: The Future of Penal Policy Reform," *Texas Law Review* 84 (2005): 1693 (noting that tough crime policies continued in severe fiscal crisis).

113. Marie Gottschalk notes that recidivism rates among older offenders who have served lengthy prison sentences are comparatively lower but are not (and never will be) at zero. Gottschalk argues that risk-averse politicians and a public immersed in years of crime-control rhetoric are significant impediments to the revitalization of parole and clemency. She further suggests that the shift toward retribution has marginalized the potential role of mercy and the rehabilitative ideal. While public officials could prepare the public to be less risk averse through public education about risk assessment, Gottschalk notes that the entrenched retributive impulse will be more difficult to dismantle. *See* Marie Gottschalk, "No Way Out? Life Sentences and the Politics of Penal Reform," chap. 7 in this volume.

114. For a highly influential and persuasive account of the shift in the United States toward a retributive and punitive penal culture, see David Garland, *The Culture of Control: Crime and Social Order in Contemporary Society* (Chicago: University of Chicago Press, 2002).

115. Dolovich, "Creating the Perfect Prisoner."

116. There have been modest attempts to address certain obstacles to reentry, but these efforts are inconsistent and have been limited in scope and in funding. *See* Jessica S. Henry, "A Second Look at the Second Chance Act," *Criminal Law Bulletin*, Summer 2009, 45; Jessica S. Henry, "Criminal History on a 'Need to Know' Basis: Employment Policies That Eliminate the Criminal History Box on Employment Applications," *Justice Policy Journal* 5 (2008): 2, http://www.cjcj.org/justice_policy_journal. But the obstacles to reentry are complex, and reform efforts have only begun to scratch the surface of the challenges. Michael Pinard, "Collateral Consequences of Criminal Convictions: Confronting Issues of Race and Dignity," *New York University Law Review* 85 (2010): 457; Jessica S. Henry, "Closing the Legal Services Gap in Reentry," *Criminal Justice Studies: A Critical Journal of Crime, Law, and Society* 21:1 (2008): 15–27.

3

Creating the Permanent Prisoner

SHARON DOLOVICH

I. American Penality's Exclusionary Project

Every year, hundreds of thousands of people churn through the great revolving door of the American penal system. In 2006 alone, more than 840,000 people were convicted of felonies and sentenced to some period of confinement.[1] Of these, approximately 460,000 were sent to state prison, with an average sentence of 4 years and 11 months.[2] By contrast, as of 2008, only slightly more than 41,000 people were serving life without parole (LWOP) sentences,[3] a mere 1.7% of the total incarcerated population.[4]

Based on these numbers, one might well regard LWOP as the anomaly, and certainly not emblematic of the system as a whole. In this chapter, however, I argue that it is LWOP that most effectively captures the central motivating aim of the contemporary American carceral system. LWOP promises permanent exclusion. In one move, it guarantees that the targeted offender will never reemerge, never reintegrate, never again move freely in the shared public space. Of course, not every person convicted of a felony can receive an LWOP sentence. Instead, the vast majority of prison terms are time limited, and even many people who get life sentences retain the promise of parole eligibility. The penal system thus operates, at least formally, on the principle of temporary removal—a principle that fits neatly with a host of other more familiar penological theories (retribution, deterrence, etc.). But a closer look at the system itself, taking into account the way it actually functions and the experience of the people inside it, tells a different story, one more consistent with the ideal of wholesale banishment that LWOP embodies.

At issue is what might be called society's collective disposition toward the people the state has incarcerated. The range of possible such dispositions can be imagined as along a spectrum. At one end is a commitment to meaningful reintegration. At the other is a commitment to permanent exclusion. Every polity that punishes crime with imprisonment must lie somewhere on this spectrum. To determine exactly where a given polity falls, one must look beyond aspirational statements and rhetorical claims to the actual practices that collectively mediate the interaction between the society at large and those people who are or have been incarcerated.

Consider first the ideal types. In a society fully committed to meaningful postrelease reintegration—call this a *reintegrationist* system—the state would help people in custody to develop prosocial skills consistent with successful reentry and to remedy or mitigate whatever antisocial traits or tendencies are likely obstacles to their living healthy and productive lives on the outside.[5] A reintegrationist system would institute a meaningful parole process through which, perhaps after a custodial term proportionate to the crime, individuals would have the chance to show that they could be released without any appreciable risk to public safety—and would actually be released subsequent to such a showing. On release, people would be helped to assemble the components of a successful postcustody existence: a job, a place to live, the means to reunite with family, etc. On the other end of the spectrum, a society committed to permanent exclusion—call this an *exclusionist* system—would do precisely the opposite.

Given the complexity of modern society, the inevitable scarcity of resources, and the intractability of many social problems known to lead to violence and other antisocial conduct,[6] a fully reintegrationist society may be an impossible ideal. But my claim in this chapter is that the American carceral system, once to some extent at least rhetorically committed to reintegration, has ceased even to gesture in that direction. Instead, in the past three decades, this system has come explicitly to embrace the opposite approach, that of permanent exclusion. Innumerable aspects of the American penal experience speak to this exclusionist commitment. In American prisons, there is little if any programming to help people in custody to address the incapacities that led them to prison in the first place. To the contrary, prison conditions today tend to exacerbate whatever antisocial tendencies people brought with them into custody and to undermine the development of the skills needed to succeed outside prison. Even those people who are parole eligible and capable of living productive and law-abiding lives out in the community are persistently denied not only release but even the opportunity to make the case that they could be safely freed. And those fortunates who *are* released will face a host of state-imposed obstacles making it extremely difficult for them to construct stable and law-abiding lives on the outside.

Viewed through this lens, what may otherwise appear as unrelated if unfortunate features of the current penal climate turn out to be mutually reinforcing components of a particular kind of carceral system. This exclusionist system has no real investment in the successful reentry of the people the state has incarcerated. Instead, a variety of forces (legal, political, economic, and cultural) array themselves against any meaningful loosening of state control, taking different forms depending on the context but all directed toward the ultimate aim of denying readmission to the shared social space to those people once marked out as prisoners.

In this way, the American carceral system has become a key instrument of social organization, a central means (if not *the* central means) by which the state manages both deviant behavior and perceived threats to the social order.[7] The logic of this organizational system is simple: those who are judged undesirable or otherwise unworthy lose their status as moral and political subjects and are kept beyond the bounds of mainstream society. And once excluded in this way, it becomes difficult, if not impossible, for people ever fully to return. In the American context, the experience of having been incarcerated thus can no longer be construed as simply one aspect of a person's life history. With few exceptions (the Martha Stewarts, the Conrad Blacks), a person who has once donned the telltale orange jumpsuit acquires a new, fixed social identity, that of *inmate*, and is thereby transformed into someone who is simultaneously outside society's moral circle and a perennial subject of state control.[8] At a rhetorical level, the fact of the crime itself justifies the subsequent social exclusion. But given the profile of the people most likely to wind up in prison—disproportionately drug addicted, mentally ill, illiterate, unskilled, indigent, and/or people of color—the criminal justice system may simply represent the most obvious sorting mechanism for officially branding as noncitizens those populations with whom, for whatever reason (hatred, fear, or even simple distaste), mainstream society would prefer not to have to deal.

Once the carceral system is understood on these terms, it becomes unsurprising that people of color—African Americans in particular—are dramatically overrepresented in the nation's prisoner population.[9] As Loïc Wacquant has forcefully argued, from slavery to Jim Crow to the northern ghetto, the history of race relations in America has been one of racial segregation officially and violently enforced.[10] On Wacquant's telling, the American prison expansion of the 1980s and 1990s was a direct response to the declining demand for labor in the postindustrial economy and the consequent emergence of a predominantly black urban underclass, the threat of which the ghetto could no longer contain.[11] Yet one need not regard the need for a new form of racial control as the only possible explanation for mass incarceration to recognize that African Americans bear a considerable disproportion of the exclusionary burdens imposed by the current carceral system—and that, as a consequence, this system has emerged as the preeminent mechanism by which African Americans without social or economic capital are "define[d], confine[d], and control[led]."[12] Nor, once this feature of the system is acknowledged, is it possible to deny that the exclusionary imperative of the American carceral system has a profoundly racial cast.

LWOP is the most obvious and expeditious way to effect permanent exclusion. But as already noted, not everyone convicted of a crime can get LWOP. In an exclusionary system, an LWOP sentence is only one of many penal strategies in place to maintain the boundary between inmates and the broader society. In what follows, I chronicle some of these strategies, which together ensure a life of struggle at the margins of society even for those people who manage on release to avoid subsequent reincarceration.[13] First, I explore the character of prison conditions and argue that the experience of incarceration in American prisons today exacerbates the antisocial behavior of those in custody and undermines their ability to live healthy and productive lives on the outside. In these ways, the institutional shape of American prisons ensures that people with time-limited sentences—the vast majority of the people in prison—will find it hard after being released to avoid reoffending and thus being reincarcerated. Second, I examine some of the strategies that have been adopted to constrain the parole prospects of even those people who manage against the odds to preserve or develop prosocial skills while in custody and who would thus pose little or no public safety threat on release. Third, I consider the collateral consequences of felony convictions and explore the way these consequences heavily burden the prospects of newly released offenders—even those former prisoners who are able to avoid reoffending. In this way, society's commitment to permanent exclusion proves to reach beyond the prisons, keeping on society's margins even those formerly incarcerated individuals capable of living lawfully on the outside. Indeed, as the work of Katherine Beckett and Steve Herbert demonstrates, the drive to exclude extends still further, so that even people without criminal convictions but who are perceived as "disorderly" or otherwise socially "undesirable" have been finding themselves forced out of the public space.[14]

This way of framing American penal policy may seem to sideline inappropriately the more legitimate penological purposes—retribution, deterrence, etc. As will be seen, however, there is a strikingly poor fit between these more familiar penological justifications and the actual practices of the penal system. This mismatch strongly indicates the need for an alternative explanation—hence my central claim, that the American carceral system, although perhaps rhetorically motivated by more familiar penological goals, is in practice designed to mark certain undesirables as social deviants and consign them to lives beyond the boundaries of mainstream society. For many of those so marked—more than 2.3 million at last count[15]—this extrasocietal existence is lived in locked institutions clearly distinct from the social space shared by the privileged persons who retain full political status as citizens. Others, freed (often only temporarily) from custody, exist on society's margins: skid rows, homeless shelters, "inner cities," some public housing projects, etc. If these noncustodial marginal spaces are preferable to prison, their inhabitants are still often reduced to what Italian political theorist Giorgio Agamben calls "bare life,"[16] i.e., naked physical being without political, legal, or social status.[17] Agamben's division between bare life and political existence maps the divide between exclusion and inclusion that, I argue, forms the foundational logic of the American carceral state.[18] Only once this logic is recognized does it become possible really to understand—and thus effectively to challenge—the seemingly disparate exclusionary practices that together define the terms of existence for people marked as criminals.

But first, some historical context.

II. The Emergence of the Exclusionary Ideal: A Brief, Partial History

According to the standard historical account, American penological practice for much of the 20th century was informed by a rehabilitative ideal, on which "the criminal was conceived of as a flawed but fixable individual and the state's responsibility was to provide the expertise and resources needed to remediate those flaws."[19] In the 1970s, however, there was a sudden assault on this model from multiple directions, and the void created by its swift abandonment was filled by the highly punitive and unforgiving approach that reigns today.[20]

As it happens, recent work has challenged this "monotonic" account,[21] exposing as mythic the notion of a widespread national commitment to a rehabilitative ideal.[22] Instead, penological practices seem to have varied by region, with the rehabilitative model reigning in "the Northeast, Midwest and coastal West," while the South and states in the "Sunbelt"—including, among others, Arizona, Nevada, New Mexico, and Utah—cleaved to an approach more consistent with the harsh penal practices that currently define American penality.[23] Still, if historically the motivating conceptions of penal practice nationwide have hardly been uniform, the evolution of sentencing policy in the United States since the 1960s nonetheless reveals a notable change in the governing conception of the penal subject,[24] consistent with a shift from some acceptance of reintegration to a wide embrace of wholesale exclusion.

In the sentencing context, this shift was most obviously expressed by the move from indeterminate to determinate penalties. For most of the 20th century, criminal sentencing in the United States was "indeterminate": for any given crime, legislatures would stipulate statutory ranges (e.g., 5 to 15 years, 10 years to life), and judges would exercise their discretion to sentence within that range in particular cases.[25] This was true even in Arizona,[26] where the commitment to rehabilitation was at best "fragil[e] and fleeting."[27] And in some contexts—most notably, California, which "[b]y the early 1970s . . . sentenced nearly all serious offenders to an indeterminate term of between one year and life in prison"—even the judge would sentence within a broad range, leaving it to parole boards to determine the precise length of time an individual would actually serve.[28]

As Joan Petersilia explains, during this period, "[i]ndeterminate sentencing coupled with parole release was a matter of absolute routine and good correctional practice."[29] Even in places with shallow commitments to rehabilitation, these two systems acted in concert, reflecting the belief that custody decisions should be individualized and that people who committed crimes could be "reformed."[30] Together, they gave individuals found suitable for release the chance to build stable lives on the outside.[31] Consistent with this approach, people could earn time off their sentences for good behavior, an incentive promoting the development of skills and habits compatible with successful reentry. Crediting time for good behavior also had a positive effect on the prison environment, making it safer, more orderly, and thereby less destructive of (and less scary for) the people who lived inside.

Under this system, it was expected that even people with life sentences would at some point be released. As recently as 1980, the Supreme Court could justify upholding a Texas decision imposing a life sentence for passing a bad check in part because that state's "relatively liberal policy of granting 'good time' credits" meant that lifers "become eligible for parole in as little as 12 years."[32] But even as Justice Rehnquist wrote those words, strong opposition toward indeterminate sentencing had already emerged from several points on the political spectrum.[33] And one point on which diverse critics agreed was that the penal goal of rehabilitation was wrongheaded and should be abandoned.

The broader aim of the rehabilitative model was "to effect changes in the characters, attitudes, and behavior of convicted offenders" so that they could safely and productively be returned to society on completion of their sentences.[34] True, as Craig Haney notes, even in the heyday of programmatic efforts to rehabilitate people behind bars, "very few prisons anywhere in the United States ever really functioned as full-fledged treatment or program-oriented facilities."[35] But there was nonetheless a belief among many corrections professionals that society's interests could best be served by providing prisoners with tools to help them become productive citizens. The broad-based commitment to rehabilitation, coupled with recognition of the limits of individualized therapies in isolation from community, even led prison administrators to call for broader adoption of alternative "community-based programs" and for the use of institutionalization as "a last resort to be used only when the system had [demonstrated] that it was necessary."[36]

If in practice, prison treatment programs were unable to live up to their advocates' highest aspirations, the widespread institutional commitment to the rehabilitative ideal at least signaled a recognition—key for our purposes—that penal subjects were fellow human beings with, as Mona Lynch puts it, "all of the psychological and sociological complexity inherent in being human."[37] As such, they were thought to be capable of change and growth, and worthy targets for state investment and intervention.[38] Consistent with this view was the sense that antisocial behavior was a collective problem requiring a collective solution. Indeed, during this period, it was not uncommon to find official acknowledgment of the possibility that individual criminal behavior was "produced much more by social than individual pathology"[39] and thus that to prevent crime, society itself would need to change.

This way of construing crime and criminal offenders was thus recognizably reintegrationist. Of course, the extent of the reintegrationist commitment should not be overstated; a society truly disposed toward meaningful reintegration would have been unwilling in the first place to deploy a penal strategy against society's most disadvantaged citizens and would instead have opted for meaningful social programs to assist those who are mentally ill, drug addicted, illiterate, etc., to deal with those problems without involving the criminal justice system.[40] This difference must be acknowledged if we are to have an accurate sense of where American society pre-1980 fell on the spectrum between reintegration and exclusion. Still, during this period, it was generally expected even in the most punitive states that people imprisoned for their crimes would at some point rejoin society.[41]

As noted, however, by the mid-1970s, the rehabilitative model informed by this seemingly reintegrationist conception was coming under major criticism from multiple quarters. The combined effect of these assaults was a rapid and dramatic shift in penological priorities toward a more punitive approach, even in those jurisdictions previously committed to rehabilitation.[42] One casualty of this shift was the then-widespread regime of indeterminate sentencing. What emerged instead was a system of "determinate" or mandatory sentences, in which penalties stipulated a specific term and any official discretion to authorize early release was strongly curtailed. Consistent with this new approach, many states entirely abolished discretionary parole, and others considerably narrowed its scope.[43] By 2002, "just 16 states still gave their parole boards full authority to release inmates through a discretionary process."[44]

The turn to mandatory sentencing proved a signal event in the emergence of the exclusionary ideal in American penology. The previous open-ended model was certainly not perfect. For one thing, the wide discretion afforded prison officials produced a pattern of inconsistent and arguably discriminatory outcomes that ultimately pushed even the political left to advocate fixed terms. But whatever the shortcomings of a system of indeterminate sentencing combined with meaningful parole review, it at least embodied an inclusionary disposition toward the people the state incarcerated. By contrast, in a determinate sentencing system, individual character and capacities are irrelevant,[45] as is the question of whether a given person might be able to live safely and productively in society. A mandatory sentence is a commitment to the social exclusion of the sentenced person for the stipulated period, irrespective of anything he or she might do or not do, be or not be. Any understanding of prisoners as people drops out of the picture.

The stripped-down conception of the penal subject reflected in mandatory sentencing schemes stands in stark contrast to the animating vision of the indeterminate approach. This shift was no accident. It reflected a broader transformation in attitudes toward convicted offenders, consistent with the self-consciously punitive penal policies—concerned less with social welfare than with the infliction of "penal harm"[46]—broadly adopted following the repudiation of the rehabilitative project. This new model found intellectual foundation in the work of James Q. Wilson, who argued that the function of the penal system was not to reform offenders but "to isolate and . . . punish" them.[47] Whereas the rehabilitative approach emphasized the social inputs of individual criminal behavior, Wilson argued that the problem was the individuals themselves. As he put it, "Wicked people exist. Nothing avails except to set them apart from innocent people."[48] Although Wilson's phrasing implies that "wicked people" are still "people"—i.e., psychologically complex beings with "rich, multi-layered identities and motivations"[49]—his broader account suggests otherwise. As he framed the issue, criminal offenders are evil, plain and simple. If they do bad things, it is because of who they are and what they therefore choose to do, and no interventions, however well meaning, can change them. Seen in this way, criminal conduct is no longer a collective problem but an individual one. And if individual actors choose to do wrong, not only is there no help for them, but the rest of us need have no sympathy for them. In this way, the punitive penality heralded by Wilson's model recast not only the nature of penal subjects but also society's moral obligations to those subjects. On the earlier model, criminal offenders were still regarded as people, able to change and grow and as such deserving of collective understanding and investment. In the new punitive climate, by contrast, to commit a criminal act is to reveal oneself as essentially and uniformly bad and thus not entitled to the consideration or respect otherwise due fellow human beings.

Wilson's deracinated and unidimensional account fit perfectly with the Reagan era's radical individualism. It also helped justify a sharp ideological shift away from any thought of reintegrating convicted offenders and toward permanent exclusion. Consistent with this shift, legislatures across the country, explicitly rejecting the goal of rehabilitation,[50] set about revising their sentencing laws. By the mid-1990s, many states had adopted policies such as "truth in sentencing," "three strikes," and other schemes designed to impose fixed terms and to increase the length of time served. Predictably, following these changes, prison populations soared, and the people sent to prison found themselves facing longer and longer periods of banishment.

Still, the system that emerged during the 1980s and 1990s did retain some avenues for release and reentry. So long as sentences remained temporally limited, even people with long fixed terms could at some point expect to hit their deadlines and be legally entitled to release. Many life sentences, moreover, retained the possibility of parole. And although going forward, sentenced offenders would be mostly subject to the new mandatory regime, there remained in custody many people sentenced under the previous approach who retained parole eligibility.

The American criminal justice system in the late 20th century was thus to some extent a patchwork, with some avenues remaining for the possible reintegration of former prisoners. In a system without a strong exclusionary disposition, the fact that some prisoners could continue to earn their way back to society (whether through time served or demonstration of personal reform) would provoke no backlash. When permanent exclusion *is* the motivating aim, however, such a backlash may be expected to emerge, along with various legal and institutional strategies designed to plug the gaps. As I argue in the sections that follow, this is precisely what has occurred, in ways consistent with the aim of exclusion and the normative vision of penal subjects as something less than human.

III. The Reproductive Effects of the American Prison

First, consider prison conditions.[51] A system committed to meaningful reintegration postrelease would treat the period of custody as a chance to help people overcome the personal difficulties and incapacities that informed whatever antisocial behavior first brought them within the ambit of the criminal justice system. Yet in American prisons today, one finds just the opposite. In fact, it is hard to imagine institutional conditions less well designed to facilitate successful reentry. There is little effective drug treatment, although as many as half or more of incarcerated offenders have reported problems with drug and/or alcohol addiction.[52] Nor is there anything like sufficient mental health care to provide adequate treatment for the estimated 56% of state prisoners who suffer from serious mental illness.[53] The emphasis on custody over rehabilitation means that whatever skills people may have had on admission are likely to deteriorate during their prison term[54] and also that few people are likely to develop new skills while in prison that will be useful to themselves or others on release. Strict limits on visiting, combined with the high cost of phone calls from prison[55] and the widespread practice of siting prisons far from the urban centers where prisoners' families are most likely to live,[56] mean that few people in prison are able to retain close family ties[57]—even though "one of the strongest predictors of post-release success is the quality of a prisoner's ongoing contact with loved ones."[58] Grossly inadequate medical care[59] leaves many people in custody with serious and/or chronic medical conditions, which can impair successful reintegration. Severe overcrowding in often unhygienic conditions, together with what is frequently an absence of institutional strategies for preventing the spread of disease, means that prisoners face infection rates for HIV, hepatitis C, tuberculosis, and even staph that are far in excess of infection rates on the outside,[60] thereby further burdening not only their health but also their capacity to escape the social marginalization that often attends the poor and chronically ill.

These material effects are not the only barriers to successful reentry that prisons systematically create. Equally debilitating is the severe emotional and psychological toll of the day-to-day custodial experience. As Terry Kupers observes, this experience can "destroy[] prisoners' ability to cope in the free world," leaving them "broken, with no skills, and a very high risk of recidivism."[61] Worse still, the experience of living under the conditions that currently define life in many of the nation's prisons and jails can leave at least some people resembling the image of the angry, unstable, antisocial, and potentially dangerous deviant that already justifies mass incarceration. And having been subjected to this transformative process, affected individuals will become even less able to successfully rejoin society on release.

Take, for example, the matter of personal space. As Justice Marshall noted in his dissent in *Rhodes v. Chapman*, "long term inmate[s]" require a minimum amount of personal space if they are "to avoid serious mental, emotional, and physical deterioration."[62] But American prisons today are often chronically overcrowded, which means that people routinely live jammed into dormitories[63] or doubled up in tiny cells designed for a single person, a situation that alone may seriously compromise an individual's "mental [and] emotional" capacities[64] and that can readily give rise to anger, tension, and hostility—and thus to disorder and violence—even among people not typically prone to aggression.[65]

At the same time, the increased use of punitive isolation, whether in supermax prisons[66] or under less extreme conditions, means that the damaging effects of isolation are being experienced by more and more detainees, many of whom will at some point be released.[67] Studies show that people who have lived in extended solitary confinement are likely to be not only more erratic and violent in their behavior but also more angry. Haney's research involving prisoners in the "secure housing unit" (SHU) of California's Pelican Bay facility found that almost 90% of SHU residents "had difficulties" with "irrational anger, compared with just 3% of the . . . population [outside prison]."[68] These combined effects on residents can lead to longer stays in isolation. But the self-perpetuating character of supermax prisons and other forms of solitary confinement has also meant that in a growing number of cases, prisoners are completing their sentences while in highly restrictive solitary confinement and being released directly to the community. Unsurprisingly, when people are freed straight from any type of solitary confinement, "there is often trouble," since "[t]he anger that has been mounting during their stints in isolation causes many prisoners great difficulty controlling their tempers just after being released."[69] Thus, both crowding and isolation contribute to the reproductive logic of the prison, producing inmates whose anger, volatility, and general inability to function successfully in a social milieu are very likely to prompt disruptive and antisocial behavior both out in the free world and in the prisons themselves, which in turn serves to justify the incarceration (or reincarceration) of those who act out in this way.

There is still another component of life in the modern American prison that powerfully contributes to the exclusionary project: the ever-present possibility of violence. Although this phenomenon has many explanations, prison violence is frequently traceable to a complex set of institutional dynamics, found especially in higher-security men's facilities, reflecting what might be thought of as a culture of hypermasculinity.[70] In this culture, there is a premium placed on being "manly," a behavioral code that "says carry yourself like a man, be hard and tough, and don't show weakness."[71] Those who act against this code, who show emotion, express need, or otherwise reveal themselves as "soft," risk being labeled a "punk"[72] and, as such, a target for all manner of abuse, ranging from intense verbal harassment and theft of personal property to serious physical assault and rape.[73] Men in prison thus work hard at seeming tough and avoiding any word or act that might suggest weakness or vulnerability.[74]

Being forced to maintain a constant front of hypermasculinity over a long period can take a profound psychological toll. Men who have lived under these circumstances report corrosive effects on the possibility for meaningful interpersonal interaction, since "[w]ithout trust or letting someone know at least some of your weaknesses, no strong bonds can develop."[75] The effect of these emotional barriers is more than just loneliness. Over time, the need to project a tough image and thus to build emotional walls compromises one's ability, whether inside or outside the prison, to forge any meaningful bonds with anyone. Yet this ability is crucial to a stable, healthy life. As Derrick Corley reasonably asks, "If it is true that healthy people have healthy relationships, and, if [as a consequence of these cultural dynamics] these relationships are systematically denied prisoners, then how can [they] be expected to eventually live in society as normal, law-abiding, productive people?"[76]

But the cultural code of hypermasculinity does not only impose obstacles to emotional connections with others. In addition, the unrelenting need to project an image of "hardness and toughness"[77] demands a constant readiness to use violence to prove one's own "manliness." And this posture too can become instinctual if sustained long enough. Such instincts may serve one well in a carceral context, but their likely accompaniments—belligerence; insensitivity; a hair-trigger temper; an inability to admit error, back down, compromise, or work through differences in a mutually respectful way—are precisely the antisocial tendencies that society fears to see in former prisoners. They are also tendencies that are very likely to keep their possessors caught in the cycle of incarceration even after they have served their initial prison terms.

There is an even worse malignancy in all this pressure to seem tough: the direct link between the culture of hypermasculinity and the fear of rape. Although not true of all prisons,[78] in many facilities—especially the overcrowded ones—the threat of rape motivates a gendered economy of respect in which the more masculine one appears, the more respect one gets and thus the greater one's protection from victimization. In this system, sexual predators show themselves by their predation to be real men, and those prisoners facing a threat of rape who seek protection from correctional officers will often be told by the officers to "fight or fuck."[79] In such a climate, those individuals with the physical strength to defend themselves from attack—even those not otherwise prone to violence—must be constantly prepared to fight.[80] As for those who are unable to protect themselves, they can escape their dilemma only by hooking up with a more powerful prisoner (sometimes known as a "wolf"),[81] who will protect them from violent rape by other prisoners in exchange for unlimited sexual access and other wifely duties such as cooking and cleaning.[82] This last resort, sometimes referred to as "protective pairing," has also perhaps more aptly been described as "sexual slavery."[83]

It is important to note that not all prison environments reproduce these dynamics. Nor, even in those that do, are all prisoners caught up in them.[84] But for those people who are not so lucky, the experience of living in such a culture will be deeply degrading and dehumanizing and can do serious emotional and psychological damage. Prisoners facing such conditions are not free just to walk away. They instead must remain locked inside the site of their abuse, often in close proximity to their abuser, in what can only be a permanently traumatized and terrorized state bereft of any peace of mind.[85] It should come as no surprise if, having endured such conditions for months or even years on end, a man might be so full of rage and self-loathing as to have trouble (re)building stable, healthy relationships or even navigating ordinary social interactions on the outside. Given the important role played by close personal relationships in successful reintegration, an inability to form close personal bonds is likely to mean the continued social marginalization of those who have been traumatized in this way. And the propensity to anger and violence that anyone subjected to such treatment is likely to develop will only contribute to the possibility of further antisocial conduct and eventual reincarceration.

As this brief sketch suggests, incarceration in the American prison is not an experience designed to promote the successful social reintegration of the people who have served their time. To the contrary, such a system is far more likely to have the opposite effect, so that people who have once been caught in its net will be unable to break free and rejoin society on terms of equal citizenship and belonging. For a polity committed to meaningful reintegration, this state of affairs would be intolerable. It does, though, seem wholly consistent with the goal of permanent exclusion. It is also not difficult to recognize in these conditions a particular normative view of the people subjected to them. Plainly put, these are not conditions that would be imposed on people widely regarded as fellow citizens and fellow human beings. They are instead the conditions of Agamben's "state of exception," in which bare biological life is all that is left, in which one may be killed without being either sacrificed (because, not being a person of value, one's death demands no ritual) or murdered (because one's death has no legal significance).[86] Agamben locates this status in the figure of the "wolfman" or "werewolf," a "monstrous hybrid of human and animal," which, although bearing the outward appearance of man, is widely recognized not to be human.[87] As such, these creatures may be killed without ceremony or at the very least banned from the community without a second thought. Indeed, the exclusion of such monsters becomes precisely what must be done to protect those who *are* regarded as fully human (and thus as full citizens)— an imperative consistent with Jonathan Simon's characterization in this volume of "total incapacitation" as a means to guard society from the "contamination" thought to emanate from prison inmates.[88] Notice, moreover, what Agamben's image of the wolfman/werewolf suggests about the appropriate conditions of confinement for the contaminated: if the werewolf is successfully trapped, he may perhaps be kept alive, but no efforts need be expended to ensure his well-being while caged or to help him flourish despite his constraints. He is nonhuman, an animal, and thus merits no such consideration.

IV. Life Means Life: The Gradual Disappearance of Parole

The conditions just explored, although perhaps officially bemoaned, are in fact fully consistent with the exclusionary project. Still, despite the debilitating effects of prison, some people do—against the odds—manage to find a way while in custody to develop or strengthen prosocial skills. This is especially true of lifers, who tend to be better able to screen out the toxic and often violent gamesmanship of the younger inmates and to be left alone to do their time in peace. This means that, over time, even long-term inmates who once posed a threat to public safety may become fully capable of leading healthy and productive lives on the outside.

In a society committed to meaningful reintegration, a showing that individuals in custody could be safely returned to society would prompt their ready release. By contrast, in a society committed to permanent exclusion, such a showing would only be unwelcome. This is particularly so when the exclusionary project is cloaked by a rhetorical commitment to reintegration when possible, since in such a system, it would be hard to justify keeping behind bars someone capable of living safely in society. Indeed, from an exclusionary perspective, every person who succeeds in demonstrating the capacity to safely reintegrate exposes the gaps in a system that cannot punish every convicted offender with LWOP. For an exclusionist system, the challenge is closing the gaps.

Over the past two decades, jurisdictions across the U.S. have met this challenge with various strategies to limit parole grants even for those people who can demonstrate their rehabilitation.[89] The most obvious development in this regard was the introduction and swift adoption of LWOP sentences. LWOP is the perfect exclusionary strategy. In one stroke, the target is permanently exiled, foreclosed from ever making a case for release. It is thus to be expected that a system committed to permanent exclusion would embrace the use of LWOP. And sure enough, one finds a substantial recent increase in the use of this sentence. According to the Sentencing Project, in 1992, there were 12,453 people serving LWOP sentences in the United States. By 2003, there were over 33,000, and by 2008, over 41,000.[90] Every state save one has made LWOP an available penalty,[91] and as of 2009, at least six states and the federal system have eliminated parole eligibility entirely for people receiving life sentences, making LWOP the norm in those jurisdictions.[92] Between 2003 and 2008, the number of LWOP sentences grew at a rate "nearly four times [that] of the parole-eligible life sentenced population,"[93] a change consistent with an emerging commitment to permanent exclusion.[94]

Still, many people have continued to receive life *with* the possibility of parole: 5,471 between 2003 and 2008 out of a total of 12,933 life sentences imposed.[95] This fact may seem to cut against the notion of a widespread commitment to exclusion. But too much should not be made of the persistence of life with parole eligibility. For one thing, given that LWOP is a relatively recent innovation, it is striking that well over half the life sentences imposed during this period were LWOP sentences. More significant still, the fact that the possibility of parole is retained as a formal matter turns out in today's penal climate to make little practical difference. What in the middle decades of the 20th century was a meaningful process in which parole boards seriously considered individual claims of rehabilitation has become in most cases a meaningless ritual in which the form is preserved but parole is rarely granted.

California is a case in point. In California, life sentences typically take the form of some minimum number of years (typically 7, 15, or 25) to life. Prisoners do not become parole eligible until they have served the minimum. Once they serve that time, the governing regulations require the Board of Parole Hearings (the Board) to consider parole eligibility. Directed by law to take account of a wide range of circumstances, including the crime itself, the individual's criminal and "social" history, and his or her behavior while incarcerated,[96] the Board is to consider whether the prisoner "pose[s] an unreasonable risk of danger to society."[97] If not, a parole date is to be set.[98] Given the population at issue, it would not be surprising if many people who came before the Board were found ineligible for parole at their earliest possible release date. But, assuming meaningful review, one might expect the Board to see some appreciable number of people, especially by the third or fourth time around, who could be released with minimal public safety risk. And yet, for the past decade, the Board has denied 98% of the petitions it hears.[99] From this, one might conclude that lifers in California are especially dangerous. But in fact, the evidence suggests that the Board's practice of routinely denying petitions is a product not of the meaningful review of the merits of each case but of a determination not to grant parole except in the rarest instances.

This sort of resistance to granting parole is not unique to California. Across the country, parole boards and governors have grown increasingly reticent to release even people with strong cases that their release would pose a minimal threat to public safety. As a result, "it has become increasingly difficult for persons serving a life sentence to be released on parole."[100] Why should this be? One possible explanation is the nature of prison conditions sketched earlier. Having been systematically subjected to degrading, destructive conditions, fewer and fewer prisoners may be able to demonstrate that they are fit for release. And to some extent, this may well be the case. But research into the relevant population—lifers who retain the possibility of parole—strongly indicates that in many cases, the obstacle is not the individual's inability to safely reintegrate but political resistance to granting release. As Ashley Nellis notes, lifers often mature in custody, are generally more well adjusted than younger prisoners, and "are frequently lauded by corrections administrators as easier to manage."[101] As long-term inmates, moreover, lifers typically age out of crime, and those who have managed to get out on parole have been persistently found to pose a relatively lower risk of recidivism.[102] Finally, the growing willingness of the federal courts to intervene and reverse parole denials by state parole boards[103] strongly suggests that one must look beyond prison conditions—destructive though they may be—to understand the dramatic decline in parole grants in recent years.

In practical terms, this decline is best understood as a political phenomenon. Parole decisions require all-things-considered judgments as to the ability of an individual to live safely in society. This enterprise necessarily carries some risk that errors will be made. This was as true in the mid-20th century as it is today. But politicians have increasingly come to pay a serious political price for any such mistakes. Most famously, in 1988, the presidential campaign of Democratic nominee Michael Dukakis was derailed by revelations that while Dukakis was governor of Massachusetts, a state prisoner escaped from a weekend furlough and went on to commit violent rape and aggravated assault. It is unlikely that Dukakis had ever heard of Willie Horton before the campaign of Republican nominee George H. W. Bush brought Horton to the attention of the American public, but no matter. The furlough had happened on Dukakis's watch, so he was held politically accountable for all that followed.

Politicians' fear of being "Willie Horton-ed" has arguably had a direct and serious impact on parole in the United States. Although the parole structure differs among jurisdictions, in many states the governor has considerable control over the process, whether indirectly through the appointment of parole board members or directly through veto power over their decisions. Many state executives have preferred to dramatically curtail the granting of parole rather than risk the single mistake that might threaten their career. But—and here is the key point—it is unlikely that this trend would have emerged were it not consistent with the prevailing propensity to exclude. Were people in prison widely viewed as human beings just like anybody else, it might be regarded as beyond cruel, not to mention an indefensible waste of taxpayer dollars, to maintain in custody those who could show themselves to be reformed. It is understandable that parole boards would want to be sure that petitioners would pose little public safety threat. Still, when a person has spent decades behind bars and when the evidence of suitability for release is strong, a society committed to meaningful reintegration would take for granted that he or she should be released.

Judging from the policies and practices that currently govern the parole context, however, American society at present takes a very different view of the matter. What one finds instead are demands for fewer parole grants and even for parole-eligible individuals to have fewer opportunities to present their cases for parole. In California, for example, a recently adopted ballot initiative known as "Marsy's Law" greatly extended the time between parole hearings. Prior to the law's passage, there was a presumption of annual hearings,[104] although the Board retained the discretion to delay a hearing for an additional year on a finding that "it is not reasonable to expect that parole would be granted at a hearing during the following year" and for four additional years if this finding is made and "the prisoner has been convicted of murder."[105] Marsy's Law extends the default between parole hearings to 15 years and flips the presumption. The Board retains the authority to reduce the waiting time but can do so only if it "finds by clear and convincing evidence" that "consideration of the public and victim's safety does not require a more lengthy period of incarceration."[106] And that discretion is limited: the shortest possible period between hearings is now 3 years (the other stipulated alternatives are 5, 7, and 10).[107] In theory, after Marsy's Law, the most someone who is able to show clear and convincing evidence of parole eligibility would need to wait between hearings would be 3 years. But the restrictions the new law creates dovetail too well with the Board's existing inclination to refuse parole in almost all cases for a 3-year delay to become standard. Those familiar with the process report that post–Marsy's Law, most people denied parole are receiving subsequent hearing dates at least 5 years from the time of a denial.[108]

Implicit in this shift is not only a commitment to longer sentences but also an insistence that, despite statutory schemes creating an entitlement to parole consideration, people in prison must and will be kept behind bars as long as the state can possibly keep them there. One might frame this disposition as indifference to the fate of society's prisoners, and that attitude is certainly part of the story. But in some cases, such a neutral term seems inadequate to capture what appears rather to be affirmative hostility to the prospect of any reintegration. This hostility was vividly on display recently in North Carolina, when—to the apparent surprise of both the courts and the legislature—it emerged that over a hundred lifers convicted in the 1970s would soon be legally entitled to release. At issue were life sentences imposed between 1974 and 1978. During those years, the governing statute fixed a life term at 80 years.[109] But in 1981, the state legislature passed a law allowing prisoners the opportunity to earn up to 50% off their sentences through good behavior.[110] And in 1983, the state's Department of Corrections expanded the "day-for-a-day" provision of the 1981 law to apply retroactively to those who were convicted prior to 1981.[111] Taken together, these provisions established that, assuming uniformly good behavior, people sentenced to life under the 1974 law could be entitled to release once they had served 40 years.

In 2005, North Carolina prisoner Bobby Bowden made just this argument in a habeas petition, and he prevailed in the state court of appeals.[112] Because in 1978 the North Carolina legislature amended its statute, redefining life as the indeterminate sentence of life with the possibility of parole,[113] the ruling in *State v. Bowden* potentially applied only to an estimated 120 or so people sentenced to life between 1974 and 1978.[114] Predictably, however, opponents of the outcome in *Bowden*—including the state's governor, leading newspapers, the North Carolina Fraternal Order of Police, and victims' rights advocates— quickly lined up to condemn the decision.

What is interesting here is that this opposition *was* so predictable, despite the fact that those people whose sentences stood to be affected had uniformly committed their crimes more than three decades previously. Admittedly, there may have been grounds for concern regarding the release of so many lifers without any individualized determinations as to a possible public safety threat. But as noted, available research suggests that, given the age and lengthy confinement of those individuals whose sentences were affected, the risk of recidivism they posed was relatively low.[115] Indeed, Bowden himself had only hit the statutory deadline because of his accumulated good-time credit,[116] which in total suggested someone who had lived in an orderly and peaceable manner for over 30 years. And the same would have to be true of anyone entitled to early release in the foreseeable future on the statutory scheme on which Bowden relied.

Yet rather than press for individualized hearings to determine suitability for release, Governor Bev Perdue fought any release at all.[117] In terms consistent with the exclusionary project, she asserted that "life should mean life, and, even if a life sentence is defined as 80 years, getting out after [40 years] is simply unacceptable."[118] Thomas Bennett, executive director of the North Carolina Victims Assistance Network, had a similar take. As Bennett put it after *Bowden*, "we've got a hole in the law, and these felons are going to use it to crawl out of prison."[119]

It is through its policies and practices that a state reveals its position on the spectrum between meaningful reintegration and permanent exclusion. For this reason, one should perhaps not make too much of the statements of Perdue and Bennett. But these statements are nonetheless telling, especially read alongside the state's refusal even to consider releasing people who were found to have a strong legal claim to freedom and who, after decades in prison, may well have posed no public safety threat. Both sets of comments lay bare the exclusionary imperative motivating the opposition to *Bowden*, and Bennett's statement in particular makes plain the conception of prisoners that undergirds the relentless impulse to exclude. Not only, as James Q. Wilson had it, are incarcerated offenders essentially "wicked," but they are insects or worms crawling in the dirt. This imagery exposes two basic beliefs that seem to animate the exclusionary project: people in prison are subhuman, and they are polluted and unclean. They must therefore be kept away from society, lest they defile the rest of us. Viewed in this light, recent events in North Carolina seem further to vindicate Simon's construal of the penal push for "total incapacitation" as motivated less by a desire to prevent crime than by a fear of "contamination" from contact with people who have spent time in prison.[120]

V. The Exclusionary Effects of Collateral Consequences

Despite LWOP's eclipse of parole-eligible life sentences and the relative rarity in today's carceral climate of parole grants even for those individuals who retain the possibility of parole, the time-limited nature of most custodial sentences means that most people sent to prison will at some point be released.[121] But the challenges facing people with felony convictions do not end with the custodial term. Even apart from the long-term harmful effects of prison conditions,[122] former prisoners will face many serious obstacles to successful reentry. Many will find themselves without the support of friends or loved ones who over the years may have died or become estranged or just moved on.[123] Employers may be reluctant to hire them.[124] People newly released from prison are also likely to have little or no money on which to rely while trying to set themselves up with the components of a postcarceral life.[125] After living for long periods—sometimes years—making few decisions and taking no responsibility for the provision of even basic personal needs, they may feel themselves at sea and unable to manage the endless details of daily life on the outside. And to make matters worse, they may yet be wrestling with the temptations of substance abuse after years without effective drug treatment. In short, for many if not most people, successful reentry is sure to be extremely hard.

A society committed to meaningful reintegration would regard these difficulties as collective problems demanding public attention and state action. In the American context, however, far from working to alleviate the burdens of reentry, the state instead exacerbates them.[126] As a consequence, people newly released from prison face not only the psychological, material, and structural obstacles already noted but also a host of state-imposed disabilities that make it even harder for them to successfully reintegrate.[127] Among other impediments, these disabilities can include "[b]ans on entry into public housing, restrictions on public-sector employment, limits on access to federal loans for higher education, and restrictions on the receipt of public assistance."[128] Those with felony convictions may also be "ineligible for many federally-funded health and welfare benefits," including food stamps.[129] They "may no longer qualify for certain employment and professional licenses."[130] Their driver's licenses may be automatically suspended,[131] making it hard in some jurisdictions for them to make meetings with their parole officers, get to work, etc., thus risking revocation of their parole. In many cases, people with felony convictions cannot vote, serve on juries, or enlist in the military.[132] Formerly incarcerated people also face legal obstacles to getting access to their own children. Before regaining custody, newly released parents may be required, among other things, to attend parenting classes, complete drug-treatment programs, and provide stable residences. Given the obstacles they face, it can be difficult for people just out of prison to find work and housing, which means that in practice, even those committed to reconstituting their families may be unable to do so.[133]

It is hard to overstate the breadth of the legal disabilities placed on people with felony convictions in the United States. The American Bar Association Criminal Justice Section recently embarked on a project to catalogue all state and federal statutes and regulations that impose legal consequences on the fact of a felony conviction. As of May 2011, the project had catalogued over 38,000 such provisions,[134] and project advisers estimate that the final number could reach or exceed 50,000.[135] Many of these restrictions will likely prove unobjectionable, particularly those that carefully tailor the restriction to the nature of the crime. To take an example at random: § 4842(d) of the California Business and Professional Code allows the licensing board to deny an application for a prospective "registered veterinary technician" if the applicant has "[b]een convicted of a crime substantially related to the qualifications, functions and duties" of someone in that position.[136] But in many other instances, the restrictions are far broader and seemingly gratuitous. For example, under federal law, anyone convicted of drug possession or drug trafficking may permanently lose access to all "federal benefits."[137] As Gabriel Chin notes, this blanket exclusion potentially applies to over 750 federal benefits, "including 162 by the Department of Education alone."[138]

People coming home from prison already face long odds. The combined effect of these various obstacles makes it that much harder for former prisoners to piece together the components of a stable life (home, family, work, schooling, etc.) and only increases the chances that they will slip back into the patterns and behaviors that led them to prison in the first place. But the practice of placing formidable impediments in the way of successful reentry does more than simply increase the likelihood of reincarceration. It also consigns to social marginalization even those people who manage to stay free. As Bruce Western and Becky Pettit observe, former prisoners have collectively become "a group of social outcasts," whose "[s]ocial and economic disadvantage, crystallizing in penal confinement, is sustained over the life course."[139] This group has "little access to the social mobility available to the mainstream."[140] The effect, moreover, is "intergenerational," so that children of incarcerated parents are more likely when young to experience poverty, dislocation, and other markers of disadvantage, setting them up for lives as "social outcasts" themselves.[141]

The socioeconomic disadvantage that dogs even those people who manage to stay out of prison may at first seem unrelated to the impulse to exclude that currently drives much penal policy in the direction of increased incarceration. But as the term "social outcast" suggests, there are many ways to exclude, of which prison is only the most obvious. The wide employment and residency restrictions many jurisdictions have lately imposed on registered sex offenders—indeed, the very notion of a sex-offender registry itself—indicates the array of noncustodial options available to a state wishing to contain those who are judged socially undesirable.

Indeed, as important recent work by Katherine Beckett and Steve Herbert reveals,[142] creative collaborations between municipal authorities and local police have begun to make it possible for the state to mark out certain people for extended exclusion from the shared public space without the need for prisons—or even for criminal conduct. In Seattle and other urban centers, multiple such tools are now operating to "explicitly create and enforce zones of exclusion."[143] For example, "off-limits" orders, which can be imposed on people merely suspected of drug or prostitution offenses, require subjects to stay out of designated neighborhoods or "zones" on pain of imprisonment.[144] In some cases, these zones "comprise significant parts of the city and may include the entire downtown core in which social and legal services are concentrated."[145]

Similar effects have also been achieved through innovative expansion of trespass laws. To commit trespass, a person must have previously received a warning or "admonishment" of limits on access. Having been so admonished, a person who returns may be subject to arrest and imprisonment. Trespass is typically used to prevent access to private property. But in Seattle, the law of trespass has been increasingly applied to a remarkably wide range of public spaces, including "public parks, libraries, recreation centers, the public transportation system, college campuses, hospitals, religious institutions, social services agencies, and commercial establishments," as well as public housing and even sidewalks and public streets.[146] The justifications for exclusion range widely. "Parks exclusion" laws allow police and park officials to impose bans on access to "one, some, or all public city parks for up to one year" for a host of minor infractions including "being present after hours, having an unleashed pet, camping, urinating, littering, or possessing an open container of alcohol."[147] In a number of municipalities, any nonresident found on public housing property may be "trespass-admonished" and subject to arrest if he or she returns. Business associations are increasingly encouraged to delegate to police officers the power to remove people from places otherwise open to the public, merely on suspicion that targeted individuals "lack 'legitimate purpose' for being there."[148] In Seattle, such an arrangement exists even as to "321 downtown parking lots"—and if a person is banned from one such lot, he or she is banned from them all and "thereby subject to arrest (for trespass) for walking through any one of them."[149]

Seattle is not alone in this creative use of exclusionary authority. According to Beckett and Herbert, some combination of the programs they describe are in force in cities as varied as New York, Los Angeles, Portland, Las Vegas, Cincinnati, Honolulu, Boston, Richmond (Virginia), and Fort Lauderdale. This panoply of exclusionary tools has a "net-widening" effect; despite the civil nature of the violations that can lead to "no-go" orders, repeated violation can land a person in jail even absent otherwise criminal conduct. In this latest twist, to be marked out for exclusion it is enough simply to be persistently "undesirable" or "disorderly."[150] Viewed alongside this range of innovative and noncustodial exclusionary mechanisms, the prison begins to appear less the necessary centerpiece of the state's response to crime than simply the most extreme and effective means to enforce a spatial segregation between, on the one hand, those people the polity is prepared to recognize as full political citizens and, on the other hand, the marginal, disorderly, aesthetically unpalatable others with whom "respectable" members of society would prefer not to have to deal.[151]

VI. Current Carceral Practice and the Purposes of Punishment

The picture painted above does not, of course, reflect the way the penal system is conventionally understood. According to the standard account, penal sanctions are not about exclusion for its own sake but are instead the essential means by which the state prevents crime and imposes just deserts on criminal wrongdoers. Indeed, to suggest otherwise may strike some readers as wrongheaded and even offensive. Prison, after all, is what we do to the people who have done awful things to innocent victims. It is where we send the rapists, the murderers, and other violent people to punish them for their wrongdoing, to keep them from reoffending, and to send a warning to others. Seen in this light, exclusion is simply a byproduct of punishment. It is what happens to criminal offenders so that society's legitimate penological interests may be vindicated.

In the abstract, this standard account may seem compelling. But closer inspection reveals a remarkably poor fit between the actual practices of the American carceral state and the most frequently invoked penological purposes. These stated purposes center on individual actors and their crimes. At base, retribution asks what the actor did and what penalty he or she deserves as a result. Deterrence asks what it would take to dissuade other similarly situated actors from committing the same crime. Even incapacitation focuses on the offenders themselves and considers whether, to what extent, and for how long those individuals must be kept separate from society in order to ensure public safety. Yet many of the most significant burdens imposed on people with felony convictions, including many noted here, have at best an attenuated connection either to the original offense or to the character of the offender. Prison conditions are borne equally by all residents of a given facility, whatever their offense of conviction. Specific harms experienced by individual prisoners—say, denials of urgently needed medical care or sexual assault at the hands of fellow inmates or guards—are in practice inflicted randomly, with no connection to the sufferer's original crime.[152] Likewise, the collateral consequences of felony convictions are frequently imposed across the board regardless of the precise nature of the felony—and in cases in which this is not so, it is not necessarily the worst offenders who are most heavily burdened.[153] And, as we have seen, what currently passes for parole review in many jurisdictions systematically denies release even to people who would pose a minimal public safety threat, without any effort to justify the denial in terms of the purposes of punishment. Perhaps in some cases the parole denial could be so justified, but the almost total absence of thoughtful consideration in this vein strongly undermines any claims of meaningful individualized determinations in each case, which is what standard penological justifications would require.

The move to determinate sentencing—whether LWOP or less extreme mandatory minimums—equally suggests an unconcern with the particulars of individual cases, the relative culpability of individual offenders, or the actual threat individuals pose. The length of many fixed sentences, although perhaps in some individual cases consistent with assessments of the actor's desert or the demands of public safety, often seems wildly excessive and thus hard to justify on these terms. More generally, given the wide range of acts currently punished with extended prison time, not to mention the general absence of concerted efforts to ensure that the range of penalties imposed reflects considered moral judgments as to the greater or lesser severity of the various crimes, it is hard to argue that the penal system today is motivated by a commitment to imposing morally proportionate punishment. Nor is there any apparent effort to determine whether and to what extent x years in prison—or, for that matter, any prison sentence at all—would yield meaningful deterrence or otherwise serve public safety.

LWOP is just one obvious example. Even assuming that some offenses are atrocious enough to justify the extreme step of incarcerating the offenders for the rest of their natural lives—a premise at least called into question by the historically contingent character of the penalty and its wholesale rejection by many European and Latin American countries[154]—the wide range of crimes currently punishable with LWOP in the United States,[155] not to mention the racial disproportion in the application of the sentence,[156] makes it hard to credit the notion that LWOP sentences are imposed only when proportionate to the offense and deserved by the offender. LWOP sentences are also hard to justify on grounds of incapacitation; in any given case, it is impossible at the time of sentencing to gauge the threat the offender will pose decades down the road, thus making the denial of parole eligibility up front at best penologically gratuitous. As to deterrence, any claim that imposing a permanent life sentence on a given set of offenders will discourage other people from committing similar crimes is wholly speculative, as is the notion, implicit in the LWOP sentence, that no lesser penalty—say, life with the (meaningful) possibility of parole—would serve as well.

The claim here is not that no legitimate public interests are realized by criminal punishment. Some criminal offenders certainly deserve serious punishment. No doubt, too, many citizens are dissuaded from criminal activity by the threat of penal sanctions. But given the highly imperfect fit between conventional penological justifications and the actual practices of the American carceral state, it seems clear that something more is going on and that contemporary penal practices are serving some other purpose.[157] Nor is my claim that the state may never legitimately inflict punishment, even severe punishment, on convicted criminal offenders. To be legitimate, however, penal sanctions should at a minimum be justifiable on some valid penological theory, held and applied in good faith.[158] Moreover—and here is perhaps the key point—the imposed sanction must be consistent with an acknowledgment that the object of punishment is a fellow citizen and human being who, notwithstanding the crime, is entitled to equal consideration and respect as such.[159]

To approach criminal punishment from this perspective would demand a radical rethinking of many practices that are taken for granted in the current penal climate, including many of those examined here. Consider what would have to change if prisoners were widely understood to be fellow human beings and fellow citizens: Prison conditions would necessarily be humane and the opportunities for human development meaningful, notwithstanding the (temporary) deprivation of freedom. Parole applications would be seriously scrutinized, and, perhaps after some period of confinement proportionate to the crime, those individuals found to pose no future public safety risk would be released. And once released, people with felony convictions would not be burdened with gratuitous civil disabilities and might even be assisted by the state with the enterprise of reentry.

If these possibilities seem familiar, it is because we have seen them once already, when contemplating the likely policies of a system committed to meaningful reintegration.[160] It turns out, in other words, that to challenge current penal practices as illegitimate, it is necessary to reject the assumption currently driving the American carceral system, that individuals subject to criminal punishment have thereby forfeited their status as political citizens and moral equals.[161] It is this assumption that underpins the exclusionary project and that must be disavowed if this project is to be abandoned and its destructive effects reversed.

VII. Death and Life

Societies that punish with imprisonment may yet commit themselves to the meaningful reintegration of the people who have served their time. The American carceral system in the early 21st century takes the opposite approach, committing itself as much as possible to the social exclusion of convicted offenders. Viewed in this light, LWOP is the emblematic criminal penalty. LWOP affords permanent exile. By foreclosing the targets from ever even making a case for release, LWOP leaves no gaps. In this sense, it is the limit case of the exclusionary impulse.

To this, one might argue that the death penalty is an even more extreme mechanism for exclusion, and in one obvious sense this is so: not only will people sentenced to death have no opportunities to press their case for release, but they will also be executed. Still, there are grounds for regarding these two penalties as fundamentally distinct in ways that make LWOP and not capital punishment the logical extreme of the exclusionary ideal. One telling difference lies in the temporal implications of each. When the death penalty is imposed, the state commits to destroying the offender, to ending his life. Not only has the offender been judged irredeemable, beyond reform, but the destructive character of the sentence forecloses the possibility that he might one day prove the state wrong. His life is over, and he will have no more chances. LWOP, too, reflects a judgment that the target is irredeemable; for what she has done, she will spend the rest of her life in prison. But the sentence, by its very nature, creates the space within which the targeted offender can continue to exist. And with that ongoing existence—that life—comes the possibility of growth and change. This means that, notwithstanding the finality of an LWOP sentence, subsequent events may rebut the judgment of irredeemability that originally justified the penalty. Yet at the same time, the sentence also deprives the subject, ex ante, of any future opportunity to show that she has changed sufficient to justify release.

It is this finality *in spite of the possibility of change* that in key part distinguishes LWOP from death. Of course, in reality, the pronouncement of a death sentence is typically followed by decades in custody, during which people on death row could well change and mature. Viewed in this light, the differences in this respect begin to narrow. But what in the death penalty context is only an accidental effect of a lengthy appeals process is an essential feature of LWOP, and this essential feature makes LWOP the defining sentence of an exclusionary system. Even a reintegrationist system would maintain in custody those who could not be safely released. What distinguishes a system committed to permanent exclusion is the determination to refuse reentry *even to those who could be productively reintegrated.* And what better way to guarantee this refusal than to foreclose in advance any possibility of review?

There are other respects in which recipients of LWOP are more profoundly excluded from the body politic than those who are sentenced to death. People who get death immediately embark on a lengthy appeals process, often with high-powered pro bono legal representation for which they never could have afforded to pay, and which they receive only because of their death sentences. During this period, they will receive regular and perhaps even searching review of their legal claims. To be sure, this attention is limited, as is the scope for legal redress. And any attention accorded capital defendants by the state during the appeals process is only in the service of clearing the way for their ultimate execution. Still, when a death sentence is imposed, the threat of state-sponsored execution means the law remains engaged. If a death sentence reflects a collective rejection of the subject's right to coexist with others in society, it also affirms his ongoing status as citizen and legal subject.

By contrast, with a sentence of LWOP, the law withdraws, taking with it the acknowledgment of shared membership that ongoing legal engagement provides. The individual sentenced to LWOP thus finds herself permanently outside the legal and political world, facing what is in practice unmitigated official discretion. In this way, the people who get LWOP come to occupy a version of Agamben's "state of exception,"[162] a zone of "bare life" into which the law does not reach, and in which the sovereign—here, in the guise of prison officials—has assumed permanent custody and control over subjects "ripped out of their social contexts and gutted of their politics and identities."[163] To be sure, people doing LWOP retain some (minimal) constitutional protections, available to those few claimants able to overcome high procedural hurdles, defeat official claims to immunity, and satisfy demanding and extremely deferential standards for recovery. Yet even when successful, such claims will bear only on the custodial conditions in which these permanent prisoners will spend the rest of their natural lives. What is not open to considered review is the sentence itself. As a formal matter, current Eighth Amendment doctrine provides for judicial review of noncapital sentences for "gross disproportionality."[164] In practice, however, this review is cursory at best, and the finality embodied in the sentence itself generally reflects the fate of the subject, notwithstanding the formal availability of direct appeal and habeas review. Thus, unlike a death sentence, which affords the subject continued meaningful engagement with the legal system, an LWOP sentence in all but the rarest of cases brings an immediate and final excision of the subject from the body politic.[165]

Capital defendants, moreover, retain a moral status, an affirmation of their essential humanity, in a way that subjects of LWOP do not. Certainly, one should not overstate the degree of this affirmation in the death penalty context. Indeed, given the natural human aversion to killing another person,[166] the dehumanization of those people sentenced to death may be a necessary prelude to their execution by those men and women charged with performing this task. But there are nevertheless ways that targets of capital punishment remain very much present to the collective consciousness as fellow human beings. This awareness is evident from the outset, in the seriousness of purpose with which the state approaches even the possibility of imposing a death sentence. As I. Bennett Capers describes in this volume,[167] in the U.S. Attorney's office where he worked, he and his fellow Assistant U.S. Attorneys (AUSAs) followed detailed protocols ensuring many layers of consideration and review merely to decide whether to bring a death case in the first place.[168]

This sort of careful and solemn attention is evident at every stage of a capital case: the decision to file, the many levels of judicial review, the ceremony brought to bear on the execution itself, not to mention the frequently intense public expressions of doubt and misgiving as to the propriety and legitimacy of state-sponsored killing in general. Each step reflects at least some collective awareness of the gravity of the undertaking—the proposed execution of a human being. In this recognition is a bridge between the subject of punishment and the rest of us; like us, he can die and can suffer both in death and in the knowledge beforehand that death is upon him. Indeed, the very notion that an offender deserves to die for what he has done—perhaps the most frequent and powerful justification for capital punishment—affirms his place in the human community; as a full moral agent, he is responsible for his actions and must bear the consequences. In these ways, even in death, the executed are accorded and thereby retain a place in the shared moral world.

These features contrast starkly with official practices and public attitudes in the context of LWOP. Capers recounts that he and his fellow AUSAs "barely gave . . . a thought" to those defendants facing LWOP, who were tried "as if they were . . . on an assembly line."[169] Although Capers took his death cases so seriously that "the names of [his] death-eligible defendants" remain with him to this day, he has "trouble remembering even one of [his] LWOP defendants."[170] Unlike death sentences, LWOP sentences are not rationed; as Jessica Henry's catalogue of the arbitrary and excessive imposition of LWOP and other DIP (death-in-prison) sentences makes clear,[171] they are meted out readily and seemingly with little reflection as to either the extreme severity of the penalty or its proportionality to the crime. Once sentenced, those individuals serving LWOP are generally ignored by the public at large, as is the normative question of the propriety of the LWOP sentence itself. In contrast to the implicit acknowledgment of a capital defendant's moral subjectivity and the public debate over the appropriateness of capital punishment, society scarcely considers either the question of what a person getting LWOP did to deserve such a severe punishment or the fact of his or her continued existence and thus ongoing suffering in prison. In the case of LWOP, these issues, and the individuals they most immediately and urgently concern, are instead swept away like the insects and worms invoked by North Carolinian Thomas Bennett after *Bowden*.[172]

The animating question of this volume is whether LWOP is the new death penalty. As a practical matter, the numbers do suggest something like LWOP's displacement of capital punishment. Today, over 41,000 people are serving LWOP sentences, compared with approximately 3,100 people on death rows nationwide.[173] There are of course innumerable legal and political explanations for this shift. But the impulse to social exclusion evident in the policies and practices explored in this chapter raises the possibility that, more than simply a policy shift toward a different penal regime, these numbers may also indicate a shift in the collective disposition toward the targets of penal harm.

In recent discourse on penal practices, one senses an additional emotional driver alongside the more familiar hatred and rage often expressed against criminal offenders: a profound unconcern with what ultimately happens to the individuals caught by the criminal justice system—or the juvenile justice system, or immigration detention, or at Guantánamo, or any of the other "states of exception"[174] that currently dot the American landscape. If there is something to this sense, it suggests that the challenge for advocates of criminal justice reform is not only that of confronting public anger, hatred, and fear toward criminals, although these emotions are still very present and must be acknowledged and addressed. It is also that of somehow overcoming the denial of a shared social membership, and of a common humanity, that lies at the heart of the impulse to exclude. Here the rhetoric of the "reentry" movement seems to hold much promise. By reminding observers that the people we send away "all come back,"[175] reentry efforts aim to construct an understanding of former prisoners as fellow members of society, fellow human beings who, once "back," have the same aspirations—for a stable home, a family, employment, personal betterment, etc.—as everybody else. If the material commitments to this enterprise have thus far been less than one might wish, the normative thrust of the movement begins to appear precisely what is necessary to challenge the project of permanent exclusion that, I have argued, drives current penal practice from LWOP on down.

Thanks to Austin Sarat and Charles Ogletree for inviting me to contribute to this collection; to my fellow contributors and to Keith Wattley and the other participants in the conversation organized by the Stanford Parole Project, for very helpful feedback on an earlier draft of this chapter; and to Scott Dewey, Max Kamer, Katie Strickland, and the fabulous reference librarians at the UCLA Hugh and Hazel Darling Law Library for excellent research assistance.

1. Sean Rosenmerkel, Matthew Durose, and Donald J. Farole, Jr., *Felony Sentences in State Courts, 2006—Statistical Tables* (Washington, DC: U.S. Department of Justice, Bureau of Justice Statistics, December 30, 2009), 9, table 1.6. This figure does not include misdemeanants.

2. Ibid., 5–6, tables 1.2.1 and 1.3.

3. See Ashley Nellis and Ryan S. King, *No Exit: The Expanding Use of Life Sentences in America* (Washington, DC: Sentencing Project, July 2009), 3.

4. See ibid.; Heather C. West, *Data Brief: Prisoners at Yearend 2009—Advance Counts* (Washington, DC: U.S. Department of Justice, Bureau of Justice Statistics, June 2010), 1; Todd D. Minton, *Jail Inmates at Midyear 2009—Statistical Tables* (Washington, DC: U.S. Department of Justice, Bureau of Justice Statistics, June 2010), 1.

5. Of course, such a society would be unlikely in the first place to create a penal system that captured high numbers of people with such personal disadvantages, opting instead for meaningful social programs to assist those who are mentally ill, drug addicted, illiterate, etc. to deal with these problems without involving the criminal justice system. Here, however, my aim is to contrast the possible dispositions, vis-à-vis the people who have been incarcerated, of systems that rely on incarceration. To motivate this contrast, it is necessary to posit a system that incarcerates regardless of social disadvantages yet takes steps to address those disadvantages to facilitate successful reentry.

6. See generally Nkechi Taifa and Catherine Beane, "Integrative Solutions to Interrelated Issues: A Multidisciplinary Look behind the Cycle of Incarceration," *Harvard Law & Policy Review* 3 (Summer 2009): 283–306.

7. For more on this point, see Sharon Dolovich, "Foreword: Incarceration American-Style," *Harvard Law & Policy Review* 3 (Summer 2009): 237–39.

8. For more on the moral economy of this exclusionary dynamic, see Sharon Dolovich, "Exclusion and Control in the Carceral State," *Berkeley Journal of Criminal Law* 16 (2011): 259.

9. African Americans make up no more than 13% of the American population, but they constitute close to 40% of the people behind bars in the United States. See William J. Sabol and Heather Coutre, *Prison Inmates at Midyear 2007* (Washington, DC: U.S. Department of Justice, Bureau of Justice Statistics, June 2008), 7, table 9 (estimating that of 2,090,800 people behind bars in the United States in 2007, 814,700 were black males and 67,600 were black females); see also *Facts about Prisons and Prisoners* (Washington, DC: Sentencing Project, December 2010) (estimating that 38% of persons in jails or prisons in 2009 were black).

10. See, e.g., Loïc Wacquant, "From Slavery to Mass Incarceration: Rethinking the 'Race Question' in the US," *New Left Review* 13 (January–February 2002): 41–60; Loïc Wacquant, "Class, Race and Hyperincarceration in Revanchist America," *Daedalus* (Summer 2010): 74–90; Loïc Wacquant, "Deadly Symbiosis: When Ghetto and Prison Meet and Mesh," *Punishment & Society* 3 (January 2001): 95–133.

11. In the postindustrial economic climate, the ghetto "lost its economic function of labor extraction and proved unable to ensure ethnoracial closure." The prison was therefore "called on to help contain a dishonored population widely viewed as deviant, destitute and dangerous." Wacquant, "Class, Race, and Hyperincarceration," 81.

12. Wacquant, "From Slavery to Mass Incarceration," 41.

13. See, e.g., Jennifer Gonnerman, *Life on the Outside: The Prison Odyssey of Elaine Bartlett* (New York: Farrar, Straus and Giroux, 2004) (recounting the struggle of Elaine Bartlett to reunite her family and build the components of a stable life after her release from prison).

14. See Katherine Beckett and Steve Herbert, *Banished: The New Social Control in Urban America* (New York: Oxford University Press, 2010), 8.

15. See Jenifer Warren et al., *One in 100: Behind Bars in America 2008* (Washington, DC: Pew Center on the States, 2008), 5 ("With 1,596,127 in state or federal prison custody, and another 723,131 in local jails, the total adult inmate count at the beginning of 2008 stood at 2,319,258.").

16. Giorgio Agamben, *Homo Sacer: Sovereign Power and Bare Life*, trans. Daniel Heller-Roazen (Stanford: Stanford University Press, 1998), 8–10 and generally.

17. Agamben seems in his work to want to exclude prisons from what he calls "states of exception," law-free zones where the sole protections occupants enjoy lie in the discretion of their keepers, who have license to do what they will without (legal) restraint. See ibid., 15–29, 57; Giorgio Agamben, *State of Exception*, trans. Kevin Attell (Chicago: University of Chicago Press, 2005), 1–4, 11–22, and generally. Certainly, there is a great distance between modern-day American prisons and the Nazi-run concentration camps that represent Agamben's archetypal state of exception. But a full understanding of the way the law operates in contemporary prisons and the scope of the discretion extended as a practical matter to corrections officials; of the stark division between prisoners and citizens that has become a taken-for-granted feature of modern American penality; and of the degree to which, again as a practical matter, convicted felony offenders are abandoned by political society to their fate, strongly suggests that prisons *are*, at least to some degree, states of exception in Agamben's sense. If in some ways the law actually does shape life on the inside, in other ways it has for all practical purposes withdrawn entirely. Although making this case is well beyond the scope of the present project, my sense is that the current state of the law vis-à-vis life in the prisons supports the conclusion that the "state of exception" Agamben theorizes is better understood as a matter of degree, so that the characteristics of existence in such a state (i.e., "bare life") can coexist with (limited) political subjectivity. But see Agnes Czajka, "Inclusive Exclusion: Citizenship and the American Prison and Prisoner," *Studies in Political Economy* 76 (2005): 130–32 (arguing that supermax prisons constitute states of exception in which subjects have been "absolute[ly] delet[ed] from the sphere of citizenship," although suggesting that people held in "standard prisons . . . remain at least partly within the purview of legal and social structures").

18. Agamben, *Homo Sacer*, 8 ("The fundamental categorial pair of Western politics is not that of friend/enemy but that of bare life/political existence, *zoē/ bios*, exclusion/ inclusion.").

19. Mona Lynch, *Sunbelt Justice: Arizona and the Transformation of American Punishment* (Stanford: Stanford Law Books, 2010), 9.

20. See ibid., 10.

21. Ibid., 13.

22. For example, Robert Perkinson makes a strong case in his history of the Texas prison system that the punitive cast of contemporary American penal practice has historical roots in the southern plantation prisons, with their commitment to "subjugationist discipline." Robert Perkinson, *Texas Tough: The Rise of America's Prison Empire* (New York: Picador, 2010), 8. And Mona Lynch convincingly shows in *Sunbelt Justice*, her rich account of Arizona penal policy over the past century, that the rehabilitationist model, although not without influence in the early years of Arizona's correctional bureaucracy, never really took hold there. See Lynch, *Sunbelt Justice*, 77–78. Instead, deep cultural currents in that state—most notably a stern ethos of "individualism and self-reliance" and a pronounced fiscal frugality (ibid., 46–47)—informed a century of punitive penality more consistent with today's "harsh, postrehabilitative, mass incarcerative warehouse-style prison system" than with the more progressive model typically associated with the American penal system in the mid-20th century (ibid., 4).

23. Lynch, *Sunbelt Justice*, 50.

24. See Mona Lynch, "The Contemporary Penal Subject(s)," in *After the War on Crime: Race, Democracy, and a New Reconstruction*, ed. Mary Louise Frampton, Ian Haney López, and Jonathan Simon, 89–105 (New York: NYU Press, 2008).

25. Kate Stith and José A. Cabranes, *Fear of Judging: Sentencing Guidelines in the Federal Courts* (Chicago: University of Chicago Press, 1998), 18–19.

26. See Lynch, *Sunbelt Justice*, 95 (explaining that legislative revision of the Arizona penal code in 1977 "dramatically decrease[d] judicial discretion in sentencing," suggesting that prior to 1977 state judges had considerable discretion in this arena).

27. Ibid., 111.

28. Stith and Cabranes, *Fear of Judging*, 21. Joan Petersilia reports that by 1927, all but three states (Florida, Mississippi, and Virginia) had parole systems in place, and by 1942, these three states and the federal system had joined the majority. See Joan Petersilia, *When Prisoners Come Home: Parole and Prisoner Reentry* (New York: Oxford University Press, 2003), 58.

29. Petersilia, *When Prisoners Come Home*, 62.

30. Ibid., 60–63. See also Lynch, *Sunbelt Justice*, 125–26 (explaining that even in Arizona, where no meaningful commitment to rehabilitation ever took hold, "it was generally accepted that [the criminal actor] was both capable of being returned to the broader community and in most cases deserved to have the opportunity upon reformation").

31. Petersilia, *When Prisoners Come Home*, 60–63.

32. Rummel v. Estelle, 445 U.S. 263, 265–67, 280 (1980).

33. Petersilia, *When Prisoners Come Home*, 65 (explaining that "[t]he political Left was concerned about excessive discretion that permitted vastly different sentences in presumably similar cases, and the political Right was concerned about the leniency of parole boards").

34. Francis Allen, *The Decline of the Rehabilitative Ideal: Penal Policy and Social Purpose* (New Haven: Yale University Press, 1981), 2 (quoted in Craig Haney, "Counting Casualties in the War on Prisoners," *University of San Francisco Law Review* 43 (2008): 93).

35. Haney, "Counting Casualties," 93.

36. Ibid., 97; see also California Board of Corrections, *Report: Coordinated California Corrections* (1971), v.

37. Lynch, "Contemporary Penal Subject(s)," 90.

38. Ibid., 90–91 ("[S]ince the penal subject's offending behavior or deviant acts fell within a continuum of human behavior, this conception of the penal subject held the potential for productive change and was generally viewed as worthy of state efforts to impel that change.").

39. Haney, "Counting Casualties," 95–96. As Haney describes, in 1968, the "primary message" of the politically diverse President's Commission on Law Enforcement and Administration of Justice was that "crime needed to be addressed by rebuilding the cities, eliminating slum conditions, and transforming lingering racial segregation to improve the lives of poor and minority citizens" (ibid., 96).

40. See generally Taifa and Beane, "Integrative Solutions to Interrelated Issues," 283–306.

41. Petersilia, *When Prisoners Come Home*, 60–63.

42. The flashpoint for this dramatic change is widely thought to have been a 1974 essay, published in the journal *Public Interest*, by sociologist Robert Martinson. See Jerome Miller, "Criminology: Is Rehabilitation a Waste of Time?," *Washington Post*, April 23, 1989 (discussing Robert Martinson, "What Works? Questions and Answers about Prison Reform," *Public Interest* 35 (Spring 1974): 22–54).

43. See Petersilia, *When Prisoners Come Home*, 65.

44. See ibid., 65–67 and table 3.1.

45. Steven Donziger, ed., *The Real War on Crime: Report of the National Criminal Justice Commission* (New York: HarperPerennial, 1996), 24.

46. Todd R. Clear, *Harm in American Penology: Offenders, Victims, and Their Communities* (Albany: SUNY Press, 1994), 4.

47. James Q. Wilson, *Thinking about Crime* (New York: Basic Books, 1985), 193 (quoted in Petersilia, *When Prisoners Come Home*, 64).

48. Wilson, *Thinking about Crime*, 193 (quoted in Petersilia, *When Prisoners Come Home*, 64).

49. Lynch, "The Contemporary Penal Subject(s)," 95.

50. The preamble to the California Determinate Sentencing Law, adopted in 1977, made this shift explicit, announcing that the purpose of prison was "punishment" and not "rehabilitation." See Petersilia, *When Prisoners Come Home*, 65.

51. This section is largely drawn from Dolovich, "Incarceration American-Style," 245–53.

52. See Christopher J. Mumola and Jennifer C. Karberg, *Drug Use and Dependence, State and Federal Prisoners 2004* (Washington, DC: U.S. Department of Justice, Bureau of Justice Statistics, October 2006; revised January 19, 2007), 6; Jennifer C. Karberg and Doris J. James, *Substance Dependence, Abuse, and Treatment of Jail Inmates, 2002* (Washington, DC: U.S. Department of Justice, Bureau of Justice Statistics, July 2005), 1–5.

53. Doris J. James and Lauren E. Glaze, *Mental Health Problems of Prison and Jail Inmates* (Washington, DC: U.S. Department of Justice, Bureau of Justice Statistics, September 2006), 1.

54. See Bruce Western, Becky Pettit, and Josh Guetzkow, "Black Economic Progress in the Era of Mass Imprisonment," in *Invisible Punishment: The Collateral Consequences*

of Mass Imprisonment, ed. Marc Mauer and Meda Chesney-Lind (New York: New Press, 2002), 176 (noting that "incarceration erodes job skills").

55. See Donald Braman, "Families and Incarceration," in Mauer and Chesney-Lind, Invisible Punishment, 120.

56. See Tracy Huling, "Building a Prison Economy in Rural Areas," in Mauer and Chesney-Lind, Invisible Punishment, 197–99.

57. See Braman, "Families and Incarceration," 117–18.

58. Terry A. Kupers, "Prison and the Decimation of Pro-Social Life Skills," in The Trauma of Psychological Torture, ed. Almerindo E. Ojeda (Westport, CT: Praeger, 2008), 10.

59. See, e.g., Benjamin Fleury-Steiner with Carla Crowder, Dying Inside: The HIV/AIDS Ward at Limestone Prison (Ann Arbor: University of Michigan Press, 2008); Plata v. Schwarzenegger, No. C01-1351 TEH, 2005 U.S. Dist. LEXIS 43796, at *2–3 (N.D. Cal., Oct. 3, 2005).

60. See, e.g., Silja J. A. Talvi, "Deadly Staph Infection 'Superbug' Has a Dangerous Foothold in U.S. Jails," Alternet, December 4, 2007, http://www.alternet.org/story/69576/%20?page=entire; Brent Staples, "Treat the Epidemic behind Bars before It Hits the Streets," New York Times, June 22, 2004; Jessica R. MacNeil, Mark N. Lobato, and Marisa Moore, "An Unanswered Health Disparity: Tuberculosis among Correctional Inmates, 1993 through 2003," American Journal of Public Health 95 (October 2005): 1800–05; James A. Inciardi et al., "Developing a Multimedia HIV and Hepatitis Intervention for Drug-Involved Offenders Reentering the Community," Prison Journal 87 (March 2007): 111–42.

61. Kupers, "Prison and the Decimation of Pro-Social Life Skills," 129.

62. Rhodes v. Chapman, 452 U.S. 337, 371 (1981) (Marshall, J., dissenting).

63. As of 2006, over 15,000 California inmates were sleeping in prison common areas "such as prison gymnasiums, dayrooms and program rooms." Governor Arnold Schwarzenegger, Prison Overcrowding State of Emergency Proclamation, October 4, 2006, http://gov.ca.gov/news.php?id=4278.

64. Rhodes, 452 U.S. at 371 (Marshall, J., dissenting).

65. See Kupers, "Prison and the Decimation of Pro-Social Life Skills," 130.

66. On supermax prisons, see generally Lorna Rhodes, Total Confinement: Madness and Reason in the Maximum Security Prison (Berkeley: University of California Press, 2004); Leena Kurki and Norval Morris, "Supermax Prisons," Crime and Justice: A Review of Research 28 (2001): 385–424.

67. "[F]or just about all prisoners [even those without documented mental health histories], being held in isolated confinement for longer than 3 months causes lasting emotional damage if not full-blown psychosis and functional disability." Terry Kupers, "What to Do with the Survivors? Coping with the Long-Term Effects of Isolated Confinement," Criminal Justice and Behavior 35 (August 2008): 1005–06.

68. Atul Gawande, "Hellhole: The United States Holds Tens of Thousands of Inmates in Long-Term Solitary Confinement: Is This Torture?," New Yorker, March 30, 2009, http://www.newyorker.com/reporting/2009/03/30/090330fa_fact_gawande.

69. Kupers, "What to Do with the Survivors?," 1010.

70. Terry A. Kupers, "Rape and the Prison Code," in Prison Masculinities, ed. Don Sabo, Terry A. Kupers, and Willie London (Philadelphia: Temple University Press, 2001), 114–15.

For further discussion of the prison culture of hypermasculinity, see Sharon Dolovich, "Strategic Segregation in the Modern Prison," *American Criminal Law Review* 48 (2011): 11–19.

71. Derrick Corley, "Prison Friendships," in Sabo, Kupers, and London, *Prison Masculinities*, 106.

72. See Stephen "Donny" Donaldson, "A Million Jockers, Punks, and Queens," in Sabo, Kupers, and London, *Prison Masculinities*, 119 (explaining that punks are "prisoners who 'have been forced into a sexually submissive role,' usually through rape or convincing threat of rape") (quoting Wayne S. Wooden and Jay Parker, *Men behind Bars: Sexual Exploitation in Prison* (New York: Da Capo, 1982)).

73. See Kupers, "Rape and the Prison Code," 114.

74. Don Sabo, "Doing Time, Doing Masculinity: Sports and Prison," in Sabo, Kupers, and London, *Prison Masculinities*, 64.

75. Corley, "Prison Friendships," 106.

76. Ibid., 107.

77. Sabo, "Doing Time, Doing Masculinity," 65.

78. See Allen J. Beck and Paige M. Harrison, *Sexual Victimization in State and Federal Prisons Reported by Inmates, 2007* (Washington, DC: U.S. Department of Justice, Bureau of Justice Statistics, December 2007; revised April 9, 2008), 2, 6 (of the 146 prison facilities participating in the national inmate survey on sexual victimization in prison, 6 facilities had no reports of sexual victimization).

79. See James E. Robertson, "'Fight or F . . .' and Constitutional Liberty: An Inmate's Right to Self-Defense When Targeted by Aggressors," *Indiana Law Review* 29 (1995): 339 n. 3 ("'[I]n the prison vernacular, [prison correctional officers] seem to offer little assistance to inmates except the age-old advice of 'fight or fuck.'"") (quoting Helen M. Eigenberg, "Rape in Male Prisons: Examining the Relationship between Correctional Officers' Attitudes toward Rape and Their Willingness to Respond to Acts of Rape," in *Prison Violence in America*, ed. Michael C. Braswell, Reid H. Montgomery, Jr., and Lucien X. Lombardo (Cincinnati, OH: Anderson, 1994), 159).

80. See James Gilligan, *Violence: Reflections on a National Epidemic* (New York: Vintage, 1996), 163.

81. See Alice Ristroph, "Sexual Punishments," *Columbia Journal of Gender & Law* 15 (2006): 150.

82. Donaldson, "A Million Jockers, Punks, and Queens," 120. This assumes, of course, that a person threatened with rape has the time to choose a protector before he is raped and thereby recast in the prison culture as the property of his rapist.

83. Ibid., 119 (explaining that punks are, "for all practical purposes, slaves and can be sold, traded, and rented or loaned out at the whim of their 'Daddy'"); see also *No Escape: Male Rape in U.S. Prisons* (New York: Human Rights Watch, April 1, 2001), 71–72 and generally (documenting cases of sexual slavery in prisons in various states).

84. Older prisoners, prisoners known to be connected to powerful people inside or outside the facility, and others who for whatever reason are respected and left alone may be able to shield themselves from the sexual violence of prison culture.

85. See Judith Herman, *Trauma and Recovery* (New York: Basic Books, 1992), 74 (explaining that "[p]rolonged, repeated trauma . . . occurs only in circumstances of cap-

tivity") (quoted in Nell Bernstein, *All Alone in the World: Children of the Incarcerated* (New York: New Press, 2005), 182).

86. Agamben, *Homo Sacer*, 105. As Agamben explains, the state of exception, the sphere of pure sovereign power, "is the sphere in which it is permitted to kill without committing homicide and without celebrating a sacrifice" (ibid., 83 (emphasis omitted)). See also Lorna A. Rhodes, "Supermax Prisons and the Trajectory of Exception," *Studies in Law, Politics, and Society* 47 (2009): 196–98.

87. Agamben, *Homo Sacer*, 104–05.

88. See Jonathan Simon, "Dignity and Risk: The Long Road from *Graham v. Florida* to Abolition of Life without Parole," this volume, 304.

89. One might well wonder what social benefits come from imposing such limits. But the presence of strategies that operate to constrain meaningful reentry absent plausible justifications for ongoing exclusion is the hallmark of an exclusionary system.

90. See Nellis and King, *No Exit*, 9–10 and figure 2.

91. Ibid., 6, table 1. The exception is Alaska.

92. Ibid. The six states are Illinois, Iowa, Louisiana, Maine, Pennsylvania, and South Dakota.

93. Ibid., 3.

94. Indeed, according to the Sentencing Project, "during the 1990s the growth of persons serving life without parole [was] precipitous, an increase of 170%, between 1992 and 2003. Overall, one of every six lifers in 1992 was serving a sentence of life without parole. By 2003, that proportion had increased to one in four." Marc Mauer, Ryan S. King, and Malcolm C. Young, *The Meaning of "Life": Long Prison Sentences in Context* (Washington, DC: Sentencing Project, May 2004), 11.

95. See Nellis and King, *No Exit*, 7, figure 1, and 10, figure 2.

96. See 15 California Code of Regulations (CCR) § 2281(c)(1), (c)(3), (d)(2), (d)(9) (2008); 15 CCR § 2402 (c)(1), (c)(3), (d)(2), (d)(9) (2008).

97. See 15 CCR § 2281(a) (2008); 15 CCR § 2402(a) (2008).

98. The relevant statute provides that "[o]ne year prior to the inmate's minimum eligible parole release date a panel of two or more commissioners or deputy commissioners shall . . . meet with the inmate and shall normally set a parole release date." Cal. Penal Code § 3041(a).

99. See Keith Wattley, *Introduction to Life Sentences in California* (presentation at UCLA School of Law, November 10, 2010). According to one survey of 300 lifers in custody, only 2 had been granted release dates by the state parole board, while a further 6 had had their parole denials overturned by the courts. See Jennifer Chaussee, "For Paroled Lifers, Release Dates May Come Only with the Courts," *Capitol Weekly*, January 13, 2011, http://www.capitolweekly.net/article.php?_c=zoljk3t6h7py52&xid=zezqccws115j0p&done=.zoljrhdo6nhzvs.

100. Nellis and King, *No Exit*, 6.

101. See Ashley Nellis, "Throwing Away the Key: The Expansion of Life without Parole Sentences in the United States," *Federal Sentencing Reporter* 23 (October 2010): 28–29.

102. Ibid.

103. Wattley, *Introduction to Life Sentences in California*. But see Swarthout v. Cooke, 131 S. Ct. 859 (2011) (holding that California's "some evidence" standard is not constitutionally required, thereby foreclosing the federal courts from reversing California parole

denials unless a prisoner has not been "allowed an opportunity to be heard" or "provided a statement of the reasons why parole was denied").

104. Cal. Penal Code § 3041.5(b)(2) (2007).

105. Cal. Penal Code § 3041.5(b)(2)(A)–(B) (2007).

106. Cal. Penal Code § 3041.5(b)(3)(A)–(C) (2010).

107. Cal. Penal Code § 3041.5(b)(A)–(C) (2010).

108. Keith Wattley, personal communication, February 4, 2011 (reporting that the breakdown of the 6,760 prisoners who received parole denials in California in 2009 in terms of number of years until their next parole hearing date was as follows: 3 years: 1,942; 5 years: 4,229; 7 years: 303; 10 years: 191; 15 years: 91).

109. N.C. Gen. Stat. § 14-2 (1974).

110. North Carolina Fair Sentencing Act (1981), N.C. Gen. Stat. § 15A-1340, enacted as Chapter 760 of the 1979 Session Laws. For further background on this act, see Dee Reid, "The Fair Sentencing Act: Setting the Record Straight," *North Carolina Insight* 9 (March 1987): 42–49.

111. See Bruce Mildwurf, "Sentencing Policy at Center of Convicts' Release," Associated Press, October 23, 2009 (updated November 19, 2009), http://www.wral.com/news/state/story/6272596/.

112. State v. Bowden, 193 N.C. App. 597, 668 S.E.2d 107 (November 4, 2008). Although Bowden had done 30 and not 40 years when he filed his habeas petition, he had earned enough time off his sentence under companion programs to qualify him for release.

113. *Bowden*, 668 S.E. 2d at 109, note 1 (explaining that N.C. Gen. Stat. § 15A-2002 (2007) currently provides that "a sentence of life imprisonment means a sentence of life without parole").

114. Robbie Brown, "North Carolinians Bridle over Plan to Free Inmates," *New York Times*, October 17, 2009.

115. See Nellis, "Throwing Away the Key," 28 (reporting that "recidivism rates are low among [released] older inmates, including lifers," because of "the duration of their imprisonment, the maturity they are likely to gain in prison, and their age upon reentry into the community"). Nellis describes the results of two such studies. First, "a study in Ohio of twenty-one people released in 2000 who were 50 years of age or older and had served twenty-five years or more at the time of release found that none of these individuals committed a new crime during the three years after their release" (ibid., 29). Second, in Pennsylvania, "the recidivism rate of individuals convicted of new offenses who were 50 years of age or older and released in 2003 was 1.4% in the first twenty-two months after release" (ibid., 29).

116. The relevant figure included both the "day-for-a-day" credit created by the 1981 statute as well as other credits accumulated through the state's parole regulations. See *Bowden*, 668 S.E.2d at 108–10.

117. Although the state's supreme court upheld the *Bowden* decision, the governor had another chance when the next affected prisoner filed for release. This time, the state prevailed, and the resulting North Carolina Supreme Court opinion foreclosed the release of any other affected prisoners. See Jones v. Keller, 364 N.C. 249, 698 S.E.2d 49 (2010).

118. Ken Smith, "Perdue Has No Plans to Release Life Inmates," Associated Press, October 22, 2009 (updated November 19, 2009), http://www.wral.com/news/state/story/6261276/.

119. Brown, "North Carolinians Bridle."

120. See Simon, "Dignity and Risk," 304.

121. Recall that the average sentence for the more than 460,000 people sent to prison in 2006 was 4 years and 11 months. See note 3 above and accompanying text.

122. See Part III above.

123. This is especially likely to be the case with older inmates. See Goodwill Industries International, *Road to Reintegration: Ensuring Successful Community Re-entry for People Who Are Former Offenders*, June 10, 2009, 4–5, 9; "Help for Older Ex-Prisoners," *Christian Science Monitor*, January 14, 2002.

124. See Devah Pager, *Marked: Race, Crime, and Finding Work in an Era of Mass Incarceration* (Chicago: University of Chicago Press, 2007), 24; Becky Pettit and Christopher J. Lyons, "Status and the Stigma of Incarceration: The Labor-Market Effects of Incarceration, by Race, Class, and Criminal Involvement," in *Barriers to Reentry? The Labor Market for Released Prisoners in Post-industrial America*, ed. Shawn Bushway, Michael A. Stoll, and David F. Weiman (New York: Russell Sage Foundation, 2007), 203–05 ("Employers express a reluctance to hire inmates, and ex-inmates face earning penalties of between 10 to 30 percent." (citations omitted)).

125. See Nancy G. La Vigne, Elizabeth Davies, Tobi Palmer, and Robin Halberstadt, *Release Planning for Successful Reentry: A Guide for Corrections, Service Providers, and Community Groups* (Washington, DC: Urban Institute Justice Policy Center, September 2008), 10–11 (explaining the financial implications of incarceration for individuals relying on state assistance and other reasons why former prisoners tend to face financial difficulties upon release).

126. True, in 2008, President George W. Bush signed the Second Chance Act of 2007, Pub. L. 110-199, April 9, 2008, 122 Stat. 657 (see also 42 U.S.C. § 17501 et seq.). And certainly, this law is welcome. But its practical effects have thus far been limited. See Jessica S. Henry, "The Second Chance Act of 2007," *Criminal Law Bulletin* 45 (Summer 2009): 430–32. And given how much is spent annually on incarceration across the country, the total funding of $360 million authorized thus far to implement this law is ultimately a drop in the bucket (ibid.).

127. As Webb Hubbell put it in an op-ed in the *San Francisco Chronicle* shortly after his release from federal prison in 2001, these restrictions—collectively "called the mark of Cain . . . in the prison reform movement"—are commonly referred to as "civil disabilities" but "[m]ore realistically" would be known as "'civil death,' a condition that, for many of us, offers little option but to return whence we came: to prison." Webb Hubbell, "The Mark of Cain," *San Francisco Chronicle*, June 10, 2001.

128. See Pager, *Marked*, 24. For detailed discussion of the various forms these burdens can take, see Michael Pinard, "Collateral Consequences of Criminal Convictions: Confronting Issues of Race and Dignity," *New York University Law Review* 85 (May 2010): 489–94.

129. American Bar Association, Task Force on Collateral Sanctions, *Introduction: Proposed Standards on Collateral Sanctions and Administrative Disqualification of Convicted Persons*, draft, January 18, 2002, quoted in Marc Mauer and Meda Chesney-Lind, introduction to *Invisible Punishment*, 5.

130. Ibid.

131. See Gabriel J. Chin, "Race, the War on Drugs, and the Collateral Consequences of a Drug Conviction," *Journal of Gender, Race & Justice* 6 (Fall 2002): 260.

132. Ibid., 253, 259. In addition, noncitizens increasingly face deportation upon the completion of their sentences—another form of wholesale exclusion (ibid., 253).

133. To make matters worse, in many jurisdictions, parents must reimburse foster parents, and even the government, for support their children received during their incarceration. Unable to meet these unrealistic demands, many parents find their parental rights permanently terminated. See Bernstein, *All Alone in the World*, 154–55.

134. See the project's website: http://isrweb.isr.temple.edu/projects/accproject/.

135. Gabriel Chin, "Citizenship and Community," panel presentation, "Symposium: The Constitution in 2020: The Future of Criminal Justice," Florida State University College of Law, Tallahassee, Florida, October 8, 2010.

136. Cal. Bus. & Prof. Code, § 4842(d) (2010).

137. See G. Chin, "Race, the War on Drugs," 259 (citing 21 U.S.C. § 862(a)(1)(A) (1999)).

138. Ibid., 259–60.

139. Bruce Western and Becky Pettit, "Incarceration and Social Inequality," *Daedalus* (Summer 2010): 8.

140. Ibid.

141. Ibid., 8, 14–16.

142. Beckett and Herbert, *Banished*.

143. Ibid., 37.

144. Ibid., 45–46.

145. Ibid., 46. Such restrictions may also be imposed as a condition of probation or pretrial release (ibid., 45–46).

146. Katherine Beckett and Steve Herbert, "The Punitive City Revisited: The Transformation of Urban Social Control," in Frampton, López, and Simon, *After the War on Crime*, 114. See also Beckett and Herbert, *Banished*, 48–49.

147. Beckett and Herbert, *Banished*, 47.

148. Ibid., 51.

149. Ibid.

150. Ibid., 33. Indeed, the removal of such individuals from the shared public space is arguably the motivating impulse behind the "broken windows" approach popularized by James Q. Wilson and others. The ostensible aim of that policing strategy was to reduce crime by targeting the physical signs of disorder—graffiti, broken windows, abandoned buildings, etc. But as Beckett and Herbert astutely observe, in practice, the targets of broken-windows policing are not features of the "built environment" but "disreputable or obstreperous or unpredictable *people*: panhandlers, drunks, addicts, rowdy teenagers, prostitutes, loiterers, the mentally disturbed" (ibid., 33 (quoting James Q. Wilson and George F. Kelling, "Broken Windows: The Police and Neighborhood Safety," *Atlantic Monthly*, May 1982, 32) (emphasis added)).

151. As Beckett and Herbert observe, one consequence of the exclusionary mechanisms they describe is that "those who are unwanted—which includes those who merely offend our aesthetic sensibilities—feel continually harassed and unwelcome. The moral division between the respectable and not-so-respectable is reinforced daily by a spatial division between the included and the excluded." Beckett and Herbert, *Banished*, 21–22.

152. If a prisoner's offense does have any bearing on his or her prison experience, it is likely the opposite of that imagined by retribution or deterrence, since it is typically prisoners who have committed serious violent crimes and therefore are perceived as possible threats who receive the most respect from both correctional officers and fellow inmates. For more on this point, see Sharon Dolovich, "Cruelty, Prison Conditions, and the Eighth Amendment," *New York University Law Review* 84 (October 2009): 919–20.

153. For example, under federal law, anyone with a felony drug conviction is automatically permanently banned from Temporary Aid to Needy Families assistance and food stamps, although no such restriction applies to people convicted of more serious crimes such as murder, rape, or armed robbery. See Gwen Rubenstein and Debbie Mukamal, "Welfare and Housing—Denial of Benefits to Drug Offenders," in Mauer and Chesney-Lind, *Invisible Punishment*, 41.

154. See Jessica S. Henry, "Death-in-Prison Sentences: Overutilized and Underscrutinized," this volume, 78–79.

155. See ibid., 83–87.

156. African Americans make up almost 40% of the American prison population (see note 9 above), 45% of the parole-eligible lifers, and 56.4% of people serving LWOP sentences. See Nellis and King, *No Exit*, 11–14 and tables 3 and 4. In the juvenile LWOP (JLWOP) population, the disparity is equally pronounced. Of those juveniles serving LWOP sentences, 56.1% are African American (ibid., 20–24 and table 9). In 17 states, more than 60% of the JLWOP population is African American. In Alabama, for instance, 75 of the 89 people with JLWOP sentences (84.3%) are African American, and in Maryland, 15 of the 19 (70.9%) people serving JLWOP sentences are African American. In the federal system, that number is 19 out of 35 (54.3%). In South Carolina, it is 11 out of 14 (78.6%) (ibid., 23–24 and table 9).

157. The widespread assumption of a connection between penological practices and the conventional justifications for punishment seems best understood as the artifact of an inevitable overlap between the legitimate moral sentiments that motivate the impulse to punish (in particular, the desire to condemn bad acts and to deter their repetition) and the illegitimate impulse—most notably the withdrawal from certain individuals of their moral status as human—that drives the exclusionary project.

158. For an in-depth examination of what precisely is required for state punishment to be legitimate, see Sharon Dolovich, "Legitimate Punishment in Liberal Democracy," *Buffalo Criminal Law Review* 7 (2004): 307–442.

159. For (much) more on this point, see ibid.

160. See 97.

161. An assertion of the moral equality of penal subjects does not preclude the imposition of (legitimate) punishment on convicted offenders for their crimes. For an extended argument defending this position, see Dolovich, "Legitimate Punishment," 336–41, 374–78.

162. See Agamben, *State of Exception*, 3–4.

163. See Czajka, "Inclusive Exclusion," 129.

164. Harmelin v. Michigan, 501 U.S. 957, 997–98 (1991) (Kennedy, J., concurring).

165. The Supreme Court has repeatedly emphasized that successful constitutional challenges to noncapital sentences are "'exceedingly rare.'" Ewing v. California, 538 U.S. 11, 21 (2003) (quoting Rummel v. Estelle, 445 U.S. 263, 272 (1980)). *Graham v. Florida*, in which

the Court held that LWOP sentences are per se unconstitutional as applied to juveniles convicted of nonhomicide offenses, was one notable exception. See Graham v. Florida, 130 S. Ct. 2011 (2010). But *Graham* is an outlier. In the majority of LWOP cases, there is a strong presumption of constitutionality, as *Graham's* carefully limited holding indicates.

166. See Dave Grossman, *On Killing: The Psychological Cost of Learning to Kill in War and Society* (New York: Little, Brown, 1995), 35–36, 249–62 (explaining the way the U.S. military had to learn how to break down the instinctive aversion of its soldiers to killing fellow human beings, an effort that bore especial fruit during the Vietnam War).

167. See I. Bennett Capers, "Defending Life," this volume, 167–89.

168. Ibid., 167.

169. Ibid., 169.

170. Ibid.

171. See Henry, "Death-in-Prison Sentences," 82–87.

172. See notes 118–120 and accompanying text. This dehumanization may be a function of the form of the punishment. Imprisonment entails confining people in enclosed spaces, behind bars and walls, and keeping them there against their will. This is something society does as a matter of course to animals and insects, but not to humans. Recall Agamben's "wolfman" or "werewolf"—a decided nonhuman—who if confined, need not be spared a second thought. I thank Katie Strickland for helpful discussion on this point.

173. See Tracey L. Snell, *Capital Punishment 2009—Statistical Tables* (Washington, DC: U.S. Department of Justice, Bureau of Justice Statistics, December 2010), 1.

174. See Agamben, *State of Exception*, 1–4, 22.

175. Jeremy Travis, *But They All Come Back: Facing the Challenges of Prisoner Reentry* (Washington, DC: Urban Institute Press, 2005).

4

Life without Parole under Modern Theories of Punishment

PAUL H. ROBINSON

I. Introduction

Almost 10% of U.S. prisoners are serving life terms. In some states the figure is 17% or more; in California it is 20% of all prisoners.[1] Of the prisoners sentenced to life terms, almost 30% have no possibility of parole, and the number of prisoners serving life without parole (LWOP) has tripled in the past sixteen years.[2] Life sentences arise from a wide variety of offenses. A majority of life sentences are for offenses other than homicide,[3] which is to be expected given that life is a common sentence under habitual offender statutes, such as so-called three-strikes laws.[4]

The underlying rationales for LWOP sentences include all three of the most common distributive principles for punishment: general deterrence, incapacitation of the dangerous, and deserved punishment.[5] Some theorists have relied on general deterrence to support LWOP, arguing that it provides a serious deterrent effect that in some sense is even harsher than the death penalty. "[I]f most death row inmates surveyed, who obviously were not deterred from committing murder by the threat of capital punishment, maintain that LWOP is a worse sanction than death, does it not stand to reason that the penalty that is perceived as being the harshest will have been the greatest deterrent effect, whatever that effect might be?"[6] Incapacitation rationales also are frequently relied on, often in support of habitual offender statutes, for example.[7] As Danya Blair argues, "The release of offenders who present a danger to society is not a rare mistake, but rather an inherent flaw in an unworkable system, resulting from a general inability of parole boards to make intelligent predictions about an offender's future behavior. Parole ineligibility for certain offenders operates to protect against this inefficiency by recognizing that some offenders are so dangerous that we cannot leave the question of their release to the vagaries of the parole system."[8]

As an alternative to these instrumentalist distributive principles, desert or justice principles may be offered as a rationale for LWOP sentences. Desert has gained increasing prominence in recent years. The American Law Institute recently amended the Model Penal Code to set desert as the dominant distributive principle for punishment.[9] Some courts have followed suit, as when the Supreme Court cited retributivism as the "primary justification for the death penalty."[10] In the LWOP context, some people have argued that LWOP is the sort of tough punishment needed for the most blameworthy offenders—especially if a jurisdiction lacks the death penalty. "If the death penalty is to be abolished, a replacement sanction of sufficient gravity needs to be provided by the law."[11]

However, close analysis suggests that none of these rationales in fact supports current LWOP practice. To signal those conclusions up front: The existence of the prerequisites of effective general deterrence commonly are the exception in LWOP cases, rather than the rule. Incapacitation of the dangerous would be cheaper and more effective for the community and fairer to detainees if done through an open civil preventive detention system that admitted its preventive detention purpose rather than being dressed up to look like criminal justice for past offenses. And fair and effective preventive detention would not likely support the common use of LWOP found in current practice. Finally, a system of deserved punishment requires careful attention to setting the extent of punishment to match the relative blameworthiness of the offender. Imposing LWOP, the highest punishment (or second highest, if the death penalty is available), on a wide range of cases—especially on 10% to 20% of all prisoners—is to trivialize important differences in the moral blameworthiness among serious cases. Further, the empirical evidence suggests that the doctrines that produce LWOP sentences regularly and seriously conflict with the community's shared intuitions of justice. That conflict, through the high use of LWOP, undermines the criminal law's moral credibility with the community it governs and thereby undermines the law's crime-control effectiveness.

II. Justifying LWOP under Distributive Principles of Deterrence or Incapacitation

LWOP sentences are commonly justified under rationales of general deterrence or incapacitation of the dangerous, but there is good reason to doubt that these purposes are well served by the current common use of LWOP.

A. Deterrence

It is easy enough to see the attraction of general deterrence as a means of crime control. Under the right conditions, a system of general deterrence can avoid future crime. Indeed, it has the potential for enormous efficiency. For the cost of punishing just the offender at hand, one can deter thousands of others who hear about the case and heed its warning.

On the other hand, it may well be that general deterrence will be effective in only a limited number of instances. For it to work, three prerequisites must be satisfied. First, the deterrence-based rule can deter only if the intended targets are aware of the rule, directly or indirectly. Second, even if the target audience knows of the deterrence-based rule, a deterrent effect results only if they have the capacity and inclination to rationally calculate what is in their best interests. Finally, even if potential offenders know of the deterrence-based rule, are able to rationally calculate the conduct that is in their best interests, and do in fact make such a calculation, the rule will deter only if they conclude that the costs of committing the offense exceed its anticipated benefits. As discussed later, it may be rare that these three prerequisites are satisfied, thus casting doubt on the ability to realize the potential benefit of deterrence.[12]

The first prerequisite requires that the potential offender be aware of the deterrence-based rule. However, evidence suggests that this commonly is not the case. For example, a primary justification for the felony murder rule—treating even accidental killings during a felony as murder—is its presumed deterrent effect on potential felons. But few potential offenders are likely to know whether their jurisdiction has such a rule or what its terms might be. The adoption and formulation of the rule vary widely.[13] The same is true of habitual offender statutes.[14] The same may be true for LWOP generally. How many potential offenders will actually know their own state's practices relating to LWOP sentences? That sentence's threat cannot have a deterrent effect if the target of the threat does not know of it.

Studies suggest that most people assume the criminal law tracks their intuitions of justice. Therefore, deterrence will have its greatest difficulty in cases in which it *deviates* from what people intuitively think is just (empirical desert), because people are least likely to know the law when it conflicts with common intuitions. As part III.A of this chapter makes clear, habitual offender statutes, drug offenses, and felony murder statutes generating LWOP are just such deviations from desert as the community perceives it, and these deviations will not be anticipated by potential offenders unless they are specially advised of them.

Further, even in cases in which the potential offender knows of the rule intended to deter, he or she must be able and inclined to do the balancing of costs and benefits on which deterrence relies, the second prerequisite. Again, the evidence suggests that this commonly is not the case. Potential offenders as a group are less inclined than most people to think carefully about the future consequences of their conduct and are more likely to be under the distorting influence of drugs, alcohol, or mental illness. Indeed, the habitual offenders caught up in three-strikes statutes commonly are just the kinds of persons suffering such distortions in rational calculations, which is why they have repeatedly offended despite having endured past convictions and punishments. The same is true of many people involved in felony murders. Intentional killings are often fueled by drug or alcohol use, emotion, or mental illness, all of which inevitably cloud reasoning.[15] Persons committing drug offenses are, not surprisingly, commonly involved in drug use, which distorts rational calculation.[16] General deterrence threats of LWOP can have little effect when aimed at persons not inclined toward rational calculation.

The last prerequisite also reveals problems for the general deterrence program of LWOP threats: even if a potential offender knows the deterrence-based rule and is able to calculate his or her best interests, a variety of factors commonly lead potential offenders to conclude that the perceived benefits of committing a crime outweigh its perceived costs. In fact, capture and punishment rates are exceptionally low for most offenses, even low for the serious offenses that lead to LWOP sentences. While the frequency of LWOP sentences is high and increasing, it is nothing like the frequency of serious drug offenses or of homicide or aggravated assaults that may lead to homicide. Of the 1,745,712 drug violations in the U.S. in 2004,[17] only 288,160 of them (16.5%) result in felony convictions.[18] Even the most serious offenses often have low punishment rates. Of the 451,500 homicides and aggravated assaults in the U.S. in 2004,[19] only 103,537 of them (22.9%) resulted in a felony conviction.[20] And of course, of people convicted of a felony offense, only a small percentage are given an LWOP sentence. A rational calculator might conclude that this distant risk of receiving an LWOP sentence is not sufficiently serious as to justify passing up the immediate benefit of committing the offense.

Even if actual punishment rates were not so low, a deterrent effect depends not on the reality of the deterrent threat but rather on its perception. Thus, even if the deterrent threat were significant, deterrence may fail if the intended target does not appreciate the true likelihood of punishment. Unfortunately, people show a natural tendency to discount future detriments just as they discount future benefits, and many offenders are likely to overestimate their ability to avoid capture and punishment.[21] These natural human predilections are not good for a general deterrence program.

In sum, for general deterrence to effectively achieve its aims, three prerequisites must be satisfied. Yet satisfying each prerequisite encounters its own challenges, which general deterrence may have difficulty overcoming. And, even if the prerequisites are satisfied and some general deterrent effect results, the crime-control benefit of the effect may be outweighed by the crime-control cost that results from being in conflict with the community's intuitions of justice. More on this later.

B. Incapacitation

While there are serious concerns about the crime-control effectiveness of general deterrence, no similar doubts exist for incapacitation as a distributive principle. Incapacitation can reduce crime by the person detained even if he or she cannot or does not calculate cost-benefit analysis. Admittedly, incapacitation lacks the enormous potential efficiency of general deterrence. That is, it can have a crime-control effect only on the offender at hand. However, it does work.

The problem here is that, first, the current practice in the application of LWOP sentences may be difficult to justify and, second, it may be difficult more generally to justify incapacitation as a distributive principle for criminal liability and punishment. As a mechanism for preventive detention, criminal sentencing may be inefficient and unfair; preventive detention can be efficient and fair only when done in a civil commitment system that openly admits it is in the preventive detention business and adheres to the limits and procedures that logically follow from that purpose.[22]

For incapacitation to be effective as a distributive principle, one must be able to identify persons who will commit offenses in the future, preferably with a minimum of "false positives" (persons predicted to be dangerous who in fact would not commit an offense). Presently, however, the behavioral sciences have only a limited ability to make such predictions accurately. "False positives" commonly exceed "true positives." They are problematic both because they are costly—one estimate put the average cost of each life sentence at $1 million[23]—and because they seriously intrude on liberty when no crime justifying such intrusion would have in fact occurred.

Instead of examining each offender to determine the person's actual present dangerousness, the current system uses prior criminal records as a proxy for dangerousness—prompted by a perceived need to "cloak" preventive detention to make it look like criminal justice. Prior record has some correlation with dangerousness but is only a rough approximation, and its use in preventive detention guarantees errors of both inclusion and exclusion. A behavioral scientist's ability to predict future criminality using all available data is poor;[24] using the proxy of prior criminal history as the basis for prediction is even less accurate. It is often true that a person who has committed an offense will do so again. But it is also frequently false—many offenders do not commit another offense.[25] An explicit assessment of dangerousness would reveal that many second-time offenders are no longer dangerous, yet these offenders can receive long preventive terms under habitual offender statutes and criminal-history-based guidelines. At the same time, a direct and explicit reliance on dangerousness, rather than its proxy of criminal record, would reveal that many first-time offenders are dangerous, but these offenders are not preventively detained under habitual offender statutes and criminal-history-based guidelines.[26]

Indeed, this particular cloaking device stands good prevention on its head. Evidence suggests that criminality is highly age related.[27] Whether due to changes in testosterone levels or something else, the offending rate drops off steadily for individuals beyond their twenties. The prior-record cloak leads us to ignore younger offenders' crimes when they are running wild and to begin long-term imprisonment, often life imprisonment under three-strikes, once the natural forces of aging would naturally rein in the offenders. Offenders with their criminal careers before them are not detained because they have not yet compiled their criminal résumés, whereas offenders with their criminal careers behind them are detained because they have the requisite criminal records. Such a scheme produces a costly and wasteful prevention system of prisons full of geriatric or soon-to-be geriatric life-termers. Simultaneously, the scheme leads to ineffective prevention, because the system does little or nothing during that period in a criminal's life when the need for preventive detention is greatest. A rational and cost-effective preventive detention system would more readily detain young offenders during their crime-prone years and release them for their crime-free older years. Yet the need to cloak preventive detention with deserved punishment prompts the use of prior records as a substitute for actual dangerousness.

An equally counterproductive aspect of the cloaked system is its mandating of fixed ("determinate") sentences soon after a guilty verdict or plea. In determining the length of a deserved sentence, all the relevant information is known at the time of sentencing—the nature of the offense and the personal culpability and capacities of the offender. Thus, sentencing judges determining deserved punishment have little reason to impose any sentence other than a fully determinate one (that is, one that sets the actual release date) soon after trial. A system that instead allows a subsequent reduction of sentence, as by a parole board, undercuts deserved punishment. Citizens become cynical that a just sentence will be undermined by early release. It is this cynicism that gives rise to the demands for "truth in sentencing" and the legislative response of establishing determinate terms and abolishing early release on parole.[28]

The cloaked preventive detention system, to maintain its justice cloak, must follow this practice of imposing determinate sentences soon after trial. But this practice is highly inappropriate for effective preventive detention. It is difficult enough to determine a person's present dangerousness—whether he or she would commit an offense if released today. It is all the more difficult to predict an offender's future dangerousness—whether he or she would commit an offense if released at some future date, such as at the end of the deserved punishment term. It is still more difficult, if not impossible, to predict precisely how long the future preventive detention will need to last. Yet that is what determinate sentencing demands: the imposition of a fixed term that predicts preventive detention needs far in the future.

A sentencing judge or guideline drafter is left to the grossest sort of speculation, inevitably doomed to setting either a term too long—thus unfairly detaining a nondangerous offender and wasting preventive resources—or a term too short—thus failing to provide adequate prevention. In deciding between these two bad choices, decision-makers commonly opt for errors of the first sort rather than the second, with the result, as has recently been the case, of harsher prison terms. A rational preventive detention system would do what current civil commitment systems do: make a determination of present dangerousness in setting detention for a limited period, commonly six months, and then periodically revisit the decision to determine whether the need for detention continues.[29]

A preventive detention system hidden behind the cloak of criminal justice not only fails to protect the community efficiently but also fails to deal fairly with those who are being preventively detained. As noted earlier, the inaccuracies created by the use of prior records as a substitute for actual dangerousness result in the unnecessary detention of a greater number of nondangerous offenders. The inaccuracies created by the use of determinate sentences can have the same effect. In cases in which a nonincarcerative sentence would provide adequate protection, the use of a prison term provides one more example of needless restraint.

The irrationalities of the cloak of criminal justice extend to other aspects of the preventive detention system, such as the conditions of detention. Punitive conditions are entirely consistent with a punishment rationale for incarceration. But if an offender has served the portion of his or her sentence justified by deserved punishment and continues to be detained for preventive reasons, punitive conditions become inappropriate. Similarly, an offender being preventively detained should logically have a right to treatment, especially if such treatment can reduce the length or intrusiveness of the preventive detention—a specialized application of the principle of minimum restraint. If treatment can reduce the necessary individual sacrifice,[30] the offender ought to receive it.

One might achieve the preventive detention goal with greater accuracy, fewer wasted resources, and less unjustified intrusion on liberty—avoiding the criminal justice system's regular conflict with desert—by relying instead on an open civil preventive detention system, as currently exists to civilly commit persons who are dangerous because they are mentally ill or have a contagious disease or drug dependency. If preventive detention can be more effective when performed apart from the criminal justice system, and if such separation avoids the crime-control cost of conflicts with empirical desert (discussed later), it seems difficult to justify using incapacitation as a distributive principle for criminal liability and punishment.

III. Justifying LWOP under a Distributive Principle of Desert

An alternative justification for a sentence of LWOP is that the offender simply deserves the extreme sentence, to match the extreme seriousness of his or her crime. The traditional desert rationale sees doing justice as a value in itself, which requires no further justification. Such "deontological desert," as it has been called, focuses on the extent of the offender's moral blameworthiness for his or her offense and seeks punishment that mirrors that degree of blameworthiness. Unfortunately, many of the offenses on which LWOP sentences are based, especially under habitual offender statutes, drug offenses, and felony murder rules, do not involve intentional killings, the most serious offenses, and thus are not appropriate under a desert analysis for this most serious sentence.

A different form of desert—what has been called "empirical desert"— focuses on doing justice not for its own sake but rather for its crime-control potential. Perhaps LWOP sentences can find better justification under a distributive principle of empirical desert? Unfortunately for LWOP, it does not.

On the contrary, the studies only highlight how badly the current practice of common LWOP sentences deviates from lay intuitions of justice, thus having the effect of undermining the criminal law's moral credibility with the community it governs and thereby undermining its crime-control effectiveness.

A. LWOP and the Ordinal Ranking Demands of Desert

The central concern for both deontological and empirical desert is not the absolute amount of punishment to be imposed but rather the relative amount of punishment among cases of differing degrees of moral blameworthiness.[31] The focus is on ensuring that the offender receives the amount of punishment that puts the offender in his or her proper ordinal rank among all other offenders of greater and lesser blameworthiness.[32] Of course, once a society has committed itself to a particular high-end point for its punishment continuum, which all societies must do (be it the death penalty or life imprisonment or something less), the ordinal rank of any given case necessarily converts to a specific amount of punishment: the amount of punishment that sets the offender at his or her appropriate ordinal rank. (The limited punishment continuum must accommodate a very high number of cases of distinguishable degrees of blameworthiness.) However, the amount of punishment itself has no magical significance. If the end point of the punishment continuum changes, the amount of punishment that an offender deserves also changes, to that amount of punishment that is necessary for the offender to keep his or her proper ordinal rank. This is why, even though different jurisdictions may have different high-end points on the punishment continuum, each can set a specific amount of punishment that each offender deserves depending on the offender's degree of relative blameworthiness.

The problem with current LWOP practice under a desert distributive principle is that it fails to take account of the sometimes dramatic differences in moral blameworthiness among serious offenses. As has already been noted, many LWOP sentences are imposed under habitual offender statutes when the current offense (and past offenses) are not even killings. While the offense at hand might well be serious, it is not as serious as a planned intentional killing, and to treat the two cases the same is to trivialize the greater blameworthiness of the more serious offense. For example, when thirty-year-old William James Rummel offered to fix a bar's broken air conditioner for $129.75 with no intention of doing so—continuing his career of petty larceny and fraud—he was caught and convicted of theft, a felony under then-existing state law. After the state presented evidence of two prior felonies, a three-strikes recidivist statute required that Rummel receive a sentence of life in prison. The U.S. Supreme Court denied his appeal, concluding that the statute did not violate the Eighth Amendment's prohibition against cruel and unusual punishment. Rummel's crime, a minor fraud, hardly seems to deserve life imprisonment. Indeed, the cumulative effect of his entire criminal career—whether or not he had been formally sanctioned and punished for his earlier crimes—does not seem to merit such severe liability, at least on desert grounds.[33]

Similarly, many drug offenses may be serious, but it would be a gross distortion of desert to say they are as blameworthy as a planned intentional killing of a human being. The case of Ronald Allen Harmelin is on point. Harmelin was driving through Detroit in the early morning when he made an illegal U-turn through a red light. After he was pulled over and arrested for marijuana possession, a police search uncovered 672 grams of cocaine in the car's trunk—an amount approximately equal in size to one and half soda cans. Harmelin, who had no prior police record, was convicted under a Michigan drug statute and was sentenced to a mandatory term of life in prison without the possibility of parole, which the Supreme Court upheld as constitutional in *Harmelin v. Michigan*.[34]

The same is true for LWOP sentences even for homicide—they commonly disregard the greater blameworthiness of planned intentional killings. Under the felony murder rule, an offender may have played no role in the killing; the offender's homicide liability may rest entirely on his or her complicity in the underlying offense, such as a theft or a robbery. While that may well be a serious offense, it is not as serious as an intentional killing, and to treat it the same is to trivialize the greater blameworthiness of the intentional killing. Even among killers there may be vastly different degrees of blameworthiness. Under the felony murder rule, offenders may have been at most negligent or reckless in causing the death, which makes them markedly less blameworthy than an offender who planned to kill.[35]

Consider the case of Jerry Moore, who agreed to help an acquaintance burglarize a house while its owner was away.[36] Although neither man was armed when they arrived at the house, Moore's acquaintance found a gun in the house and shot the owner upon his unexpected return. At trial, the prosecution relied on Louisiana's felony murder rule to convict Moore. He was sentenced to life imprisonment at hard labor without the possibility of parole.

The disproportionality between life sentences generally and the seriousness of the underlying offenses is illustrated by the broader statistics on their use. A majority of the life sentences in state courts are imposed for nonhomicide offenses.[37] At the same time, three-quarters of state murder sentences are less than life.[38] In other words, the majority of life sentences that are for offenses other than homicide are being punished more severely than three-quarters of murders. Desert requires that the uniquely high sentence of life imprisonment be reserved for the most egregious cases.

B. The Utility of Desert

The preceding desert analysis suggests that LWOP sentences are commonly imposed on offenders who are significantly less blameworthy than the most serious cases—cases that deserve this most serious punishment. However, the analysis is based on a reasoned notion of moral blameworthiness—desert as reasoned from principles of right and good by moral philosophers. Perhaps LWOP cases, while not justified under this notion of desert, might be justified under "empirical desert," in which the measure of what is deserved is not derived from principles of moral philosophy but rather is measured from the shared intuitions of the community governed by the law. That is the subject of part III.C. A preliminary question, however, is why one might want to rely on such an empirical view of desert, rather than a deontological view.

Clearly, empirical desert is not "true justice" in a transcendent sense. It is not justice but only what the community's intuitive principles think is justice. The community could be wrong. The difference between deontological desert—derived from the reasoned analysis of moral philosophy—and empirical desert—derived from the shared intuitions of justice of the community to be bound by the law—can produce important differences in liability and punishment rules. For example, moral philosophers disagree about the significance of resulting harm, and each side of the debate has plausible arguments to make.[39] In contrast, all available data suggest there is a nearly universal and deeply held view among laypersons that resulting harm, such as a resulting death, does matter. The absence of a resulting death reduces an offender's blameworthiness, and its presence increases it, even if the actor's conduct and culpable state of mind are the same.[40]

One set of reasons offered to support empirical desert as the distributive principle for criminal liability and punishment rests on notions of democracy: it ought to be the people's view of desert that controls, not that of the moral philosophy elite.[41] That dispute is one of political theory, which will not be pursued here.

A different rationale that has been offered is purely utilitarian. It looks to the crime-control benefits of relying on criminal liability and punishment rules that are perceived as just by the community they govern and thus have a greater ability to harness the powerful forces of normative influence and internalized norms. If current LWOP practice conflicts with community views, as the following section suggests it does, it may do more harm than good in fighting crime because it undermines the criminal law's moral credibility and thereby its crime-control effectiveness. Indeed, there is reason to believe that normative crime-control mechanisms can be more powerful and effective than traditional mechanisms of coercive crime control (i.e., deterrence, rehabilitation, and incapacitation of the dangerous). This is due in part to the strength of the normative forces that arise from criminal law's moral credibility and in part to the practical limitations and weaknesses of traditional coercive crime-control mechanisms.[42] Let me try to summarize the practical attraction of empirical desert.[43]

Some of us have argued that empirical desert is an attractive distributive principle because by building the moral credibility of the system, it can promote cooperation and acquiescence with it, harness the powerful social influences of stigmatization and condemnation, and increase the criminal law's ability to shape societal and internalized norms.

Some of the system's power to control conduct derives from its potential to stigmatize violators—with some potential offenders this is a more powerful, yet essentially cost-free, control mechanism when compared to imprisonment. Yet the system's ability to stigmatize depends on its having moral credibility with the community. That is, for a conviction to trigger community stigmatization, the law must have earned a reputation for following the community's view on what does and does not deserve moral condemnation. Liability and punishment rules that deviate from a community's shared intuitions of justice undermine this reputation.

The effective operation of the criminal justice system depends on the cooperation, or at least the acquiescence, of those involved in it—offenders, judges, jurors, witnesses, prosecutors, police, and others. To the extent that people see the system as unjust—as in conflict with their intuitions about justice—that acquiescence and cooperation is likely to fade and be replaced with subversion and resistance. Vigilantism may be the most dramatic reaction to a perceived failure of justice, but a host of other less dramatic (but more common) forms of resistance and subversion have shown themselves. Jurors may disregard their jury instructions. Police officers, prosecutors, and judges may make up their own rules. Witnesses may lose an incentive to offer their information or testimony. And offenders may be inspired to fight the adjudication and correctional processes rather than participating and acquiescing in them.

Criminal law also can an have effect in gaining compliance with its commands through another mechanism: if it earns a reputation as a reliable statement of what the community perceives as condemnable, people are more likely to defer to its commands as morally authoritative and as appropriate to follow in those borderline cases in which the propriety of certain conduct is unsettled or ambiguous in the mind of the actor. The importance of this role should not be underestimated; in a society with the complex interdependencies that characterize ours, a seemingly harmless action can have destructive consequences. When the action is criminalized by the legal system, a citizen ought to respect the law and forbear the action, even though he or she may not immediately intuit the law's rationale. Such deference will be facilitated if citizens believe that the law is an accurate guide to appropriate prudential and moral behavior.

Perhaps the greatest utility of empirical desert comes through a more subtle but potentially more influential mechanism. The real power to gain compliance with society's rules of prescribed conduct lies not in the threat of official criminal sanction but in the influence of the intertwined forces of social and individual moral control. The networks of interpersonal relationships in which people find themselves, the social norms and prohibitions shared among those relationships and transmitted through those social networks, and the internalized representations of those norms and moral precepts control people's conduct. The law is not irrelevant to these social and personal forces. Criminal law in particular plays a central role in creating and maintaining the social consensus necessary for sustaining moral norms. In fact, in a society as diverse as ours, the criminal law may be the only societywide mechanism that transcends cultural and ethnic differences. Thus, the criminal law's most important real-world effect may be its ability to assist in the building, shaping, and maintaining of these norms and moral principles. It can contribute to and harness the compliance-producing power of interpersonal relationships and personal morality but will only be effective in doing so if it has sufficient credibility.

The extent of the criminal law's effectiveness in all these respects—in bringing the power of stigmatization to bear; in avoiding resistance and subversion to a system perceived as unjust; in gaining compliance in borderline cases through deference to its moral authority; and in facilitating, communicating, and maintaining societal consensus on what is and is not condemnable—is to a great extent dependent on the degree to which the criminal law has gained moral credibility in the minds of the citizens governed by it. Thus, the criminal law's moral credibility is essential to effective crime control and is enhanced if the distribution of criminal liability is perceived as "doing justice"—that is, if it assigns liability and punishment in ways that the community perceives as consistent with its shared intuitions of justice. Conversely, the system's moral credibility, and therefore its crime-control effectiveness, is undermined by a distribution of liability that conflicts with community perceptions of just desert.

As the next section demonstrates, recent studies show that many modern crime-control doctrines, especially those regularly resulting in LWOP, seriously conflict with the community's shared intuitions of justice, that this conflict undermines the criminal law's moral credibility, and that this loss has practical consequences that undermine the criminal justice system's crime-fighting effectiveness.[44] The findings are consistent with previous studies.[45]

A greater appreciation for the value of desert as criminal law's distributive principle, and a greater appreciation for the limits and costs of alterative distributive principles, such as deterrence and incapacitation, may help explain the dramatic American Law Institute amendment of the Model Penal Code for the first time in the forty-eight years since its enactment.

As is well known, since 1962, the Code has been the model for the codification of criminal law in three-quarters of the states and, for the most part, has represented the epitome of instrumentalist thinking. The Code's original section 1.02 made clear its preventive focus. While the original Code was not entirely indifferent to the offender's moral blameworthiness, it did not direct liability and punishment to track desert but rather looked to a wide range of goals, touching on both deterrence and incapacitation of the dangerous.[46] The new Model Penal Code's "purposes" provision, in contrast, sets desert as the primary distributive principle for criminal liability and punishment— that is, the blameworthiness of the offender. Alternative distributive principles such as deterrence, incapacitation, or rehabilitation may be pursued only to the extent that they remain within the bounds of desert.[47]

This rather dramatic turnabout is in part the result of a growing recognition of the weaknesses and limitations of the traditional mechanisms of coercive crime control. As noted in part II, deterrence may work under the right conditions, but those conditions may be the exception rather than the rule,[48] and incapacitation of the dangerous clearly does work but generally can be achieved more effectively and more fairly when done through a civil system that operates apart from the criminal justice system and that openly admits its preventive detention purpose.[49] However, the Model Penal Code's turn to desert also may reflect a growing appreciation that doing justice is an attractive distributive principle because it advances both justice and instrumentalist crime control.

C. LWOP and the Disutility of Injustice

Does the current LWOP practice conflict with the community's shared intuitions of justice? The available evidence suggests that it does. Consider, for example, a recent study of the most common and politically popular crime-control doctrines, including three-strikes and other habitual offender legislation, felony murder, and drug-offense sentencing. As noted previously, many LWOP sentences result from these doctrines.

Subjects were first asked to rank and then assign a specific punishment to a wide range of cases, from minor theft to minor assault to robbery to aggravated assault to manslaughter to various versions of intentional killings. This ranking established "milestones" along the continuum of punishment. There was high agreement among the subjects on the relative rankings of these "milestone" cases. Subjects were then asked to add to the rankings another set of cases involving the crime-control doctrines just noted and then to assign specific punishments to them. These included two felony murder cases, *Moore* (J on fig. 4.1) and *Heacock* (H), in which sentences were given of LWOP and forty years, respectively; a three-strikes case, *Rummel* (F), in which a sentence of life was given; a drug case, *Harmelin* (G), in which LWOP was given; and two cases in which the abolition or severe narrowing of the insanity defense led to convictions of mentally ill persons, *Yates* (K) and *Clark* (I), who both received life sentences.

The results of the participants' rankings and sentencing are summarized in figure 4.1. The "milestone" cases are on the left; the crime-control cases are on the right. The subjects' sentences are shown in solid lines; the law's actual sentences are shown in dotted lines. As is apparent, the subjects ranked the crime-control cases dramatically less seriously than the law provided. Compare the subjects' judgments, represented by the solid lines on the right, to the law's determination, represented by the dotted lines on the right. Each numbered point on the scale represents about a doubling of punishment, so the difference between the solid and the dotted lines is dramatic—with the law sometimes imposing a sentence many times more severe than the subjects' sentence.[50] While the sentences imposed by the law were fully consistent with the law's requirements—that is, these were not rogue judges but rather judges following the law's direction to provide the sentences that

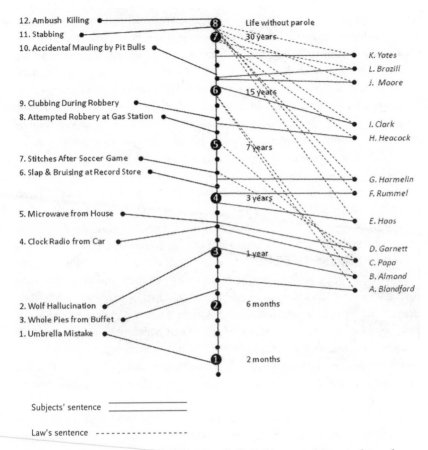

12. Ambush Killing
11. Stabbing
10. Accidental Mauling by Pit Bulls

Life without parole

30 years

K. Yates
L. Brazill
J. Moore

15 years

9. Clubbing During Robbery
8. Attempted Robbery at Gas Station

I. Clark
H. Heacock

7. Stitches After Soccer Game
6. Slap & Bruising at Record Store

7 years

G. Harmelin
F. Rummel

3 years

5. Microwave from House

E. Haas

4. Clock Radio from Car

1 year

D. Garnett
C. Papa
B. Almond
A. Blandford

2. Wolf Hallucination
3. Whole Pies from Buffet
1. Umbrella Mistake

6 months

2 months

Subjects' sentence ——————

Law's sentence - - - - - - - - - - -

Fig. 4.1. Comparison of layperson judgments of relative blameworthiness to those of modern crime-control doctrines

would express the doctrine—they clearly are dramatically higher than what the subjects thought was just.

For example, in the *Moore* case (J on fig. 4.1), the felony murder case discussed earlier, the subjects rated the offense as being more serious than a clubbing during a robbery but less serious than an accidental mauling by pit bulls, and gave it an average sentence of 17.7 years.[51] In the *Heacock* case (H on fig. 4.1), another felony murder case, the defendant was given a *de facto* life sentence of forty years, yet the subjects, in contrast, thought that the offense was more serious than an assault that required stitches but less serious than an attempted robbery at a gas station, and gave the defendant an average sentence of 10.7 years.[52] The three-strikes case shows a similar pattern. In *Rummel* (F), the defendant is given a sentence of life, yet the subjects see the offense, a minor fraud after a string of previous offenses, as more serious than stealing a microwave from a house but less serious than an assault involving a slap that bruised, and on average gave a sentence than 3.1 years, even while knowing of Rummel's criminal history.[53] The same pattern is apparent in the drug cases. In *Harmelin* (G), the offender gets life without parole for transporting a pound and a half of cocaine in his car, even though he had no criminal record. In contrast, the subjects saw the offense as more serious than a slap with bruising but less serious than an assault causing stitches, and gave an average sentence of 4.2 years.[54]

Does it matter that current practice conflicts with the community's shared intuitions of justice? The available evidence suggest that it does. Another part of the same recent study tested this issue. The study asked subjects the extent of their willingness to assist and to defer to the criminal law in a variety of situations. For example, the questions asked the extent of the subjects' willingness to help police by reporting a crime, to turn in contraband they found, to accept and internalize judgments that the law made about the condemnability of certain conduct, or to conform their own conduct to what the law requires.[55] The subjects were told of cases in which the law's punishment judgments conflicted with those of the community, as in the cases just discussed. When subjects were later asked again about their willingness to assist or to defer to the criminal law, they showed a marked lower willingness to assist or to defer than they had originally.

While the surveys were taken over the Internet with likely little pressure for subjects to do what they might have thought the experimenters wanted, the experimenters reexamined the same issue without using the baseline comparison technique. In this version of the study, subjects were randomly divided into a "high disillusionment" group and a "low disillusionment" group. The first group was exposed to the sentences that we know they would see as unjust. The second group was given cases in which the sentences would be less likely to conflict with what the subjects would think just. Both groups were then asked the questions regarding their willingness to assist or to defer to the criminal law. The results are shown in table 4.1, reproduced from the original study.[56]

The results show that the "high disillusionment" subjects' willingness to assist or to defer was significantly lower than that of the "low disillusionment" group, which in turn was lower than that of the no-disillusionment condition (when the subjects were asked the same questions without being exposed to any sentencing).[57] The results show how people's perceptions that the criminal justice system is unjust serves to reduce their willingness to

TABLE 4.1
Study 2a Baseline and Study 2b Results

Question	No disillusionment	Low disillusionment	High disillusionment
1. Life sentence means heinous	6.46[a]	6.59[a]	5.35[b]
2. Posting was condemnable	6.14[a]	5.38[b]	5.59[a,b]
3. Financial move was condemnable	5.25[a]	5.16[a]	4.34[b]
4. Report arrowhead theft	5.93[a]	5.65[a]	4.95[b]
5. Turn in hand gun found	6.66[a]	5.40[b]	4.32[c]
6. Report dogs violation	5.15[a]	4.75[a,b]	4.43[b]
7. Return to gas station to correct	7.05[a]	6.63[a]	5.63[b]
8. Return to restaurant to correct	7.15[a]	6.47[b]	5.84[c]

Note: Where two cells on a row do not share the same letter, their values are statistically different.

assist or to defer to it and thereby undermines the criminal justice system's crime-control effectiveness.

The divide between the sentences that courts often impose and the expectations of the community might be illustrated by the case of Clarence Aaron, who in 1993 was convicted of three charges linked to a drug distribution ring.[58] At the time a promising student athlete at Southern University at Baton Rouge but in need of cash to support himself, Aaron introduced a high school friend looking for drugs to an acquaintance drug dealer. Paid $1,500 for arranging the meeting, Aaron became the center of the police's investigation. He was convicted on the testimony of his co-conspirators, all of whom received reduced sentences. The court sentenced Aaron to three consecutive life sentences without the possibility of parole.

The PBS documentary program *Frontline* interviewed one of Aaron's jurors, Willie Jordan, who before the interview did not know the severity of Aaron's sentence:

INTERVIEWER: What kind of sentence do you think he deserves?
JORDAN: Well, I wouldn't have thought a large number of years, no. Just . . . just . . . probably a short sentence. Now, what a short sentence is I don't know—three to five years, maybe something like that. I don't know.

INTERVIEWER: Do you know that he got life?

JORDAN: Life!

INTERVIEWER: Three concurrent life sentences.

JORDAN: Three concurrent life sentences. With no hope of parole?

INTERVIEWER: No hope of parole.

JORDAN: Well, that's more than I thought it would be. But see, I had no idea. Well, I'm surprised at that, I really am, that harsh a sentence. He seemed to be a pretty promising boy. Why did they get such a high sentence, I wonder? I wish I didn't know that they'd [*sic*] got life.[59]

If the goal of the desert distribution is not only to do justice but also to build the criminal law's moral credibility with the community in order to harness the powerful forces of social and normative influence, the perception and shock of injustice that one sees in juror Jordan suggests that such common use of LWOP is hurting not helping the effectiveness of the criminal justice system.

IV. Conclusion

General deterrence and incapacitation of the dangerous have traditionally been used to justify the sentencing rules that produce sentences of LWOP. Yet the best available evidence suggests that neither of these is an attractive or wise distributive principle for liability and punishment. The existence of the prerequisites for effective general deterrence are the exception rather than the rule, especially in the kinds of cases that give rise to life sentences. Incapacitation as a distributive principle—setting an offender's punishment according to his dangerousness rather than according to his blameworthiness for a past offense—is simply a form of preventive detention, and an open civil preventive detention system would be more effective in protecting society and more fair to detainees than our present system of using criminal justice as cloaked preventive detention.

While desert provides a defensible distributive principle for criminal liability and punishment, the current practice in which LWOP sentences are common cannot be justified under either principle. The central demand of desert is that greater punishment be imposed on an offender of greater blameworthiness. Current practice imposes the same LWOP sentence on offenders of significantly different degrees of blameworthiness, thereby violating desert's proportionality principle and trivializing the greater blameworthiness of the more serious case. LWOP sentences ought to be reserved for the most egregious case or, if the death penalty is available, the second most egregious case. Cases of less egregious blameworthiness ought to receive serious sentences, but sentences proportionally less than LWOP.

Nor does a distributive principle of specifically empirical desert support the current practice of common LWOP sentences. First, many, if not most, of the kinds of doctrines leading to a life sentence—such as felony murder, habitual offender statutes, and high penalties for drug offenses—have been shown to seriously conflict with the community's shared intuitions of justice. More broadly, lay intuitions of justice are quite nuanced and sophisticated. Small differences in facts regularly produce predictable differences in lay assessments of blameworthiness. As a result, the current practice of imposing the same LWOP sentence on a wide range of offenders with noticeably different degrees of blameworthiness produces regular conflicts with the community's shared intuitions of justice, which in turn undermines the criminal law's moral credibility and, thereby, its crime-control effectiveness.

As a separate matter, what is proposed here—seriously limiting the use of LWOP sentences—would also make good correctional policy. LWOP deprives inmates of hope, but hope can have powerful, positive effects. For instance, biologist Curt Richter found that rats immersed in water tended to keep themselves afloat for as many as eighty-one hours when they had previously been freed from confined areas. Rats who had not had that prior experience, thus had little hope, died within minutes.[60] Positive psychologists have seen similar, if less dramatic, effects of hope among humans.[61] High levels of hope have been shown to correlate with academic performance, athletic success, better coping abilities, and psychological adjustment.[62] "Low hopers," moreover, "are often depressed and vegetable-like in their demeanors, especially after encountering impediments."[63] They are "lethargic and have an 'I don't give a damn' attitude."[64]

Thus, it is no stretch to think that some hope of future life outside of prison, even a distant hope, can improve inmate behavior and corrections efforts. Correspondingly, taking away all hope—the hallmark of the LWOP sentence—can create difficult problems for prison administration that can affect not only the rehabilitation of the offender but also the safety and quality of life of other prisoners and correctional staff. Even the "truth in sentencing" movement, as reflected in the Sentencing Reform Act of 1984, did not go all the way to require that offenders serve all of the sentence imposed but rather directed that offenders serve only 85% of the sentence imposed, under the reasoning that the potential for a 15% discount for good behavior gave correctional officials the ability to create a more productive and safer prison environment.[65]

In other words, both justice and effective crime control, as well as sound correctional policy, support a sentencing policy that rarely imposes LWOP sentences, reserving them for only the most egregious case imaginable. This does not require a system that releases offenders early, before they have served the sentence that they deserve. It simply requires that the sentence imposed be one that does not fall at the extreme end point of the punishment continuum but rather falls on that point on the punishment continuum that puts each offender at his appropriate ordinal rank in relation to the blameworthiness of all other offenders.[66]

If we value doing justice, fighting crime, and having safe and productive correctional facilities, we should prefer a sentencing system that rarely imposes sentences of LWOP.

NOTES

The author thanks Sean E. Jackowitz, University of Pennsylvania Law School class of 2012, for his valuable research assistance.

1. Ashley Nellis and Ryan S. King, *No Exit: The Expanding Use of Life Sentences in America* (Washington, DC: Sentencing Project, 2009), 9, table 2, http://www.sentencing-project.org/doc/publications/publications/inc_noexitseptember2009.pdf. Nellis and King survey state and federal departments of corrections to compile statistics on the size of the life and LWOP populations in the country's prisons.

2. Ibid., 9–10. See also Kathleen McGuire and Ann L. Pastore, eds., *Sourcebook of Criminal Justice Statistics 1992* (Washington, DC: Bureau of Justice Statistics, 1993), 633, table 6.81s. Appleton and Grøver showed the same high growth rate for LWOP as of 2007:

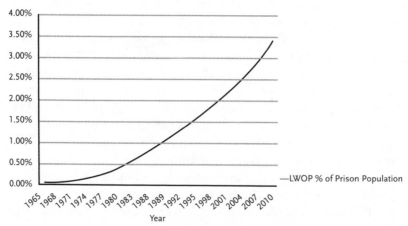

LWOP growth in relation to the U.S. prison population (actual and estimated U.S. data)

Catherine Appleton and Bent Grøver, "The Pros and Cons of Life without Parole," *British Journal of Criminology* 47 (2007): 600, fig. 1.

3. Matthew Durose and Patrick Langan, *State Court Sentencing of Convicted Felons, 2002* (Washington, DC: Bureau of Justice Statistics, 2005), tables 1.2, 1.4, http://bjs.ojp. usdoj.gov/index.cfm?ty=pbdetail&iid=1534. In 2002, only 41.2% of people serving life sentences in state prisons had been convicted of homicide. The remaining 58.8% included those whose most serious offense was some other violent crime such as rape or robbery (29.8%), a drug offense (15.4%), burglary (3.8%), or a weapons offense (0.6%).

4. See, e.g., Ala. Code § 13A-5-9(c) (LexisNexis 2005) (mandating LWOP for fourth-time defendants convicted of a Class A felony when one of the previous convictions is a Class A felony); Ark. Code Ann. § 5-4-501(d)(1)(A) (LexisNexis 2006) (mandating LWOP for defendants convicted of a Class Y felony with two prior violent felony convictions); Ga. Code Ann. § 17-10-7(b)(2) (LexisNexis 2008) (mandating LWOP upon conviction of a second "serious violent felony"); Miss. Code Ann. § 99-19-83 (West 2006) (mandating LWOP for third felony conviction when defendant has already served at least one year in prison and one of the prior convictions was for a violent felony); Wash. Rev. Code § 9.94A.570 (West 2003) (mandating LWOP for "persistent offender[s]," i.e., an offender convicted of a "most serious offense" who has been twice previously convicted of a most serious offense).

5. It would seem difficult to justify LWOP under rehabilitation or special deterrence rationales because both of those presume that the offender will be released back to society at some point. They are being rehabilitated against or deterred from further offenses upon their release.

6. Julian H. Wright, Jr., "Life without Parole: The View from Death Row," *Criminal Law Bulletin* 27 (1991): 353. For a compilation of other arguments building on general deterrence rationales (as well as incapacitation and desert rationales), see Appleton and Grøver, "Pros and Cons," 597–615.

7. For instance, former Senate majority leader Trent Lott explained the need for a federal three-strikes statute by noting that "there is no doubt that a small hardened group of criminals commit most of the violent crimes in this country" and that "many of the people involved in these crimes are released again and again because of the 'revolving door' of the prison system." 139 Cong. Rec. 27,822–23 (1993).

8. Danya W. Blair, "A Matter of Life and Death: Why Life without Parole Should Be a Sentencing Option in Texas," *American Journal of Criminal Law* 22 (1994): 198–99. See also Appleton and Grøver, "Pros and Cons," 603–4.

9. See n. 47 below.

10. Spaziano v. Florida, 468 U.S. 447, 461 (1984). For a collection of authorities citing desert as a primary distributive principle, see Paul H. Robinson, "Competing Conceptions of Modern Desert: Vengeful, Deontological, and Empirical," *Cambridge Law Journal* 67 (2008): 145–46nn. 4–9.

11. Appleton and Grøver, "Pros and Cons," 605.

12. For a more detailed discussion, see Paul H. Robinson, "Does Criminal Law Deter?," chap. 3 in *Distributive Principles of Criminal Law: Who Should Be Punished How Much?* (New York: Oxford University Press, 2008).

13. See Paul H. Robinson, "Felony-Murder," sec. 14.3 in *Criminal Law* (New York: Aspen, 1997). The traditional felony murder rule has two components. First, it imposes liability for murder for any killing that occurs in the course of the attempt, commission, or flight from a felony. Second, accomplices to the felony are considered accomplices in

the murder. Although nearly every jurisdiction limits the traditional felony murder in some way, the limitations are far from consistent. For example, some require the killing to be a probable consequence of the unlawful act. Others may also require that underlying felony be a *malum in se* offense, an offense evil in and of itself.

14. See John Kimpflen, "Application; Federal 'Three Strikes' Law," sec. 6 in *American Jurisprudence*, 2nd ed., vol. 39, *Habitual Criminals and Subsequent Offenders* (New York: Thomson Reuters, 2008). For instance, habitual offender statutes may apply, depending on the jurisdiction, when a defendant has committed any prior felony offense or when he or she commits a felony within a certain time after a previous felony conviction. Furthermore, jurisdictions may specify enhanced penalties only for certain offenses or require a showing of a pattern of criminal conduct.

15. See Kathleen McGuire, ed., *Sourcebook of Criminal Justice Statistics Online*, table 3.120.2008, http://www.albany.edu/sourcebook/pdf/t31202008.pdf. In 2008, of instances of nonnegligent homicide for which data was available, 42.0% of victims were killed during an argument, and 7.6% were killed in circumstances involving alcohol or drugs. Regarding mental illness, one UK study found that of the five hundred homicide offenders for which psychiatric data could be obtained, 44% had a lifetime history of mental disorder, and 14% had symptoms of mental disease at the time of the homicide. Jenny Shaw et al., "Mental Disorder and Clinical Care in People Convicted of Homicide: National Clinical Survey," *British Medical Journal* 318 (1999): 1240–44.

16. According to data collected between 2002 and 2004, 60.1% of persons aged 18 or older who were arrested for homicide, forcible rape, robbery, aggravated assault, burglary, larceny theft, motor-vehicle theft, and arson reported illicit drug use in the year before their arrest. National Survey on Drug Use and Health, *Illicit Drug Use among Persons Arrested for Serious Crimes* (Washington, DC: Substance Abuse and Mental Health Services Administration, 2005), 2.

17. Federal Bureau of Investigation, *Crime in the United States 2004* (Washington, DC: Federal Bureau of Investigation, 2005), 280, table 29.

18. Federal courts convicted 25,310 defendants of felony drug offenses. See McGuire, *Sourcebook*, table 5.17.2004, http://www.albany.edu/sourcebook/pdf/t5172004.pdf. State courts convicted 262,850 defendants of felony drug offenses. See ibid., table 5.44.2004, http://www.albany.edu/sourcebook/pdf/t5442004.pdf.

19. FBI, *Crime in the United States 2004*, 280, table 29.

20. Federal courts convicted 757 defendants of felony homicide and assault offenses. See McGuire, *Sourcebook*, table 5.17.2004, http://www.albany.edu/sourcebook/pdf/t5172004.pdf. State courts convicted 102,780 defendants of felony homicide and assault offenses. See ibid., table 5.44.2004, http://www.albany.edu/sourcebook/pdf/t5442004.pdf.

21. David A. Anderson, "The Deterrent Hypothesis and Picking Pockets at the Pickpocket's Hanging," *American Law & Economic Review* 4 (Fall 2002): 295–313.

22. For a more detailed discussion, see Robinson, "Incapacitation of the Dangerous," chap. 6 in *Distributive Principles of Criminal Law*.

23. Marc Mauer, Ryan S. King, and Malcolm C. Young, *The Meaning of "Life": Long Prison Sentences in Context* (Washington, DC: Sentencing Project, 2004), 25.

24. Cf. Stephen J. Morse, "Blame and Danger: An Essay on Preventive Detention," *Boston University Law Review* 76 (1996): 126n. 39. Morse concludes that even in the closely supervised environment of a mental health institution, "the ability of mental health

professionals to predict future violence among mental patients may be better than chance, but it is still highly inaccurate, especially if these professionals are attempting to use clinical methods to predict serious violence" (ibid., 126).

25. See *Recidivism of Adult Felons*, report 97-01 (St. Paul: Office of the Legislative Auditor, State of Minnesota, 1997), 55, http://www.auditor.leg.state.mn.us/ped/1997/pe9701. htm. The Minnesota Office of the Legislative Auditor reported that 55% of all felony offenders in its study were not convicted of a subsequent offense during the three years after their initial arrest. It further found that homicide offenders had one of the lowest recidivism rates. See also Allen J. Beck and Bernard E. Shipley, *Bureau of Justice Statistics Special Report: Recidivism of Prisoners Released in 1983* (Washington, DC: Bureau of Justice Statistics, 1989), http://bjs.ojp.usdoj.gov/content/pub/pdf/rpr83.pdf.

26. The chronic spouse abuser who turns to obsessive violence when the battered spouse leaves may have no criminal history—battering spouses are often able to persuade their victims not to press criminal charges—yet the abuser may present a clear and immediate danger. Similarly, a stalking and threat offense, depending on its circumstances, may suggest a high risk of serious danger. See, e.g., John Douglas and Mark Olshaker, *Obsession: The FBI's Legendary Profiler Probes the Psyches of Killers, Rapists, and Stalkers and Their Victims and Tells How to Fight Back* (New York: Scribner, 1998), 266. Yet most such offenses would not trigger the dangerousness add-on provisions that are components of recent reforms. That is, even if the circumstances and nature of the offense suggest a life-threatening level of violence, a system that looks to criminal history rather than to dangerousness will have no grounds to detain the perpetrator.

27. For example, only 15% of people arrested for crime in 1994 were in their forties or older, although that age group made up 40% of the U.S. population. Kathleen McGuire and Ann L. Pastore, eds., *Sourcebook of Criminal Justice Statistics 1995* (Washington, DC: Bureau of Justice Statistics, 1996), 397, table 4.4. In contrast, persons in their thirties made up 25.3% of arrests but accounted for only 16.9% of the population (ibid.). Persons between the ages of nineteen and twenty-nine made up 37.1% of arrests but only 15.9% of the population (ibid.). Homicide arrest rates suggest an even greater drop-off in criminality with age: in 1993, 11.9 of 100,000 males in the thirty-five-to-forty-four age bracket were arrested for homicide (ibid., 423, table 4.18). Of those aged twenty-five to twenty-nine, the rate was more than two and a half times higher, 30.0 per 100,000 (ibid.). For those between twenty-one and twenty-four, the rate was almost five times higher, 56.8 (ibid.). Of those between eighteen and twenty, the rate was almost eight times higher, 91.3. The trend of the past several decades has been toward even less criminality by middle-aged persons. In 1970, the homicide arrest rate for males between thirty-five and forty-four was two-thirds higher than it was in 1993—19.5 per 100,000 versus 11.9 per 100,000 (ibid.). Yet the current reforms will detain a greater number of middle-aged offenders for a longer period of time.

28. One of the prime motivations for the federal Sentencing Reform Act of 1984, which among other things abolished the United States Parole Commission, was an attempt to reestablish credibility with an emphasis on "truth in sentencing" that determinate sentences bring. See, e.g., U.S. Sentencing Guidelines Manual ch. 1, pt. A, introductory cmt. (2009). The Sentencing Commission stated in its introductory notes that "Congress first sought honesty in sentencing . . . to avoid the confusion and implicit deception" arising out of the then-extant indeterminate sentencing system.

29. See, e.g., Idaho Code 66-337(a) (Michie 2000) (requiring department directors to examine a patient's need for commitment at the end of the first 90 days and every 120 days thereafter); R.I. Gen. Laws 40.1-5.3-4(f) (1997) (permitting courts to commit dangerous persons but requiring courts to review such orders every six months); S.D. Codified Laws Ann. 27A-10-14 (Michie 2000) (requiring a board to review a patient who has been committed for mental illness at least once every six months for the first year and at least once every twelve months thereafter).

30. For example, a number of encouraging studies have recently suggested that comprehensive treatment of pedophilia has a 90% or better success rate. See Robert E. Freeman-Longo, "Reducing Sexual Abuse in America: Legislating Tougher Laws or Public Education and Prevention," *New England Journal on Criminal & Civil Confinement* 23 (1997): 323.

31. For a discussion of the alternative forms of desert, including a third kind— "vengeful desert"—which has few if any supporters among modern writers, see Robinson, "Competing Conceptions of Modern Desert," 146–55.

32. Andrew von Hirsch, *Past or Future Crimes: Deservedness and Dangerousness in the Sentencing of Criminals* (New Brunswick: Rutgers University Press, 1985), 39–46. With regard to deontological desert, von Hirsch explains, "Desert should be treated as a determining principle in deciding *ordinal* magnitudes" (ibid., 39).

33. Rummel v. Estelle, 498 F. Supp. 793 (W.D. Tex. 1980). The case is described in Paul H. Robinson, Geoffrey P. Goodwin, and Michael D. Reisig, "The Disutility of Injustice," *New York University Law Review* 85 (2010): sec. II.A.

34. 501 U.S. 957 (1991). See also Robinson, Goodwin, and Reisig, "Disutility," sec. II.B.

35. For a general discussion of the felony murder rule, see Robinson, "Felony-Murder."

36. For a description of Moore's crime, see State v. Moore, No. 2006-KA-1979, 2007 WL 914637, at *1 (La. Ct. App., Mar. 28, 2007). The case is also described in Robinson, Goodwin, and Reisig, "Disutility," sec. II.F.

37. See Durose and Langan, *State Court Sentencing*, tables 1.2, 1.4.

38. Ibid., table 1.4.

39. Those who argue that resulting harm should matter include Leo Katz, "Why the Successful Assassin Is More Wicked Than the Unsuccessful One," *California Law Review* 88 (2000): 806 (arguing by hypothetical that principled moral analysis suggests that harm should be considered when assessing blameworthiness); Ken Levy, "The Solution to the Problem of Outcome Luck," *Law and Philosophy* 24 (2005): 263; Michael S. Moore, "The Independent Moral Significance of Wrongdoing," *Journal of Contemporary Legal Issues* 5 (1994): 267–71 (positing that our own experiences—we feel more guilty about our own completed misdeeds than we do about attempts, and we are dissatisfied with reasonable moral choices that produce undesirable consequences—suggest that "results matter" in the moral arena).

However, there is significant disagreement in this area. See, e.g., Joel Feinberg, "Equal Punishment for Failed Attempts: Some Bad but Instructive Arguments against It," *Arizona Law Review* 37 (1995): 119; Sanford H. Kadish, "The Criminal Law and the Luck of the Draw," *Journal of Criminal Law & Criminology* 84 (1994): 686 ("[P]unishing attempts and completed crimes differently makes no sense insofar as the goal of the criminal law is to identify and deal with dangerous offenders who threaten the public."); Stephen J. Morse, "The Moral Metaphysics of Causation and Results," *California Law Review* 88 (2000): 879.

40. For a report of empirical studies, see Paul H. Robinson and John M. Darley, *Justice, Liability, and Blame: Community Views and the Criminal Law* (Boulder, CO: Westview, 1995), 14–28, 181–96.

41. See, e.g., Andrew E. Taslitz, "Empirical Desert: The Yin and Yang of Criminal Justice," in *Criminal Law Conversations*, ed. Paul H. Robinson, Steve P. Garvey, and Kimberly Kessler Ferzan (New York: Oxford University Press, 2009), 56; Adil Ahmad Haque, "Legitimacy as Strategy," in ibid., 57.

42. Robinson, "The Strengths and Weaknesses of Alternative Distributive Principles," chap. 10 in *Distributive Principles*.

43. For a fuller account, see Paul H. Robinson and John M. Darley, "Intuitions of Justice: Implications for Criminal Law and Justice Policy," *Southern California Law Review* 81 (2007): 1–67; Robinson, "The Utility of Desert," chap. 8, and "A Practical Theory of Justice: Proposal for a Hybrid Distributive Principle Centered on Empirical Desert," chap. 12, in *Distributive Principles*; Paul H. Robinson, "Empirical Desert," in Robinson, Garvey, and Ferzan, *Conversations*, 29–39; Robinson, Goodwin, and Reisig, "Disutility," part I.

44. See Robinson, Goodwin, and Reisig, "Disutility," parts V and VI.

45. See ibid., sec. V.F.

46. The original "purposes" section of the code read,

> (1) The general purposes of the provisions governing the definition of offenses are:
>> (a) to *forbid and prevent conduct* that unjustifiably and inexcusably inflicts or threatens substantial harm to individual or public interests;
>> (b) to *subject to public control* persons whose conduct indicates that they are disposed to commit crimes;
>> (c) to safeguard conduct that is without fault from condemnation as criminal; . . .
>> (e) to differentiate on reasonable grounds between serious and minor offenses.
> (2) The general purposes of the provisions governing the sentencing and treatment of offenders are:
>> (a) to *prevent the commission* of offenses;
>> (b) to promote the *correction and rehabilitation* of offenders;
>> (c) to safeguard offenders against excessive, disproportionate or arbitrary punishment.

Model Penal Code § 1.02 (Proposed Official Draft 1962) (emphasis added).

47. The new provision reads,

> (2) The general purposes of the provisions governing the sentencing and corrections, to be discharged by the many official actors within the sentencing and corrections system, are:
>> (a) in decisions affecting the sentencing and correction of individual offenders:
>>> (i) to render punishment within a range of severity *proportionate to the gravity of offenses, the harms done to crime victims, and the blameworthiness of offenders;*

(ii) when possible with realistic prospect of success, to serve goals of offender *rehabilitation, general deterrence, incapacitation of dangerous offenders, and restoration of crime victims and communities,* provided that these goals are pursued within the boundaries of sentence severity permitted in subsection (a)(i); and

(iii) to render sentences no more severe than necessary to achieve the applicable purposes from subsections (a)(i) and (ii).

Model Penal Code § 1.02 (amended 2007) (emphasis added).

48. See Robinson, *Distributive Principles*, 21–46; Paul H. Robinson and John M. Darley, "Does Criminal Law Deter? A Behavioural Science Investigation," *Oxford Journal of Legal Studies* 24 (2004): 173–205; Paul H. Robinson and John M. Darley, "The Role of Deterrence in the Formulation of Criminal Law Rules: At Its Worst When Doing Its Best," *Georgetown Law Journal* 91 (2003): 949–1002.

49. See Robinson, *Distributive Principles*, 130–33; Paul H. Robinson, "Punishing Dangerousness: Cloaking Preventive Detention as Criminal Justice," *Harvard Law Review* 114 (2001): 1429–56.

50. The following table, from Robinson, Goodwin, and Reisig, "Disutility," sec. III.D, table 4, describes all the cases shown in fig. 4.1.

Subjects' Mean Sentences for Scenarios Compared to Actual Sentences

Scenario	Subjects' Mean Sentence	Actual Court Sentence
12. Ambush shooting	between life and death	
11. Stabbing	essentially life	
10. Accidental mauling by pit bulls	20.6 years	
L. Accidental teacher shooting (juvenile)	19.2 years	28 years w/o parole
K. Drowning children to save them from hell (insanity)	26.3 years	life
J. Accomplice killing during burglary (felony murder)	17.7 years	life at hard labor w/o parole
9. Clubbing during robbery	12.0 years	
8. Attempted robbery at gas station	9.1 years	
I. Killing officer believed to be alien (insanity)	16.5 years	life
H. Cocaine overdose (felony murder)	10.7 years	40 years
7. Stitches after soccer game	5.0 years	
6. Slap & bruising at record store	3.9 years	
G. Cocaine in trunk (drugs)	4.2 years	life w/o parole
F. Air conditioner fraud (3 strikes)	3.1 years	life

Scenario	Subjects' Mean Sentence	Actual Court Sentence
5. Microwave from house	2.3 years	
E. Sex with female reasonably believed over-age (strict liability)	*2.9 years*	*40 to 60 years*
4. Clock radio from car	1.9 years	
D. Underage sex by mentally retarded man (strict liability)	*2.3 years*	*5 years*
C. Marijuana unloading (drugs)	*1.9 years*	*8 years*
B. Shooting of TV (3 strikes)	*1.1 years*	*15 years w/o parole*
3. Whole pies from buffet	8.3 months	
A. Incorrect lobster container (regulatory)	*9.7 months*	*15 years to life*
2. Wolf hallucination	1.1 years	
1. Umbrella mistake	1.8 months	

51. Ibid., sec. II.F.

52. Ibid.

53. Ibid., sec. II.A. Similarly, in the Almond case (B), the defendant was given a sentence of fifteen years without parole, yet the subjects thought that his offense, shooting his television, was more serious than taking (two) pies from an all-you-can-eat buffet in violation of the rules but less serious than stealing a clock radio from a car, and gave a sentence of 1.1 years on average, even while knowing of Almond's criminal history (ibid.).

54. Ibid., sec. II.B.

55. Ibid., table 7.

56. Ibid., the figure, on the opposing page, which is reprinted from sec. V.D.

57. See ibid., tables 8 and 10.

58. Details taken from Jennifer Lawinski, "Locked Up for Life, Part One: The Case of Clarence Aaron," *Fox News*, December 4, 2008, http://www.foxnews.com/story/0,2933,461747,00.html.

59. Ofra Bikel, "Snitch: How Informants Have Become a Key Part of Prosecutorial Strategy in the Drug War" (includes interview with Willie Jordan), *Frontline*, PBS, January 12, 1999, http://www.pbs.org/wgbh/pages/frontline/shows/snitch/.

60. Curt P. Richter, "On the Phenomenon of Sudden Death in Animals and Man," *Psychosomatic Medicine* 19, no. 3 (1957): 191–98.

61. One prominent researcher in the field defined hope as "a positive motivational state that is based on an interactively derived sense of successful (a) agency (goal-directed energy) and (b) pathways (planning to meet goals)." C. R. Snyder, "Hope Theory: Rainbows in the Mind," *Psychological Inquiry* 13 (2002): 250. In other words, Snyder defines hope with reference to our abilities to set and pursue goals. When those goals are frustrated, Snyder speculates that "the resulting disruptive negative emotions cycle back to register on the person's dispositional and situational hopeful thinking" (ibid., 255).

62. Hope has been shown to influence students' grade expectancies, which in turn influence academic performance. Kevin L. Rand, "Hope and Optimism: Latent Structures

and Influences on Grade Expectancy and Academic Performance," *Journal of Personality* 77 (2009): 232–60. Division I college athletes with high hope scores outperformed their low-hope peers. Lewis A. Curry et al., "Role of Hope in Academic and Sport Achievement," *Journal of Personality and Social Psychology* 73 (1997): 1257–67. Adventitiously blind military veterans with high hope measures were better able to cope with their disability and enjoyed more functional ability. Warren T. Jackson et al., "Negotiating the Reality of Visual Impairment: Hope, Coping, and Functional Ability," *Journal of Clinical Psychology in Medical Settings* 5 (1998): 173–85. Lower levels of hope have been shown to be associated with greater dysphoria, depression proneness, and maladjustment. Paul Kwon, "Hope, Defense Mechanisms, and Adjustment: Implications for False Hope and Defensive Hopelessness," *Journal of Personality* 70 (2002): 207–31.

63. Snyder, "Hope Theory," 265.

64. Ibid.

65. Report on Sentencing Reform Act of 1983, S. Rep. No. 98-225, at 146–47 (1983).

66. Nor does the approach require the abolition of parole. There are good reasons why every offender released from prison should remain under correctional supervision for a period of time to assist in the transition and to help the offender construct a new life without criminality. And if there is need to preventively detain dangerous offenders beyond the term of imprisonment that they deserve as punishment for their past offenses, that preventive detention ought to be done openly and forthrightly, in a civil commitment system with all the procedures and safeguards that preventive detention logically requires.

5

Defending Life

I. BENNETT CAPERS

I have never been a defense lawyer, let alone a capital defense lawyer. Before becoming a law professor, however, I was a prosecutor. At the time, my feet were "firmly" planted on the side of seeking death.[1] The invitation to contribute to this book has prompted me to reflect on those days and on capital punishment's often-neglected step-sister, life without parole. But perhaps more interestingly, this book has prompted me to think about what it means to defend life.

I. Seeking Death

I am no stranger to seeking death. As a federal prosecutor in the U.S. Attorney's Office for the Southern District of New York, I spent several years prosecuting violent gangs, and by virtue of the Federal Death Penalty Act of 1994 (FDPA),[2] several of my cases were death eligible. What this means is that we went into death penalty mode. As required by the FDPA, we would make arrangements to have two attorneys appointed to such defendants, ensuring that one was "learned in the law applicable to capital cases."[3] We would take steps to ensure that we were complying with the Department of Justice protocol concerning death-eligible cases.[4] Defense counsel was provided the opportunity to submit any facts, including any mitigating factors, for the government's consideration in determining whether to seek the death penalty. We would then complete a Death Penalty Evaluation form and draft a recommendation to first the U.S. Attorney and then to the Attorney General's Capital Case Review Committee, detailing the strength and weaknesses of the government's case, as well as our assessment of statutory aggravating and mitigating factors. Afterward, we would travel to Washington, DC, for meetings with the Department of Justice's Capital Review Committee, then back to New York to await the Attorney General's decision whether to file a notice of intent to seek the death penalty.

Hanging over the entire process was the way race did and did not matter. Officially, the review process was carried out in a "color-blind" manner.[5] And yet race was invariably present. It was present in a defendant's name or in his gang affiliation or in the mitigating circumstances summarizing his upbringing. We were acutely aware of race and of the overrepresentation of blacks and Hispanics among the defendants who were death eligible. Race was particularly salient for me. In an office of approximately 241 prosecutors, I was one of six blacks, and many of the defendants facing death looked like me. Still, those of us on our side of the table, the side that laid claim to seeking justice, pretended that race did not matter. Looking back, I probably pretended harder than most.

For most of my defendants, the Attorney General ultimately decided against pursuing the death penalty. This is not to say there were not close calls, especially under Attorney General John Ashcroft, who was more hawkish about seeking death than his predecessor Janet Reno. There was Eladio Padilla, aka "Caco," a gang leader who, among other things, dismembered one of his victims before burying the body parts. There was Jose Erbo, aka "Pinguita," who ran a drug crew that also had a side business of murder for hire. We indicted him for carrying out nine murders. At trial, I introduced evidence of nine additional murders as evidence of the racketeering enterprise, giving him a total tally of eighteen homicides. Erbo was a prime candidate for the death penalty. What saved him was his flight to the Dominican Republic. Although I extradited him and prosecuted him in New York, the Dominican Republic made it a condition of his extradition that he not be executed.

Other times, the Attorney General directed us to seek death. For these, we really went into death penalty mode. One such defendant was Charles Michael Kee, aka "O.G. Mike." In addition to committing murder, Kee kidnapped and held hostage a sixteen-year old girl whom he kept handcuffed to a bed for two days, over which time both he and his girlfriend raped her. Kee then allowed his cousin to rape the girl before selling her to a stranger he met on the street.[6]

Mostly though, the individual defendant mattered less than the process. Once a case was approved for the death penalty, staffing was increased, additional resources were allocated, and the real adversarial process began.[7] We knew that the defense would put together a barrage of motions requiring a counterbarrage of responses. We knew that the trial judge would consider each motion with unusual care, issuing a written opinion on each. We knew that our every step would be subjected to heightened scrutiny on appeal. We knew we were in for the long haul.

As a prosecutor, I unquestioningly accepted the line that "death is different" and hence justified this heightened care and scrutiny.[8] My other defendants, either because they killed before September 13, 1994, the effective date of the FDPA, or because their involvement was limited to the drug side of the business, faced the "lesser" punishment of life without parole (LWOP),[9] but I barely gave these defendants a thought. Part of this had to do with sheer numbers. For every death-eligible defendant I prosecuted, I had a dozen or so more who were *only* facing life without parole. (Even defendants who were not officially facing life without parole might unofficially face life; for some defendants, including white-collar defendants, we would literally consult actuarial life-expectancy tables to provide us a floor for plea negotiations, the goal being to achieve the equivalent of life without parole.) But part of this also had to do with the cult of death. Our obsession with death. We—and by we, I mean prosecutors, defense lawyers, and judges—had repeated the mantra "death is different" for so long that we had come to accept it as necessarily true. We prosecuted our LWOP defendants as if they were interchangeable widgets on an assembly line, and it was clear that they were often defended the same way too. Even now, though I can remember the names of my death-eligible defendants, I have trouble remembering even one of my LWOP defendants. And no one lost sleep over racial disparities, which were even more pronounced than in death penalty cases. (All my LWOP defendants were black or Hispanic.)

Here is the thing. The whole time I was prosecuting death-eligible cases, I used to wonder what if.[10] Would prosecuting a death penalty case all the way through to the penalty phase change me? Would playing a role in a state-authorized killing change me? I never wondered that about my LWOP cases. Now, I do.

II. Life/Death

As Rachel Barkow, Marie Gottschalk, and several other contributors to this book have observed, the history of life without parole as punishment is incomplete without an understanding of the movement to abolish the death penalty. In short, one consequence of the turn from death has been a turn to life without parole.

This connection between death and life without parole is perhaps most evident in the response to *Furman v. Georgia*,[11] which effectively invalidated all existing death penalty sentencing regimes.[12] Prior to *Furman*, the punishment of life without parole was rare. The punishment of life imprisonment existed, but "life" usually meant a term of years and then eligibility for parole. *Furman,* by removing, at least temporarily, the specter of death, changed that. Unable to sentence defendants to death, states responded in two ways. They scrambled to fashion new capital punishment schemes that might pass constitutional muster.[13] And they enacted "the next best thing": LWOP statutes.

Consider Alabama. In Alabama life without parole originated as an option in capital cases in the early 1970s, resulting from general public dissatisfaction with murderers serving "life" terms and leaving prison early on parole. No specific, egregious incident sparked the Alabama legislature's adoption of life without parole. Rather, a general attitude of frustration toward a "revolving door" parole system made worse by *Furman,* with an increased fear of the paroling of violent murderers, led to Alabama moving quickly to legislate LWOP in the post-*Furman* era.[14]

Other states, similarly frustrated by *Furman's* invalidation of then-existing death penalty schemes, also passed LWOP statutes.[15] But *Furman's* effect extended beyond capital cases. States not only revised their statutes to make life without parole the default punishment for crimes that previously carried the possibility of death. They also added life without parole as punishment for many crimes previously punishable by mere "life." The result was not just a rise in the number of LWOP sentences for murderers but a rise in the number of LWOP sentences for all defendants.

When the Supreme Court decided *Gregg v. Georgia*[16] four years later and in effect ended the moratorium on the death penalty, this symbiotic relationship between the death penalty and LWOP statutes continued, but in reverse. Armed once again with the ability to seek death, prosecutors now argued *against* the adoption of LWOP statutes.[17] The reason for their opposition was simple. In trying to convince sentencing jurors to impose the ultimate punishment of death, it helped that the only alternative included the specter of parole and the risk that the defendant might one day be back out on the street to kill again.[18] In contrast, many defense lawyers and abolitionists urged the enactment of LWOP statutes: with LWOP statutes, defense lawyers could argue for a less scary alternative to death. If future danger to the public was a concern, it need concern jurors no longer; a vote for life would keep the defendant behind bars until death.

The debate over LWOP statutes in Texas illustrates this often counterintuitive relationship—that death penalty advocates would often oppose the availability of tougher incarceratory sentences, while death penalty abolitionists would often support them. In Texas, prosecutors long opposed legislative efforts to pass LWOP statutes, while death penalty abolitionists pushed for such statutes. The fight became particularly intense when an LWOP bill was introduced in the Texas legislature. A local paper explained, "Several big-city prosecutors and victims-rights groups opposed it because it would make death sentences harder to obtain, and civil liberties groups [and others] pushed for its passage to give juries more choices."[19] What caused the balance to shift decidedly in favor of the bill was a death penalty decision. In 2005, the Supreme Court decided *Roper v. Simmons*,[20] ruling that the execution of individuals for crimes committed before the age of eighteen was inconsistent with evolving standards of decency. Faced with this contraction of the death penalty, Texas prosecutors softened their opposition to the LWOP bill, ensuring its passage.[21] Many death penalty abolitionists, for their part, celebrated the new "tough-on-crime" measure, since it made the availability of a sentence of life imprisonment a real alternative to the possible sentence of death. The *Dallas Morning News* joined in the celebration, noting, "Death penalty reformers, including this newspaper, have pushed for life without parole for several years."[22]

In short, arguing that "[t]he sentence of life without parole is a stronger, fairer, and more reliable punishment"[23] and "shamelessly promot[ing] LWOP as the better option,"[24] death penalty abolitionists have often played a consequential role in advocating for LWOP statutes. In an effort to respond to the argument of death penalty advocates and prosecutors that capital punishment is the only way to ensure that rapists and murderers are not released on parole to rape and murder again,[25] many death penalty abolitionists have championed LWOP statutes. The prosecutor's ace card in urging jurors to vote death ("Do you really want to risk this man being let back out on the street?") has now given way to a strong defense argument ("Ladies and gentlemen, vote life with the confidence that this man will never be released again and will die in prison").

But again, it is not just life sentences in lieu of death. The move to enact LWOP statutes as an alternative to capital punishment has also been accompanied by a move for harsher punishments in general. We have moved to life sentences in lieu of lesser sentences. This is not to diminish the role of the so-called war on drugs and other "tough on crime" measures.[26] But this is to suggest that the move to life without parole as a substitute for capital punishment facilitated the normalization of LWOP sentences across the board. By the time the Court rejected a cruel and unusual punishment challenge to the sentence issued in *Harmelin v. Michigan*,[27] in which a first-time drug offender received a sentence of mandatory life imprisonment without the possibility of parole for the possession of 672 grams of cocaine, tough drug sentences were becoming routine. Life sentences were becoming part and parcel of our incarceratory turn.

Perhaps nowhere is this more apparent than in the rash of three-strikes laws that began to sweep the nation in the early 1990s and that were (in)famously upheld in *Ewing v. California*[28] and *Lockyer v. Andrade*.[29] In *Ewing v. California*, the Supreme Court ruled that a prison term of twenty-five years to life under California's "Three Strikes and You're Out" law did not offend the Eighth Amendment's cruel and unusual punishments clause. Never mind that Gary Ewing's sentence was for shoplifting three golf clubs, each worth about $399—or rather, as Justice O'Connor put it, "felony grand theft for stealing nearly $1,200 worth of merchandise after previously having been convicted of at least two 'violent' or 'serious' felonies." The sentence the Court upheld in *Andrade* was even more extreme and, though set as a term of years, was effectively too a life sentence. Andrade's crime was being a recidivist petty thief with a drug habit. His last outing, stealing four videotapes from Kmart when he was thirty-seven, landed him a sentence of fifty years to life. We have become a country where serving de facto life no longer seems extreme, let alone cruel or unusual. De facto life has become the new normal. And death penalty abolitionists have played a significant role in this change.

Justice O'Connor's opinion in *Ewing* acknowledges our incarceratory turn. "When the California Legislature enacted the three strikes law, it made a judgment that protecting the public safety requires incapacitating criminals who have already been convicted of at least one serious or violent crime."[30] "Recidivism is a serious public safety concern in California and throughout the nation."[31] "The State's interest in deterring crime also lends some support to the three strikes law. We have long viewed both incapacitation and deterrence as rationales for recidivism statutes."[32] What was left unsaid is that we have always been a nation of recidivist offenders. What was also left unsaid is that any claimed increase in recidivism rates seems to correlate to our increasing incarceration rates—in short, to the fact that our prisons have become criminogenic.[33] *Ewing* juridically documents our incarceratory turn and sanctions it with the well-worn shibboleths of deterrence and incapacitation. In doing so, it conveniently elides the role prison unions have played in this state of affairs[34] or the complicity of the media in fostering a culture of fear. We respond by embracing, at least when it comes to crime and policing, a culture of control.[35] We respond by governing through crime.[36] And we respond by incarcerating defendants, even petty criminals, for life or something like life. Even when we forgo death, or when the death penalty is not available, we are still controlling the manner of death, the place of death. We have gone from state-imposed executions to state-imposed death behind bars. Indeed, the only thing that seems to have tempered our incarceratory turn is our pocketbooks. Unable to afford new prisons to handle prison overcrowding, California is now granting early releases to nonviolent offenders—or at least to a few, lucky nonviolent offenders.

I wonder about the nonviolent offenders who are not so lucky. I wonder what Ewing is doing now. I wonder what Andrade is doing now. And I wonder too about all the other faceless, nameless, but numbered prisoners serving life sentences.

III. Seeking Life

The current state of affairs would not exist, I am convinced, but for the role many death penalty abolitionists have played in attempting to eradicate capital punishment. Indeed, the term "abolitionists"—suggestive of slavery abolitionists—is a telling one.[37] There is the racial connection, to be sure. Slavery in this country was decidedly color coded, but so has been the imposition of the death penalty, from the antebellum laws that reserved capital punishment for black defendants[38] to the extralegal lynchings that plagued the country until the 1930s[39] to the continued influence of race as revealed in *McCleskey v. Kemp*[40] and *Miller-El v. Dretke*.[41] But what is also telling is that "abolitionist" suggests something that goes well beyond advocacy. It often suggests something beyond dedication or commitment. Often, it suggests something that approaches fanaticism or religious fervor. One thinks of Frederick Douglass and Harriet Beecher Stowe, but one also thinks of John Brown and the guerrilla warfare of Bloody Kansas and of the insurrectionist raid on Harper's Ferry. It often suggests commitment to a cause—in this case the elimination of the death penalty—at whatever costs.[42] And here, one of the costs has been the acceptance of death behind bars. Death penalty abolitionists—again, not all, but many—have defended life without parole as a commendable alternative to death. And in doing so, they have assisted in the promulgation of an array of LWOP sentences that extend well beyond capital crimes.

I once wrote that we have a curious fascination with death, including state executions.[43] Scheduled death intrigues us. I observed, "How else can we explain why so many went on-line, or to video stores, like prurient consumers of snuff films, to view the beheadings of Daniel Pearl and Nicholas Berg, in all their theatricality? During the French Revolution, women called *tricoteuses* would knit while watching executions. Now, we are the *tricoteuses*."[44]

At the time, I was referring to us, the larger public. Now, it occurs to me that, to a certain extent, the same is true of many death penalty abolitionists.[45] For too many abolitionists, state-imposed death is the bête noire. State-imposed death is all that matters. Nothing else.

All of this has gotten me thinking about the recent "successes" of the abolitionist movement. On January 11, 2003, Illinois governor George Ryan declared before an audience at Northwestern Law School,

> [Because of] questions about the fairness . . . in sentencing; because of the spectacular failure to reform the system; because we have seen justice delayed for countless death row inmates with potentially meritorious claims; because the Illinois death penalty system is arbitrary and capricious—and therefore immoral—I no longer shall tinker with the machinery of death. . . . The legislature couldn't reform it. Lawmakers won't repeal it. But I will not stand for it. I must act. Our capital system is haunted by the demon of error—error in determining guilt, and error in determining who among the guilty deserves to die. Because of all of these reasons today I am commuting the sentence of all death row inmates.[46]

Governor Ryan's decision—which in one fell swoop removed 171 Illinois inmates from death row—reverberated beyond Illinois. It brought to national attention the growing reality of wrongful convictions and DNA exonerations. The fact that Governor Ryan had previously seemed steadfast in support for the death penalty added to the significance of his decision. It mattered little that his motivation may have been to deflect attention from a growing corruption scandal. Death penalty abolitionists heralded him. But in heralding the decision to remove 171 inmates from death row, abolitionists seemed untroubled by the fact that the inmates would, for the most part, be removed instead to death behind bars, what we euphemistically call life without parole.[47] Nor was Governor Ryan concerned, stating, "I will sleep well tonight knowing I made the right decision."[48] If the concern is truly "the demon of error," then the message appears to be that to sentence someone to die behind bars as a result of error is one thing, but to sentence someone to die by execution as a result of error is another thing entirely. We are willing to play the odds and risk life, but we are unwilling to play the odds and risk death.

Or consider North Carolina's attempt to address racial discrimination in capital punishment. In 2009, North Carolina enacted the Racial Justice Act, allowing death-row inmates to use statistical data to challenge their sentences on the basis of racial discrimination, including discrimination in jury selection.[49] While the Racial Justice Act has much to commend it, it must be noted that the petitioner who demonstrates racial discrimination does not receive a new trial; rather, he or she receives a commutation of sentence to life imprisonment without the possibility of parole.[50]

I have a similar concern with the Innocence Project and what Carol and Jordan Steiker rightfully critique as the "seduction of innocence."[51] In our binary of guilty or not guilty, the focus on innocence places undue weight on exonerations, lulling us into a kind of indifference with respect to defendants who are guilty but serving unconscionably lengthy sentences. But that is only one shortcoming. The greater shortcoming is that it reifies and legitimizes a binary that should strike us as deeply problematic. As such, the movement to dismantle capital punishment by establishing that some defendants have been wrongfully executed is not a challenge to the system but a buy-in to the system. It allows lawmakers to hold as a goal the prospect of making capital punishment error free. It allows lawmakers to point to examples of actual guilt to justify the imposition of death in particular cases. And it encourages too many of us to accept guilt as sufficient alone for no-further-questions-asked imprisonment.[52]

When a defendant is sentenced to death behind bars because he was convicted of a noncapital offense and sentenced to LWOP—perhaps he was convicted of a drug crime or under a state's three-strikes law—we are not even *tricoteuses*. There is nothing to see, nothing to hold our interest. A few civil libertarians may lament the harshness of the system, but there is no collective hand-wringing. On the other hand, when a death-eligible defendant is sentenced to life without parole, or something amounting to life, because a jury determines that the mitigating factors outweigh the aggravating factors or because of reversal on appeal or as a result of executive clemency, we bring out the champagne. We engage in collective back-slapping. In high-fives. We won. We escaped death. Job well done. We go home. But for the defendant who originally faced life and the defendant who originally faced the possibility of death, the "we" is still a limited "we." He does not go home. Fresh off our indifference in the former scenario or our victories in the latter, we rarely pause to think through the significance of life without parole. We do not even recognize the irony that death behind bars is called life.

IV. Rethinking Life

Perhaps it is curious that, in thinking about life without parole, I find myself thinking about our imaginative capabilities. Some years ago, in an essay on

Andy Warhol's electric chair paintings, I wrote that what was missing from our discussions about the death penalty was something both simple and complex, "something that implicates race and gender and religion and disability and age and comfort. . . . Who are we comfortable visualizing in the chair?"[53] Now, as I think about that claim, it occurs to me that when it comes to punishment, there is at least one area where our imagination is inadequate. We can easily imagine someone sitting in an electric chair or in a gas chamber or strapped to a gurney awaiting lethal injection or even standing against a wall, awaiting death by firing squad.[54] We can imagine a death-row prisoner being escorted to his execution, a dead man walking the green mile.[55] We can even imagine a death-row inmate eating his last meal. How many of us have not wondered what last meal we would request? Where our imagination often seems inadequate is in imagining life behind bars.[56]

What do we know about life without parole? Not much, though a survey of prisoners serving life sentences in Utah is revealing. The twenty-two "lifers" surveyed were asked which sentence they would prefer: death or their current sentence of life without the possibility of parole. Eight prisoners chose the death penalty. As one lifer put it, "Despite my best efforts, I lead a pointless, monastic existence with no end in sight. . . . I live in hell." Another six prisoners were ambivalent. Only eight of the twenty-two would choose their current predicament of life without parole.[57]

We also know a little about solitary confinement. EEG studies have shown that, in as little as a week, individuals in solitary confinement exhibit diffuse slowing of brain waves.[58] The brains of those who have been confined for six months can show brain impairment on par with someone who has incurred traumatic injury.[59] Craig Haney's study of inmates at a California supermax prison revealed that many prisoners "begin to lose the ability to initiate behavior of any kind—to organize their own lives around activity and purpose."[60] Chronic apathy, depression, and despair are often the product of solitary confinement; some inmates become in effect catatonic.[61] Isolation can also lead to paranoid psychosis.[62] Tellingly, Atul Gawande, a writer and professor of surgery at Harvard, has compared solitary confinement to torture.[63]

I am opening myself up to the charge that the comparison I am making is imperfect, that the deprivations endured by those who are confined to their cells is qualitatively different from the conditions endured by lifers, many of whom are permitted interaction with other inmates. Still, it stands to reason that long-term inmates develop some of the same psychological symptoms as those in solitary confinement.[64] This is to say nothing of the overlap between those doing both or of the dehumanizing conditions endured by many inmates in general population, including the perpetual threat of violence and rape.[65] Moreover, those inmates doing stints in solitary confinement as part of a term of years have one important advantage over inmates serving life sentences without the possibility of parole. They have hope.

Hope is not a trivial thing. And one thing that we have yet to address as a society is our decision, in imposing sentences of life without parole, to remove hope. In 2009, the Court decided *Graham v. Florida*,[66] which was immediately heralded as "indisputably the Court's most important non-capital Eighth Amendment decision."[67] The issue before the Court was straightforward: whether sentencing a juvenile to life without parole for a nonhomicide offense was cruel and unusual punishment. In ruling such sentences unconstitutional, the Court noted that sentences of life without parole share characteristics with death sentences "that are shared by no other sentences." The state does not execute the offender, "but the sentence alters the offender's life by a forfeiture that is irrevocable."[68] Then the Court made a curious observation: life without parole deprives juveniles of hope. What the Court chose not to observe is this: what is true for juveniles is true of all prisoners. Hope matters.

What the Court also chose not to observe is the curious state of affairs we are in. After all, prisoners sentenced to death likely have more hope than those individuals serving life sentences without the possibility of parole or those individuals serving a term of years approaching life. After all, noncapital defendants are rarely successful in efforts to secure postconviction relief. In fact, according to one study from the 1980s, the rate of success from denial of habeas corpus relief in noncapital cases is around 7%. By contrast, as a result of the heightened scrutiny given to capital cases, the rate of some form of success for capital defendants is closer to 73%.[69] Law firms often tout the pro bono work they do on capital cases. There are far fewer people defending those who are facing "merely" life.

V. Invisible Cities and New Cities

There is another concern I have about the turn to life sentences, both LWOP and de facto life, not just for murderers in lieu of capital punishment but for almost any offender. I am concerned about the way it allows us to sideline issues of race.

The link between capital punishment and race is inescapable. Just consider our history of executing convicted rapists. Many of the early laws were racially explicit about punishments. The Virginia Code, for example, authorized the death penalty for a black man convicted of raping a white woman but set the maximum punishment for a white man convicted of rape at twenty years' imprisonment.[70] Other states followed a similar practice, removing capital punishment in rape cases for white defendants but retaining it for slaves and in some cases for all blacks, slave and free, convicted of either raping or attempting to rape white women.[71] After ratification of the Reconstruction Amendments, explicit laws racializing the death penalty disappeared, only to be replaced by what I have termed elsewhere "white-letter laws"[72] that had a similar effect. Thus, between 1930 and 1967, 89% of all of the men *officially* executed for rape in the United States were black men accused of raping white women.[73] This does not include unofficial executions committed through lynchings, which prior to 1930 already numbered in the thousands.[74] Perhaps most revealing: no one, white or black, has been executed for raping a black woman, notwithstanding the absence of significant variation in the rate of victimization of white women and black women.[75]

Even after *Coker v. Georgia*'s elimination of rape as a capital offense, the death penalty remains very much racialized, as *McCleskey v. Kemp* reminded us. Indeed, a strong argument can be made that, but for our racialized history and the continuing salience of race—in the value we put on certain lives and the indifference we show to particular deaths—this country would have followed the trend of other Western nations in abolishing the death penalty. Public support for the death penalty would have waned. One thing that keeps the death penalty alive is that we continue to imagine violent criminals as black and their victims as white and, God forbid, female.

Because of this history, capital defendants today have an important advantage over noncapital defendants, even those sentenced to life without parole. When it comes to the death penalty, the Court, for the most part, has been vigilant with respect to racial discrimination. Indeed, as I have argued elsewhere, much of the criminal-procedure protections we enjoy today are the result of this attention to race.[76] In the Scottsboro Boys case, in which nine black youths were accused of raping two white women, the Court invalidated convictions and sentences of death when blacks had been systematically excluded from the jury pool[77] and when no lawyers had been appointed to represent the defendants until the eve of trial.[78] In *Brown v. Mississippi*,[79] involving three black sharecroppers sentenced to death for murdering their white landlord, the Court overturned the convictions and death sentences when the sole evidence was confessions extracted through torture. In *Coker v. Georgia*,[80] in which the undercurrent was race even though the parties were all white, the Court ruled that the imposition of the death penalty for the crime of raping an adult woman was grossly disproportionate. In *Miller-El v. Dretke*,[81] the Court granted habeas relief to a black death-row inmate convicted of murder after finding that prosecutors had engaged in purposeful discrimination to ensure an almost-all-white jury. An even though McCleskey's statistical evidence of racial bias proved unavailing in *McCleskey v. Kemp*, it at least brought race to the forefront of every capital trial, especially when the victim is white and the defendant is not.

In short, given our history, we are vigilant when it comes to race and the death penalty. But one collateral effect of the turn to life without parole and de facto life as an alternative to death is that it renders race less visible, less pressing, less noticeable in LWOP cases. We have yet to bring the kind of concern we have brought to the imposition of the death penalty along racial lines to the imposition of life sentences or of de facto life sentences. Consider California's three-strike law. African Americans are sentenced under the three-strikes law at ten times the rate of whites.[82] Hispanics are sentenced at double the rate of whites.[83] We all know that Ewing was sentenced to twenty-five years to life for stealing three golf clubs, that Andrade was sentenced to fifty years to life for stealing four videocassettes. What the cases elide is that both defendants are black.

We live in a country that, between 1970 and 2005, increased its prison population by 628%. We live in a country where one in every one hundred persons is behind bars, where our prisons and jails now hold about 2.4 million individuals. This is more than the population of New Hampshire, more than the population of Wyoming, more than the population of Vermont. Part of this increase is attributable to the war on drugs, to be sure, but part is surely attributable to our turn to longer and longer sentences, including life without parole and de facto life. Consider more numbers. Since 1992 and 2009, the number of prisoners serving LWOP sentences has risen from about 12,400 to 41,000, an increase of more than 300%. The number of prisoners serving life sentences is more staggering. As of 2009, one in every eleven prisoners was serving a life sentence. Nationally, 35% of the individuals sentenced to death since *Gregg* have been black.[84] By contrast, nearly 50% of the individuals sentenced to life without parole are black.[85] In short, it appears that the turn to life without parole has had racial consequences that we are only beginning to attend to.

All of this makes me think of how we create invisible cities, so that we can live in new cities. It is one thing to ask what it means when the state kills. But it also has to be asked what it means when the state banishes. What does it mean when the state creates prisons that function as banishment zones, as prison cities, as invisible cities, as cities whose occupants become faceless and numbered and forgotten, as cities whose occupants are overwhelmingly black or Hispanic and overwhelmingly poor? And what does it mean for us to live in our newly configured, sanitized, and purged cities? These whiter cities? I have previously written that *how* we police and *what* we police perpetuate residential segregation along race lines.[86] But it seems that how we imprison and our incarceratory turn also function in ways that have the effect of racially reconfiguring our cities. In short, our new and improved criminal justice system plays a role in "disappearing" those who are black, those who are Hispanic, and those who are poor.[87]

And all of this brings me back to the link between slavery abolitionists and death penalty abolitionists. It is not only that we have begun to refer to this country's death penalty as our "new 'peculiar institution,'"[88] when in fact the "peculiar institution" is not the death penalty but our entire criminal justice system. It is not only that others have compared the work death penalty abolitionists do to the work slavery abolitionists did on the Underground Railroad.[89] It is the fact that, despite slavery abolitionists' commitment to ending slavery, many of them accepted the alternative of repatriating blacks[90]—of banishing blacks. It is my concern that many death penalty abolitionists, in their commitment to ending the death penalty, accept a similar alternative, except this time with more success. Now, we really are repatriating blacks, and Hispanics as well. Along racial lines, we are banishing them and, through disenfranchisement and other collateral moves, marking them as subcitizens. They are cast out to live and die in invisible, racialized prison cities, while we accept the "benefit" of now living in newly purged, whiter cities.

VI. Rethinking Punishment

In 2003, when Governor Ryan commuted the death sentence of 171 Illinois death-row inmates, commuting their sentences to LWOP, he backed his decision with the declaration, "I no longer shall tinker with the machinery of death." His choice of words, of course, was deliberate, recalling Justice Blackmun's declaration nearly a decade earlier: "From this day forward I no longer shall tinker with the machinery of death."[91] What lay behind Justice Blackmun's declaration, and in turn Governor Ryan's decision, was the realization that achieving the desired level of fairness in the death penalty—fairness from error, fairness from our racialized history, fairness from class disadvantages—was simply not achievable. Justice Blackmun was largely right, of course, as was Governor Ryan, about the "demon of error." But in an important respect, they were both wrong. In focusing on capital punishment, they were missing the forest for the trees. The problem is not simply the death penalty. Nor is the problem simply the turn to LWOP. The problem is with our entire system of punishment.

Allow me to invoke another Justice. In *Baze v. Rees*, a case upholding lethal-injection protocols, Justice Stevens posited that capital punishment in America may be the "product of habit and inattention rather than an acceptable deliberative process that weighs the costs and risks of administering that penalty against identifiable benefits."[92] The same can be said of our entire system of punishment. With 2.4 million persons in U.S. prisons and jails, with the U.S. incarcerating 25% of the world's prisoners, with our creation of invisible, racialized prison cities, of a nation of subcitizens within our larger nation, the numbers *are* the argument.

We have reached a point where if someone does something that offends our sensibilities, we arrest him for breaking the law, or if there is no law that prohibits his activity, we create one or bend existing law to serve our purposes.[93] (Consider how we have extended aiding and abetting liability, conspiracy liability, *Pinkerton*, while at the same time contracting traditional defenses such as insanity, necessity, and entrapment.) If our sentence of imprisonment is not enough to keep him from reoffending, we imprison him again and create stiffer punishments, three-strikes laws, life, LWOP, anything that the Supreme Court, with its Eighth Amendment jurisprudence, will allow. Still dissatisfied, we confine even in the absence of crime, confining preemptively, calling it civil confinement, as we did in *Kansas v. Hendricks*.[94] And we clamor for more, to the point of logical absurdities. When Bernard Madoff was sentenced to 150 years' imprisonment without the possibility of parole for carrying out an elaborate Ponzi scheme, many of us still complained that his sentence was too short. And as Jessica Henry observes in her chapter in this book, the Madoff example is but one of many.[95]

Indeed, we have reached a point where incarceration is the go-to punishment, even when incarceration cannot possibly address, or even deter, the underlying offense. (Increasing the period of incarceration for someone who commits a hate crime, for example, does nothing to address the underlying hate other than to fuel it. Similarly, incarcerating a drug addict cannot possibly deter other drug addicts from committing crimes to feed their addiction.)

And we have reached a point where the rate that we incarcerate blacks— we incarcerate blacks at a greater rate now than we did at the time of *Brown v. Board of Education*[96] and at eight times the rate we incarcerate whites—dwarfs other black/white disparities such as in unemployment (2:1), wealth (1:4), out-of-wedlock births (3:1), and infant mortality (2:1).[97]

The challenge, then, is not only to rethink the death penalty or LWOP but also to rethink our entire system of punishments. We need to rethink the current alignment of death penalty abolitionists and "tough on crime" advocates when it comes to LWOP and foster a realignment of death penalty abolitionists and sentencing reformers. We need to question, as Rachel Barkow has so eloquently done,[98] the collateral consequences to noncapital sentences as a result of the heightened scrutiny given to death penalty cases. We need to admit where the traditional rationales for punishment—the justifications now offered by the Court for sanctioning "extreme punishments"[99]—fail on their own merits, as Paul Robinson has demonstrated in the case of LWOPs,[100] and how they fail to capture other dynamics at play, such as agitation for stiffer penalties from prison unions, such as race, and such as our media-fueled culture of fear. We need to bring other language to the table, including the language of norm shifting and legitimacy, to reduce the occurrence of crime so that we can spend less time worrying about the punishment for crime. We need to reorient how we teach criminal law, which marginalizes one of the most important consequences of criminal law: how we punish. We need to find common ground. It is one thing to concede life without parole for one who murders. It is another thing to concede life without parole, or its equivalent, for Ewing or for Andrade or for Harmelin or for the thousands like them. We need to be open about race, in the way the Court in *Coker v. Georgia* could not be. And we need to recognize, as network theorists have long done,[101] that all of this is interconnected.

Conclusion

I began this chapter in response to a call, or rather challenge, from Charles Ogletree and Austin Sarat, to think about "life without parole, the new death penalty." Along the way, I have found myself rethinking my own views on the death penalty and thinking anew about our turn to life without parole as both a substitute for and supplement to the death penalty. I have thought about the role many death penalty abolitionists, however unwittingly, have played in the rise of LWOP punishments and our incarceratory turn. Mostly, though, I have found myself pondering the rise of invisible cities where we banish so many of our citizens, especially those who are black or brown, and our acceptance of the newly purged, whiter cities that the rest of us inhabit. I want to end with my own call, or rather challenge, to Charles and Austin: to think about our incarceratory turn in general and these cities that we have created and inhabit, and to imagine an abolitionist movement predicated on the notion that there is something fundamentally and morally wrong with how we punish. Loïc Wacquant recently observed that our "carceral expansion is not a destiny, but a policy means that can be questioned, slowed down, and eventually reversed by other policies."[102] The task, then, is to begin the process of reversal. That is the real challenge.

NOTES

1. I put "firmly" in quotes because, even though prosecutors in my office were given the leeway to refuse being assigned to capital cases, I considered my personal views, which bordered on agnosticism, to be irrelevant. To my mind, I was representing the United States of America, not Bennett Capers. If the government wanted death, it was the job of a "good" prosecutor to get death. That is what I thought at the time. It is only on reflection that I realize how much of my zeal was tied up with being a black prosecutor in an almost entirely white prosecutor's office, and the repeated need I felt to play against expectations and prove my toughness as a prosecutor.

2. 18 U.S.C. §§ 3591–98 (1994). The act established the death penalty as a sentencing option for over sixty offenses and set forth aggravating and mitigating circumstances to be considered in determining whether a death sentence is justified, as well as setting up a system of appeal and review.

3. 18 U.S.C. § 3005.

4. U.S. Attorney's Manual § 9-10.000

5. U.S. Attorney's Manual § 9-10.080.

6. *United States v. Kee*, 2004 WL 1542233 (S.D.N.Y. July 8, 2004).

7. The cost of prosecuting and defending a capital case can run anywhere from a million dollars to several times that amount. See, e.g., *Costs of the Death Penalty and Related Issues: Hearing on H. Bill 1094 before the Colo. H. of Rep. Judiciary Comm.*, 2007 Leg., 66th Sess. (Colo. 2007); see also James S. Liebman, "The Overproduction of Death," *Columbia Law Review* 100 (2000): 2030 (observing that executions have an average cost of $5 million in California, $3.2 in Florida, $2.16 in North Carolina, $3 million in Pennsylvania, and $3.2 in Texas). New Jersey abolished the death penalty in 2007, in part over concern about escalating costs.

8. For an excellent critique of the disparate treatment that is accorded nondeath sentences vis-à-vis capital sentences, see Rachel E. Barkow, "The Court of Life and Death: The Two Tracks of Constitutional Sentencing Law and the Case for Uniformity," *Michigan Law Review* 107 (2009): 1145.

9. Parole was abolished in the federal system in 1984.

10. Since 1988, when the death penalty was reinstated for federal crimes, a total of sixty-eight individuals have been sentenced to death in the federal system. Of those

sixty-eight, three have been executed. See Death Penalty Information Center, "Federal Death Row Prisoners," updated June 16, 2011, http://www.deathpenaltyinfo.org/federal-death-row-prisoners.

11. 408 U.S. 238 (1972).

12. Although the issue before the *Furman* Court was the "fundamental claim that the punishment of death always, regardless of the enormity of the offense or the procedure followed in imposing the sentence, is cruel and unusual punishment," the plurality decision was based on the narrower ground that the capital punishment regimes that were before the Court were invalid as applied. *Gregg v. Georgia*, 428 U.S. 153 (1976).

13. For more on this scramble, see Franklin Zimring and Gordon Hawkins, *Capital Punishment and the American Agenda* (Cambridge: Cambridge University Press, 1986).

14. Julian H. Wright, Jr., Note, "Life-without-Parole: An Alternative to Death or Not Much of a Life at All?," *Vanderbilt Law Review* 43 (1990): 529, 548.

15. Marc Mauer, Ryan S. King, and Malcolm C. Young, *The Meaning of "Life": Long Prison Sentences in Context* (Washington, DC: Sentencing Project, 2004), 6.

16. 428 U.S. 153 (1976).

17. The Court's decision in *Simmons v. South Carolina* likely fueled this opposition even further. In *Simmons*, the Court held that prosecutors arguing future dangerousness in seeking a death penalty must inform the jury of an LWOP option if one exists. 512 U.S. 154 (1994).

18. Prosecutors' assumptions that jurors are more likely to impose a sentence of death when they believe that a nondeath sentence carries the possibility of parole are supported by studies. For example, a study in Virginia revealed that most capital jurors believed a defendant sentenced to life would be eligible for parole in as little as ten years and stated that knowing about the existence of parole-ineligible sentences would significantly influence their sentencing decisions. See William W. Hood III, Note, "The Meaning of 'Life' for Virginia Jurors and Its Effect on Reliability in Capital Sentencing," *Virginia Law Review* 75 (1989): 1605, 1624–25. A Georgia study reached similar conclusions. William J. Bowers and Benjamin D. Steiner, "Death by Default: An Empirical Demonstration of False and Forced Choices in Capital Sentencing," *Texas Law Review* 77 (1999): 605, 635.

19. Mike Ward, "Life without Parole among 600 Laws Signed by Governor," *Austin American-Statesman*, June 18, 2005, A15.

20. *Roper v. Simmons*, 543 U.S. 551 (2005). *Roper* reversed the Court's earlier decision in *Stanford v. Kentucky*, 492 U.S. 361 (1989).

21. Janet Elliott and Polly Ross Hughes, "Life without Parole among Raft of Bills Signed by Perry," *Houston Chronicle*, June 18, 2005, A1.

22. Editorial, "Hits and Misses," *Dallas Morning News*, June 18, 2005, 32A.

23. Note, "A Matter of Life and Death: The Effect of Life-without-Parole Statutes in Capital Punishment," *Harvard Law Review* 119 (2006): 1838 (quoting New Jerseyans for Alternatives to the Death Penalty, *The Death Penalty: Questions and Answers*); see also Douglas A. Berman, "Extreme Punishment," in *When Law Fails: Making Sense of Miscarriages of Justice*, ed. Charles J. Ogletree, Jr., and Austin Sarat (New York: NYU Press, 2009), 175; Carol S. Steiker and Jordan M. Steiker, "Opening a Window or Building a Wall? The Effect of Eighth Amendment Death Penalty Law and Advocacy on Criminal Justice More Broadly," *University of Pennsylvania Journal of Constitutional Law* 11 (2008):

156, 158 ("[I]n order to prevent death sentences and executions, abolitionists have championed LWOP as a workable and humane alternative to the death penalty.").

24. Robert Blecker, "Less Than We Might: Meditations on Life in Prison without Parole," *Federal Sentencing Reporter* 23 (October 2010): 12.

25. Until *Coker v. Georgia*, 433 U.S. 584 (1977), the death penalty was a punishment for rape in many jurisdictions. The *Coker* Court invalidated this practice in 1977, ruling that such punishment violated the Eighth Amendment's proportionality principle.

26. In the federal system, for example, not only did the war on drugs usher in statutory minimum sentences, most famously in the case of even small quantities of crack cocaine, and maximum sentences of life imprisonment for moderate quantities of drugs. It also ushered in the abolition of parole in the federal system, so that life would in fact mean life.

27. 501 U.S. 957 (1991).

28. 538 U.S. 11 (2003).

29. 538 U.S. 63 (2003).

30. *Ewing*, 538 U.S. at 25.

31. *Ewing*, 538 U.S. at 26.

32. *Ewing*, 538 U.S. at 26–27.

33. As far back as 1973, the National Advisory Committee on Criminal Justice Standards and Goals observed that "the prison, the reformatory, and the jail have achieved only a shocking record of failure. There is overwhelming evidence that these institutions create crime rather than prevent it." National Advisory Commission on Criminal Justice Standards and Goals, Task Force on Corrections, *Report* (Washington, DC: Government Printing Office, 1973), 597.

34. Sharon Dolovich, "State Punishment and Private Prisons," *Duke Law Journal* 55 (2005): 437, 531n. 367.

35. See David Garland, *The Culture of Control: Crime and Social Order in Contemporary Society* (Chicago: University of Chicago Press, 2001).

36. See Jonathon Simon, *Governing through Crime: How the War on Crime Transformed American Democracy and Created a Culture of Fear* (New York: Oxford University Press, 2007). As Simon observes, much of governance in America today is in response to the fear of crime. This fear has not only resulted in increases in police power vis-à-vis the individual. It has also shaped other areas of the law, from the right to bear arms to immigration policy to public education and charter schools to land use and zoning.

37. Others have drawn additional comparisons between slavery abolitionists and death penalty abolitionists. Charles Ogletree and Austin Sarat, for example, have referred to the death penalty as America's "new 'peculiar institution.'" Charles J. Ogletree, Jr., and Austin Sarat, introduction to *From Lynch Mobs to the Killing State: Race and the Death Penalty in America*, ed. Charles J. Ogletree, Jr., and Austin Sarat (New York: NYU Press, 2006), 14. Another scholar has compared capital defense lawyers to the underground railroad. William S. McFeely, *Proximity to Death* (New York: Norton, 2000).

38. See Stuart Banner, "Traces of Slavery: Race and the Death Penalty: Historical Perspectives," in Ogletree and Sarat, *From Lynch Mobs to the Killing State*; see also I. Bennett Capers, "The Unintentional Rapist," *Washington University Law Review* 87 (2010): 1345 (discussing race-specific punishments for rape).

39. In the nineteenth century, lynchings in fact outnumbered state-sponsored executions. In the first few decades of the twentieth century, such lynchings constituted about a third of all executions. See William J. Bowers, *Executions in America* (Lexington, MA: Lexington Books, 1974), 40–44.

40. 481 U.S. 279, 313 (1987) (declining to invalidate a Georgia death penalty statute on constitutional grounds despite statistical evidence demonstrating that, in Georgia, the imposition of death often strongly correlated with the race of the defendant and the race of the victim). See also Randall L. Kennedy, "*McCleskey v. Kemp*: Race, Capital Punishment, and the Supreme Court," *Harvard Law Review* 101 (1988): 1388 (noting the seeming indifference of the Supreme Court to the continuing pervasiveness of racial biases in the administration of criminal justice).

41. 545 U.S. 231 (2005) (granting habeas relief to a black death-row inmate after finding that prosecutors had engaged in purposeful discrimination in using their peremptory challenges to excuse ten of eleven black venirepersons, and noting "the general policy of the Dallas Country District Attorney's Office to exclude black venire members from juries").

42. The analogy gestures toward additional concerns. After all, many abolitionists, though committed to ending slavery, were opposed to the notion of social or political equality. Many abolitionists advocated relocating blacks to Africa. Here, the comparison would be to death penalty abolitionists who are committed to ending state executions but are entirely comfortable with imprisonment for life.

43. I. Bennett Capers, "On Andy Warhol's Electric Chair," *California Law Review* 94 (2006): 243.

44. Ibid., 257.

45. The Steikers have been equally blunt: "Fewer than 50 were executed and slightly over 100 people were sentenced to death nationwide in 2007, while considerably over two million people remain incarcerated in the non-capital criminal justice system. . . . By any metric, capital punishment receives a disproportionate share of popular, political, and legal attention." Steiker and Steiker, "Opening a Window or Building a Wall?," 155.

46. George Ryan, address at Northwestern University School of Law (January 11, 2003), available online at http://www.law.northwestern.edu/wrongfulconvictions/issues/death-penalty/clemency/RyanSpeech.html.

47. Of the 171 prisoners who were either on death row or awaiting resentencing for capital offenses, Governor Ryan pardoned 4. He barred the state from seeking death for 14 prisoners awaiting resentencing, commuted the sentence of 150 prisoners to LWOP, and commuted the sentence of 3 prisoners to forty years in prison. Maurice Possley and Steve Mills, "Clemency for All: Ryan Commutes 164 Death Sentences to Life in Prison without Parole," *Chicago Tribune*, January 12, 2003, 1.

48. Ryan, address at Northwestern University School of Law.

49. N.C. 15A-2010 et al.

50. N.C. 15A-2012(a)(3).

51. Carol Steiker and Jordan Steiker, "The Seduction of Innocence: The Attraction and Limitations of the Focus on Innocence in Capital Punishment Law and Advocacy," *Journal of Criminal Law and Criminology* 95 (2005): 587.

52. Doug Berman makes a similar observation. "[M]uch of the advocacy against the death penalty can often (1) distract would-be reformers from recognizing and assailing

broader extreme punishment problems and (2) desensitize moderates and conservatives to broader problems throughout the criminal justice system." Berman, "Extreme Punishment," 174. So do Carol and Jordan Steiker. "Many of the reforms generated by an innocence focus tend to reinforce the basic 'justice' of non-capital convictions and sentences of the 'guilty,' thereby deflecting more encompassing challenges to the status quo." Steiker and Steiker, "Opening a Window or Building a Wall?," 158.

53. Capers, "On Andy Warhol's Electric Chair," 257–58.

54. There is a rich body of such images in the fine arts (Brueghel's *Justitia*, Goya's *The Third of May 1808*, Manet's *The Execution of Maximilian*, to name a few) and in film (e.g., *I Want to Live*, *The Executioner's Song*, *Dead Man Walking*, *Dancer in the Dark*, *Monster's Ball*).

55. Horace Pippin's *John Brown Going to His Hanging* is an example in the fine arts. In film, there is *Dead Man Walking* and *The Green Mile*.

56. Perhaps Alexander Solzhenitsyn's *One Day in the Life of Ivan Denisovich* comes closest, though even Denisovich is only serving a ten-year sentence.

57. Robert Johnson and Sandra McGunigall-Smith, "Life without Parole, America's Other Death Penalty," *Prison Journal* 88 (June 2008): 328–46.

58. Atul Gawande, "Hellhole," *New Yorker*, March 30, 2009.

59. Ibid.

60. Craig Haney, "Mental Health Issues in Long-Term Solitary and 'Supermax' Confinement," *Crime & Delinquency* 49 (2003): 124–56.

61. Ibid.

62. Bruno M. Cormier and Paul J. Williams, "Excessive Deprivation of Liberty," *Canadian Psychiatric Association Journal* 11 (1996): 470–84.

63. Gawande, "Hellhole."

64. It is telling that Leoš Janáček titled his opera about the monotony of prisoners serving lengthy sentences *From the House of the Dead*.

65. Eva S. Nilsen, "Decency, Dignity, and Desert: Restoring Ideals of Human Punishment to Constitutional Discourse," *University of California–Davis Law Review* 41 (2007): 111 (discussing conditions of confinement); I. Bennett Capers, "Real Rape Too," *California Law Review* 99 (forthcoming 2011) (focusing on frequency of male victim rape in prisons).

66. 130 S. Ct. 2011 (2010).

67. Robert Barnes, "Supreme Court Restricts Life without Parole for Juveniles," *Washington Post*, May 18, 2010 (quoting professor Douglas Berman).

68. *Graham*, 130 S. Ct. at 2027.

69. "Background Report on Death Penalty Habeas Corpus Issues Prepared for the American Bar Association Criminal Justice Section's Task Force on Death Penalty Habeas Corpus," *American University Law Review* 40 (1990): 53, 109.

70. Capers, "The Unintentional Rapist."

71. Ibid.

72. See I. Bennett Capers, "The Trial of Bigger Thomas: Race, Gender, and Trespass," *New York University Review of Law and Social Change* 31 (2006): 1, 7–8. Unlike black-letter law, which brings to mind statutory law, written law, the easily discernible law set forth as black letters on a white page, "white-letter law" suggests societal and normative laws that stand side by side and often undergird black-letter law but, as if inscribed in white ink on white paper, remain invisible to the naked eye.

73. See Marvin Wolfgang, "Racial Discrimination in the Death Sentence for Rape," in Bowers, *Executions in America*, 110–20.

74. See NAACP, *Thirty Years of Lynching in the United States: 1889–1918* (New York: Negro Universities Press, 1919), 7–8.

75. Capers, "The Unintentional Rapist."

76. I. Bennett Capers, "Rethinking the Fourth Amendment: Race, Citizenship, and the Equality Principle," *Harvard Civil Rights–Civil Liberties Law Review* 46 (2011): 1.

77. *Norris v. Alabama*, 294 U.S. 587 (1934).

78. *Powell v. Alabama*, 287 U.S. 45 (1932).

79. 297 U.S. 278 (1936).

80. 433 U.S. 584 (1977).

81. 545 U.S. 231 (2005).

82. Scott Ehlers, Vincent Schiraldi, and Eric Lotke, "Racial Divide: An Examination of the Impact of California's Three Strikes Law on African-Americans and Latinos" (Washington, DC: Justice Policy Institute, 2004), available at http://www.justicepolicy.org/research/2022.

83. Ibid.

84. Death Penalty Information Center, "Race of Death Row Inmates Executed since 1976," updated July 8, 2011, http://www.deathpenaltyinfo.org/race-death-row-inmates-executed-1976.

85. Ashley Nellis, "Throwing Away the Key: The Expansion of Life without Parole Sentencing in the United States," *Federal Sentencing Reporter* 23 (2010): 27–32.

86. I. Bennett Capers, "Policing, Race, and Place," *Harvard Civil Rights–Civil Liberties Law Review* 44 (2009): 43.

87. Michelle Alexander, *The New Jim Crow: Mass Incarceration in the Age of Colorblindness* (New York: New Press, 2010), 174.

88. Ogletree and Sarat, introduction to *From Lynch Mobs to the Killing State*, 14; see also David Garland, *Peculiar Institution: America's Death Penalty in an Age of Abolition* (Cambridge: Harvard University Press, 2010).

89. McFeely, *Proximity to Death*.

90. If it is true, as Michelle Alexander argues in her recent book *The New Jim Crow*, that our mass incarceration along lines of race and class shares more in common with our history of Jim Crow than with slavery, then it is also the fact that slavery abolitionists were largely indifferent to Jim Crow.

91. *Callins v. Collins*, 510 U.S. 1141, 1145 (1994).

92. 128 S. Ct. 1520, 1546 (Stevens, J., concurring).

93. See, e.g., Erik Luna, "The Overcriminalization Phenomenon," *American University Law Review* 54 (2005): 703. As John Pfaff recently observed, our prison growth in the past three decades owes less to longer sentences and more to increased admissions, with many more inmates serving short sentences. John Pfaff, "The Durability of Prison Populations," *University of Chicago Legal Forum* (2010): 73.

94. 521 U.S. 346 (1997).

95. Jessica S. Henry, "Death in Prison Sentences: Overutilized and Underscrutinized," chap. 2 in this volume.

96. 347 U.S. 483 (1954).

97. James Forman, Jr., "The Black Poor, Black Elites, and America's Prisons," *Cardozo Law Review* 32 (2011): 791.

98. Barkow, "The Court of Life and Death."

99. Berman, "Extreme Punishments."

100. See Paul H. Robinson, "Life without Parole under Modern Theories of Punishment," chap. 4 in this volume.

101. See, e.g., I. Bennett Capers, "Crime, Legitimacy, *Our* Criminal Network, and *The Wire*," *Ohio State Journal of Criminal Law* 8 (2011): 459–71.

102. Loïc Wacquant, *Prisons of Poverty* (Minneapolis: University of Minnesota Press, 2009), 5.

6

Life without Parole and the Hope for Real Sentencing Reform

RACHEL E. BARKOW

In recent years, people seeking to limit the use of life without the possibility of parole (LWOP) in the United States have won significant victories. The Supreme Court in *Graham v. Florida* declared a sentence of LWOP unconstitutionally cruel and unusual for juveniles who commit nonhomicide offenses. Some state legislatures have also limited the availability of LWOP sentences for juveniles.[1] These could be early signals that LWOP is on the same path to fundamental reform that the death penalty has been on for the past thirty years. Whether or not reform ultimately means abolition in some jurisdictions, it could at least mean more limited use and procedural safeguards. In light of these developments, this book asks whether LWOP will become the "new death penalty" in the sense of being a punishment that undergoes significant reform by either the Supreme Court or politicians.

In this chapter, I explore some reasons why it is unlikely LWOP will experience the same procedural and substantive oversight that now exists for the death penalty. The chapter begins by highlighting the problem of defining LWOP in a way that will lead to meaningful reforms. If the concern with LWOP sentences is, as the Supreme Court recently suggested in *Graham*, that they eliminate the realistic hope of release,[2] then other sentences—such as natural-life sentences for which parole is just as unlikely as executive clemency of an LWOP sentence or long term-of-years sentences—would seem to be equivalent. Once one recognizes that these other sentences are comparable, problems of administrability and line drawing pose enormous obstacles to both judicial and legislative reform efforts. The next hurdle addressed by the chapter is the puzzling question of how one should limit LWOP, assuming one can define it. Although some reformers would favor outright abolition, that is exceedingly unlikely given current Supreme Court attitudes about punishment review and American politics more generally. Thus, the question becomes, who should be eligible for LWOP and which categories of offenses and offenders will create enough public sympathy to generate favorable judicial decisions or legislative reform efforts? Outside of juveniles, the pool of candidates is shallow.

After addressing these substantive questions of scope, the chapter turns to the likelihood of procedural reforms and explains why LWOP sentences are unlikely to get the same procedural protections as capital cases. The sheer number of such cases is the largest obstacle, but the line-drawing problems are also likely to deter courts and legislators. It is one thing to say that "death is different" for purposes of constitutional analysis and quite another to say that LWOP is. If the Supreme Court were to open the door to procedural protections for LWOP that do not exist for other noncapital crimes, it is hard to see what would keep that door from opening still wider to encompass all noncapital sentences. But neither the Court nor legislative bodies have shown any willingness to provide greater procedural protections in noncapital cases.

Because the central question of this book is whether LWOP is the new death penalty, the chapter next discusses an additional significant political obstacle to LWOP reform: the capital abolition movement itself. Anti-death-penalty advocates have incentives to prevent LWOP from becoming the "new death penalty" in order to abolish the "old death penalty" and keep it from coming back. The success of abolition campaigns against capital punishment have depended heavily on the existence of LWOP, and it is unlikely that most abolitionists will join the battle to reform LWOP unless and until the death penalty is off the table as an option—and with no risk of return.

Finally, the chapter concludes with a note of caution about focusing too much on what makes LWOP a unique punishment—the path paved by the Supreme Court's "death is different" jurisprudence—as opposed to emphasizing the troublesome aspects it shares with other sentences. While a majority of the Court seems to view the extinction of hope as the main problem with LWOP,[3] that concern is in many ways a distraction. The bigger problem with LWOP, in my view, is that in too many cases it is a disproportionate punishment relative to the offense or the offender. But a concern with disproportionate sentencing is hardly limited to LWOP sentences. Any term of years sentence with or without parole can be disproportionate under the Eighth Amendment. The Court created a "death is different" jurisprudence to avoid facing the hard question of disproportionality outside the capital context. It appears to be on the road to doing the same thing with LWOP. That may be the easier path for the Court's docket and judicial management more generally, but it falls short of fulfilling the Constitution's mandate, which covers all cruel and unusual punishments, not only the ones that, in the Court's view, extinguish hope.

I. What Is LWOP?

The first problem with LWOP reform involves the definitional question. We can agree what it means to put someone to death, but defining the boundaries of life without parole is harder. The first question is what counts as "life." Must the sentence explicitly be for one's natural life, or is a sufficiently long term of years before parole eligibility also included? For example, Alaska does not have LWOP as a sanction, but it requires a mandatory 99-year term of incarceration for certain homicides.[4] Is that comparable? Will an 80-year sentence count as life? Do we take into account the age of the offender at sentencing, such that a 10-year sentence for an 80-year-old counts?

Equally difficult is determining what it means to say the sentence is "without parole." In some cases, this question will be easy to answer. The federal government and many states have abolished parole outright for all offenses or some category of offenses.[5] Things get more complicated when parole is technically available but rarely if ever given in practice. For example, California's parole grant rate has been less than 5% in recent years.[6] California prisoners serving life sentences—a full 20% of the prison population in California[7]—fared even worse, with a parole grant rate of less than 1%.[8] In former governor Gray Davis's five years in office, he adopted "a virtual no-parole-for-murderers policy," freeing only six individuals, five of whom were women who had been victims of domestic abuse.[9] Is parole meaningful when there is a greater than 99% chance it will never be granted? If the remote chance of executive clemency was not enough in *Graham* to save LWOP sentences for juveniles who were guilty of nonhomicide offenses, would the equally rare possibility of parole also fall short?

There is the further question of when an offender should have the opportunity for parole. For juveniles, must it occur once he or she reaches adulthood? Would a wait of no more than 15 years be appropriate?[10] Can it happen at the end of one's life? At oral argument in *Graham*, Graham's lawyer seemed to concede that a juvenile convicted of a nonhomicide offense could be forced to wait 40 years for a parole hearing.[11]

And is parole itself always the necessary outlet for reconsideration, or could a robust executive clemency process ever serve the same ends? In *Graham*, the Supreme Court was dismissive of the idea of executive clemency as a sufficient safety valve, noting that it is rarely granted.[12] But in the nineteenth century, "the power to pardon was used liberally."[13] And even today, in some states, clemency is not an infrequent occurrence, at least as compared to the rates of parole discussed earlier. This is particularly true in states where the pardon power has been set up in a way that resembles parole, with boards that can grant a pardon without the governor's involvement.[14] Indeed, these clemency boards often combine pardon and parole authority, as is the case with the Georgia Board of Pardons and Paroles.[15] Thus, despite *Graham's* suggestion that executive clemency and parole are entirely different, the two are often quite similar. Thus, if a jurisdiction has a robust pardon regime, could that satisfy critics of LWOP?

I raise these definitional questions of scope because how they are answered will be critical to the future of LWOP reform and of noncapital sentencing reform more generally. If "life without parole" means only that in the strictest sense—and there is language in *Graham* to suggest that the Court views LWOP sentences as distinguishable from all other sentences[16]— there are gaping loopholes through which legislatures and executive officials can achieve the same ends. States could replace LWOP with 100-year terms of incarceration. Or states could start sentencing offenders to life with parole but not make them eligible for parole until 70 or 80 years into the sentence. States could also sentence offenders to life terms and offer parole in theory without ever granting it in practice, in much the same way that executive clemency now operates in most jurisdictions. Unless these types of sentences are also subject to judicial or legislative reforms for LWOP, any oversight of or limit on LWOP sentences will be essentially meaningless.

But once one recognizes that it is necessary to go beyond the strict confines of an explicit LWOP sentence for reform to have real consequences, as Jessica Henry points out in her chapter in this volume, the questions of administrability and line drawing become vexing. Judge Alex Kozinski describes the problem this way: "if we put mandatory life imprisonment without parole into a unique constitutional category, we'll be hard pressed to distinguish mandatory life with parole; the latter is nearly indistinguishable from a very long, mandatory term of years; and that, in turn, is hard to distinguish from shorter terms."[17] While Judge Kozinski views the death penalty as "unique" and something that could be cabined, LWOP in his view is "for young and old alike, only an outlying point on the continuum of prison sentences."[18]

And if the acceptability of the sentence depends on the availability of parole, how does the Supreme Court review parole to ensure that it is meaningful? In *Graham*, the Supreme Court stated that offenders need "some meaningful opportunity to obtain release based on demonstrated maturity and rehabilitation."[19] But as the dissenting Justices pointed out, the Court provided no guidance on what "meaningful opportunity" entails or how parole boards must go about their decisions.[20] The Court's prior treatment of parole suggests that a "meaningful opportunity" ultimately means very little.[21] As the Court recently reiterated, "In the context of parole, we have held that the procedures required are minimal."[22] The Court has not been willing to say that due process requires anything more than the opportunity for the prisoner to be heard and some statement of reasons for parole denial. The Court has consistently made clear that the substantive standards for release rest entirely with the states.[23] But if the parole availability standard in *Graham* is to have real significance, one might think the Court will have to fashion a more robust vision of what a "meaningful opportunity" entails.

These line-drawing questions must be lurking in the back of the minds of at least some of the Justices who signed on to the majority opinion in *Graham*. If the Court admits that sentences other than the nominal sentence of LWOP are functional equivalents and that parole must be a realistic option as opposed to a theoretical one, it is much harder to cabin judicial oversight to a limited category of cases. To be sure, many people (including me) have argued that the Court's responsibility under the Eighth Amendment is, in fact, to police all sentences and not to create artificial categories of sentences it will review and ones it will not.[24]

But the Court itself has been reluctant to go down any path of sentencing oversight that would cover too much of the criminal justice system. The Supreme Court has for decades kept its death penalty jurisprudence from bleeding into other areas of criminal justice by repeating the truism that death is different.[25] In contrast, the line between life without parole and life with parole in a state where parole is rarely granted is not so clear. Nor is the difference between life without parole and a 70-year sentence. If the Court is worried about administrability—and its Eighth Amendment jurisprudence shows that this has been one of the Court's primary concerns[26]—the Court is likely to define LWOP narrowly. That means states can achieve the result of LWOP in other ways and, more generally, all other noncapital sentences remain essentially off the table when it comes to the Court's Eighth Amendment jurisprudence.

Thus, a somewhat intractable dilemma presents itself for a Court concerned with administrability concerns: to truly police what are effectively sentences of LWOP, the Court would need to review sentences that achieve the same ends, even if they do not use the same terminology. But if the Court does that, there is no logical stopping point of what it will need to review.

II. Who, If Anyone, Deserves LWOP?

The line-drawing problems do not stop there. Even if the Court or legislative bodies define with precision what *types* of sentences are functionally equivalent to LWOP or stick only to LWOP itself as the appropriate sentence subject to reform, there remains the question of *who* merits an LWOP sentence. Answering that question presents obstacles of its own.

A. The Prospects for Abolition

In the context of the death penalty, the public debate has revolved mainly around the question of whether anyone should be sentenced to death, with abolitionists making the case that the punishment should be banned entirely,[27] as it has in other Western democracies. This strategy has been effective in some jurisdictions, with reformers successfully abolishing the death penalty through legislation or litigation in 6 states and the District of Columbia in the past 30 years, bringing the total number of abolitionist jurisdictions to 16.[28]

It is hard to imagine a similar abolitionist movement gaining political traction in the case of LWOP. While one can make colorable absolutist arguments that the state should never kill a citizen, particularly when alternatives exist for keeping offenders from reoffending, it is harder to argue credibly that the state should never be permitted to lock someone away for the rest of his or her life. Some crimes are so heinous (terrorist attacks, torture, multiple murders) or the risk of reoffending so great (for example, when an offender repeatedly commits violent crimes on parole) that removing an individual from society for the remainder of his or her life is the penalty that retributive justice or public safety requires. Thus, as Marie Gottschalk documents in her chapter in this volume, both LWOP and life sentences are prevalent throughout the United States.[29] To be sure, there may be disagreement over which offenses and offenders qualify for this harsh sanction,[30] and, as other contributors to this volume note, there is a powerful argument that LWOP is overused. But there are few individuals in America who would argue that no cases merit life sentences in the way that death penalty abolitionists argue that no cases deserve the death penalty.

Indeed, on the question of whether someone can be imprisoned for life, the United States is far from alone in finding an actual life sentence an appropriate punishment in some cases. The International Criminal Court accepts the possibility of a life sentence, as does the European Convention on Human Rights.[31] The International Criminal Tribunal for the former Yugoslavia and the International Criminal Tribunal for Rwanda also permit life sentences.[32] Life sentences are also possible in Austria, Belgium, Cyprus, the Czech Republic, Germany, Italy, Romania, Sweden, and Ukraine.[33] Indeed, some countries accept life sentences without the possibility of parole. Britain's House of Lords has observed that "there was no reason in principle why a crime, if sufficiently heinous, should not be regarded as deserving of lifelong incarceration for purposes of pure punishment."[34] Hungary, Slovakia, Russia, Turkey, Lithuania, and Bulgaria similarly provide for a sentence of life imprisonment without the possibility of parole.[35] To be sure, both LWOP sentences and actual life sentences are relatively rare in Europe and certainly as compared to the United States. (Roughly 1 in 11 incarcerated individuals— more than 140,000 people—in the United States are serving a life term.)[36] But there is broad acceptance of some offenders meriting a life sentence, something that cannot be said of the death penalty. Thus, it does not appear that international pressure would upset the already strong views in favor of life sentences in America.

Given the politics in America and the lack of international consensus against life sentences, it is hard to imagine any movement developing in the foreseeable future that would lead to the abolition of life sentences in America.[37] To be sure, one could imagine either a political or judicial effort to limit the number of life sentences from what we see today, but outright abolition seems unlikely.

Thus, to the extent that there is space for an abolition argument against LWOP in the foreseeable future, it would have to focus on the "without parole" aspect of LWOP. In other words, the question is whether a life sentence can be imposed at the initial sentencing of the offender without being revisited, or whether there always must be a subsequent reevaluation of the sentence and, if so, by whom. The major difference between the United States and some European countries is on this aspect of life sentences, not on the question of life sentences more generally.[38] So, to the extent that international opinion bears on American legal developments, this seems like the aspect of LWOP that is ripest for broad reform.

Those who would insist on the abolition of LWOP would therefore need to create a political or judicial movement for a second look at a life sentence, which is traditionally done via parole review. But to advocate for parole availability for all life sentences (that is, the abolition of LWOP in all cases) requires at least two concessions: first, that there are no crimes for which the proper punishment is a life behind bars, regardless of how the person changes over time; second, that people are capable of change and reformation, regardless of their crimes, and that it is possible to identify who those people are.

Let us consider each point in turn. The first point raises the question of whether there are crimes that merit a sentence of life behind bars with no hope of release. As an initial matter, to answer that question requires agreement on what theory or theories of punishment are valid. One can imagine an argument against LWOP grounded in deterrence if, for example, empirical evidence shows that a sufficiently long term of years achieves the same effect as LWOP or if life with the possibility of parole creates the same deterrence as LWOP.[39] Similarly, one could object to LWOP under a theory of incapacitation because parole officials would be deciding the very question of whether an offender must continue to remain behind bars for the community to be safe. And of course a belief in rehabilitation argues against LWOP because the essence of parole is to release offenders when they have been rehabilitated.

But if retribution is also accepted as a theory of punishment, as it is in the United States,[40] the case for abolishing LWOP becomes weaker. There is, of course, no universal consensus on what crimes deserve what punishments. Some people believe that no crime, no matter how heinous, merits an LWOP sentence because everyone deserves the opportunity to reform.[41] But other retributivists acknowledge that some crimes cause sufficient harm or reflect sufficient culpability of the defendant that a life sentence without the opportunity for release is an appropriate sanction. In the United States, it is hard to imagine a sufficient number of people holding the view that no crime merits LWOP such that a vibrant political movement would form against it. There are simply too many crimes that are sufficiently horrendous that, regardless of whether the person genuinely changes or is no longer dangerous, the public will demand that the person forfeit life in free society as a just desert. Again, this view does not appear to be an example of American exceptionalism in the way the death penalty has become. The Netherlands, France, Switzerland, England, and Wales also allow life sentences without requiring a realistic opportunity for release.[42]

A strong endorsement of retribution also helps explain both the continued support for the death penalty in America and why death penalty abolitionists have so frequently endorsed LWOP. Even as studies show that the deterrent effect of the death penalty is weak or nonexistent,[43] support for the death penalty remains, largely on retributive grounds.[44] Death penalty abolitionists understand this dynamic, and that is why they have embraced LWOP: it is the only punishment other than the death penalty that the public will accept for some crimes.[45]

Because of the centrality of retribution to the philosophy of punishment in the United States, it is hard to envision a majority of the Supreme Court categorically rejecting it as a rationale for punishment, including as a rationale for LWOP.[46] And in a political climate that is notoriously "tough on crime," it should go without saying that political reform would be even harder. Thus, the first concession is a difficult one to make because courts are likely to accept LWOP for at least some crimes and some offenders.

When one considers the second concession that has to be made—that offenders are capable of reform, and we are able to recognize when reform is genuine—it becomes even less likely that broad-scale LWOP abolition will occur.

The fate of LWOP is tied to the fate of parole (because, as noted, the life sentence itself is unlikely to undergo dramatic change). Thus, LWOP's fate is tied to views on rehabilitation.[47] The history of rehabilitation as a punishment goal in the United States is one of a tremendous rise, followed by a crashing fall.[48] For more than a century, faith in the rehabilitation of offenders pushed the country toward indeterminate sentencing and the use of parole boards.[49] Indeed, rehabilitation was seen as the primary goal of the prison system (thus the use of the word "corrections" to describe penal institutions).[50] The downfall of this movement in the 1970s came from two sides. On the right, conservatives rejected rehabilitation as insufficiently harsh to deter crime. On the left, liberals rejected indeterminate sentencing and the discretion associated with rehabilitation as creating too many opportunities for discrimination and arbitrary distinctions among offenders.[51]

Buttressing both sides was mounting evidence that the experts did not really know how to rehabilitate offenders. Beginning in the 1950s, criminologists began to question the effectiveness of treatment programs in reducing the recidivism rates of offenders.[52] The skepticism continued to grow and reached its peak with the publication of Robert Martinson's influential 1974 essay "What Works: Questions and Answers about Prison Reform" and his accompanying book.[53] Martinson analyzed 231 studies performed between 1945 and 1967 on the efficacy of different treatment programs.[54] His study assessed existing research on academic and vocational programs for inmates,[55] individual and group counseling both inside prison[56] and outside prison in wilderness or community settings,[57] medical treatments,[58] and probation or parole with varying levels of supervision.[59] He reached a sobering conclusion: nothing works.[60] Although Martinson himself later retreated somewhat from this extreme view,[61] his original article remained highly influential on criminologists, and a strong consensus that efforts at rehabilitation were futile has persisted for decades.[62]

The current research on rehabilitation and treatment programs is more promising, but it can only go so far in allaying public doubts. A growing number of academics have seriously questioned Martinson's results and whether they are still applicable over the past twenty years,[63] but even among this group, the consensus now seems to be that while certain treatments (either alone or in combination) lower rates of recidivism,[64] recidivism remains relatively high even after treatment.[65]

Some of the most positive findings involve drug treatment programs and drug courts, which target first- or second-time offenders who have been charged with minor crimes and have drug problems. The research indicates that through careful case management, incentives for good behavior, and supervision, recidivism rates for drug offenders can be lowered by as much as 25%.[66]

In the case of juveniles, there are also some promising results from rehabilitation programs, though the treatment program itself seems to matter less than the simple fact that most juvenile offenders age out of crime.[67] That is, time itself thus seems to have a large effect, regardless of whether any effort is made to rehabilitate them. That said, some programs are more effective than others at reducing recidivism. For example, Mark Lipsey's research on interventions for violent and nonviolent juvenile offenders found that real-world efforts to reform juvenile offenders reduced recidivism by an average of 6%.[68] Among the most successful programs, with recidivism reduction of between 10% and 25%, are the ones that emphasize intensive probation supervision, restitution, counseling, intensive aftercare and parole supervision, some school-sponsored programs (such as law-related education programs and athletic programs), community-based counseling and casework, programs emphasizing the improvement of academic skills, and community-based brokerage services that connect juveniles with the appropriate service providers.

But results are offender and offense specific. In some areas, rehabilitation brings more modest gains or none at all. Results of treatment on certain categories of sex offenders, for example, are generally disappointing. A decade-long, government-funded study of the effects of treatment programs on sex offenders in California concludes that we are still far from understanding how and when treatment works.[69] From 1985 to 1995, the Sex Offender Treatment & Evaluation Project (SOTEP) collected data on a group of 700 offenders, drawn randomly from a sample of 16,000 offenders and consisting of 78% molesters and 22% rapists.[70] The treatment group received intensive, state-of-the-art therapy, which included a variety of cognitive, behavioral, and skill-training elements.[71] The study concluded that the therapy did not have any effect at all on the rate of recidivism among low- and high-risk rapists and molesters.[72] More recent meta-analysis of sex-offender treatment provides some modest signs of improvement,[73] but the lifetime recidivism rates remain relatively high for some types of sex offenders even with interventions.[74]

More fundamentally for purposes of political change, even when rehabilitation programs are successful at reducing recidivism, they do not "cure" criminal behavior such that recidivism rates drop to zero. Recidivism and risk remain. Of course, some people believe that "the essential core of humanity is that everyone is redeemable,"[75] and that view drives the law in those countries that require reconsideration of life sentences after a term of years. As Dirk van Zyl Smit observes, these countries believe that "[n]o human being should be regarded as beyond improvement and therefore should always have the prospect of being released."[76] But this view has not been prevalent in America for decades, at least with respect to adults who commit violent crimes. This cynicism, moreover, does not come out of nowhere; it is a judgment based at least in part on the facts on the ground about recidivism reduction. Only some offenders appear to change, even with the best treatment programs.

Thus, to abolish LWOP would require not just a faith in the power of individuals to change but also faith in experts to identify which offenders have been reformed such that the opportunity for parole in every case makes sense. Here, too, the history is helpful. At the National Congress on Penitentiary and Reformatory Discipline held in 1870—an event many scholars associate with rehabilitation's rise—one of the delegates explained that the creation of prisons or parole boards was necessary precisely because, in their absence, the decision about whether an offender had changed would be handled by elected officials who lacked the time or expertise to know how to address a particular case.[77] Rehabilitation's rise was thus premised on the view that decisions about sentencing and release required expert judgment.

But this vision of parole boards composed of experts who could better assess the rehabilitated state of an offender did not come to pass. Parole boards have often been staffed with political appointees, "too often selected based on party loyalty and political patronage, rather than professional qualifications and experience."[78] These parole boards do not use objective criteria in making their determinations, resulting in major sentencing disparities and racial and gender bias.[79]

Even when experts are the ones making assessments of future dangerousness, they have high rates of error. Reviewing the research in 1981, John Monahan found that experts were worse than chance at predicting which individuals would go on to commit future violent behavior.[80] Reevaluating the state of clinical predictions in 2006, Monahan observed that "[l]ittle has transpired in the intervening decades to increase confidence in the ability of psychologists or psychiatrists, using their unstructured clinical judgment, to accurately assess violence risk."[81] There is evidence that actuarial predictions of risk—statistical predictions based on risk factors that are scored—are more accurate. But even if actuarial assessments are more accurate than clinical predictions, they are not foolproof.

The state of rehabilitation today is that many—perhaps the majority of—existing programs fall far short of what the empirical research tells us we should be doing to maximize recidivism reduction.[82] And while some programs successfully reduce recidivism, none eliminates reoffending. Nor do even the best actuarial models guard against the risk of releasing someone who will go on to commit a serious violent crime. And that brings us to one of the biggest obstacles to reform based on a renewed faith in rehabilitation and parole.

In the political climate of the United States today, it takes just one high-profile mistake to call the entire enterprise of rehabilitation and parole into question. Every instance in which a paroled or pardoned individual goes on to commit a violent crime further shatters the public's confidence that decision-making about dangerousness deserves deference, even if the decisions are right much of the time. Take the politically infamous case of Willie Horton, which many people believe played a major role in costing Michael Dukakis the presidency. Horton was allowed to participate in a weekend furlough program while serving an LWOP sentence and took the opportunity to commit a violent armed robbery and rape. But Horton was an outlier; the program had an overall success rate of 99.5%. This statistic mattered little in the public debate, particularly when Horton's victims declared that "when you're dealing with people that are this dangerous and this violent, anything short of 100 percent is not successful."[83]

We live in a society that is risk averse about letting offenders out without knowing with full confidence that it is safe to do so. And what we know about rehabilitation and expertise in identifying those who have been reformed is unlikely to convince the electorate or the judiciary that it is time to enter a new age of rehabilitation and, concomitantly, parole eligibility across the board. Because risk remains, it is unlikely to be accepted in those cases in which a sentence as severe as life is already in play. Because the sentence is life, if parole is not available, there is no risk of the offender committing additional crimes outside of prison. Faced with a choice between no risk of additional crimes outside of prison and even a slight, but ever-present, risk of additional crimes being committed when an offender is granted parole, voters overwhelming opt to err on the side of keeping the offender incarcerated and removing discretion from any official to change that determination.

Skepticism over parole officials' abilities may help explain the failures of several recent efforts to overhaul LWOP. For example, in Arizona, a bill that would have retroactively granted the possibility of parole to certain lifers convicted before August 8, 1973,[84] was pulled in January 2010 in anticipation of defeat.[85] Recently, a bill was introduced in Alabama to reduce the maximum sentence for certain first-time felony offenders from LWOP to life with the possibility of parole.[86] At the time of this writing, the bill remains in committee.[87]

The case for abolition of LWOP would thus require wholesale rethinking of the American system of punishment. It would require a rejection of retribution as a goal of punishment. And it would require renewed faith in the capacity of people to change and faith in experts to effectuate and recognize that change and make risk assessments. There is nothing to indicate that the courts, policymakers, or the American people are ready for that in the context of violent crime.

B. The Case for Categorical Limits

As long as retribution is a valid theory of punishment and our knowledge of rehabilitation and the risk of violence remains limited, LWOP abolition seems unlikely. But a concern with just deserts leaves plenty of room for limiting LWOP, as Paul Robinson convincingly points out in his contribution to this volume. Courts and legislators (who respond to public attitudes) may view particularly sympathetic categories of offenders and offenses as undeserving of LWOP sentences. Indeed, this targeted approach of limiting LWOP has been the strategy of reform thus far, with a focus on juvenile LWOP offenders as the ones most amenable to change.[88] That is where LWOP reform has had its greatest legislative success, though even there many efforts at reform have stalled.[89]

But to understand how difficult even targeted reform is likely to be, consider the factors that had to align for LWOP reform for juveniles to become possible. First, this is an area where there is an international consensus, reflected in the Convention on the Rights of the Child, that children should be given the opportunity to rehabilitate themselves.[90] Second, the empirical evidence that children have the capacity for growth, maturity, and reformation is strong.[91] The recent decision in *Graham* built on this evidence to disallow LWOP for juvenile offenders. Third, juvenile LWOP has received an enormous amount of press coverage.[92] Fourth, these sentences have been disproportionately imposed on juvenile offenders of color, particularly African Americans,[93] so they raise questions of racial injustice. And, finally, public opinion is quite favorable to reform in this area because 89% of people surveyed believe "[a]lmost all youth who commit crimes have the potential to change."[94]

Even with these powerful forces lining up behind juvenile LWOP reform, it has been relatively limited, as *Graham* attests. *Graham* limited its holding to juveniles who have not committed a homicide. But homicides make up a large percentage of the LWOP pool,[95] including the LWOP pool of juveniles.[96] The number of offenders actually affected by the Court's decision is small: nonhomicides made up only 129 of the 2,589 juvenile LWOP sentences.[97] The Court's decision to carve out homicide offenses suggests that the Court may be reluctant to rule out LWOP completely for juveniles. In addition, the Court did not consider sentences that are functionally equivalent to LWOP sentences for juveniles, such as terms of incarceration that would cover a juvenile's natural life.[98] As Richard Frase has observed, the Court has set the stage to be able to say in future cases lacking any of these three factors (a juvenile offender, a crime other than homicide, or a sentence other than LWOP) that "*Graham* was different."[99]

That said, it remains possible that the Court will follow some of its capital cases and carve out additional offenders or offenses from LWOP's purview. For instance, the Court may ultimately rule out LWOP for all juveniles under the logic of *Roper*, or at least those juveniles who are convicted of felony murder and do not play a major role in the killing,[100] as the Court has done with the death penalty.[101] The Court may also exempt individuals with mental retardation from LWOP, just as it has exempted them from capital punishment.[102]

But it is harder to imagine LWOP reform going further than that, if it even goes that far. There have been no indications from the Court or legislative reformers that either would be more sympathetic to the other categories of cases and offenders who are most often sentenced to LWOP, even in those cases in which an LWOP sentence is likely to be viewed as excessive by the public.[103] The Court has accepted the death penalty for homicides committed by adults, even when the killing is unintentional, so undoubtedly it would condone LWOP sentences for these homicides as well. In fact, Justice Kennedy, a crucial vote for *Graham*, has already written that "no sentence of imprisonment would be disproportionate"[104] for felony murder, let alone other types of homicide. Thus, homicide, a main category of LWOP sentences, seems off the table for reform.

Habitual offenders are subject to LWOP sentences in many states,[105] but legislative and judicial reforms to these laws have been few and far between. For example, attempts at legislation to ameliorate the often draconian results in application of the three-strikes law in California have repeatedly failed,[106] and future attempts at reform seem just as unlikely to succeed.[107] Indeed, legislative proposals merely to study the costs and benefits of the three-strikes law have been vetoed.[108] The Supreme Court has been just as reluctant to place limits on recidivist laws, even when they impose 50-year-to-life sentences for minor offenses.[109]

Drug trafficking can yield an LWOP sentence in many jurisdictions, including at the federal level, but here, too, there is little reason to anticipate broad reform. Although drug courts and treatment options have proliferated recently,[110] most are limited to first-time and low-level offenders.[111] For those engaged in the trafficking of larger quantities—even if they are minor players in a conspiracy—LWOP sentences and their equivalent are still handed out.[112] There are few signs that the judiciary or legislators will change course. Courts have routinely upheld LWOP sentences for drug-trafficking offenses.[113]

The Supreme Court, for its part, has shown little sympathy for individuals charged with drug-trafficking crimes. Consider that many of the Justices in the majority in *Graham*, including its author, Justice Kennedy, have already suggested that drug trafficking by a kingpin might be the kind of nonhomicide crime committed by an adult that could be death eligible.[114] If these Justices were not prepared to say one cannot get the death penalty for high-level drug trafficking, it seems unlikely that they would rule out LWOP, let alone any lesser sentence, for such a crime. And of course, in *Harmelin*, the Court already approved a mandatory LWOP sentence for a first-time offender who possessed 672 grams of cocaine.[115] The legislative front has been similarly bleak for reforming LWOP for drug offenders, as jurisdictions continue to provide for LWOP sentences for drug trafficking.[116]

The prospect for reform of LWOP for violent crimes short of homicides is just as unlikely. Consider the rape of a child or adult, crimes that the Court ruled out of bounds for the death penalty in *Kennedy* and *Coker*, respectively. It is hard to imagine the Court finding LWOP for an adult sex offender to cross the line into unconstitutionality. The evidence of a national consensus against such a sentence is far weaker than it was for LWOP for nonhomicides by juveniles,[117] making it unlikely that the Court will nevertheless exercise its "independent judgment" to rule such a sentence unconstitutional as a categorical matter. And given the rates of recidivism for sex offenders and the difficulty identifying which offenders are likely to pose a threat going forward,[118] this does not appear to be a category for which the Court is likely to view character transformation as sufficiently likely to support parole eligibility as a categorical matter.

Graham stands apart from these other categories because it drew from two lines of authority: the cases holding juveniles less culpable and the cases viewing nonhomicides as less serious. Cases that do not rest at a similar intersection are unlikely to be placed beyond the reach of LWOP as a categorical matter.[119]

If successful categorical challenges cannot be mounted, defendants will be relegated to contest their particular sentences under the proportionality test from *Harmelin* that the *Graham* decision left intact for noncapital sentences. *Graham* allowed the more defendant-friendly proportionality standard from capital cases to be used only when a defendant could frame his or her sentencing challenge as one to "a sentencing practice itself" "as it applies to an entire class of offenders who have committed a range of crimes."[120] When challenges are framed in these categorical terms, the Court will consider "objective indicia of society's standards, as expressed in legislative enactments and state practice," and also apply its "own independent judgment" to determine whether a sentence is disproportionate under the Eighth Amendment.[121]

But if a defendant cannot make a categorical challenge and can realistically only argue that a sentence is grossly disproportionate as applied to him and his circumstances, the test from *Harmelin* is far more difficult to overcome. This test requires noncapital defendants to show, as a threshold matter, that the state had no "reasonable basis for believing" that its sentence would serve deterrent, retributive, rehabilitative, or incapacitative goals.[122] The Court will not even consider the objective indicia of society's standards if this threshold is not satisfied, much less exercise its independent judgment. This test effectively renders the Eighth Amendment a nullity for noncapital sentences. Indeed, it has been almost three decades since the Court found a noncapital sentence unconstitutional. Using the *Harmelin* test, the Court has condoned an LWOP sentence for a first-time drug offender and a 50-year-to-life sentence for a recidivist petty thief who stole nine videotapes.[123] To put it mildly, the prospects for successful challenges to LWOP sentences outside of categorical challenges are dim.

III. Are Additional Procedural Protections Required before LWOP Sentences Are Imposed?

The other avenue for LWOP reform involves procedural reforms as opposed to substantive limitations. Currently, LWOP sentences receive no special procedural protections or judicial oversight but are instead treated like every other noncapital sentence.

In contrast, capital defendants enjoy numerous procedural protections and particular scrutiny by the courts. Capital defendants, for example, are entitled to review by the highest state court on appeal as a matter of right, whereas noncapital defendants can obtain review only at the highest court's discretion.[124] Capital defendants generally have access to state-appointed counsel in postconviction litigation, whereas noncapital defendants do not.[125] The Supreme Court has also more rigorously reviewed ineffective assistance of counsel claims in capital cases.[126]

Defendants in capital cases also receive more substantive checks on their sentences that do not exist for LWOP or any other noncapital sentence. In capital cases, the discretion of the sentencer must be guided by clear and objective standards.[127] Mandatory sentences are not permissible in death penalty cases.[128] Defendants must have an opportunity to present mitigating evidence. And in challenges to a death sentence, the Supreme Court will always consider how other jurisdictions treat the crime at issue and how the same jurisdiction treats other crimes. The Court will also exercise its independent judgment to assess whether the gravity of the offense and culpability of the defendant warrant a death sentence, regardless of the consensus in other jurisdictions. In noncapital cases, as noted, the Court has applied the much more stringent test of proportionality from *Harmelin*, requiring a finding as a threshold matter that the sentence is grossly disproportionate to the crime before even engaging in the interjurisdictional or intrajurisdictional assessments. *Graham* represented the Court's only departure from that bifurcation in proportionality tests, and the Court stated that it would apply the capital test only when defendants raise categorical challenges to the sentence.

The more rigid test will continue to apply when a defendant asserts that the sentence is disproportionate on the facts of his or her case.

It is hard to imagine judges or legislators insisting on all of the same procedural protections in LWOP cases that are provided in death penalty cases. The sheer number of LWOP cases would make these requirements inordinately expensive. There were 33,633 people serving LWOP sentences in 2003, and by 2008, that number had risen 22%, to 41,095.[129] This can be compared with the number of people sentenced to death during the same five-year period: 784.[130]

Thus, even if the Court were to define LWOP strictly—as a sentence of life without the possibility of parole without accounting for functional equivalents—it would be enormously costly to provide counsel to all these individuals in postconviction proceedings or to open the highest court of each state to their claims. The costs of capital cases alone have strained many state systems;[131] adding LWOP cases to the mix would be crushing. For every death sentence, there are at least three LWOP sentences, and there are 10 times as many LWOP sentences as executions.[132] Legislators are generally unsympathetic to procedural protections in criminal cases, and they are unlikely to see LWOP sentences—reserved for some of the worst offenders—as justifying large financial outlays for procedural guarantees.

For reform to come, it would most likely have to come from the Supreme Court, as it has in the death penalty. But the Court has not yet shown a willingness to extend procedural protections from death penalty cases to any area that would involve a large number of cases. Indeed, thus far, when faced with the question of additional procedural protections for LWOP along the lines of those for capital cases, the Court has been clear in its answer. Although mandatory LWOP sentences are particularly troubling, as Josh Bowers points out in his contribution to this volume, the Court has already refused to treat mandatory LWOP sentences as it treated mandatory capital sentences. In *Harmelin*, the Court concluded that defendants were not entitled to have mitigating factors considered at sentencing in LWOP cases, even though the Court had required the allowance of mitigating evidence in capital cases.[133] A mandatory sentence of LWOP for a first-time offender was deemed acceptable. There are few signs from the Court that it is going to rethink this decision or be more sympathetic to other claims for procedural protections. Nor are there indications that the Court will abandon the threshold requirement of gross disproportionality when defendants challenge their specific sentences. The Court seems too concerned with opening the floodgates and administrative costs.

IV. The Zero-Sum Relationship between LWOP and Capital Punishment

The story so far is hardly promising for significant LWOP reform. And yet there is still more to stand in the way of LWOP's path to follow on the heels of the death penalty and undergo significant reform. Indeed, a large obstacle to reforming LWOP through the judicial or political process is that such reforms may conflict with the goals of death penalty reform.

LWOP's rise is inextricably linked with capital punishment reform. In response to the Supreme Court's decision in *Furman*, several states adopted LWOP for the first time.[134] Kansas's LWOP statute, passed in 2004, was signed by an anti-death-penalty governor because she viewed it as an alternative to the death penalty.[135] New Mexico's recent decision to abolish the death penalty was directly tied to its embrace of LWOP.[136] When Texas passed its LWOP statute in 2005, it was due to an alliance of death penalty reformers and prosecutors concerned about the Court's decision ruling the death penalty unconstitutional for juveniles in *Roper*.[137] In addition, there is empirical evidence that the availability of LWOP has led to a reduction in death sentences in jurisdictions that have both punishments.[138]

Although some death penalty abolitionists also oppose LWOP,[139] many other capital punishment abolitionists have led the charge for the availability of life without parole because having that option has been critical to gaining acceptance for the narrowing of the death penalty.[140] As Richard Dieter, the executive director of the Death Penalty Information Center, puts it, "Having a stated alternative that sounds tough makes a big difference."[141] James Liebman, a leading scholar of the death penalty, has similarly observed that the availability of LWOP "has been absolutely crucial to whatever progress has been made against the death penalty."[142] When Justice Stevens wrote separately in *Baze* to declare that he had come to the view that the death penalty was unconstitutional, he specifically noted that it could not be justified on incapacitation grounds because of the availability of LWOP.[143] Thus, as Carol and Jordan Steiker have put it, many death penalty abolitionists have embraced LWOP and other lengthy sentences "as a 'lesser' evil instead of as an evil in itself" and, in turn, have helped create the impression that LWOP is not such a harsh sentence.[144] "Even the lengthiest sentences lose their horror when they are so avidly sought and so victoriously celebrated by the (rarely) successful capital litigant."[145]

If LWOP is no longer available as an option, one could imagine more calls for death sentences, either as a matter of incapacitation, retribution, or deterrence. And it is that threat that may keep many death penalty abolitionists from pressing too hard on LWOP reforms in general.

This is not to say that the only obstacle standing in the way of LWOP reform is the abolitionist movement or that death penalty abolitions are exclusively responsible for LWOP. LWOP reform would be a difficult political battle even if death penalty abolitionists were opposed to LWOP. Reform of the death penalty has been possible because of a coalition of various interested groups,[146] but it is harder to see a similarly politically strong coalition emerging that would seek parole eligibility or a reduction in sentence severity. Again, a main problem is definition and scope—most Americans believe as a matter of retributive justice that some crimes are so heinous that they merit life sentences without the prospect of release—so it is harder to make abolition a rallying cry. At most, targeted reforms might be sought—such as eliminating LWOP for juveniles (even in homicide cases) or the mentally disabled—but these would fall far short of the energetic movement that has existed for decades to eliminate the death penalty altogether. Those who are against the death penalty have been steadfast in their moral and human rights claims and have had the language of absolutes at their disposal. Those who are against LWOP have to rely on much more nuanced and subtle arguments that focus on redemption, hope, or disproportionality in specific cases and contexts. In American criminal justice politics, it is hard to see those arguments winning the day even if death penalty abolitionists agreed with them.

V. The Dangers of Isolating "LWOP as Different"

Because this book focuses on the links between LWOP and the death penalty, I want to end with a note of caution about any LWOP reform movement that follows the "death is different" blueprint and thus focuses on what makes LWOP a unique punishment, separate from all others, instead of on the problem of disproportionality that exists for many noncapital punishments.

When the Supreme Court began reforming the death penalty, it made clear that its jurisprudence was limited to that specific context because "death is different." The Court created two tracks of sentencing jurisprudence, one for death and one for everything else. By bifurcating its Eighth Amendment jurisprudence, the Court freed itself to address its anxiety over its role in capital cases while ignoring similar dangers in noncapital cases. This approach has allowed the Court, for example, to say in the death penalty context that "the fundamental respect for humanity underlying the Eighth Amendment requires consideration of the character and record of the individual offender and the circumstances of the particular offense as a constitu-tionally indispensable part of the process,"[147] while ignoring those very same considerations in every other sentencing case. It has allowed the Court to say a mandatory sentence of death is unacceptable, but any other manda-tory sentence (including LWOP) is fine. While sentencing discretion must be guided in capital cases, according to the Court, there are no similar require-ments for noncapital cases. And the list goes on.[148]

Graham is noteworthy in part because it involved a merger of those two tracks. For the first time, the Court was willing to use its more defendant-friendly proportionality test from the capital context in noncapital cases, albeit only to the extent the noncapital defendant presented a categorical challenge to the punishment. If *Graham* is the first step toward a greater blending of these two tracks, that is cause for celebration. But there is rea-son to believe that *Graham* will end up being more of the same, with LWOP occupying a third track of sentencing jurisprudence.

Graham can be read, and has been read, to focus on what the Court sees as unique to LWOP: the deprivation of hope. By identifying the problem with LWOP as lack of hope of release, the Court's solution is to provide some glimmer of it, even if nothing comes of it. And in most cases, nothing will. All *Graham* does is kick the responsibility for individualized assessment—at some unspecified date in the course of a defendant's sentence—to parole boards that are unlikely to grant release. The Court itself has already made clear that when "the state holds out the *possibility* of parole," it "provides no more than a mere hope that the benefit will be obtained."[149] Thus, all *Graham* gives is that "mere hope."

The real problem with LWOP is not what makes it unique from other sen-tences but the danger it shares with all sentences: it is in some cases a dispro-portionate sentence, just as life with the availability of parole is dispropor-tionate in some cases and terms of years are disproportionate in others. As Josh Bowers explains in his chapter in this volume, LWOP is often imposed as a mandatory sentence, leaving no room for consideration of individual circumstances. Whether it is mandatory LWOP or a mandatory minimum term of years, these sentences are often disproportionate in particular cases because their one-size-fits-all approach ends up not fitting the facts or cir-cumstances of a particular case. And even when LWOP is discretionary, it is often disproportionate to the facts of the case.

To be sure, the Court's first extension of the proportionality test from capital cases to noncapital cases is an important development that may ultimately lead the Court to strike down other sentences as disproportionate under the Eighth Amendment. *Graham* could be the beginning of more robust proportionality review across the board.

But if the Court were focused on the injustice of disproportionate sentences, it likely would have gone further. Indeed, the Court could have addressed the problem of disproportionality by making clear that the proportionality test from its capital cases applies to all Eighth Amendment challenges to noncapital sentences, whether they are framed in categorical terms or not. Chief Justice Roberts seems to have adopted this approach. He considered Graham's sentence without bothering to engage in the threshold inquiry that *Harmelin* requires. His methodology would thus allow a more generous test of proportionality to be used in all noncapital sentencing challenges, not just those that can be phrased in categorical terms. Thus, even if a life sentence might not be off the table as a categorical matter for all drug offenders, it might be found disproportionate as applied to a particular offender given the circumstances of his or her offense. In contrast, the majority's categorical bar benefits only those who can say that a sentence is per se disproportionate for an entire category.[150] As explained earlier, that is going to be a hard test to satisfy, even if one focuses only on LWOP.

It may turn out that the Court's use of the categorical test from *Graham* results in far more sentencing reform than my gloomy predictions here. And I will happily be proven wrong. But it is important not to lose sight of the costs of reading *Graham* as a case about hope and resting a reform movement on that same fact. If we focus too much on LWOP and its diminishment of hope as the problem, we miss what is really wrong with noncapital sentences today. The problem is that sentences in some cases are disproportionate, and a theoretical check by a parole board is not an answer to Eighth Amendment shortcomings. The correction needs to come before that, with judges insisting on rational sentencing laws that are proportionate to the offense or offender. LWOP is the starkest manifestation of that problem, but the disease is far more widespread than that. And just as clemency falls short as a check, so does parole. But the Court seems poised to do little more than provide prisoners with the platitude of hope, instead of the promise of real proportionality review. Just as the "death is different" jurisprudence has allowed the Court to avoid hard questions of noncapital sentencing review, an emphasis on lack of hope might provide the Court with a similar escape hatch.

Conclusion

It is difficult to imagine LWOP undergoing the fundamental structural reform that we have witnessed in the context of the death penalty. While death penalty abolitionists have succeeded in eliminating the death penalty as an option in 16 jurisdictions, it is hard to envision a similar pattern of success for LWOP. For starters, there are functional equivalents to LWOP that simply do not exist for the death penalty. But in addition, the moral arguments against LWOP as a categorical matter are simply not as powerful.

Even targeted cutbacks on the use of LWOP seem unlikely. In the death penalty context, the Supreme Court has led the way in this regard, carving out substantive categories unfit for the death penalty as well as procedural protections that must be observed. But neither of these paths seems likely for LWOP. On the substantive front, it is hard to imagine the Court going the same distance with LWOP that it has gone with the death penalty in holding certain categories of offenses off the table. To be sure, the Court followed this course in *Graham*, but Graham sat at the intersection of two lines of authority: he both was a juvenile and had committed a nonhomicide. If either of those factors were missing, it is hard to see the Court taking the same step. Adults who have committed nonhomicides have garnered almost no sympathy from the Court over the years, outside the limited context of death penalty cases. And juveniles who commit homicides seem to have been so deliberately carved out of *Graham*'s scope that it will probably take a significant social movement in the states against LWOP sentences for juveniles convicted of homicide before the Court will act.

It is even harder to imagine the Court taking the procedural protections it has established for the death penalty—protections which have dramatically curtailed the pace and frequency of executions in the United States—and extending them to noncapital cases, even when LWOP is the sentence. The number of cases at issue and the line-drawing problems are likely to deter the Court from going down that road. And the political process is even more unlikely to yield such protections.

At the most fundamental level, true reform of LWOP requires a rethinking of the capacity of parole and the value of giving offenders an opportunity to show that they are not a risk to society—not to mention some faith in our ability to assess those claims. But in America today, there is not the political appetite for taking a chance on law violators when a mistake can mean a violent crime. Death penalty reform has not required the same leap of faith precisely because LWOP has been available as an alternative. Unless there is a similar foolproof alternative for LWOP that protects public safety to the same extent, we are unlikely to see any real changes.

But even if we were to see a scaling back of LWOP, that would hardly scratch the surface of the problems with noncapital sentencing. The Supreme

Court seems to see the problem with LWOP as the denial of hope. But the real focus of the Court and criminal justice reformers should be on LWOP's disproportionality. It is insufficient to rely on parole officials to make individualized assessments of blameworthiness to ensure that sentences are not cruel and unusual. The Constitution places that responsibility with the judiciary. That the Court continues to ignore that duty in the context of individual challenges to noncapital sentences is perhaps the greatest cause for hopelessness when it comes to criminal justice reform.

NOTES

Thanks to Jonathan Grossman and David Lin for superb research assistance. I am grateful to all the contributors to this volume for helpful feedback on an earlier draft of this chapter and to participants at faculty workshops at NYU School of Law and Temple University Beasley School of Law. I owe particular thanks to Josh Bowers and Richard Greenstein, who commented on earlier versions of this chapter, and to Ryan Goodman and Marie Gottschalk for pressing me to think harder about the cultural contingency of sentence lengths.

1. For example, in 2004, Kansas exempted child offenders from LWOP. Kan. Stat. Ann. §21-4622 (West 2007) (effective April 16, 2004). Colorado followed in 2006. Colo. Rev. Stat. Ann. §18-1.3-401(4)(b) (2009) (effective July 1, 2006). And Texas repealed its juvenile LWOP law in 2009. Tex. Penal Code Ann. §12.31 (West Supp. 2009) (effective Sept. 1, 2009).

2. See Graham v. Florida, No. 08-7412, slip op. at 19 (May 17, 2010) (Life without parole "deprives the convict of the most basic liberties without giving hope of restoration, except perhaps by executive clemency—the remote possibility of which does not mitigate the harshness of the sentence" (citing Solem v. Helm, 463 U.S. 277, 300–01 (1983))).

3. Alice Ristroph, "Hope, Imprisonment and the Constitution," 23 Federal Sentencing Reporter 75 (Oct. 2010).

4. Alaska Stat. § 12.55.125 (2006).

5. Graham, No. 08-7412, slip op. at 14 (Thomas, J., dissenting) (noting that the federal government and 16 states had abolished parole for all offenses by the end of 2000 and that an additional 4 states abolished parole for certain offenses).

6. Jenifer Warren, "Justices Seem Divided on Parole Board Policy," L.A. Times (Nov. 5, 2004), http://articles.latimes.com/2004/nov/05/local/me-parole5.

7. Ashley Nellis & Ryan S. King, No Exit: The Expanding Use of Life Sentences in America 3 (Sentencing Project, July 2009).

8. Harriet Chiang, "Governor Paroles Killer—Apparent New Policy: Schwarzenegger, Unlike Davis, Heeds Judgment of Board," S.F. Chronicle (Nov. 22, 2003), at A1. Compare these statistics with New York's parole grant rate of 40.9% in 2009. New York State Department of Correctional Services, Parole Board and Presumptive Release Dispositions 1 (2009), available at http://www.docs.state.ny.us/Research/Reports/2010/Parole_Board_Dispositions_2009.pdf. For another point of comparison, Texas's parole grant rate was 30.3% in 2009. Texas Board of Pardons and Paroles, Annual Report FY 2009, 16 (2009).

During California governor Gray Davis's administration, only eight people sentenced to life were released between 1999 and 2003. Nellis & King, *No Exit*, 27.

9. Carol J. Williams, "When California Denies a Murderer Parole, Should It Need a Reason?," *L.A. Times* (Dec. 13, 2009), *available at* http://articles.latimes.com/2009/dec/13/local/la-me-parole-suits13-2009dec13.

10. *See* Model Penal Code: Sentencing § 305.6 (Discussion Draft No. 2, 2009); Juvenile Justice Accountability and Improvement Act, H.R. 4300, 110th Cong. § 3(a)(1), (d)(2) (2007) (proposed legislation would condition federal funding on states reviewing life sentences for juveniles after 15 years and then every three years).

11. Tr. of Oral Arg., *Graham v. Florida*, at 6–7, available at http://www.supremecourt.gov/oral_arguments/argument_transcripts/08-7412.pdf.

12. *Graham*, No. 08-7412, slip op. at 19 (noting that the "remote possibility" of executive clemency does not "mitigate the harshness" of a sentence of life without parole).

13. Dirk van Zyl Smit, *Taking Life Imprisonment Seriously* 32 (Kluwer 2002).

14. Rachel E. Barkow, "The Politics of Forgiveness," 23 *Federal Sentencing Reporter* 154 (Oct. 2010).

15. Ga. Const. art. IV, § 2, II; Ga. Comp. R. & Regs. R. 475-3-.10.

16. Graham v. Florida, 130 S. Ct. 2011, 2027 (2010) (noting that LWOP and capital sentences have traits "shared by no other sentences" and that LWOP "deprives the convict of the most basic liberties without giving hope of restoration"). *Cf. id.* at 2052 n. 10 (Thomas, J., dissenting) (observing that "it seems odd that the Court counts only those juveniles sentenced to life without parole and excludes from its analysis all juveniles sentenced to lengthy terms-of-years sentences" because those sentences "effectively den[y] the offender any material opportunity for parole").

17. Harris v. Wright, 93 F.3d 581, 584–85 (9th Cir. 1996).

18. *Id.* at 585.

19. *Graham*, No. 08-7412, slip op. at 24.

20. *Id.* at 27–28 (Thomas, J., dissenting).

21. *See, e.g.*, Greenholtz v. Inmates of Nebraska Penal & Correctional Complex, 442 U.S. 1, 7 (1979) ("There is no constitutional or inherent right of a convicted person to be conditionally released before the expiration of a valid sentence."); *id.* ("[N]othing in the due process concepts as they have thus far evolved . . . requires the Parole Board to specify the particular 'evidence' in the inmate's file or his interview on which it rests the discretionary determination that an inmate is not ready for conditional release."); Board of Pardons v. Allen, 482 U.S. 369, 381 (1987) (quoting *Greenholtz* and noting that "the release decision is . . . 'necessarily subjective . . . and predictive'" and "the discretion of the Board is 'very broad'").

22. Swarthout v. Cooke, 562 U.S. ___ (2011); No. 10-333, slip op. at 4–5 (Jan. 24, 2011).

23. *Id.*, at 4 ("Whatever liberty interest exists is, of course, a *state* interest created by [state] law. There is no right under the Federal Constitution to be conditionally released before the expiration of a valid sentence, and the States are under no duty to offer parole to their prisoners.").

24. Rachel Barkow, "The Court of Life and Death: The Two Tracks of Constitutional Sentencing Law and the Case for Uniformity," 107 *Michigan Law Review* 1145 (May 2009); Richard S. Frase, "Excessive Prison Sentences, Punishment Goals, and the Eighth Amendment: 'Proportionality' Relative to What?," 89 *Minnesota Law Review* 571 (2005); Youngjae

Lee, "The Constitutional Right against Excessive Punishment," 91 *Virginia Law Review* 677 (2005).

25. Barkow, "The Court of Life and Death."

26. *See, e.g.,* Harmelin v. Michigan, 501 U.S. 957, 988 (1991) (opinion of Scalia, J., joined by Rehnquist, C.J.) (lamenting that noncapital offenses cannot be compared because "there is no objective standard of gravity"); McCleskey v. Kemp, 481 U.S. 279, 319 (1987) (denying a challenge to a capital sentence and noting that legislatures, not courts, are best qualified to weigh evidence to "determine the appropriate punishment for particular crimes"); Solem v. Helm, 463 U.S. 277, 315 (1983) (Burger, C.J., dissenting) (worrying that the majority's opinion "will flood the appellate courts with cases in which equally arbitrary lines must be drawn"); Rummel v. Estelle, 445 U.S. 263, 275–76 (1980) (rejecting a challenge to a noncapital sentence and noting that "the lines to be drawn are indeed 'subjective,' and therefore properly within the province of legislatures, not courts").

27. *See, e.g.,* Callins v. Collins, 510 U.S. 1141, 1145 (1994) (Blackmun, J., dissenting from denial of certiorari) ("[T]he inevitability of factual, legal, and moral error gives us a system that we know must wrongly kill some defendants, a system that fails to deliver the fair, consistent, and reliable sentences of death required by the Constitution."); McCleskey v. Kemp, 481 U.S. 279, 320 (1987) (Brennan, J., dissenting) (arguing that the fact that "murder defendants in Georgia with white victims are more than four times as likely to receive the death sentence as are defendants with black victims" demonstrates "the intractable reality of the death penalty: 'that the effort to eliminate arbitrariness in the infliction of that ultimate sanction is so plainly doomed to failure that it—and the death penalty—must be abandoned altogether'" (quoting Godfrey v. Georgia, 446 U.S. 420, 442 (1980) (Marshall, J., concurring in judgment))); Brief for Petitioner at 61, Aikens v. California, 406 U.S. 813 (1972) (No. 68-5027) (The death penalty, "inflicted on the smallest handful of murderers is no part of the regular criminal law machinery of any state. It is a freakish aberration, a random, extreme act of violence, visibly arbitrary and discriminatory, a penalty reserved for unusual application because if it was usually used it would affront universally shared standards of public decency."); David C. Baldus, George Woodworth & Charles A. Pulaski, Jr., *Equal Justice and the Death Penalty: A Legal and Empirical Analysis* 2 (Northeastern Univ. Press 1990) (arguing that "although the levels of arbitrariness and racial discrimination in capital sentencing have declined in the post-*Furman* period, none of" the promises of death penalty reform have been fulfilled); Jeffrey H. Reiman, "Justice, Civilization, and the Death Penalty: Answering van den Haag," 14 *Philosophy & Public Affairs* 115, 131–32 (1985) (footnote omitted) ("Since I believe that the vast majority of murders in America are a predictable response to the frustrations and disabilities of impoverished social circumstances, and since I believe that that impoverishment is a remediable injustice from which others in America benefit, I believe that we have no right to exact the full cost of murders from our murderers until we have done everything possible to rectify the conditions that produce their crimes.").

28. Death Penalty Information Center, *States with and without the Death Penalty*, http://www.deathpenaltyinfo.org/states-and-without-death-penalty (last visited April 14, 2011) (listing Illinois, New Mexico, New Jersey, New York, Massachusetts, Rhode Island, and the District of Columbia as jurisdictions without the death penalty since 1980).

29. Marie Gottschalk, "No Way Out? Life Sentences and the Politics of Penal Reform," this volume, 227.

30. Although there is widespread agreement on the relative blameworthiness of different types of crimes, there is less convergence on the appropriate sanction that should apply. Paul H. Robinson & John M. Darley, "Intuitions of Justice: Implications for Criminal Law and Justice Policy," 81 *Southern California Law Review* 9 (2007).

31. Marie Gottschalk, "Dismantling the Carceral State: The Future of Penal Policy Reform," 84 *Texas Law Review* 1716 (2006). Van Zyl Smit, *Taking Life Imprisonment Seriously*, 189 (noting that "life imprisonment was included as a penalty that could be imposed by the International Criminal Court"); Dirk van Zyl Smit & Sonja Snacken, *Principles of European Prison Law and Policy* 328 (Oxford Univ. Press 2009) (noting that life sentences have "been recognized by the EComHR and the ECtHR as not being inherently incompatible with the ECHR"). The support for life sentences is broad but not universal. Norway, Portugal, Spain, and Brazil, for example, disallow life imprisonment, and many Western countries that authorize it use it infrequently. Gottschalk, "Dismantling the Carceral State," 1717, 1732; van Zyl Smit, *Taking Life Imprisonment Seriously*, 189. But even in countries that disallow life imprisonment, alternative sentences might achieve the same ends. Dirk van Zyl Smit, "Abolishing Life Imprisonment?," 3 *Punishment and Society* 299, 304 (2001) (noting a 360-year sentence handed down in Brazil, where life sentences are unconstitutional).

32. Agnes Bruszt, "Right to Hope? Legal Analysis of Life Imprisonment without Parole" 24–25 (unpublished paper 2009), *available at* http://www.etd.ceu.hu/2010/bruszt_agnes. pdf.

33. *Id.* at Annex No. 3.

34. Van Zyl Smit, "Abolishing Life Imprisonment?," 299.

35. Bruszt, "Right to Hope?," 8–9.

36. Nellis & King, *No Exit*, 3.

37. Robinson & Darley, "Intuitions of Justice," 18 ("We must face the reality that human beings will demand justice for serious wrongdoing, and that the absence of a system that allows for the imposition of deserved punishment would produce intolerable consequences, such as people undertaking to do justice themselves.")

38. Catherine Appleton & Bent Grøver, "The Pros and Cons of Life without Parole," 47 *British Journal of Criminology* 604, 610 (July 2007) (noting that in Germany, France, Italy, and Namibia, individuals with life sentences must be considered for release). The European Court in *Kafkaris v. Cyprus* determined that life imprisonment could be valid as long as the sentence was not "irreducible." The Court noted that "a life sentence does not become 'irreducible' by the mere fact that in practice it may be served in full." ECHR 21906/04 (Feb. 12, 2008).

39. In England, the rates of recidivism for individuals originally sentenced to life who were released under supervision are lower than for any other sanction. Appleton & Grøver, "The Pros and Cons of Life without Parole." Marie Gottschalk's chapter in this volume points out that the recidivism rates for lifers in the United States is similarly lower than for other offenders. Gottschalk, "No Way Out?"

40. *Graham*, No. 08-7412, slip op. at 20 ("Retribution is a legitimate reason to punish."); Ewing v. California, 538 U.S. 11, 25 (2003) (plurality opinion) (citations omitted) ("A sentence can have a variety of justifications, such as incapacitation, deterrence, retribution, or rehabilitation. . . . Some or all of these justifications may play a role in a State's sentencing scheme."); *Harmelin*, 501 U.S. at 999 (Kennedy, J., concurring in part and concurring in

judgment) ("[T]he Eighth Amendment does not mandate adoption of any one penological theory. . . . The federal and state criminal systems have accorded different weights at different times to the penological goals of retribution, deterrence, incapacitation, and rehabilitation.").

41. Van Zyl Smit, *Taking Life Imprisonment Seriously*, 214 Hans-Jörg Albrecht, "Post-adjudicative Dispositions in Comparative Perspective," in *Sentencing and Sanctions in Western Countries* 302–03 (Michael Tonry & Richard S. Frase eds., Oxford Univ. Press 2001).

42. Dirk van Zyl Smit, "Outlawing Irreducible Life Sentences: Europe on the Brink?," 23 *Federal Sentencing Reporter* 39, 40–41 (Oct. 2010) (describing whole-life sentences in the Netherlands, England and Wales, France, and Switzerland). Switzerland is somewhat different because it allows release "if new scientific knowledge were to show that [the offender] could be treated in order to render them not dangerous." But the expert giving such a view would be "personally responsible if the offenders reoffended." *Id.* at 41.

43. E.g., John J. Donohue & Justin Wolfers, "Uses and Abuses of Empirical Evidence in the Death Penalty Debate," 58 *Stanford Law Review* 791, 794 (2005) ("[T]he death penalty—at least as it has been implemented in the United States since Gregg ended the moratorium on executions—is applied so rarely that the number of homicides it can plausibly have caused or deterred cannot be reliably disentangled from the large year-to-year changes in the homicide rate caused by other factors."); Jeffrey Fagan, "Death and Deterrence Redux: Science, Law and Causal Reasoning on Capital Punishment," 4 *Ohio State Journal of Criminal Law* 255, 315 (2006) ("[T]he fragility of the new deterrence evidence, a function of the fundamental empirical and theoretical errors in this body of work, raises concerns greater than simply just 'doubt': the conclusions in this body of work are wrong, there is no reliable evidence of deterrence."); Robert Weisberg, "The Death Penalty Meets Social Science: Deterrence and Jury Behavior under New Scrutiny," 1 *Annual Review of Law & Social Science* 151, 163 (2005) ("We can . . . conclude with more confidence, now that critics have begun to weigh in on the most recent research, that the relationship between executions and murders still lacks clear proof.").

44. Baze v. Rees, 553 U.S. 35, 79–80 (2008) (Stevens, J., concurring in the judgment) ("We are left . . . with retribution as the primary rationale for imposing the death penalty. And indeed, it is the retribution rationale that animates much of the remaining enthusiasm for the death penalty."); David Garland, *Peculiar Institution: America's Death Penalty in an Age of Abolition* (Belknap Press of Harvard Univ. Press 2010) (explaining the continued vitality of the death penalty in America).

45. Gottschalk, "Dismantling the Carceral State," 1731.

46. The Court in *Graham*, in exercising its "independent judgment" to determine the constitutionality of a sentence of life without parole for juvenile nonhomicide offenders, focused on retributive concerns. *Graham*, No. 08-7412, slip op. at 16. The Court argued that "a juvenile offender who did not kill or intend to kill has a twice diminished moral culpability." *Id.* at 18. Noting the importance of age, the Court reaffirmed *Roper's* holding that juveniles have diminished culpability because of a "lack of maturity and an underdeveloped sense of responsibility." *Id.* at 17 (quoting Roper v. Simmons, 543 U.S. 551, 569 (2005)). The Court also factored in the nature of the crime, reaffirming previous holdings which recognized "that defendants who do not kill, intend to kill, or foresee that life will be taken are categorically less deserving of the most serious forms of punishment than

are murderers." *Id.* at 18. The Court concluded that "[r]etribution is a legitimate reason to punish, but it cannot support the sentence at issue here." *Id.* at 20.

47. Hayward v. Marshall, 603 F.3d 546, 570 (2010) (Berzon, J., concurring in part and dissenting in part) (noting that "a parole system assumes, as its basic premise, that some rehabilitation is at least possible").

48. Francis A. Allen, *The Decline of the Rehabilitative Ideal: Penal Policy and Social Purpose* (Yale Univ. Press 1981); van Zyl Smit, *Taking Life Imprisonment Seriously.*

49. Van Zyl Smit, *Taking Life Imprisonment Seriously*, 46.

50. *See, e.g.,* Francis T. Cullen & Paul Gendreau, "Assessing Correctional Rehabilitation: Policy, Practice, and Prospects," in *Criminal Justice 2000, Volume 3: Policies, Processes, and Decisions of the Criminal Justice System* 109, 118 (Julie Horney ed., U.S. Dept. of Justice, National Institute of Justice 2000).

51. Katherine Beckett & Bruce Western, "Governing Social Marginality: Welfare, Incarceration, and the Transformation of State Policy," 3 *Punishment & Society* 43, 46 (2001); Marc Mauer, "The Causes and Consequences of Prison Growth in the United States," 3 *Punishment & Society* 9, 11 (2001).

52. Cullen & Gendreau, "Assessing Correctional Rehabilitation," 120–22.

53. Douglas Lipton, Robert Martinson & Judith Wilks, *The Effectiveness of Correctional Treatment: A Survey of Treatment Evaluation Studies* (Praeger 1975).

54. Robert Martinson, "What Works? Questions and Answers about Prison Reform," 35 *Public Interest* 22 (1974).

55. *Id.* at 24–28.

56. *Id.* at 29–35.

57. *Id.* at 38–40.

58. *Id.* at 35–36. Martinson quotes a well-known Danish study that found that castration reduced rates of recidivism by sex offenders to 3.5%, compared with 30% among those treated with therapy and hormones.

59. *Id.* at 40–44.

60. *Id.* at 25 ("With few and isolated exceptions, the rehabilitative efforts that have been reported so far have had no appreciable effect on recidivism.").

61. *See* Cullen & Gendreau, "Assessing Correctional Rehabilitation," 130–31.

62. *Id.* at 121 (quoting D. A. Andrews & James Bonta, *The Psychology of Criminal Conduct* (Anderson 1998)).

63. *See* D. A. Andrews et al., "Does Correctional Treatment Work? A Clinically Relevant and Psychologically Informed Meta-analysis," 28 *Criminology* 369 (1990); *see also* T. Ward et al., "Reconstructing the Risk-Need-Responsivity Model: A Theoretical Elaboration and Evaluation," 12 *Aggression & Violent Behavior* 208, 209 (2007) ("[T]he Andrews et al. meta-analysis . . . was conducted to refute the 'nothing works' perspective that had dominated since Martinson's (1974) famous report."); Francis T. Cullen & Cheryl Lero Jonson, "Rehabilitation and Treatment Programs," in *Crime and Public Policy* 293 (James Q. Wilson and Joan Petersilia eds., Oxford Univ. Press 2011) (noting how meta-analysis shows that "nothing works" is not an accurate description of rehabilitation and treatment).

64. *See, e.g.,* R. Karl Hanson, Guy Bourgon, Leslie Helmus & Shannon Hodgson, *A Meta-analysis of the Effectiveness of Treatment for Sexual Offenders: Risk, Need, and Respon-*

sivity i (Public Safety Canada 2009) ("[I]t is widely agreed that certain forms of human service interventions reduce the recidivism rates of general offenders.").

65. Mark W. Lipsey, "Can Rehabilitative Programs Reduce the Recidivism of Juvenile Offenders? An Inquiry into the Effectiveness of Practical Programs," 6 *Virginia Journal of Social Policy & the Law* 611, 624 (1998–1999).

66. Douglas Young, Reginald Fluellen & Steven Belenko, "Criminal Recidivism in Three Models of Mandatory Drug Treatment," 27 *Journal of Substance Abuse Treatment* 313, 313–16, 320 (2004); *see also* Cary Heck, Aaron Roussell & Scott E. Culhane, "Assessing the Effects of the Drug Court Intervention on Offender Criminal Trajectories: A Research Note," 20 *Criminal Justice Policy Review* 236, 244 (2009).

67. Robert J. Sampson & Janet L. Lauritsen, "Violent Victimization and Offending: Individual-, Situational-, and Community-Level Risk Factors," in *Understanding and Preventing Violence: Social Influences* 3:1, 18 (Albert J. Reiss & Jeffrey A. Roth eds., National Academy Press 1994); Darrell J. Steffensmeier, Emilie Allan, Miles Harer & Cathy Streifel, "Age and the Distribution of Crime," 94 *American Journal of Sociology* 803 (1989); *see also* R. Karl Hanson, "Recidivism and Age: Follow-Up Data from 4,673 Sexual Offenders," 17 *Journal of Interpersonal Violence* 1046 (2002) (detailing the lower recidivism rates among violent offenders released from prison at an older age); Stephen Porter, Angela R. Birt & Douglas P. Boer, "Investigation of the Criminal and Conditional Release Profiles of Canadian Federal Offenders as a Function of Psychopathy and Age," 25 *Law & Human Behavior* 647 (2001) (analyzing the negative relationship between recidivism rates and age for psychopathic criminals).

68. Lipsey, "Can Rehabilitative Programs Reduce the Recidivism of Juvenile Offenders?," 624.

69. Janice K. Marques et al., "Effects of a Relapse Prevention Program on Sexual Recidivism: Final Results from California's Sex Offender Treatment and Evaluation Project (SOTEP)," 17 *Sexual Abuse: A Journal of Research & Treatment* 79, 98–99 (2005).

70. *Id.* at 84.

71. *Id.* at 86.

72. *Id.* at 98–99.

73. Keith Soothill, "Sex Offender Recidivism," 39 *Crime and Justice* 155–88 (2010).

74. *Id.* at 187. *See also* Eric Beauregard & Roxanne Lieb, "Sex Offenders and Sex Offender Policy," in *Crime and Public Policy* 348–50 (James Q. Wilson & Joan Petersilia eds., Oxford Univ. Press 2011).

75. Appleton & Grøver, "The Pros and Cons of Life without Parole," 611 (quoting Rod Morgan, Emeritus Professor of Criminal Justice, University of Bristol, United Kingdom, and former Chair of the Youth Justice Board of England and Wales).

76. Van Zyl Smit, "Outlawing Irreducible Life Sentences," 40. For a summary of the arguments against LWOP, as well as an overview of the international consensus against LWOP, *see* Appleton & Grøver, "The Pros and Cons of Life without Parole." *See also* U.N. Secretary-General, *Capital Punishment and the Implementation of the Safeguards Guaranteeing Protection of the Rights of Those Facing the Death Penalty: Report of the Secretary-General,* ¶ 10, U.N. Doc. E/2010/10 (Dec. 18, 2009) (compiling data from 56 countries that replaced the death penalty with lighter sanctions, and finding that not a single country replaced capital punishment with LWOP); Andrew Coyle, "Replacing the Death Penalty:

The Vexed Issue of Alternative Sanctions," in *Capital Punishment: Strategies for Abolition* 92 (Peter Hodgkinson & William A. Schabas eds., Cambridge Univ. Press 2004).

77. Van Zyl Smit, *Taking Life Imprisonment Seriously*, 36–37.

78. Joan Petersilia, "Parole and Prisoner Reentry in the United States," 26 *Crime & Justice* 479, 491 (1999). *See also* Gottschalk, "No Way Out?," 227–67 (observing that in two-thirds of the states, there are not professional qualifications for parole board membership).

79. Petersilia, "Parole and Prisoner Reentry in the United States," 491.

80. John Monahan, *The Clinical Prediction of Violent Behavior* 47–49 (U.S. Dept. of Health & Human Services 1981) (finding that experts were accurate "in no more than one out of three predictions of violent behavior over a several-year period among institutionalized populations that had both committed violence in the past (and thus had high base rates for it) and who were diagnosed as mentally ill").

81. John Monahan, "A Jurisprudence of Risk Assessment: Forecasting Harm among Prisoners, Predators, and Patients," 92 *Virginia Law Review* 391, 406 (2006).

82. Cullen & Jonson, "Rehabilitation and Treatment Programs," 327 (noting that multiple studies of more than 400 existing programs in the U.S. and Canada show that a large percentage of them—as high as 70% in one study—fail or need significant improvement).

83. Joseph E. Kennedy, "Monstrous Offenders and the Search for Solidarity through Modern Punishment," 51 *Hastings Law Journal* 829, 887–97 (2000).

84. A state law passed at that time extending parole eligibility had left out this group. *See* Ariz. Rev. Stat. Ann. §13-751(A) (West 2010) (distinguishing between prisoners serving natural-life sentences, who are not eligible for parole, and those serving "life" sentences, who are eligible for parole after 25 years).

85. National Organization of Victims of Juvenile Lifers, *HB2525 Pulled in Arizona, Facing Certain Legislative Defeat* (press release, Jan. 28, 2010), *available at* http://www. willsworld.com/HB2525%20Defeated%20in%20AZ%20press%20release.pdf.

86. H.B. 532, 2010 Regular Session (Al. 2010).

87. Alabama Legislative Information System Online, http://alisondb.legislature.state. al.us/acas/ViewBillsStatusACASLogin.asp?BillNumber=HB532.

88. *See, e.g.,* Wayne A. Logan, "Proportionality and Punishment: Imposing Life without Parole on Juveniles," 33 *Wake Forest Law Review* 710–13 (Fall 1998).

89. In 2008, a proposed bill in Illinois would have allowed all juvenile LWOP (JLWOP) prisoners the right to apply for review of their case by a Prisoner Review Board. The board, in turn, would decide whether to grant the prisoner parole eligibility. H.B. 4384, 95th General Assembly (Ill. 2008). The legislation died when the session of the General Assembly adjourned without voting on the bill. Illinois General Assembly, "Bill Status of HB4384: 95th General Assembly," http://www.ilga.gov/legislation/BillStatus.asp?DocNum =4384&GAID=9&DocTypeID=HB&LegId=34892&SessionID=51&GA=95. The California Senate has a similar two-step bill, first introduced almost two years ago, still pending. If it passes, it will grant every prisoner sentenced to JLWOP the right to apply for resentencing after serving 10 years. S.B. 399, 2009–10 Session of the Senate (Ca. 2009), *available at* http://info.sen.ca.gov/pub/09-10/bill/sen/sb_0351-0400/sb_399_bill_20090625_amended_ asm_v93.pdf. In Pennsylvania as well, two bills intended to cut back on JLWOP are still pending. H.B. 1994, 1999 Gen. Assembly (Pa. 2009) (granting parole eligibility to anyone serving a JLWOP sentence who served at least 10 years), *available at* http://www.legis.

state.pa.us/cfdocs/legis/PN/Public/btCheck.cfm?txtType=HTM&sessYr=2009&sessInd=
0&billBody=H&billTyp=B&billNbr=1994&pn=2694; H.B. 1999, 1999 Gen. Assembly (Pa.
2009) (abolishing JLWOP completely), *available at* http://www.legis.state.pa.us/cfdocs/
legis/PN/Public/btCheck.cfm?txtType=HTM&sessYr=2009&sessInd=0&billBody=H&bill
Typ=B&billNbr=1999&pn=2699. The Michigan legislature has yet to vote on four JLWOP
bills introduced over a year ago. Email from Susan Stutzky, Legislative Analyst, Michigan
House Fiscal Agency, to Jonathan Grossman (June 10, 2010) (on file with author) (noting that the House package had stalled in committee); H.B. 4518, 95th Leg. Reg. Session
(Mich. 2009) (abolishing JLWOP), *available at* http://www.legislature.mi.gov/docu-
ments/2009-2010/billintroduced/House/pdf/2009-HIB-4518.pdf; H.B. 4594, 95th Leg.
Reg. Session (Mich. 2009) (listing crimes for which juveniles can be sentenced as adults,
with the exception of an LWOP sentence), *available at* http://www.legislature.mi.gov/
documents/2009-2010/billintroduced/House/pdf/2009-HIB-4594.pdf; H.B. 4595, 95th
Leg. Reg. Session (Mich. 2009) (listing factors to be taken into account when sentencing
juvenile offenders, reiterating that juveniles cannot receive LWOP sentence), *available at*
http://www.legislature.mi.gov/documents/2009-2010/billintroduced/House/pdf/2009-
HIB-4595.pdf; H.B. 4596, 95th Leg. Reg. Session (Mich. 2009) (retroactively granting
parole eligibility to offenders sentenced to LWOP for crimes committed as juveniles
after 10 years served), *available at* http://www.legislature.mi.gov/documents/2009-2010/
billintroduced/House/pdf/2009-HIB-4596.pdf. It should be noted that H.B. 4518, which
abolishes JLWOP, states explicitly that it will not take effect unless the other three bills
are enacted into law. Most significantly, a bill proposed in the U.S. Congress that would
abolish JLWOP in all states and the federal system has stalled in the House Judiciary
Committee. Juvenile Justice Accountability and Improvement Act of 2009, H.R. 2289,
111th Cong. (2009) (requiring that every juvenile sentenced to life in prison receive at
least one parole hearing during the first 15 years of incarceration and at least one hearing
every 3 years thereafter), *available at* http://frwebgate.access.gpo.gov/cgi-bin/getdoc.
cgi?dbname=111_cong_bills&docid=f:h2289ih.pdf. The bill was referred to the Subcommittee on Crime, Terrorism, and Homeland Security over a year ago. "H.R. 2289: Juvenile
Justice Accountability and Improvement Act of 2009," Govtrack.us, http://www.govtrack.
us/congress/bill.xpd?bill=h111-2289.

90. Van Zyl Smit, *Taking Life Imprisonment Seriously*, 2–13, 212. The United States and
Somalia are the only major countries that have not signed on to the Convention on the
Rights of the Child. *Id.*

91. Brief for J. Lawrence Aber et al. as Amici Curiae Supporting Petitioner at 30,
Graham, No. 08-7412, slip op. ("Conduct Disorder, a high-risk psychiatric condition
in which a child repeatedly violates basic social rules and which was once believed to
be impervious to treatment, has been proven treatable through intervention programs" (citing Paul J. Frick, "Effective Interventions for Children and Adolescents with
Conduct Disorder," 46 *Canadian Journal of Psychiatry* 597, 605 (2001))); Linda S. Chan
et al., *Evidence Report/Technology Assessment No. 107: Preventing Violence and Related
Health-Risking Social Behaviors in Adolescents* 2, 4 (Agency for Healthcare Research
and Quality, Oct. 2004) (finding five of six interventions "targeted to youth who have
already demonstrated violent or seriously delinquent behavior" to be effective); Bruce
D. Perry, *Inaugural Lecture at the Margaret McCain Lecture Series: Maltreatment and
the Developing Child: How Early Childhood Experience Shapes Child and Culture* (Sept.

23, 2005), *available at* http://www.lfcc.on.ca/mccain/perry.pdf ("[T]he brain altered in destructive ways by trauma and neglect can also be altered in reparative, healing ways. Exposing the child, over and over again, to developmentally appropriate experiences is the key."); President's New Freedom Commission on Mental Health, *Achieving the Promise: Transforming Mental Health Care in America* 29 (2003) ("Emerging evidence shows that a major Federal program to establish comprehensive, community-based systems of care for children with serious emotional disturbances has . . . generated positive clinical and functional outcomes."); U.S. Public Health Service, *Executive Summary, Youth Violence: A Report of the Surgeon General* (2001), *available at* http://www.surgeongeneral. gov/library/youthviolence/sgsummary/summary.htm ("Research clearly demonstrates that prevention programs and strategies can be effective against both early- and late-onset forms of violence in general populations of youths, high-risk youths, and even youths who are already violent or seriously delinquent."); Robert J. Sampson & John H. Laub, "A Life-Course View of the Development of Crime," 602 *Annals of the American Academy of Political & Social Science* 12–13 (2005) (examining the question of whether "adolescent delinquents persist or desist from crime as they age across the adult life course" and finding that "life-course desistance is the norm").

92. Scott Hechinger, "Juvenile Life without Parole (JLWOP): An Antidote to Congress's One-Way Criminal Law Ratchet?," 35 *N.Y.U. Review of Law & Social Change* 436–40 (2011).

93. Michelle Leighton & Connie de la Vega, *Sentencing Our Children to Die in Prison* 7 (Center for Law and Global Justice 2007).

94. Center for Children's Law and Policy, *Potential for Change: Public Attitudes and Policy Preferences for Juvenile Justice Systems Reform* 1 (2007), http://www.macfound.org/ atf/cf/%7Bb0386ce3-8b29-4162-8098-e466fb856794%7D/POLLINGWASH.PDF.

95. Julian H. Wright, Jr., "Life-without-Parole: An Alternative to Death or Not Much of a Life at All?," 43 *Vanderbilt Law Review* 533 (1990) (observing that the largest number of states use LWOP as a sentence for capital or first-degree murder); Ashley Nellis, "Throwing Away the Key: The Expansion of Life without Parole Sentences in the United States," 23 *Federal Sentencing Reporter* 27 (2010) ("[M]ost individuals serving LWOP sentences have been convicted of murder.").

96. *See Graham*, No. 08-7412, slip op. at 11 (noting that "sentences of life without parole for juvenile nonhomicide offenders" are "most infrequent"). About 2,466 of the 2,589 juvenile offenders serving sentences of life without parole were committed for homicide offenses. *See Graham*, 130 S. Ct. at 2024; Human Rights Watch, *State Distribution of Youth Offenders Serving Juvenile Life without Parole (JLWOP)* (Oct. 2, 2009), http://www.hrw.org/en/news/2009/10/02/ state-distribution-juvenile-offenders-serving-juvenile-life-without-parole.

97. Ibid.

98. *Graham*, 130 S. Ct. at 2052 n. 10 (Thomas, J., dissenting) (criticizing Court for not considering functional equivalent sentences to LWOP such as "lengthy terms-of-years sentences").

99. Richard S. Frase, "*Graham's* Good News—and Not," 23 *Federal Sentencing Reporter* 54, 55 (Oct. 2010).

100. A quarter of juveniles serving LWOP sentences were convicted of felony murder. Human Rights Watch, *Rest of Their Lives: Life without Parole for Youth Offenders in the United States in 2008* 2–5 (2008).

101. Enmund v. Florida, 458 U.S. 782 (1982) (holding that the death penalty is disproportionate as applied to felony murder when the defendant did not participate or attempt
to participate in the killing and lacked an intent to kill); Tison v. Arizona, 481 U.S. 137
(upholding the death penalty for defendant convicted of felony murder who did not actually kill but who exhibited a reckless disregard for human life).

102. Atkins v. Virginia, 536 U.S. 304 (2002). *But see* Rachel E. Barkow, "Categorizing
Graham," 23 *Federal Sentencing Reporter* 49, 50 (2010) (pointing out that *Graham* rested
in part on the capacity of juveniles to change and observing that the Court may not find
individuals with mental retardation as having a "similar capacity to reform because of
their mental disability").

103. Paul H. Robinson, "Life without Parole under Modern Theories of Punishment,"
this volume, 138–166, (noting that felony murder, habitual offender, and drug cases are
those for which a sentence of LWOP is disproportionate).

104. *Harmelin*, 501 U.S. at 1004 (Kennedy J., concurring in part and concurring in the
judgment).

105. Wright, "Life-without-Parole," 532.

106. *See, e.g.*, Hearing on AB 112 before the Assembly Comm. on Pub. Safety, 2003–04
Reg. Sess. 1 (Cal. Feb. 25, 2003) (requiring "that the current conviction be a 'serious' or
'violent' felony in order to subject a defendant to an enhanced sentence"); Hearing on SB
1517 before the Senate Comm. on Pub. Safety, 2001–02 Reg. Sess. 2 (Cal. Apr. 16, 2002) (providing "that a defendant shall not receive a sentence under the Three Strikes law where he
or she has been convicted of a specified non-violent felony offense in the current prosecution"); Hearing on AB 1790 before the Assembly Comm. on Pub. Safety, 2001–02 Reg. Sess.
1 (Cal. Mar. 12, 2002) (same); Hearing on AB 1652 before the Assembly Comm. on Pub.
Safety, 2000–01 Reg. Sess. 1 (Cal. Apr. 24, 2001) (prohibiting "a felony conviction for the
simple possession of a controlled substance from being used as a second or third strike").

107. "With the sole exception of associations of defense attorneys, the single-issue politicians in criminal justice form an alliance for penal severity that regards the Three Strikes
law as iconic orthodoxy." Franklin E. Zimring, Gordon Hawkins & Sam Kamin, *Punishment and Democracy: Three Strikes and You're Out in California* 222 (Oxford Univ. Press
2001). Furthermore, popular support for the three-strikes law seems to be rooted in the
belief that it "*feel*[s] right," not that it is particularly effective. *Id.* at 221. It will be particularly hard to reform the law in California because any modification of the three-strikes
law requires a supermajority. Cal. Penal Code §§ 667(j), 1170.12 (4) (West 2004). As one
commentator observes, three-strikes laws are "here to stay." Michael Vitiello, "Three
Strikes," 87 *Journal of Criminal Law & Criminology* 395, 458 (1997). Habitual offender legislation has "flourished" in the United States since the 1920s, when legislators "selectively
appl[ied] criminology to support their political claims." V. F. Nourse, "Rethinking Crime
Legislation: History and Harshness," 39 *Tulsa Law Review* 925, 931 (2004); Michael G.
Turner, Jody L. Sundt, Brandon, K. Applegate & Francis T. Cullen, "'Three Strikes and
You're Out' Legislation: A National Assessment," 59 *Federal Probation* 16, 17 (1995). The
movement toward habitual offender legislation survives today, as "[e]very state [now] has
some form of recidivist sentencing law." Erwin Chemerinsky, "Cruel and Unusual: The
Story of Leandro Andrade," 52 *Drake Law Review* 1, 4 (2003).

108. *See, e.g.*, Hearing on SB 2048 before the Assembly Comm. on Pub. Safety, 1997–98
Reg. Sess. (Cal. June 30, 1998).

109. *Ewing*, 538 U.S. at 30 (holding that a sentence of 25 years to life in prison for a third strike of stealing golf clubs does not violate the Eighth Amendment); *Lockyer v. Andrade*, 538 U.S. 63, 70, 77 (2003) (holding that "it was not an unreasonable application of . . . clearly established law" for the California Court of Appeal to affirm a sentence of "two consecutive terms of 25 years to life in prison" for "stealing approximately $150 in videotapes" under California's three-strikes law); *Rummel*, 445 U.S. at 276, 285 (holding that a "mandatory life sentence" imposed for "obtaining $120.75 by false pretenses" under Texas's recidivist statute does not violate the Eighth Amendment).

110. *See, e.g.*, Ryan S. King & Jill Pasquarella, *Drug Courts: A Review of the Evidence* 1 (Sentencing Project 2009) ("Since 1989, drug courts have spread throughout the country; there are now over 1,600 such courts operating in all 50 states."); Eric J. Miller, "Drugs, Courts, and the New Penology," 20 *Stanford Law & Policy Review* 417, 420–24 (2009) (describing the rise of drug courts as "low-level and localized judicial responses to the incarcerative consequences of national drug policies"); Richard Boldt & Jana Singer, "Juristocracy in the Trenches: Problem-Solving Judges and Therapeutic Jurisprudence in Drug Treatment Courts and Unified Family Courts," 65 *Maryland Law Review* 82, 85 (2006) ("Hundreds of drug treatment courts have been established throughout the United States. There is a National Association of Drug Court Professionals with a membership in the thousands; annual conferences are held, and professional publications abound.").

111. *See, e.g.*, Avinash Singh Bhati, John K. Roman & Aaron Chalfin, *To Treat or Not to Treat: Evidence on the Prospects of Expanding Treatment to Drug-Involved Offenders* 7 (Urban Inst. 2008) (citation omitted), *available at* http://www.urban.org/Uploaded-PDF/411645_treatment_offenders.pdf ("Despite the pervasiveness of the drug treatment court model, drug courts routinely exclude most of the eligible population. A survey of adult drug courts in 2005 found that only 12% of drug courts accept clients with any prior violent convictions."); Gov't Accountability Office, GAO-05-219, *Adult Drug Courts: Evidence Indicates Recidivism Reductions and Mixed Results for Other Outcomes* 37 (2005) ("Criteria for legal eligibility typically include charging offense, prior convictions, pending cases, and supervision status. Drug courts generally accept defendants charged with drug possession or other nonviolent offenses such as property crimes."); King & Pasquarella, *Drug Courts*, 3–4 (describing the "narrow criteria for drug court participation").

112. Sasha Abramsky, "Lifers," *Legal Affairs* 42 (April 2004) (noting that 150 of Louisiana's natural-life sentences are for heroin trafficking); Wright, "Life-without-Parole," 532 ("A growing number of states and the federal government apply LWOP against drug kingpins and persons trafficking in large amounts of narcotics.").

113. *See, e.g.*, Ott v. Kaiser, 17 F. App'x 829 (10th Cir. 2001); Young v. Miller, 883 F.2d 1276 (6th Cir. 1989); United States v. Milburn, 836 F.2d 419 (8th Cir. 1988); United States v. Valenzuela, 646 F.2d 352 (9th Cir. 1980).

114. Kennedy v. Louisiana, 128 S. Ct. 2641, 2659 (2008) (noting that the Court does not reach crimes against the State, which the Court defines to include "treason, espionage, terrorism, and drug kingpin activity").

115. *Harmelin*, 501 U.S. 957

116. *See, e.g.*, 21 U.S.C.A. § 841(b) (West 2010) (life without parole for manufacturing, distributing, or possessing with intent to manufacture or distribute a controlled substance after being convicted of two or more felony drug offenses); Mich. Comp. Laws Ann.

§ 333.7401 (West 2010) (life imprisonment for manufacturing, distributing, or possessing with intent to manufacture or distribute a controlled substance in an "amount of 1,000 grams or more of any mixture containing that substance"); Nev. Rev. Stat. Ann. §§ 453.3385, 453.339, 453.3395, (West 2010) (life without parole for manufacturing, distributing, or constructively possessing a specified amount of a controlled substance); Okla. Stat. Ann. tit. 63, § 2-415 (West 2010) (life without parole for "trafficking in illegal drugs" after being convicted of two or more felony drug offenses).

117. At least for repeat offenders, there is a broad consensus among states that LWOP is an acceptable punishment: 36 states, the District of Columbia, and the federal government authorize LWOP for child sex offenders who have committed a previous offense; 32 states authorize LWOP for recidivist offenders who rape an adult.

118. *See supra* note 58.

119. Barkow, "Categorizing Graham," 50–51.

120. *Graham*, 130 S. Ct. 2022–23.

121. *Roper*, 543 U.S. at 563–64.

122. *Ewing*, 538 U.S. at 28 (plurality opinion)

123. Barkow, "Categorizing Graham," 51.

124. Carol S. Steiker and Jordan M. Steiker, "Opening a Window or Building a Wall? The Effect of Eighth Amendment Death Penalty Law and Advocacy on Criminal Justice More Broadly," 11 *University of Pennsylvania Journal of Constitutional Law* 156 (2008).

125. *Id.*; Emily Bazelon, "Arguing Three Strikes," *N.Y. Times* (May 17, 2010) (noting the contrast between capital and three-strikes cases in California, including the fact that the state pays for habeas counsel in capital cases).

126. Steiker and Steiker, "Opening a Window or Building a Wall?," 190–200.

127. Barkow, "The Court of Life and Death," 1151–53.

128. *Id.*

129. Nellis & King, *No Exit*, 3.

130. Bureau of Justice Statistics, *Statistical Tables: Capital Punishment 2008* 17 (Dec. 2009), *available at* http://bjs.ojp.usdoj.gov/content/pub/pdf/cp08st.pdf.

131. *See, e.g.*, Brenda Goodman, "Georgia Murder Case's Cost Saps Public Defense System," *N.Y. Times* (Mar. 22, 2007), at 16A ("A high-profile multiple-murder case has drained the budget of Georgia's public defender system and brought all but a handful of its 72 capital cases to a standstill."); Editorial, "High Cost of Death Row," *N.Y. Times* (Sept. 28, 2009), at A22 (California's "death row costs taxpayers $114 million a year beyond the cost of imprisoning convicts for life. The state has executed 13 people since 1976 for a total of about $250 million per execution."); Ian Urbina, "Citing Costs, States Consider End to the Death Penalty," *N.Y. Times* (Feb. 24, 2009), at A1 (describing a number of state efforts to abolish the death penalty in order to cut costs).

132. Jeffrey Fagan, "Death and Deterrence Redux: Science, Law and Causal Reasoning on Capital Punishment," 4 *Ohio State Journal of Criminal Law* 270 (Fall 2006).

133. *Harmelin*, 501 U.S. at 994–95.

134. Steiker and Steiker, "Opening a Window or Building a Wall?," 176.

135. Note, "A Matter of Life and Death: The Effect of Life-without-Parole Statutes on Capital Punishment," 110 *Harvard Law Review* 1838, 1842 (2006).

136. Shari Allison, Cathy Ansheles & Angelyn C. Frazer, "Taking Death off the Table in the Land of Enchantment," 33 *Champion* 43 (June 2009) (noting that "replacing the death

penalty with a sentence of life without parole was necessary" to abolish the death penalty in New Mexico).

137. "A Matter of Life and Death," 1844; Steiker and Steiker, "Opening a Window or Building a Wall?," 176.

138. Marilyn Peterson Armour & Mark S. Umbreit, "The Ultimate Penal Sanction and 'Closure' for Survivors of Homicide Victims," 91 *Marquette Law Review* 390 (Fall 2007) (noting that after LWOP became available in 1996, Ohio's death sentences were cut by nearly one-third and that North Carolina experienced a 65% drop in death sentences after LWOP became available). LWOP has not had a significant effect on the number of executions. "A Matter of Life and Death," 1850.

139. Gottschalk, "Dismantling the Carceral State," 1734 (citing American Friends Service Committee, Amnesty International, and the ACLU among abolitionist groups that have "denounced LWOP or expressed deep reservations about it"). *See also* Hugo Bedau, "The Controversy over Public Support for the Death Penalty: The Death Penalty versus Life Imprisonment," in *The Death Penalty in America: Current Controversies* (Hugo Bedau ed., Oxford Univ. Press 1997), 87.

140. *See, e.g.*, Carol S. Steiker, "The Marshall Hypothesis Revisited," 52 *Howard Law Journal* 539 (Spring 2009); David McCord, "Imagining a Retributivist Alternative to Capital Punishment," 50 *Florida Law Review* 9 (Jan. 1998); Gottschalk, "Dismantling the Carceral State," 1733; "A Matter of Life and Death."

141. Abramsky, "Lifers," 41.

142. Adam Liptak, "Serving Life, with No Chance of Redemption," *New York Times* (Oct. 5, 2005).

143. *Baze*, 553 U.S. at 78 (Stevens, J., concurring in the judgment).

144. Steiker and Steiker, "Opening a Window or Building a Wall?," 175.

145. *Id.* at 190.

146. Barkow, "The Court of Life and Death," 1193–95.

147. Woodson v. North Carolina, 428 U.S. 280, 304 (1976) (plurality opinion).

148. I explore these two tracks in detail in Barkow, "The Court of Life and Death."

149. *Greenholtz*, 442 U.S. at 11.

150. Or the Court in *Harmelin* could have disallowed mandatory sentences in noncapital cases, as it has done in capital cases, because "the character and record of the individual offender and the circumstances of the particular offense [are] a constitutionally indispensable part" of any sentencing determination. *Woodson*, 428 U.S. at 304 (plurality opinion).

7

No Way Out?

Life Sentences and the Politics of Penal Reform

MARIE GOTTSCHALK

The Great Recession has raised expectations that the United States will begin to empty its jails and prisons because it can no longer afford to keep so many people behind bars.[1] As Attorney General Eric Holder told the American Bar Association in August 2009, the country's extraordinary incarceration rate is "unsustainable economically."[2] The economic crisis has sparked a major rethinking of U.S. penal policies that may eventually result in significant cuts in the country's incarceration rate, which for years has been the highest in the world. Enthusiasm for the "war on drugs" appears to be waning at the federal and state levels. States have enacted a slew of penal reforms aimed at shrinking their prison populations, including expanding the use of alternative sentences and drug courts, loosening restrictions on parole eligibility, and reducing revocations of parole and probation for minor infractions.[3] Dozens of states have cut their corrections budgets the past few years, and many have proposed closing penal facilities to save money.[4] In 2009, the total state-prison population in the country dipped for the first time since 1972.[5]

Although the economic crisis has been a catalyst to reexamine many penal policies, the political obstacles to seriously reconsidering the widespread use of life sentences in the United States remain formidable. The United States continues to be deeply attached to condemning huge numbers of offenders to the "other death penalty" despite mounting evidence that lengthy sentences have minimal impact on reducing the crime rate and enhancing public safety. Moreover, some of the recent successes of penal reformers seeking to soften the hard edge of the U.S. carceral state, including opponents of capital punishment and foes of the war on drugs, may be coming at the cost of reinforcing the country's strong attachment to the widespread use of life sentences and life sentences without the possibility of parole (LWOP).

Life sentences have become so commonplace that about 1 out of 11 people imprisoned in the United States is serving one.[6] Nearly one-third of these life-sentenced offenders have been sentenced to LWOP.[7] The total life-sentenced population in the United States is about 141,000 people—or about twice the size of the *entire* incarcerated population in Japan. Indeed, the United States locks up people for life at a rate of about 50 per 100,000 people, which is comparable to the incarceration rate for *all* prisoners in Sweden and other Scandinavian countries, including pretrial detainees.[8] These figures on life sentences do not fully capture the extraordinary number of people who will spend all or much of their lives in U.S. prisons, as Jessica S. Henry elaborates in her chapter in this book. They do not include the "virtual lifers"—people serving so-called basketball sentences that exceed a natural life span and who will likely die in prison long before reaching their parole-eligibility or release dates.[9] Moreover, defendants serving life sentences have much in common with defendants sentenced to capital punishment. They are disproportionately poor, African American, and Hispanic and are often bereft of adequate legal representation. The conditions of confinement for prisoners serving life sentences in the United States and elsewhere "are often far worse than those for the rest of the prison population and more likely to fall below international human rights standards."[10]

The explosion in the number of lifers in the United States since the 1970s is a dramatic change in U.S. penal policy. For much of the last century, life in prison "never really meant life in prison" thanks to critical penal reforms during the Progressive era.[11] These reforms were rooted in growing enthusiasm for early release as halfway houses, work-release programs, and parole programs proliferated. In 1913, a "life" sentence in the federal system was officially defined as 15 years.[12] Many states had comparable rules.[13] Until the early 1970s, even in a hard-line state such as Louisiana, which today has the country's highest incarceration rate, a life sentence typically meant 10 years and 6 months. For almost five decades, the 10/6 law, enacted in 1926, governed life sentences in Louisiana. Lifers were routinely released in Louisiana after serving about a decade if they had good conduct records and the warden's support. The years that inmates spent in Louisiana's infamous Angola prison were oftentimes brutal and dehumanizing, but they nearly always had an end date. Almost overnight that changed. In 1973, lawmakers in Louisiana raised the minimum to be considered for clemency to 20 years. Three years later they raised it to 40 years. And in 1979 they mandated that all life sentences meant life without the possibility of parole.[14] In 1970, just 143 people were serving LWOP sentences in Louisiana. By 2009, it had mushroomed to 4,270—or to about 11 percent of the state's entire prison population.[15]

The political and legal obstacles to reducing the life-sentenced population in the United States are formidable. In the 2010 *Graham vs. Florida* decision, the Supreme Court ruled that sentencing juveniles convicted of nonhomicidal crimes to life imprisonment without the possibility of parole was unconstitutional. That decision bolstered faith in focusing on the courts to reduce the lifer population. However, this faith in legal strategies may be unwarranted. In the absence of a wider political push to challenge life sentences, the courts can be counted on at best to chip away at the life-sentenced population without making a major dent in it. Relatively speaking, the political and legislative arenas—not the courts—may be more promising forums to challenge life sentences. That said, the obstacles to convincing governors, legislators, prosecutors, parole and pardon boards, and the general public to seriously rethink the country's excessive reliance on extraordinarily long sentences are considerable.

This chapter identifies some of the key hurdles and assesses emerging legal and political strategies to reduce the number of lifers and to challenge excessive sentences more broadly. It begins by highlighting why an assault on life sentences waged primarily through the courts is not likely to reduce the lifer population significantly. The second section examines how concerns about recidivism and public safety tower over all discussions of penal reform, often to the detriment of lifers. It also discusses how the war on the war on drugs influences penal policy more generally. In particular, it may be constricting political opportunities to reduce the broader lifer population.

The third section examines how the vast heterogeneity of the life-sentenced population, as measured by offense, is an impediment to developing effective political and legal strategies to challenge the widespread use of the "other death penalty." It focuses on the political and legal challenges posed by four categories of lifers: those convicted of felony murder, juvenile lifers, California's three-strikers, and the "worst of the worst," who have been convicted of particularly brutal or heinous crimes. The fourth section analyzes why executive clemency, which used to be an important release valve for lifers, has atrophied in the United States and the obstacles to resuscitating what once was an integral feature of the criminal justice system.

The final section analyzes the long shadow that capital punishment continues to cast over penal policy in general and life sentences in particular. It assesses the degree to which the abolitionist movement has contributed to the proliferation of life sentences. It also identifies some key lessons that opponents of life sentences should draw from the setbacks and victories of the abolitionist movement.

I. No Judicial Promised Land

The public has been largely indifferent to the proliferation of life sentences and of disproportionate and arbitrary punishments in the United States. Likewise, the political process has failed to engage in a serious debate about these issues. For these reasons, the courts appear to some observers to be the most promising arena to check the "excessive punishments that emerge from a democratic process that fails to give noncapital sentencing rational consideration."[16] This confidence in the judiciary's greater potential to lead the way in curtailing extreme sentences in the United States is unwarranted. Moreover, an excessive focus on judicial strategies may come at the cost of developing successful complementary political and legislative strategies to shrink the lifer population.

The Supreme Court has a "highly unsatisfactory and disappointing" record when it comes to defining and limiting disproportionate sentences.[17] Generally, the Supreme Court has been extremely supportive of life sentences. In *Schick v. Reed* (1974), it dismissed any notion that LWOP was unconstitutional.[18] In *Harmelin v. Michigan* (1991), it ruled that LWOP sentences do not require the same "super due process" procedures mandated in capital punishment cases.[19] Thus, LWOP has become cheaper and easier to mete out than a death sentence.[20] Few LWOP prisoners "have any reasonable chance of getting their sentences overturned or reduced."[21] Offenders sentenced to life often have fewer legal resources to challenge their sentences because they are not entitled to the automatic appeals process available to prisoners on death row. Moreover, most postconviction offices and organizations focus almost exclusively on capital cases.

A life sentence has become an acceptable punishment not only for murder but also for a wide variety of other crimes, some of them quite trivial, as evidenced by the popularity of draconian versions of three-strikes legislation. In *Lockyer v. Andrade* (2003), the U.S. Supreme Court affirmed two 25-years-to-life sentences for a California man whose third strike was the theft of $153 worth of videotapes intended as Christmas gifts for his nieces. In *Ewing v. California* (2003), it sanctioned a 25-years-to-life sentence under California's three-strikes law for the theft of three golf clubs. In rendering these decisions, the Supreme Court affirmed that proportionality is a valid constitutional principle but then rejected strong proportionality limits. Its jurisprudence with respect to noncapital sentences has been a "meaningless muddle"[22] in which "no clear definition of proportionality can be found."[23] The Supreme Court has consistently given legislators and judges wide berth to impose whatever punishments they see fit—short of death—without significant judicial oversight.

The Supreme Court's persistent reluctance—or hostility—to meaningfully defining and imposing real proportionality limits on noncapital cases stands in sharp contrast to its behavior in other areas of law. With respect to fines, forfeitures, and punitive damages, it has shown itself to be willing and able to set limits and define excessiveness. Concerns about federalism, separation of powers, and judicial restraint have not prevented the Court from imposing meaningful "constitutional proportionality limits in many other areas of law," unlike in the case of noncapital sentences.[24] This suggests that the Supreme Court lacks the will—not the capability—to take up the task of reviewing noncapital sentences and to devise a meaningful definition of proportionality that limits excessive sentences.

Capital punishment is one area of criminal law where the Supreme Court has sought to define a robust oversight process and curb excessive punishment.[25] The Court requires states to have clear guidelines for the imposition of a capital sentence so that it is not imposed capriciously and arbitrarily. It has banned mandatory death sentences and insisted that capital defendants have the opportunity to present all kinds of mitigating evidence in the sentencing phase of their trial. It has sought to make the punishment fit the crime in capital cases, thus forbidding the execution of people convicted of rape and greatly restricting the use of the death penalty in felony murder cases.[26]

By contrast, life sentences are imposed today in a manner that is similar in some ways to how death sentences were imposed in the pre-*Furman* and pre-*Gregg* eras, before the Supreme Court nationalized capital punishment and began to regulate it through its new death-is-different doctrine. This has prompted some observers to argue, notably Bowers in his contribution to this volume, that pushing the courts to extend the death-is-different doctrine to lifers may be the most fruitful way to curtail use of this extreme sentence. The *Graham* decision, which was a rare instance when the Court stepped in to regulate a noncapital sentence and borrowed from the death-is-different canon to do so, has reinforced this view. However, it is doubtful that legal strategies derived from death penalty jurisprudence will significantly stem the flow of life sentences in the United States.

First, as Rachel E. Barkow argues in her contribution to this volume, the Supreme Court has been scrupulous about keeping its death penalty jurisprudence from bleeding into other areas of criminal justice by repeating the truism that death is different.[27] Second, one thing supporters and opponents of the death penalty agree on is that the Supreme Court's regulation of capital punishment has not been a success. As Supreme Court Justice Harry Blackmun declared in 1994, a decade and a half after he voted in favor of reinstating the death penalty in the *Gregg* decision, "[T]he death penalty experiment has failed."[28] Today, the death penalty is "overlaid by a web of rules and procedures that is more complex than that of any other area of criminal law."[29] Yet opponents of the death penalty complain that capital defendants are regularly denied due process and that capital punishment continues to be imposed in a capricious, arbitrary, and discriminatory fashion.[30] Stephen Bright, a leading capital defense attorney, sardonically titled one of his articles "Counsel for the Poor: The Death Sentence Not for the Worst Crime, but for the Worst Lawyer."[31] Meanwhile, supporters of capital punishment lament the lengthy, often unending, legal appeals process in death penalty cases that in their view denies victims' families the closure that a timely execution reportedly brings.

Compared to the "virtually nonexistent"[32] oversight of noncapital cases, the death penalty review process may look robust. However, on its own, the body of rules and principles that has developed over the past four decades to govern capital punishment "is notoriously hard to decipher" and oftentimes "confused and contradictory."[33] Moreover, around 1983 the Supreme Court began dismantling or weakening some of the legal protections it had erected for capital defendants over the previous decade. The U.S. Congress subsequently joined the Court in this shift toward "deregulating death."[34]

It would be a mistake to view the *Graham* decision as a major departure from these general trends or to interpret it as a signal that the judiciary is the Promised Land to roll back life sentences in the United States. In *Graham*, as in the *Atkins v. Virginia* (2002) and *Roper v. Simmons* (2005) decisions, which respectively banned the execution of the mentally retarded and juvenile offenders, the Court emphasized that it was dealing with an extremely rare sentencing practice. It noted that perhaps as few as 129 men and women currently were serving LWOP sentences for nonhomicidal crimes committed when they were juveniles.[35] The Court pointed to the rare use of this sentence as one piece of evidence that these particular LWOP sentences were at odds with "evolving standards of decency," a key pillar of its death penalty jurisprudence, and thus were cruel, unusual, and unconstitutional. To gauge "evolving standards of decency," it weighed not just how many states had this sentence on the books but also how few actually imposed it. The Court also noted that international opinion and practice were arrayed against LWOP sentences for juvenile offenders, as were some key professional associations.

Even though the Court borrowed from the capital punishment canon to invalidate LWOP for these particular juvenile offenders, "evolving standards of decency" does not look like a promising avenue to mount a broader legal challenge to LWOP or other life sentences. It is hard to make the case that the American public has become disenchanted with LWOP or life sentences more generally for most adult offenders. Prior to the 1970s, LWOP was virtually nonexistent. Today 49 states have some form of LWOP on the books, up from 16 in the mid-1990s.[36] In six states—Illinois, Iowa, Louisiana, Maine, Pennsylvania, and South Dakota—all life sentences mean life without the possibility of parole. The same is true for life sentences in the federal system, which ended parole eligibility for life-sentenced prisoners in 1987. This was a sharp reversal. A decade earlier, parole eligibility for federal lifers had been reduced to 10 years.[37] Over the past three decades, the U.S. incarceration rate has quadrupled. "However, the LWOP population in the United States has increased at an even greater rate than the overall prison population," according to Appleton and Grøver. "The ratio of the LWOP population to the U.S. prison population has increased to such an extent that it is currently a 100 times greater than it was 30 years ago."[38] Public opinion polls show growing and strong support for LWOP as an alternative to the death penalty.[39] Although international practice and opinion are decidedly against LWOP and the widespread use of other kinds of life sentences, international sentiment has been at best a second-tier consideration for the Court in gauging "evolving standards of decency." In short, LWOP and other life sentences are a widely used but unremarkable part of the sentencing toolkit in the United States. One would be hard-pressed to argue that they violate the "evolving standards of decency" as defined by the capital punishment legal canon.

In *Graham*, the Supreme Court identified the "denial of hope" as another reason to declare that these specific juvenile LWOP sentences were unconstitutional. The Court favorably quoted a lower court decision to overturn an LWOP sentence for a juvenile offender. That sentence was unacceptable because it "means denial of hope; it means that good behavior and character improvement are immaterial; it means that whatever the future might hold in store for the mind and spirit of [the convict], he will remain in prison for the rest of his days."[40] However, "denial of hope" does not look like a fruitful opening to challenge life sentences more broadly. Lifers exhibit a wide range of behaviors and coping strategies, much as one would find among the terminally ill or chronically disabled at various stages of their diagnoses and illnesses.[41] Anyone who has spent some time with lifers—especially lifers who have been incarcerated for a decade or more—cannot fail to be impressed with how hopeful many of them appear to be. Many lifers doggedly seek purpose in their lives despite what may appear to many outsiders to be bleak living conditions and bleak life prospects.

New research is substantiating this view. Until the 1980s, most studies appeared to support the claim that "long-term incarceration inevitably leads to a systematic physical, emotional and mental deterioration."[42] More recent research suggests that "lifers have survived the considerable adversity of confinement through an 'optimistic sense of personal efficacy,'" by compiling trouble-free disciplinary records, and by strictly adhering to daily routines defined by a range of activities, including educational programs, volunteer work, religious studies, mentoring, and physical fitness.[43] These are "fruits of hope" that are "crucial to their psychological survival."[44] Confined for the long haul, many lifers come "grudgingly to accept the prison as their involuntary home for life and fellow lifers as something akin to an adopted family."[45] This helps explain why lifers are "the stabilizing force for prison management and for creating a more livable atmosphere," according to one lifer.[46]

This is not to deny or minimize the severe psychological distress that often comes with a life sentence. Life sentences are like a death in slow motion for many prisoners, causing great mental and sometimes great physical distress, as Sharon Dolovich elaborates in her chapter in this book. As Lewis E. Lawes, warden of New York's Sing Sing prison in the 1920s and 1930s, once said, "Death fades into insignificance when compared with life imprisonment. To spend each night in jail, day after day, year after year, gazing at the bars and longing for freedom, is indeed expiation."[47] A survey of offenders on death row in Tennessee found that half of them perceived LWOP to be a harsher punishment than execution.[48]

In short, the courts have been persistently reluctant to engage in a serious review of noncapital sentences. The hostility of the political process to rethinking lengthy sentences is matched in some ways by the courts. Notably, in the immediate wake of *Graham*, not a single former juvenile sentenced to LWOP in Florida has found much relief in the courts. The handful who thus far have returned to the trial courts for resentencing received de facto life sentences of 50, 65, and even 90 years.[49] Although *Graham* certainly provides a legal opening, it is likely to be a very limited opening. This does not mean opponents of the proliferation of life sentences should give up on the courts. Rather judicial efforts need to be pursed in tandem with political and legislative strategies and with a clear understanding of their limitations.

The political and legislative obstacles to rethinking the widespread use of life sentences are almost as daunting as the judicial ones. The remainder of this chapter examines some of the key impediments to developing effective political and legislative strategies to end the country's excessive reliance on extraordinarily long sentences.

II. Lengthy Sentences, Recidivism, Public Safety, and the War on Drugs

The U.S. commitment to life sentences remains deep despite a formidable consensus among experts on sentencing and crime that imprisonment and lengthy sentences do not necessarily deter offenders and would-be offenders from committing crimes. State-of-the-art research in criminology is substantiating Italian philosopher Cesare Beccaria's provocative claim in the 18th century that the certainty of punishment is a far greater deterrent to crime than the severity of punishment.[50] The most persuasive studies "suggest that increases in the severity of punishment have at best only a modest deterrent effect."[51] All things being equal, the recidivism rate for people sentenced to prison, regardless of sentence length, is higher than for those who receive alternative sanctions.[52] It also appears that increasing sentence lengths considerably does not deter crime. For example, sentencing enhancements for offenders who use a gun when committing a crime apparently have not reduced the use of guns.[53]

The deterrent and incapacitative effects of lengthy sentences are so modest for several reasons. Although we still need to know much more about what determines criminal decision-making, we do know that offenders tend to be present oriented. Thus, lengthening the sentence from, say, 15 years for a certain offense to life in prison is unlikely to have much of an effect on whether someone commits that crime or not. Moreover, the evidence that people age out of crime is compelling. Researchers have persistently found that age is one of the most important predictors of criminality. Criminal activity tends to peak in late adolescence or early adulthood and then declines as a person ages.[54] Finally, many lifers are first-time offenders convicted of homicide. The phrase "one, then done" is commonly used to sum up their criminal proclivities.

Older inmates who have served lengthy sentences are much less likely to return to prison due to the commission of a serious crime than are younger inmates who have served shorter sentences. The recidivism rate for lifers is much lower by far than for other offenders. People released from a life sentence were less than one-third as likely to be rearrested as all released prisoners, according to an analysis by The Sentencing Project.[55] Two-thirds of all people released in 1994 were rearrested, compared with one in five people who were released from a life sentence.[56] Only seven of the 285 lifers in Pennsylvania who were released on parole between 1933 and 2005 after their sentences were commuted were recommitted to prison for a new crime. Of the nearly 100 commuted lifers who were ages 50 and above when they were released, only one was sent back to prison for a new crime.[57] According to a 2011 study by the New York State parole board, of the 368 people convicted of murder who were granted parole in New York between 1999 and 2003, just "six, or 1.6 percent, were returned to prison within three years for a new felony conviction—none of them a violent offense."[58] These findings are consistent with other studies documenting the relatively low recidivism rate of people convicted of murder and of people on death row.[59] For example, Hugo Adam Bedau found that less than 1 percent of released murderers were returned to prison for committing a subsequent homicide.[60]

These research findings on recidivism and public safety have not spurred a rethinking of penal policy for longtime or serious offenders. Faced with severe budgets shortfalls, many states have begun talking about how to reduce their prison populations. But their attention has been focused primarily on how to shorten the prison stays of nonviolent offenders and how to keep them out of prison altogether. Policymakers and public officials generally are not pushing to revitalize the parole and commutation processes so that even people who committed serious crimes and/or received lengthy sentences get a chance to prove they are rehabilitated and should be released. Nor have they pushed for abolishing life in prison without the possibility of parole and for making all life sentences parole eligible. Although several states have enacted new measures intended to expand the use of geriatric or compassionate release for elderly or gravely ill inmates, few inmates are actually being released under these new provisions.[61]

Life sentences and decades-long sentences contribute little to enhancing public safety and are socially and economically very costly, but rethinking their widespread use is not high up on the penal reform agenda for several reasons. One reason has to do with how the political mobilization against the war on drugs has developed. The battle against the war on drugs has been premised in part on lightening up on drug offenders and other nonviolent offenders while getting tough with the "really bad guys." This quid pro quo has reinforced the misleading belief that there are two very distinct and immutable categories of offenders, the violent ones and the nonviolent ones, which has been to the detriment of lifers. This helps obscure the fact that the United States, relatively speaking, is already quite punitive toward violent offenders and property offenders and has been so for a long time now.[62] It also fuels the misperception that the war on drugs has been the primary engine of mass incarceration in the United States and that ending it would significantly reduce the country's prison population while leaving the "really bad guys" in prison where they belong.[63]

A decade ago, Franklin Zimring argued that the era of mass incarceration that began in the 1970s was not a unitary phenomenon and could be broken down into three distinct periods driven by different engines of growth.[64] From 1973 to the mid-1980s, the main engine was a general rise in committing more marginal felons to prison, with few discernible patterns by type of crime or type of offender.[65] The 1985–92 period was the heyday of the war on drugs, when "the growth of drug commitments and drug sentences far outpaced the rate of growth of other offense commitments."[66] Zimring tentatively suggested (because of insufficient evidence at the time) that longer sentences for a range of offenses propelled the prison population upward in the third period, which began in the early 1990s. The intensely punitive political climate at the time fostered penal innovations such as "three strikes and you're out," truth in sentencing, and the growing use of life sentences.

New research by William Sabol, the chief statistician for the U.S. Bureau of Justice Statistics, more precisely identifies what has been driving up the prison population since crime rates began dropping in the early 1990s. All the attention that opponents of the war on drugs, most notably the Drug Policy Alliance, have brought to bear on the excesses of the war on drugs have fueled the public perception that the country's hard-line drug policies have been the primary engine of prison growth. Sabol's findings challenge this widespread belief. He calculates that the contribution of violent offenders to the prison population dwarfs the contribution of drug offenders. Drug offenses accounted for 16 percent of the total increase in the state prison population from 1994 to 2000 and slowed to just 7 percent from 2000 to 2006.[67] Overall, drug offenders were responsible for 13 percent of the growth in the state prison population from 1994 to 2006.[68] By contrast, in the face of plummeting violent crime rates, defendants convicted of violent crimes accounted for almost two-thirds of the overall growth in state prisoners from 1994 to 2006. The lion's share of the Drug Policy Alliance's efforts has been focused on reforming the nation's marijuana laws. But cannabis offenders, who account for one million arrests annually, comprise only 30,000 of the 2.3 million people in U.S. jails and prison today—or about 1.5 percent.[69] These figures indicate that ending the war on drugs—one of the top priorities for many penal reformers—will not necessarily end mass incarceration in the United States because drug offenders have not been the primary driver of recent growth.

Opposition to the war on drugs has dominated the penal reform movement, overshadowing the plight of the "really bad guys" left behind. On a number of occasions lawmakers have enacted comprehensive penal reform packages that reduce the penalties and/or provide alternatives to incarceration for drug possession and other nonviolent crimes while simultaneously ratcheting up the punishments for other crimes. For example, in 2010, South Carolina legislators approved a number of laudable sentencing reforms with bipartisan support. These reforms included equalizing the penalties for possession of crack and powdered cocaine, authorizing greater use of alternatives to incarceration for people convicted of nontrafficking drug offenses, and reducing the maximum penalty for burglary. But South Carolina lawmakers also added two dozen offenses to the "violent crime" list and expanded the opportunities to impose LWOP sentences.[70]

The past few years, maverick district attorneys launched into office in major urban areas with the backing of broad penal reform coalitions have served as important beachheads to engineer wider statewide shifts in penal policy. However, most of their focus has been on the shortcomings of the war on drugs. The plight of people serving lengthy sentences for serious or violent crimes has not been part of their reform agenda.

New York State is a good case in point. The Empire State has garnered enormous attention recently for its success in reducing its prison population by 20 percent between 1999 and 2009.[71] Drug offenders have constituted a much higher proportion of New York's prison population than the national average thanks to the draconian Rockefeller drug laws.[72] The decades-long "Drop the Rock" campaign centered on exposing the racial disparities in imprisonment created by enforcement of the Rockefeller drug laws. The upset victory of David Soales in Albany's 2004 district attorney contest was a "watershed event" in the fight to repeal the Rockefeller drug laws.[73] Drug policy reform was the central plank of his campaign, which drew support from both urban areas and affluent suburbs. The Pataki administration's partial rollback of the Rockefeller laws in 2003–5, the consequence of an immediate budget crisis and the "Drop the Rock" campaign, and David Patterson's assumption of the governorship after Eliot Spitzer resigned in disgrace in 2008 paved the way in April 2009 for the evisceration of what remained of the Rockefeller drug laws. The New York legislature enacted the 2009 reform package in the face of strong opposition from the New York State association of district attorneys, which criticized it as "a serious threat to public safety in our state."[74]

The extent of the rollback in the war on drugs in New York State is exceptional. In other ways, however, New York is a very typical state when it comes to penal issues. Like public officials elsewhere, its legislators have been reluctant to support proposals to decrease the time served by people convicted of violent offenses. In enacting the 2009 reform package, they rejected a recommendation from the New York State Commission on Sentencing Reform to extend "merit time" to a very limited pool of people convicted of violent offenses, making them eligible to have a few months at most shaved off their sentences.[75] Many of these offenders have served decades in the system, have stellar behavior records, and have earned college degrees and/or other markers of rehabilitation.

Notably, two of the rare victories in recent efforts to curtail the use of life sentences for adult offenders have involved drug crimes. In 1998, Michigan reformed its notorious "650-lifer" law. Enacted in 1973, it mandated LWOP for all drug offenders caught with more than 650 grams of heroin or cocaine. Under the new law, the mandatory sentence was reduced to 20 years to life. The law was made retroactive, thus permitting the 220 people then serving 650-lifer sentences to be considered for parole.[76] As part of a package of penal reforms enacted in 2001, the Louisiana legislature reduced the penalty for distribution of heroin from life imprisonment to 5 to 50 years and for distribution of cocaine from a life term to 10 to 30 years. Members of Louisiana's black caucus sponsored the legislation, which was not retroactive. In 2003, the legislature agreed to permit lifers convicted of nonviolent crimes to be considered for parole eligibility.[77]

The political strategy to draw a firm line between nonviolent drug offenders and violent offenders contributes to the further demonization of "serious" or "violent" offenders in the public imagination and in policy debates. It reinforces the misleading view that there are two clear-cut, largely immutable, categories of offenders who are defined most meaningfully by the seriousness of the offense that sent them away. However, on closer examination, these fixed categories—the nonviolent drug offender on one hand and the serious violent offender on the other—are more porous.

Certainly many drug offenders are in prison because their primary criminal activities were possession of and/or trafficking in illegal drugs. However, police, prosecutors, and some scholars claim that the drug charge often serves as a surrogate for a violent crime. The difficulties that the police and prosecutors face in trying to prosecute violent felonies in many poor inner-city neighborhoods—due to no-snitchin' norms, the vulnerability of eyewitnesses, and constitutional protections imposed in the 1960s that make it harder to extract confessions—help explain why, according to Stuntz and others. Another factor is the fall in the clearance rates for violent felonies due to the changing nature of violent crimes, notably a rise in the proportion of stranger killings and robbery-murders and a relative decline in friend-and-family murders, which are easier to solve. "For all these reasons, the substitution of drug prosecutions for violent cases was natural," explains Stuntz.[78]

Just as all drug convictions may not necessarily be what they first appear, on closer inspection, all "violent" offenders are not necessarily what they seem. Many of the people sent to prison for violent offenses are not necessarily violent offenders years later. But the widespread perception is that they still are despite stellar prison conduct records; ample evidence of rehabilitation through education, volunteering, and other programs; and the mounting research about deterrence and aging out of crime. Marc Mauer's claim a decade ago that "[p]ublic policy has all but obliterated the distinction between a violent *offender* and a violent *offense*, with Charles Manson emblematic of the former and a battered wife who attacks her abuser the latter" remains true today.[79] Witness the uproar after the North Carolina Supreme Court declined in October 2009 to review a 2008 decision by the appellate court that a life sentence is to be considered 80 years under the state's statutes. After the ruling, the state's Department of Corrections announced its intention to release dozens of lifers who were eligible for early release thanks to the good-time and merit-time credits they had accumulated.[80] Governor Beverly Perdue stepped in to stop the release amid numerous reports in the media that many "rapists and murderers" were about to go free.[81] This brouhaha spurred a spate of news stories that featured outraged victims and their families and that recounted the gruesome details of crimes committed decades earlier.[82] In August 2010, the North Carolina Supreme Court reversed course, ruling that these inmates sentenced to life in the 1970s were not eligible for parole.[83]

III. The Pizza Thief and the "Worst of the Worst"

The life-sentenced population includes not only drug offenders but also middle-aged serial killers, getaway drivers in convenience store robberies gone awry, aging political radicals from the 1960s and 1970s, women who killed their abusive partners, three-strikers serving 25 years to life for trivial infractions such as stealing two pieces of pizza, and people who killed their teenage girlfriends decades ago in a fit of jealous rage. Many of the people serving life sentences today were the main perpetrators of a violent crime such as homicide, but a great number of them were sent away for life for far less serious infractions. A central question facing any penal reform movement concerned about the lifer issue is whether to concentrate on challenging the fundamental legitimacy of all life sentences not subject to a meaningful parole review process or to concentrate on a subset of lifers who appear less culpable and more likely to garner public sympathy.

In the 1980s and 1990s, the penal reform movement among lifers at Louisiana's Angola prison splintered and floundered over this very issue. Divisive battles among the various lifers at Angola and their allies on the outside "crippl[ed] any chance for a united front in the quest for penal reform."[84] Old-timers sentenced during the more permissive 10/6 regime were at odds with more recent lifers sentenced under the tougher new statutes.[85] Angola's Lifers Association excluded "practical lifers," even though "there is little difference between a man with a life sentence and one doing 299 years without parole."[86] Lifers who were first-time offenders wearied of the all-or-nothing push for parole eligibility for all lifers and attempted to form their own organization. They believed legislators would be more receptive to consider parole eligibility for them than for repeat offenders. Their movement quickly gained momentum "despite the objection of organized penal reform groups who stood fast to the ideal that no matter what the offender status a life sentence was one in the same for all."[87] Norris Henderson, a leader of Angola's lifers who became a penal reformer on the outside, said, "Now that I'm in the free world and talk to different people and we talk about lifers, they want to know what group of lifers. Those serving first degree murder or second degree murder? The repeat offenders or the first offenders?" He continued, "While I think the life sentence is in itself the problem, I also believe we have to go for the low-hanging fruit. We've now done that with the drug lifers, so the next thing might be to see how many 10/6 lifers are here and work on them. Then how many 20-year lifers and work on them."[88]

The enormous heterogeneity of the life-sentenced population presents an enormous political challenge. It renders political and legal arguments based on going after the "low-hanging fruit" by emphasizing degrees of culpability and relative fairness extremely attractive. However, such strategies could be costly over the long term. They potentially sow divisions among lifers and also among their advocates on the outside. Moreover, they also threaten to undermine more universalistic arguments about redemption, rehabilitation, mercy, and aging out of crime that would encompass a broader swath of the life-sentenced population. Narrowly tailored arguments may win the release of individual lifers or certain categories of lifers but may worsen the odds of other lifers left behind. Four categories of lifers sharply illustrate this point: offenders convicted of felony murder, juveniles sentenced to life without the possibility of parole (JLWOP), people sent away for life for trivial offenses under California's "three-strikes" law, which is the toughest in the country, and, finally, the "worst of the worst," convicted of particularly brutal, offensive, or noteworthy crimes.

Felony Murder. The United States is exceptional not only for its widespread use of life sentences but also for the persistence of the felony murder rule, which has its origins in English common law. The British Parliament abolished felony murder in 1957, and other common law countries, except the United States, followed suit. There are many variants of the felony murder doctrine, which generally refers to an unintended killing during a felony and/or an accomplice's role in a murder. An accomplice can be considered as liable as the triggerman for any murder committed during the commission of another felony such as burglary or robbery. And the definition of accomplice can be quite capacious. Lending your car to a friend who ends up using it to commit a murder can send you away for life in some states.[89] Prosecutions for felony murder have been relatively common in the more than 30 states that allow them.[90]

Political and legal strategies highlighting the lesser culpability of people convicted of felony murder and the gross disproportionality of their sentences can end up pitting one group of lifers and their advocates against another. One lifer appears more deserving of release by highlighting how less deserving other lifers are. This may win the eventual release of that offender who had only minimal involvement in a particular crime but perhaps at the cost of bolstering the view that the main perpetrators—or the "really bad guys"—got what they deserved and should be forever defined by the crime they committed. As such, arguments about rehabilitation, redemption, mercy, and aging out of crime are pushed even further to the wayside.

Juvenile Lifers. The plight of juvenile lifers sentenced to life without the possibility of parole is another good case in point. Approximately 2,500 people are currently serving LWOP sentences for offenses committed when they were juveniles. This sentencing practice violates the 1989 United Nations Convention on the Rights of the Child and other international human rights agreements and norms.[91] The United States is the only country "in the world today that continues to sentence child offenders to LWOP terms."[92] In 2007, the United Nations General Assembly passed a resolution by a 183-to-1 vote urging member states to outlaw JLWOP as soon as possible. The United States was the only dissenting vote.[93] Many youths sentenced to LWOP are incarcerated in adult facilities while they are still juveniles. Youths as young as 14 years of age who are convicted of murder in Michigan are automatically sent to adult prisons.[94] Despite efforts to segregate these juveniles from the adult population, often in supermax-type conditions until they turn 18, many youths in adult prison are still subject to physical and other abuses, including rape, by adult inmates.[95]

States are beginning to rethink JLWOP. In recent years, legislation that would eliminate or restrict the use of JLWOP has been introduced in at least nine states.[96] In 2006, Colorado banned JLWOP, and Texas followed suit three years later. Montana recently changed its laws to hold out the possibility of parole for some juvenile lifers.[97] After a lengthy, emotional debate in August 2010, the California State Assembly defeated a proposal that would have allowed juvenile lifers to petition for sentence modification. The California State Senate had approved a more liberal version of the proposal by a wide margin.[98] Developments at the federal level have been mixed. In 2009, legislation was introduced to abolish JLWOP at the federal and state levels through the use of financial incentives.[99] However, leading conservatives on the Senate Judiciary Committee have been pushing legislation to make it easier to prosecute juvenile defendants as adults.[100]

As discussed earlier, *Graham v. Florida* and *Roper v. Simmons* have been major catalysts for the reconsideration of JLWOP sentences. These two cases rested on persuasive new research in brain science and psychology about adolescent brain development, most notably that the prefrontal cortex of the brain, which regulates impulse control, is not fully developed in teenagers. Opponents of executing juveniles and of condemning them to life in prison argue that children and teenagers should not be considered fully culpable for the crimes they commit, however heinous or violent, because their brains are not fully developed until they are in their 20s. As a consequence, they have greater trouble controlling their impulses and resisting peer pressure.

Political and legal strategies rooted in arguments about the underdevelopment of teenage brains have proven to be an extremely promising avenue to end or at least limit the use of JLWOP sentences. However, these strategies could be costly over the long term for those offenders who were sent away for life for crimes they committed as adults and thus who presumably had fully developed brains. Stressing that teenagers are not fully culpable reinforces in a backhanded way the idea that adults who commit serious crimes should have known better and thus are fully culpable. The brain-scan approach to criminal justice bolsters narrow biologically deterministic arguments about why people commit crimes, arguments that are enjoying a renaissance in criminology and in public debates about crime and punishment to a degree not seen since the heyday of the eugenics movement a century ago. This approach reinforces the popular view that people who commit serious crimes are biologically incapable of fundamentally changing.

Pennsylvania has about 450 juvenile lifers, or one-fifth of the country's total, which is more than any other jurisdiction in the world.[101] Under Pennsylvania law, mandatory life is the only sentence available to adults and youths convicted of first- or second-degree murder, and there is no minimum age for which a juvenile can be tried as an adult.[102] The recent case of Jordan Brown, initially charged as an adult in early 2010 for killing his father's pregnant girlfriend when he was 11 years old, put an unflattering national spotlight on JLWOP in Pennsylvania.[103] In keeping with national trends, Pennsylvania's juvenile lifer population is disproportionately African American. A black juvenile in Pennsylvania is 1.48 times more likely to receive an LWOP sentence than a white juvenile is.[104] Pennsylvania has been persistently unwilling to commute the sentences of juvenile lifers who have served decades behind bars, even in instances when members of the homicide victim's family have called for mercy and release.[105] A newly formed statewide coalition is currently engaged in an uphill battle to get Pennsylvania legislators to reconsider the state's widespread use of JLWOP sentences. At a legislative hearing in August 2010, JLWOP opponents focused extensively on the adolescent brain development argument. As Robert G. Schwartz, executive director of the Juvenile Law Center testified, "Kids are different."[106]

The relative culpability of juveniles convicted of felony murder was also a central issue at the hearing. One of the main witnesses testifying in favor of the legislation was Anita Colón, a charismatic, articulate woman whose brother, Robert Holbrook, is serving a life sentence in Pennsylvania for a felony murder conviction when he was 16. Decades ago, her brother was the lookout in a drug deal gone awry that resulted in the death of a young woman. In her testimony, Colón underscored that almost 60 percent of Pennsylvania's juvenile lifers were first-time offenders who had never been convicted of a previous crime and that about a third of them were sent away for life for a felony murder conviction.[107] This is slightly above the national average of about 25 percent.[108] She and other supporters of the legislation stressed that rehabilitation and treatment have a greater impact on juveniles than they do on adults and thus juveniles are not "beyond redemption." Members of the

House Judiciary Committee focused much of their attention in their comments and questions on the relative fairness of felony murder for juvenile lifers rather than on alternative arguments raised by Colón and other witnesses about redemption, aging out of crime, and the huge economic cost of incarcerating so many youths until the end of their days.

In opposing the legislation, the Pennsylvania District Attorneys Association (PDAA) commended the House Judiciary Committee's recent efforts to reduce the state's prison population by focusing on diversionary and other programs directed at people convicted of less violent offenses. "That is the cohort group our collective attention should be focused on—not on letting murderers out early," the association declared in its written testimony. The association also emphasized that the state's Board of Pardons provides adequate means for offenders to prove "they are rehabilitated and seek release through the commutation process."[109]

The PDAA and other opponents framed the proposed legislation as a violation of the rights of victims and of Pennsylvania's commitment to truth in sentencing. "It would be devastating and unfair to change the rules long after families of murder victims who were told that the person who murdered their child, spouse, parent or other family members would spend the rest of his or her life behind bars," the PDAA argued.[110] Representatives of victims' organizations and other opponents of the legislation echoed this view and devoted much of their testimony to recounting gruesome details of crimes committed by juvenile lifers.[111] Charles D. Stimson of the Heritage Foundation used the term "juvenile killers" half a dozen times in his brief testimony opposing the bill.[112] However, Julia Hall, representing the Pennsylvania Prison Society, questioned, among other things, the primacy that victims and their families have had in debates over JLWOP. "A serious question arises about whether personal grief is an appropriate basis for public policy and legislation," she testified.[113]

The debate over JLWOP illustrates how the death penalty continues to cast a long shadow over the broader politics of punishment and penal reform. As *Roper v. Simmons* wound its way through the courts, organizations representing the victims of juvenile offenders generally did not mobilize in support of executing juvenile offenders. Assurances that juveniles who were spared the death penalty would spend all their remaining days behind bars were an important reason why. At the Pennsylvania hearing, representatives of victims' organizations portrayed ending JLWOP retroactively and making juvenile lifers eligible for parole consideration as a betrayal. They contended that many victims' families agreed not to push for the death penalty because of assurances from prosecutors that the perpetrator would be locked up for life, thus sparing the family the seemingly endless appeals process of capital punishment cases. At the Pennsylvania hearing on JLWOP legislation, Bobbi Jamriska, a prominent spokesperson for the National Organization of Victims of "Juvenile Lifers" (NOVJL), charged that ending JLWOP in Pennsylvania would be tantamount to "torturing" victims whose loved ones were murdered, forcing them "to relive the trauma over and over" again with each parole hearing.[114]

Striking Out in the Golden State. California has been teetering at the brink of fiscal Armageddon for several years now and is contending with a federal court order to release tens of thousands of prisoners to relieve overcrowded, unconstitutional prison conditions or else to build more prisons to house them. Nonetheless, the state's commitment to incarcerating people for lengthy or life sentences at an average cost of nearly $50,000 per year has not diminished. California has the largest state prison system and also the highest number of life-sentenced prisoners—about 34,000, or about one-quarter of the nation's total.[115] This is more than triple the number in 1992, before the state enacted the country's toughest three-strikes legislation.[116] About one in five prisoners in California is serving a life sentence, or about double the national average.[117]

California's life-sentenced population is exceptional not only for its sheer size but also for its extreme heterogeneity as measured by sentencing offense. The three-strikes law in California, which has become a towering symbol of the state's commitment to crime victims and of its uncompromising stance toward offenders, poses a huge hurdle to devising effective political and legislative strategies to dismantle the "other death penalty" in the Golden State.

California's 1994 three-strikes law doubles the minimum sentence for anyone convicted of a felony who has one prior serious or violent felony. For those with two or more prior serious or violent strikes, a third conviction for *any* felony generally means a minimum sentence of 25 years to life if a prosecutor chooses to invoke the three-strikes law. Unlike three-strikes statutes in many other states and the federal system, in California the third strike need not be for a serious or violent offense. Moreover, California has an extremely permissive definition of what constitutes a felony, and prosecutors have enormous leeway to upgrade misdemeanors to felonies. As a consequence, the state's prison population includes a considerable number of people convicted under the three-strikes law who are serving lengthy sentences for trivial infractions such as petty theft, minor drug possession, or minor drug sales. In one of the most infamous cases, Jerry Dewayne Williams received a

25-years-to-life sentence for stealing pizza from some children.[118] In another, a defendant was sentenced to life for stealing a dollar in change from the coin box of a parked car.[119]

The proportion of three-strikers in California's prisons increased dramatically between 1994 and 2001, going from about 2.5 percent to about 25 percent, where it has stabilized.[120] The readiness of California's district attorneys to invoke their three-strikes prerogative varies enormously around the state and even between seemingly like cases in a single county.[121] Offenders sentenced under the state's three-strikes law receive on average sentences that are nine years longer than they would have received otherwise.[122] A recent study by the state's auditor estimated that the 43,500 inmates currently serving time under California's three-strikes law will cost the state approximately $19 billion in additional costs.[123] More than half of the people convicted under three strikes are imprisoned for a felony that is not considered violent or serious, at an additional cost of $7.5 billion.[124] A significant number of them are not necessarily habitual offenders.[125] Rather, prosecutors chose to invoke three strikes in instances of multiple serious or violent offenses committed on a single day, often in a single incident. For example, an armed robbery committed by a first-time offender could, through creative prosecutorial accounting, be considered three strikes that warrant a sentence of 25 years to life.

The last major attempt to reform the state's three-strikes law went down to a resounding defeat in 2004. Proposition 66 would have required that all strikes under the revised law be for serious or violent offenses. Offenders serving 25-years-to-life sentences for nonviolent or trivial infractions would be eligible for resentencing. Proposition 66 also included provisions that would have made it more difficult to invoke the draconian three-strike penalties in instances of multiple infractions stemming from a single criminal incident such as an armed robbery.

Just two weeks before the 2004 election, polls showed that two-thirds of likely voters supported Proposition 66. However, the ballot initiative was defeated 53 percent to 47 percent on Election Day after the political establishment in California, including then governor Arnold Schwarzenegger and former and current governor Jerry Brown, rallied against the measure in the final days before the election. They joined a well-funded campaign against Proposition 66 spearheaded by conservative victims' groups allied with the California Correctional Peace Officers Association (CCPOA), arguably the most powerful union in the state and unquestionably the country's savviest prison guards' union. A fund developed by Schwarzenegger to pay for ballot initiatives contributed over $2 million to defeat the measure, while the CCPOA spent more than three-quarters of a million dollars to kill it.[126] The well-funded eleventh-hour blitz of television and radio commercials employed "harrowing music and images of reviled criminal types like sex offenders and career criminals" to communicate "a simple yet powerful message; the initiative would lead to chaos and destroy communities and families."[127] The notorious "He Raped Me" commercial featured a white middle-aged rape victim and concluded with the warning, "Proposition 66 creates a loophole that will release 26,000 dangerous felons."[128]

California's three-strikes case raises a broader question about how best to challenge mass imprisonment in the United States. Should penal reformers concentrate on high-profile campaigns, such as undoing three strikes at the ballot box, that may go down to defeat but may help to build the foundation for a more durable political movement to challenge the carceral state? Or should they concentrate on below-the-radar efforts that attract less public attention and controversy? For example, some lawyers and law students in the state have started mobilizing to exploit a 1998 ruling by the California Supreme Court that permits trial judges, in considering a bid for leniency in a three-strikes case, to weigh whether mitigating factors such as a defendant's "background, character and prospects" place him or her outside the "spirit" of three strikes.[129] The Stanford Three Strikes Project has litigated various aspects of the administration of California's three-strikes law in both state and federal court.[130] Defense attorney Michael Romano, who helped found the Stanford clinic, argues that legal clinics should concentrate their efforts on gaining the release of sympathetic three-strikers "who haven't done terrible things, who haven't actually hurt anyone."[131] On the positive side, these below-the-radar efforts have resulted in the release of a handful of three-strikers. But given the huge size of the three-striker and life-sentenced population, it is hard to see how these below-the-radar efforts will significantly reduce the number of lifers in California.

The case of California is a stark reminder that political and institutional logic can matter as much as or more than economic logic in determining the future course of penal policy. Another ballot initiative to challenge three strikes may be in the offing. In some respects, the prospects for revising three strikes should be more promising now for several reasons. First, as mentioned earlier, California has been teetering on the brink of fiscal and social disaster for several years. Commentators have even begun to refer to it as a "failed state," a term usually associated with countries such as Congo or Afghanistan. Over the past three decades, California has gone from spending five dollars on higher education for every dollar spent on corrections "to a virtual dead-heat on spending."[132] In 2007–8, the annual expenditures for the California Department of Corrections and Rehabilitation topped $10 billion, or about 10 percent of the state's General Fund, compared to just 2 percent in 1982.[133] The state's ballooning budget deficits and deep cuts in spending on education and other key services are drawing increased attention to the state's costly prison system.

Moreover, despite all the billions spent each year on the prison system, the federal judiciary put California's prison system under federal receivership in 2006 because of extreme overcrowding and failure to provide adequate medical care to all prisoners. In August 2009, a panel of three federal judges ordered the corrections department to devise a plan that would reduce the state's prison population by more than 40,000, or to about 138 percent of capacity (compared to 200 percent in recent years). In May 2011, the U.S. Supreme Court upheld that decision by a 5–4 vote. Finally, the political establishment's support of three strikes is not as steadfast as it once was. Steven Cooley, the 2010 Republican candidate for attorney general in California, became an outspoken opponent of three strikes as district attorney of Los Angeles, earning him the umbrage of the California District Attorneys Association. Kamala Harris, who triumphed over Cooley in a tight race, brought forward relatively few three-strikes cases when she was San Francisco's district attorney.

Despite these developments, a major overhaul of three strikes in California via the ballot box remains a tough sell. When Arnold Schwarzenegger was governor, he and the state's corrections department vigorously fought the federal court order and any population caps or court-ordered early release of prisoners. They charged that the federal judges exceeded their authority under the federal Prison Litigation Reform Act. As discussed earlier, the CCPOA and its allies have been steadfast in their opposition to revising three strikes, even in the case of the pizza thief, the petty drug dealer, and other minor offenders. The prison guards provided a key campaign endorsement to Jerry Brown, the state's new governor, who has assiduously cultivated the union over the years.

California's recent record on crime-related ballot initiatives and the enormous controversy surrounding recent legislative proposals to reduce the number of nonviolent offenders in its prisons indicate that the state is not likely to begin a serious discussion about the huge and growing lifer population. Despite the state's growing fiscal crisis, in November 2008, voters narrowly approved Proposition 9, which toughens up requirements for granting parole and calls for amending the state's constitution to give crime victims unprecedented influence on criminal cases.[134] Voters soundly rejected Proposition 5, a ballot initiative that would have expanded alternative sentences for nonviolent drug offenders and saved billions of dollars.[135] Schwarzenegger and four former governors opposed the measure, including Jerry Brown, who was then attorney general.[136]

A legislative proposal in 2009 to release some nonviolent offenders in response to the federal lawsuit created a political firestorm. A watered-down compromise was nearly scuttled in the eleventh hour in the state assembly after the sensational story of Phillip Garrido became front-page news worldwide in summer 2009. Garrido was accused of kidnapping an 11-year-old girl and confining her to an undiscovered backyard encampment for nearly two decades while he was on parole for rape and kidnapping offenses dating back to 1976. The significantly weaker assembly bill eventually passed in late August without a vote to spare. The measure unleashed over-the-top rhetoric. One Republican assemblyman warned, "We might as well set off a nuclear bomb in California with what we are doing with this bill."[137] Law enforcement groups, led by the CCPOA, successfully pressed Democrats to strip the bill of provisions to reduce sentences for some nonviolent offenders and to establish a commission to revise sentencing guidelines.[138] The final bill projected to reduce the prison population by 16,000 inmates, far fewer than originally proposed.[139] In a similar vein, the case of John Wesley Ewell, charged in late 2010 with murdering four people in home-invasion robberies, has clearly set back the cause of three-strikes reform. Ewell was a "multiple felon who campaigned against California's three-strikes law and was free after managing four times to escape its harsh sentencing guidelines."[140]

In short, the political establishment's commitment to three strikes is almost theological in California. In the past, any time this faith appeared to be wavering, victims' groups working closely with the CCPOA have had the money and organizational resources to bring them back into the fold. Any future ballot initiative to reform three strikes may provide yet another occasion to demonstrate that California's prisons are full of the "worst of the worst" who should not be released for a very long time—if ever.

The "Worst of the Worst." What to do about "the worst of the worst" lurks in the background of any discussion of life sentences. Just reciting the names Charles Manson, Jeffrey Dahmer, and Ted Bundy is enough to abort any serious discussion about developing political and legislative strategies to challenge the fundamental legitimacy of *all* LWOP sentences and of *all* life sentences that are not subject to meaningful parole reviews. The two key issues here are retribution and risk. Some people mistakenly interpret calls to abolish all LWOP sentences and to entitle all prisoners to a parole eligibility hearing after a certain number of years as an assault on the whole idea of retribution, which has been a guiding principle, if not the preeminent philosophy, of the criminal justice system in the United States for decades. In affirming retribution as a legitimate reason to punish, Justice Anthony Kennedy wrote in the *Graham* decision, "Society is entitled to impose severe sanctions, . . . to express its condemnation of the crime and to seek restoration of the moral imbalance caused by the offenders."[141]

The retribution issue is a familiar one from debates over capital punishment. As demonstrated most starkly with the death penalty, what constitutes an acceptable punishment is culturally, politically, and socially constructed and thus varies enormously over time. Centuries ago, a mere execution was not enough to express society's reprobation. The condemned often were publicly tortured and mutilated, and then their bodies were dissected for good measure and left on public display. By contrast, the maximum sentence available today to the International Criminal Court, which tries the gravest of crimes, including war crimes, crimes against humanity, and genocide, is a life sentence reviewable every 25 years.[142] Under California law, Charles Manson has been getting a parole eligibility hearing every two years for decades, as has Sirhan Sirhan, the assailant of Senator Robert F. Kennedy. This is hardly a sign that California, whose prison population has increased more than 800 percent since Manson and Sirhan were incarcerated and which today operates the second-largest penal system in the country after the federal government, has somehow forsaken retribution.[143] As Dan Markel argues, retributive justice, properly understood, "hinges on modesty and dignity in modes of punishment" and is at odds with "the apparently ineluctable slide towards ever-harsher punishments in the name of justice."[144]

Unlike in the United States, a number of European countries make explicit the relative weights of retribution and risk in meting out life sentences. England and Wales, for example, have adopted a two-part process in which the court sets a minimum term for the purposes of deterrence and retribution. "However, once that period has been served, the release of the offender must be considered by a judicial body that meets the requirements of due process similar to those of a full trial but considers only the danger that the offender may still present to the public," according to Appleton and Grøver.[145] In Germany, all life-sentenced prisoners are constitutionally entitled to be considered for release after 15 years. If someone does not pose a continued major threat to public safety and was not convicted of crimes involving "exceptional gravity of guilt," he or she is generally released after serving 15 years. Crimes involving "exceptional gravity of guilt" include multiple homicides and instances of particularly cruel, brutal, reckless, or antisocial acts. "In practice, most prisoners whose guilt is so exceptionally grave will serve 18 or 20 years," according to Frieder Dünkel and Ineke Pruin.[146] As of 2007, Germany had about 2,000 prisoners serving life sentences, or about the same number as the state of Mississippi, whose total population is barely 4 percent of Germany's population.[147]

One of the country's premier penal reform groups appears to have made an important shift in its stance on the abolition of LWOP. The Sentencing Project is the author of two pathbreaking reports on life sentences, in 2004 and 2009, that were invaluable in drawing public, journalistic, and scholarly attention to this invisible issue. In the earlier report, the Sentencing Project called for abolishing LWOP "in all but exceptional cases."[148] In the follow-up report, it recommended eliminating *all* sentences of life without the possibility of parole.[149] Explaining the organization's current stance on LWOP, Marc Mauer, the executive director, said, "The argument on LWOP is very similar to that on the death penalty. Both on moral and practical terms the death penalty is cruel and ineffective and so should be eliminated, rather than each of us individually trying to determine who is actually 'the worst.'" Mauer went on to say, "Similarly for LWOP, there's no strong public safety argument supporting the policy since its elimination only opens up a possibility for release, and certainly no guarantee."[150]

To sum up, the "worst of the worst" will always present a daunting challenge to penal policy. For ages, this issue dominated discussions of capital punishment. In deciding on how best to challenge the widespread use of LWOP and whether to declare all LWOP sentences unacceptable, penal reformers certainly need to consider the realities of the broader political environment. But as Hugo Adam Bedau, a prominent death penalty abolitionist who did not endorse LWOP as an alternative to capital punishment, eloquently reminds us, "[I]t is not the task of penal reform—or of the movement against the death penalty—to present to the public whatever it will accept. The task, rather, is to argue for a punitive policy that is humane, feasible, and effective, whatever the crime and whoever the offender, and regardless of the current climate of public opinion."[151]

IV. Executive Clemency, Risk, and the Waning of Mercy

Governors and other public officials today remain deeply opposed to releasing serious and long-time offenders, no matter how many decades they have served behind bars, no matter the pile of evidence showing that they have turned their lives around, and no matter the compelling research findings about deterrence and aging out of crime. For example, in 2008 Governor Schwarzenegger and prosecutors in California vehemently opposed the compassionate release of Susan Atkins, a former follower of Charles Manson who was convicted in the infamous 1969 Tate-LaBianca murders. Atkins, who was paralyzed and dying of brain cancer, had become a model prisoner in her four decades behind bars.[152] Explaining why he refused to commute Atkins when she was gravely ill, Schwarzenegger said, "[T]hose kinds of crimes are just so unbelievable that I'm not for compassionate release."[153] For Schwarzenegger and many other politicians, the retributive endpoint for certain crimes is infinity.

Over the past four decades or so, retribution has become a central feature of U.S. penal policy, supplanting rehabilitation and even public safety as the chief aim. As a consequence, mercy, forgiveness, and redemption, which have been central considerations in religious, philosophical, and political debates about punishment for centuries—indeed millennia—have been sidelined. This is starkly evident not only in the sharp drop in the use of executive clemency today but also in the marked change in how public officials justify the few pardons and commutations that they do grant.

Pardons and commutations were vital features of the U.S. criminal justice system throughout the 19th century and much of the 20th century.[154] Presidents and governors regularly invoked their powers of executive clemency to reduce prison sentences, to remit fines, and to spare the lives of prisoners on death row. Despite the widespread view that pardons and commutations were antidemocratic and sources of corruption, executive clemency was a key mechanism to manage the prison population, to correct miscarriages of justice, to restore the rights of former offenders, and to make far-reaching public statements about the criminal justice system.[155]

Presidents and governors continued to wield their powers of executive clemency even in the face of public uproars over particular pardons or commutations. On Christmas Day in 1912, Governor George Donaghey of Arkansas, a fierce opponent of convict leasing, "pardoned 360 state prisoners in one fell swoop," in a gesture that made national headlines.[156] For years, a coalition of cotton planters, coal operators, corrupt judges, and anxious taxpayers had stymied his attempts to end the brutal system of convict leasing in Arkansas, which Donaghey considered a legalized system of murder in which the punishment so poorly fit the crime. In the 1930s at the height of Jim Crow era, Governor Mike Conner traveled to Parchman Farm to investigate the "forgotten men" of Mississippi's infamous penal farm. He "offered a personal hearing to any convict who had served a sentence of at least ten years." At his "mercy courts," Conner freed dozens of black prisoners in the face of charges that he was granting "amnesty for ancient coons." The governor was particularly affected by the sight of black children wearing prison stripes at Parchman, where one out of five inmates was under 20 years of age. He sent a number of these children home after giving them a lecture about honesty.[157]

Compare that with the modern-day commutation record of Pennsylvania, one of six states where life means life and where the lifer population has increased elevenfold since the early 1970s.[158] Between 1967 and 1994, Pennsylvania's governors and pardon board commuted the life sentences of nearly 400 inmates. Since then, only six commutations have been granted. Democrat Ed Rendell commuted only five life sentences during his two terms. Three of those were announced just weeks before he left office in early 2011.[159] By contrast, Democrat Milton Shapp commuted 251 during his eight years in office (1971–79), and Republican Raymond Shafer (1967–71) commuted 95 during his single term.[160] Pennsylvania's state officials vigorously battled a lawsuit filed on behalf of inmates sentenced prior to 1997, when the commutation rules changed significantly. Under the old rules, a commutation recommendation was forwarded to the governor if a majority of the pardon board supported it. The new rules, enacted in the wake of a high-profile double murder committed by a man whose sentence had been commuted, require a unanimous decision from the board, which includes the attorney general and a representative of victims' groups. That lawsuit dragged on for more than a decade—or almost as long as a typical lifer spent in prison in Pennsylvania in the 1970s before being released—and was eventually decided in the state's favor.[161]

In the first half of the 20th century, Woodrow Wilson, Franklin D. Roosevelt, and Harry Truman issued hundreds and in some cases thousands of pardons and commutations during their terms. The number of presidential pardons began to ebb during the Eisenhower years and severely dropped off with President George H. W. Bush and his successors.[162] Since at least the mid-1990s, the federal Bureau of Prisons has declined to take a position on the merits of clemency applications. It has abdicated its historical role in assisting the pardon attorney of the U.S. Department of Justice in identifying appropriate cases to recommend to the White House for early release.[163] As one commentator quipped, since becoming president, Barack Obama "has issued more pardons to Thanksgiving turkeys than to ex-offenders."[164]

Since the ascendancy of law-and-order politics in the 1970s, executive clemency has atrophied across the country. A survey of all commutations in noncapital cases between 1995 and 2003 found that most states averaged fewer than 100 commutations during these eight years; 34 states, including Texas, California, Ohio, and Pennsylvania, which have some of the largest prison populations, granted 20 or fewer commutations during this time.[165] The American Bar Association's Justice Kennedy Commission "reviewed the state of pardoning in the United States and found that in most jurisdictions the pardon power is rarely utilized to reduce sentences or promote reentry of individuals to the community."[166] The Kennedy Commission wisely recommended that states and the federal government revitalize the clemency process. It urged them "to establish standards and provide an accessible process by which prisoners may request a reduction of sentence in exceptional circumstances," including but not limited to "old age, disability, changes in the law, exigent family circumstances, heroic acts, or extraordinary suffering." The commission also called for ensuring that procedures are in place to aid prisoners who are unable to advocate for themselves to seek clemency.[167]

Standardizing procedures for seeking clemency and providing prisoners with more assistance to navigate the clemency process are noble goals. But they will not on their own revitalize the use of clemency and significantly reduce the lifer population. Public officials need once again to be willing to assume the political risks that come with releasing offenders early. In the past, governors and presidents were willing to weather charges of being antidemocratic or corrupt when they invoked their clemency powers. Now that crime has become such a persistent political trip wire in the United States, they need to steel themselves—and prepare the public—for the rare but inevitable instance when a released prisoner goes on to commit a front-page crime.

Although the recidivism rate for older inmates who have served lengthy sentences is comparatively lower, it is not—and will never be—zero. Despite all the attention focused these days on developing better risk-assessment tools, we will never be able to predict with complete certainty who will commit a serious crime if released and who will not. Lifers are not likely to kill or assault in prison or after release. However, some will. Of the 558 inmates (excluding those in Illinois) on death row awaiting execution whose sentences were commuted as a result of the 1972 *Furman* decision, six went on to commit murder in prison over the next decade and a half.[168] The 239 *Furman*-era capital offenders released on parole to the community, who as a group were more than 40 years old when they were released, committed 12 new violent offenses. Notably, one killed again and two raped again.[169] Those who went on to commit additional violent acts apparently were indistinguishable from those who did not in terms of their previous offense characteristics, race, age, and prior criminal history.[170] A more recent survey of the 322 former death-row inmates released on parole from the "class of '72," who had served about 18 years on average, found that five went on to kill again. Of the 164 who were not released, 9 committed homicide while in prison and 10 reportedly killed themselves.[171]

If public officials are going to revitalize executive clemency and parole, they need to reconcile themselves to "the fact that release procedures, like all other human practices, are not infallible."[172] They need to improve their rehabilitation programs and risk-assessment tools, but they also must do more to educate the public that inmates who are released after serving lengthy terms are unlikely to commit violent offenses—but they are not risk free.

Governors willing to assume that risk remain the exception today. Before she left office in 2011, Governor Janet Granholm of Michigan had commuted more sentences than had all her three predecessors combined. Nearly all of these commutations came after she ran for reelection in 2006, and the overwhelming majority involved drug offenders or seriously ill inmates.[173] During Arkansas governor Mike Huckabee's first six years in office, he granted 30 percent more clemencies than had the previous three governors combined.[174] His commutation and pardon record came under national scrutiny and spurred a spate of political obituaries for Huckabee after a man he had granted clemency in 2000 later killed four police officers in Tacoma, Washington, in 2009. After a released parolee shot and killed a Massachusetts police officer in December 2010, Democratic governor Patrick Duval sought to replace much of the parole board with law enforcement appointees and introduced legislation that would further restrict parole eligibility for lifers in the Bay State.[175] Notably, since returning to the governor's mansion in 2011, Jerry Brown of California has been paroling a much higher proportion of lifers than his predecessors did.[176]

Some public officials have expressed interest in releasing infirm elderly inmates who do not pose a threat to society. One of the major obstacles is that older prisoners are more likely to have been incarcerated for a serious violent offense. A 2006 report on North Carolina prisoners found that almost 60 percent of inmates ages 50 and above were serving time for violent or sex crimes. More than half of them were serving a sentence of life or 10 years to life.[177] By late 2009, 15 states and the District of Columbia had established provisions for geriatric release.[178] However, these jurisdictions rarely released elderly inmates due to political considerations, fears of public opposition, the narrow criteria for eligibility, Byzantine procedures that discourage inmates from applying for release, and the complicated and lengthy referral and review process that often drags on right up until the time an inmate dies in prison. Some of these jurisdictions have yet to release a single elderly inmate using the new geriatric early-release provisions.[179]

Released long-time offenders do not pose a widespread public threat. But they do pose a significant risk to political careers. Changes in the institutional structure of parole and pardon boards could provide public officials with some important political insulation from potentially controversial release decisions. States almost always staff these boards with political appointees, who are extremely vulnerable to the wrath of public opinion. Four decades ago, the President's Commission on Law Enforcement and the Administration of Justice recommended that the boards be composed of psychologists, social workers, corrections officials, and other professionals with specialized training and expertise to evaluate offenders' suitability for release. That recommendation remains largely unrealized today. In nearly every state, governors appoint all members of the parole board.[180] Two-thirds of the states have no professional qualifications for parole board membership. A notable exception is Ohio, where all parole board members "are appointed by the director of the state department of corrections, serve in civil service positions, and must have an extensive background in criminal justice."[181]

As U.S. Senator James Webb (D-VA) said at a recent conference on prisoner reentry sponsored by the Hamilton Project, "The question is about political fear. And I think it invades the political process."[182] Politicians and public officials can help neutralize that fear by educating the public about the nuances of deterrence, the limited utility of lengthy sentences for fighting crime, the phenomenon of aging out of crime, and the strengths and limits of risk-assessment tools. However, they cannot guarantee that releasing offenders will be risk free. As Glenn Martin of the Fortune Society said at the Hamilton Project conference, "[W]e need to increase our appetite for risk. . . . [W]e have to at least accept the fact that some people are going to fail and some people are going to fail pretty significantly."[183]

The public's and politicians' low appetite for risk is not the only obstacle to expanding the use of executive clemency and rethinking the widespread practice of condemning so many people to the "other death penalty." As Austin Sarat, Daniel Kobil, Elizabeth Rapaport, and others have noted, the retributive theory of clemency has been ascendant for some time now.[184] There is a widespread belief that clemency should only be used to remedy "miscarriages of justice," as U.S. Supreme Court Justice William Rehnquist famously argued.[185] Governors are largely unwilling to treat mercy as a permissible reason for granting clemency. Commutations and pardons are most commonly justified as a means to rectify some shortcoming of the judicial process: the offender is innocent or has a credible claim of innocence; he or she did not receive a fair trial; the sentence is disproportionately severe compared to what other participants in the crime received.[186] These "anti-mercy conceptions of clemency"[187] wholly reject redemption, forgiveness, reconciliation, and mercy as legitimate claims for clemency, greatly narrowing the pool of prisoners who might petition for a pardon or commutation. But they do more than that.

The impact of executive clemency extends far beyond all the individuals lucky enough—or not—to receive a pardon or commutation. Executive clemency is an important vehicle to make a statement about the criminal justice system and, more broadly, about what kind of society we want. As such, it shapes the wider political environment in which issues of crime and punishment are debated and criminal justice policy is forged. Governor Donaghey's wholesale pardon a century ago was intended as a searing denunciation of Alabama's system of convict leasing. Woodrow Wilson was an ardent supporter of temperance but opposed the Volstead Act, which imposed Prohibition. As president, he pardoned hundreds of alcohol-related offenders.[188] His pardons were widely understood at the time as an indictment of Prohibition. Governors Lee Cruce of Oklahoma (1911–15), Winthrop Rockefeller of Arkansas (1966–70), and Toney Anaya of New Mexico (1982–86) issued mass commutations to empty their death rows and justified their actions with calls for mercy for the condemned.[189] By contrast, of the four dozen people sentenced to death between 1976 and 2003 who were spared by acts of executive clemency, "only four were based on what could arguably be characterized as merciful reasons."[190] When Governor George Ryan pardoned four inmates on death row in Illinois and commuted the sentences of 167 others in 2003, he rejected "mercy and compassion as legitimate responses to criminals."[191] He said his actions were warranted because of problems in the way capital punishment was administrated, not because of the fundamental immorality of the death penalty. At the time, Ryan went out of his way to reaffirm his law-and-order credentials and to herald life in prison without the possibility of parole as a fate perhaps worse than death.[192]

U.S. Supreme Court Justice Anthony Kennedy lamented in a 2003 speech to the American Bar Association, "The pardon process, of late, seems to have been drained of its moral force."[193] As a consequence, many crimes remain eternally unforgivable and unforgettable. Their perpetrators are forever defined by the crime they were convicted of, despite all the evidence piling up over the decades that they are not the same person who committed that crime and that they do not pose a major threat to public safety.

V. Capital Punishment and the "Other Death Penalty"

The death penalty abolition movement and the tenacity of capital punishment in the United States pose two important challenges to reducing the lifer population. Thanks in part to the innocence movement, with its dramatic focus on people wrongly condemned to death, capital punishment is declining in the United States.[194] The number of people executed each year has fallen by about half since the late 1990s. Opinion polls show that support for capital punishment is waning. It now stands at about two-thirds, down from a high point of 86 percent in 1995, according to Gallup polls.[195] The innocence frame, with its related arguments about fairness, has supplanted constitutionality and morality as the dominant frame.

The anti-death-penalty movement's "obsessive focus" on the innocent, estimated to constitute anywhere from 1 percent to a third of the death-row population, has overshadowed the wider question of what constitutes justice for the guilty housed on death row and for the growing number of lifers who will likely die in prison or spend most of their lives there.[196] The number of people sentenced to death and executed has fallen sharply but at the cost of a huge spike in "death by incarceration."

Over the years, a number of leading abolitionists have ardently supported LWOP. They have uncritically accepted LWOP as a viable alternative to the death penalty and thus have helped to legitimize the wider use of a sentence that has many features in common with capital punishment. These abolitionists have helped normalize a sanction that, like the death penalty, is way out of line with human rights and sentencing norms in other developed countries. Many European countries do not permit LWOP, and those that do use it sparingly. In much of western Europe, a "life" sentence typically amounts to a dozen or so years, as it once did in practice in many U.S. states.[197] That said, the number of life sentences appears to have increased in the wake of the abolition of capital punishment in many countries.[198]

One has to be careful here about how much blame to apportion to death penalty abolitionists for the proliferation of life sentences in the United States, however.[199] Neither opponents nor supporters of capital punishment could have predicted the fierce conservative backlash after

the 1972 *Furman* decision and how it would spur the push for more punitive penal policies. For various reasons, the abolitionist movement of the
late 20th century got channeled though the courts. A string of victories in
the courts beginning in the 1960s reinforced this bias toward viewing the
judiciary as the most promising venue to abolish capital punishment.[200]
In the mid-1960s an elite-led anti-death-penalty movement began to take
shape in the United States. At the time, the leading public-interest groups
opposed to capital punishment made a key decision to launch an all-out
assault on the death penalty through the courts by challenging its fundamental constitutionality rather than by attempting to abolish it through
legislative means. As a consequence, the main arena to battle capital
punishment shifted from state legislatures to the courts. Accustomed to
fighting and winning in the courts and bereft of the necessary resources
to wage a wider political and legislative campaign, abolitionists concentrated their efforts and resources on the legal arena. As a consequence,
they were unprepared for the virulent political and legislative backlash in
the 1970s as many states moved quickly to refashion their death penalty
statutes to meet the constitutional objections that the Supreme Court had
raised in the *Furman* decision.

At the time, the abolitionist movement was not really a movement at all
but rather a consortium of elite public-interest lawyers. They could not have
done much to stem the punitive stampede in the immediate wake of *Furman* as states rewrote their death penalty statutes and began to rethink life
sentences. Moreover, executive clemency still appeared to be a viable mechanism to secure the release of many lifers. Thus, abolitionists at that time
could endorse LWOP or a life sentence as an alternative to capital punishment, figuring that most lifers—even those serving LWOP sentences—would
be released after a decade or two at the most.[201] Indeed, there was an expecta-
tion at the time that as states returned to determinate sentencing systems,
the importance of executive clemency as a release mechanism was likely to
grow.[202]

No comprehensive account exists to my knowledge that compares and
contrasts when, why, and how individual states came to enact LWOP statutes. Seven states already had LWOP statutes on the books or in practice
prior to the *Furman* decision. Some of these statutes dated back to the 19th
century.[203] Although the growing punitive climate generally explains why
states enacted LWOP or tougher life statutes in the aftermath of *Furman*,
the timing and triggering events appear to have varied enormously. Some
states embraced LWOP as an immediate response to sentencing dilemmas

created by *Furman*.[204] The public's growing frustration with what it perceived to be a "revolving door" of justice facilitated by permissive and incompetent parole boards appears to have been the catalyst elsewhere.[205] In other states, a particularly heinous crime set off the political stampede for LWOP.[206] As Mona Lynch explains, "the direct catalysts for mass incarceration generally are located in regional, state, and local conditions—historical and contemporary—whereas their proliferation is enhanced by more macro-level factors."[207]

Abolitionists likely played an important role in establishing the legitimacy of LWOP in the 1970s, 1980s, and 1990s but were probably quite incidental in most cases to the final legislative outcome. Some abolitionists ardently opposed promoting LWOP as an alternative to the death penalty. Hugo Adam Bedau, for example, declared, "The death penalty is not the only outrageous form of punishment active in our society, even if it is the worst."[208] But a number of prominent abolitionists have promoted LWOP as an equally tough—or even tougher—retributive moral sanction.[209] As such, we have had "a strange pairing of death penalty abolitionists" joining together with penal hard-liners to promote LWOP statutes.[210] In the early 1990s, Governor Mario Cuomo of New York called for wider use of LWOP and offered to sign away his clemency powers so as to neutralize public opposition to his strident anti-death-penalty stance.[211] Sister Helen Prejean of *Dead Man Walking* fame also promoted LWOP to undermine public support for the death penalty. Steven Brill, the founder of the *American Lawyer*, denounced the death penalty as "immoral and never acceptable" but called for imposing LWOP in all instances of premeditated murder and murder "committed during and in the furtherance of another crime." He faulted liberals for being "insanely permissive about murderers."[212]

Leading abolitionist organizations took ambivalent position stances. The director of the ACLU's National Capital Punishment Project declared in 1990 that his organization would "acquiesce, but not support" LWOP if it were offered as a substitute for the death penalty.[213] The head of the ACLU's southeastern regional office characterized LWOP sentences as too harsh and inflexible but nonetheless endorsed them as "a wrong step in the right direction."[214] In the early 1990s, a spokesman for the National Coalition to Abolish the Death Penalty (NCADP) refused to denounce LWOP sentences, declaring instead that the organization did not endorse particular alternatives to execution.[215]

Capital defense attorneys have been vested in retaining LWOP. Evidence suggests that the availability of parole in capital cases is often a key factor for jurors, who must decide whether to impose the death penalty or a life sentence. In those death penalty states where LWOP is an alternative option, capital defense attorneys, in making their pitch for life over death, emphasize that the defendant will never be getting out of prison and that a life sentence that stretches out for decades is actually more punitive than condemning someone to death. LWOP statutes appear to have played only a minor role in the recent drop in the number of executions in the United States.[216] But they have contributed to a doubling or even tripling of the sentence lengths for offenders who never would have been sentenced to death in the first place or even been eligible for the death penalty.[217] Lifers today serve on average 29 years in prison, up from about 21 years in 1991.[218]

Prosecutors in capital punishment states have been some of the fiercest opponents of LWOP statutes. In states where parole is a possibility—however remote—for life-sentenced offenders, prosecutors often focus their closing arguments on warnings about the future threat the defendant poses if released on parole one day. They ask jurors, "Do you really want this man back on the streets?"[219] This widespread prosecutorial strategy spurs jurors to choose death over life.[220] The *Simmons v. South Carolina* decision reinforced prosecutors' opposition to LWOP. That 1994 Supreme Court decision requires prosecutors who raise the issue of the future dangerousness of a capital defendant in their closing arguments to inform the jury if the LWOP alternative exists in a state. But jurors do not have to be informed about other parole conditions.[221] This explains why prosecutors in Texas steadfastly opposed creating an LWOP provision in the Lone Star State.[222] They preferred to maintain the state's "capital life" statute, which renders prisoners eligible for parole but only after 40 years. Thanks to *Simmons v. South Carolina*, Texas prosecutors were not required to inform capital juries about the existence of this de facto life sentence.[223] Only after the Supreme Court ruled in *Roper v. Simmons* that the execution of people who committed their crimes as juveniles was unconstitutional did Texas prosecutors soften their opposition to an LWOP bill that had stalled in the state legislature. This paved the way for its quick passage in spring 2005. Texas prosecutors acted out of a fear that juvenile offenders might become eligible for parole in the aftermath of the *Roper* decision.[224] This legislation opened the floodgates for what people in Texas began calling "life row." In a pattern familiar in other states, the list of qualifying crimes for LWOP expanded in Texas.[225]

The exploding lifer population and our growing understanding of the similarities between how life sentences and death sentences are imposed and on whom have not prompted a fundamental rethinking of the connections between death penalty abolitionism and penal policy more broadly. The abolitionist movement still operates quite independently of the growing movement against mass incarceration. Typical of many mainstream abolitionist organizations, Amnesty International remains notably agnostic on the question of alternatives to the death penalty, except in the case of JLWOP, which it forcefully opposes.[226] In 2002, Amnesty International rejected a recommendation by its own internal review committee to "initiate a thorough discussion of alternatives to the death penalty," even though its unwillingness to recommend or oppose substitute punishments might be undermining "the credibility of its overall argument for abolition."[227] As for the NCADP, on its current list of "Ten Reasons Why Capital Punishment Is Flawed Public Policy," number 10 is "Life without parole is a sensible alternative to the death penalty."[228]

Attorney Barry Scheck, one of the leading figures in the innocence movement today, continues to strongly defend LWOP as an alternative to capital punishment.[229] Scheck and other foes of capital punishment who testified before the New Jersey Death Penalty Study Commission in 2006 generally did not raise any concerns about the state's growing lifer population as they promoted LWOP as an alternative to the death penalty. In their testimony, they emphasized "evolving standards of decency," the growing number of exonerated prisoners released from death row, public opinion data showing growing support for LWOP among New Jerseyans, and the huge economic burden of capital punishment in the Garden State.[230] Echoing Sister Helen Prejean's position, a local chapter of the New Jersey ACLU declared in its written testimony to the panel that the death penalty is "the single most serious violation of civil liberties in our nation."[231] At the time, New Jersey had only nine prisoners on death row and had not executed anyone since 1963. But its lifer population numbered about 1,000.[232] A 2007 analysis by the *Newark Star-Ledger* of murder cases since 1982, when capital punishment was reinstated in New Jersey, found that about 100 people who were convicted of murder would have been punished more harshly under the LWOP bill proposed by the state's Death Penalty Commission.[233]

The Other Death Penalty Project, a new group composed exclusively of prisoners, has called on death penalty abolitionist groups to stop promoting LWOP as a "supposedly humane alternative to lethal injection." The group rejects the proposition that LWOP "is a necessary first step toward ultimate abolition of the death penalty."[234] Kenneth E. Hartman, a founder of the group, is serving an LWOP sentence in California for killing a man in a fistfight more than three decades ago when he was 19 years old. Hartman describes a life sentence as an "execution in the form of a long, deliberate stoning that goes on for as long as I draw breath."[235] In 2004, the Campaign to End the Death Penalty passed a resolution opposing LWOP. At its 2008 convention, it reaffirmed that LWOP is not a "humane or just alternative to the death penalty."[236] However, the campaign's website does not prominently feature its opposition to LWOP.

The abolitionist experience is relevant to the debate over life sentences in another respect. Those who are opposed to the proliferation of life sentences should be wary of making some of the same missteps that death penalty abolitionists made in the 1960s and 1970s by focusing primarily on judicial strategies and largely ignoring the legislative or political arenas. An exclusive focus on judicial strategies is potentially costly in several respects. It forces an issue to be framed within the constraints of prior legal texts, rules, and decisions. As a consequence, arguments and evidence that may be compelling in the political sphere fall to the wayside because the courts have been unreceptive to them. The most notable relevant example here is how the Supreme Court has dealt with the issue of race in the context of the death penalty.

Some of the most striking victories for civil rights groups from the 1920s to 1960s involved southern criminal cases marred by Jim Crow.[237] But in the landmark capital punishment cases since then, the Supreme Court has been persistently unreceptive to arguments fashioned on how capital punishment is imposed in a racially discriminatory manner. In 1963, Supreme Court Justice Arthur Goldberg made his highly calculated dissent to the denial of certiorari in *Rudolph v. Alabama*, an obscure interracial rape case, that appeared to open the way for a broader constitutional challenge to the death penalty. In his dissent, Goldberg did not cite racial discrimination "as relevant and, apparently, worthy of argument," even though Rudolph was black and 9 out of 10 men executed for this crime since 1930 had been black.[238] The racially discriminatory nature of capital punishment was not a central issue in the landmark *Furman* decision that suspended capital punishment in the United States. Four years later, when the Court revisited the issue of the constitutionality of the death penalty, it carefully chose the five cases that became collectively known as *Gregg*. Most of the lead defendants in those five cases, including Troy Leon Gregg, were white, thus "taking race, for the moment, off the table," David Oshinsky explains.[239] When the Supreme Court struck down capital punishment in instances of rape in the 1977 *Coker* decision, it cited proportionality concerns, not the racially discriminatory manner in which capital rape laws were imposed. Notably, the Court chose the case of Erlich Coker, a white male, to test the constitutionality of capital rape laws, which have been used overwhelmingly to punish black—not white—men. In the *McCleskey v. Kemp* (1987) decision, indifference and hostility characterized the majority's reaction to compelling statistical evidence that people convicted of murdering a white person in Georgia are 11 times more likely to be sentenced to death than those convicted of killing a black person. Extensive evidence about the history of racial discrimination in the imposition of the death penalty did not sway the majority's decision.[240] Racial considerations apparently were irrelevant in the recent *Graham* decision, even though Terrance Graham is African American, as is Joe Sullivan, another juvenile offender in Florida who had a companion case with Graham, and even though juvenile lifers are disproportionately African American.

Given the Court's persistent indifference and/or hostility to claims about racial discrimination in the administration of criminal justice, it is not surprising that legal strategies to challenge life sentences do not stress the racial aspects of this punishment.[241] But the fact that the life-sentenced population is disproportionately African American is an important political issue.[242] African Americans are considerably more likely to receive third-strike sentences in California, even after controlling for legally relevant variables.[243] Nationally, nearly half of all lifers are black.[244] This is considerably higher than the proportion of blacks in the general prison population, which is about 38 percent. The issue of racial disparities is even more pronounced in the case of LWOP sentences. Blacks constitute 56 percent of the LWOP population.[245] Nearly half of all juveniles sentenced to life—and about 56 percent of the juveniles serving LWOP sentences—are African American.[246] In many states, the racial disparity in juvenile life sentences is "quite severe."[247] In short, a primary or exclusive focus on judicial strategies forces the whitewashing of the problem of LWOP and life sentences.

Conclusion

Keeping so many older prisoners incarcerated does not significantly reduce the crime rate and is extremely expensive. It vacuums up dollars that might be better spent on something else. The population of imprisoned elderly adults is growing rapidly. Between 1999 and 2007, the number of people ages 55 or older in state and federal prisons grew by nearly 77 percent, and those ages 45 to 54 grew by almost 68 percent.[248] Because of elderly inmates' greater need for expensive health-care services, prisons spend two to three times more to incarcerate an elderly inmate than a younger one, or on average about $70,000 a year.[249] These elderly inmates, like nearly all inmates, do not qualify for Medicare, Medicaid, or Social Security benefits, so states must assume the entire burden of their medical and other costs. Although the current economic distress provides an important political opening to rethink these and other penal expenses, we should not assume that the crushing economic burden of the penal system will single-handedly unhinge the carceral state.

Mounting fiscal pressures will not be enough on their own to spur communities, states, and the federal government to make deep and lasting cuts in their prison and jail populations. It was mistakenly assumed four decades ago that shared disillusionment on the right and the left with indeterminate sentences and prison rehabilitation programs would shrink the inmate population. Instead, it exploded. The race to incarcerate began in the 1970s at a time when states faced dire financial straits. It persisted over the next four decades despite wide fluctuations in the crime rate, public opinion, and the economy. If history is any guide, rising public anxiety in the face of persistent economic distress and growing economic inequalities might, in fact, spur more punitiveness.[250]

In short, the current economic crisis presents an opportunity to redirect U.S. penal policy that opponents of the prison boom should exploit. However, framing this issue as primarily an economic one will not sustain the political momentum needed over the long haul to drastically reduce the prison population and to bring about the end of LWOP and the release of sizable numbers of lifers. Economic justifications also ignore the fact that a successful decarceration will cost money. The people reentering society after prison need significant educational, vocational, housing, medical, and economic support. We need to make considerable reinvestments in reentry to ensure that the communities these people are returning to are not further destabilized by waves of former prisoners whose time inside has greatly impaired their economic, educational, and social opportunities.

Reentry—that is, providing offenders with educational programs, substance-abuse treatment, job skills, and other services to help them make a successful transition back to society upon release—has caught the imagination of penal reformers, policymakers, and public officials spanning the political spectrum. But as reentry has skyrocketed to the top of the penal reform agenda, lifers are facing the prospect of a further deterioration in their conditions of confinement. Despite all the recent talk about reentry, money for treatment, programs, and services for all offenders is shockingly limited and continuing to shrink.[251] In an age of tightening budgets and a fixation on reentry, lifers are increasingly being denied programs and activities that might make their prison days without end more bearable.[252] As one lifer in California lamented, "The thinking goes that since we will never get out of prison there is no point in expending scarce resources on dead men walking."[253]

In California and elsewhere, the prospects are bleak that the plight of lifers will become a leading issue on the penal reform agenda anytime soon. This political quiescence in the face of exponential growth in the lifer population is particularly striking given the intense legal and political mobilization against capital punishment in recent years. There are currently about 3,300 inmates on death row in the United States. Nearly all of them will die in prison of natural causes or suicide—not lethal injection. Compare that with the estimated 141,000 people now serving life sentences in the United States. The reinstatement and transformation of capital punishment have been central legal and political issues for going on four decades now. Meanwhile the United States has been nonchalantly condemning tens of thousands of people to the "other death penalty" with barely a legal or political whimper.

NOTES

I especially would like to thank Rachel Barkow, Jeffrey Fagan, Julia Hall, Dan Markel, Charles Ogletree, Austin Sarat, participants in the 2011 Criminal Justice Roundtable at Yale Law School, the students in the Prison University Program at San Quentin, and the other contributors to this book for their thoughtful comments and constructive suggestions on drafts of this chapter.

1. Pew Center on the States, "One in 31: The Long Reach of American Corrections" (Washington, DC: Pew Center on the States, 2009), 2; Sara Robinson, "Five Big Ideas We Should Be Talking About," OurFuture.org, Feb. 4, 2009, http://www.ourfuture.org/blog-entry/2009020604/five-big-ideas-we-should-be-talking-about (accessed Mar. 24, 2009); Newt Gingrich and Pat Nolan, "Prison Reform: A Smart Way for States to Save Money and Lives," *Washington Post*, Jan. 7, 2011.

2. Abdon Pallasch, "Prisons Not the Answer to Crime Problems: Attorney General," *Chicago Sun-Times*, Aug. 3, 2009.

3. Ryan S. King, "The State of Sentencing 2008: Developments in Policy and Practice" (Washington, DC: Sentencing Project, 2009).

4. Nicole D. Porter, "The State of Sentencing 2010: Developments in Policy and Practice" (Washington, DC: Sentencing Project, Feb. 2011); David M. Reutter, "Economic Crisis Prompts Prison Closures Nationwide, but Savings (and Reforms) Are Elusive," *Prison Legal News* 20.4 (2010): 1, 3–10; John Gramlich, "At Least 26 States Spend Less on Prisons," Stateline.org, Aug. 11, 2009 (updated Aug. 14, 2009), http://www.stateline.org/live/details/story?contentId=418338 (accessed Oct. 16, 2009).

5. Pew Center on the States, "Prison Count 2010" (Washington, DC: Pew Center on the States, Mar. 2010).

6. Ashley Nellis and Ryan S. King, "No Exit: The Expanding Use of Life Sentences in America" (Washington, DC: Sentencing Project, July 2009), 2.

7. Ibid., 2–3.

8. Michael Tonry, *Punishing Race: A Continuing American Dilemma* (New York: Oxford University Press, 2011), 36.

9. A 2000 study estimated that about one of every four adult prisoners was serving a sentence of 20 years or more. C. G. Camp and G. M. Camp, *The 2000 Corrections Yearbook: Adult Corrections* (Middletown, CT: Criminal Justice Institute, 2000), 54, cited in Marc Mauer, Ryan S. King, and Malcolm C. Young, "The Meaning of 'Life': Long Prison Sentences in Context" (Washington, DC: Sentencing Project, May 2004), 11.

10. Penal Reform International, "Alternatives to the Death Penalty: The Problems with Life Imprisonment," *Penal Briefing* 1 (2007), http://www.penalreform.org/publications/penal-reform-briefing-no1-alternatives-death-penalty-0 (accessed May 25, 2011), 1, 6.

11. "A Matter of Life and Death: The Effect of Life-without-Parole Statutes on Capital Punishment," *Harvard Law Review* 119 (2006), 1839.

12. Peter B. Hoffman, "History of the Federal Parole System, Part 1 (1910–1972)," *Federal Probation* 61 (1997), 24, cited in "A Matter of Life and Death," *Harvard Law Review*, 1840n. 16.

13. In the early 1950s, the average life sentence was 10 years in Kentucky, 11 years in Texas, and 14 years in North Carolina. Giovanni I. Giardini and Richard G. Farrow, "The Paroling of Capital Offenders," *Annals of the American Academy of Political and Social Science* 284 (1952), 93.

14. Lane Nelson, "A History of Penal Reform in Angola, Part I: The Immovable Object," *Angolite*, Sept.–Oct. 2009, 17.

15. John Corley, "A Matter of Life," *Angolite*, Sept.–Oct. 2009, 29.

16. Rachel E. Barkow, "The Court of Life and Death: The Two Tracks of Constitutional Sentencing Law and the Case for Uniformity," *Michigan Law Review* 107 (May 2009), 1167.

17. Youngjae Lee, "The Constitutional Right against Excessive Punishment," *Virginia Law Review* 91.3 (May 2005): 681. See also Barkow, "The Court of Life and Death."

18. Julian H. Wright, Jr., "Life-without-Parole: An Alternative to Death or Not Much of a Life at All?," *Vanderbilt Law Review* 43 (March 1990): 535–37.

19. J. Mark Lane, "'Is There Life without Parole?': A Capital Defendant's Right to a Meaningful Alternative Sentence," *Loyola (Los Angeles) Law Review* 26 (1992–93): 351–53.

20. Robert M. Bohm, "The Economic Costs of Capital Punishment: Past, Present, and Future," in James R. Acker, Robert M. Bohm, and Charles S. Lanier, eds., *America's Experiment with Capital Punishment: Reflections on the Past, Present, and Future of the Ultimate Penal Sanction*, 2nd ed. (Durham, NC: Carolina Academic Press, 2003), 591–92. In Texas, each death penalty case costs taxpayers on average $2.3 million, about three times the lifetime cost of imprisoning someone at the highest level of security. Richard C. Dieter, "Millions Misspent: What Politicians Don't Say about the High Costs of the Death Penalty," in Hugo Adam Bedau, ed., *The Death Penalty in America: Current Controversies* (New York: Oxford University Press, 1997), 402.

21. "A Matter of Life and Death," 1853.

22. Lee, "The Constitutional Right against Excessive Punishment," 681.

23. Richard S. Frase, "Excessive Prison Sentences, Punishment Goals, and the Eighth Amendment: 'Proportionality' Relative to What?," *Minnesota Law Review* 89 (Feb. 2005),

574. See also Catherine Appleton and Bent Grøver, "The Pros and Cons of Life without Parole," *British Journal of Criminology* 47 (2007): 599.

24. Frase, "Excessive Prison Sentences," 629. See also Barkow, "The Court of Life and Death," 1184.

25. Barkow, "The Court of Life and Death," 1145.

26. For an excellent critical overview of the Court's "death-is-different canon," see Barkow, "The Court of Life and Death." See also Barkow's "Life without Parole and the Hope for Real Sentencing Reform," chap. 6 in this volume, as well as Henry, "Death-in-Prison Sentences," and Josh Bowers, "Mandatory Life and the Death of Equitable Discretion," chap. 1 in this volume.

27. See Barkow, "Life without Parole," this volume.

28. *Callins v. Collins* 510 U.S. 1141, at 1145 (1994), as quoted in David Garland, *Peculiar Institution: America's Death Penalty in an Age of Abolition* (Cambridge: Belknap Press of Harvard University Press, 2010), 266.

29. Garland, *Peculiar Institution*, 43.

30. See, for example, Stephen B. Bright, "Discrimination, Death, and Denial: Race and the Death Penalty," in David R. Dow and Mark Dow, eds., *Machinery of Death: The Reality of America's Death Penalty Regime* (New York: Routledge, 2002): 45–78.

31. *Yale Law Journal* 103.7 (1994): 1835–83.

32. Barkow, "The Court of Life and Death," 1145.

33. Garland, *Peculiar Institution*, 258.

34. Robert Weisberg, "Deregulating Death," *Supreme Court Review* (1983): 305–95. See also John Paul Stevens, "On the Death Sentence," *New York Review of Books*, Dec. 23, 2010, 14.

35. *Graham v. Florida*, 569 U.S. (2010), slip opinion, 2.

36. Bohm, "The Economic Costs of Capital Punishment," 591; and Nellis and King, "No Exit."

37. Peter B. Hoffman, "History of the Federal Parole System," 49, 51, cited in "A Matter of Life and Death," *Harvard Law Review*, 1839n. 8.

38. Appleton and Grøver, "The Pros and Cons of Life without Parole," 599–600.

39. Phoebe C. Ellsworth and Samuel R. Gross, "Hardening of the Attitudes: Americans' Views of the Death Penalty," in Stuart A. Scheingold, ed., *Politics, Crime Control and Culture* (Aldershot, UK: Ashgate, Dartmouth, 1997): 209–47; William J. Bowers, Margaret Vandiver, and Patricia H. Dugan, "A New Look at Public Opinion on Capital Punishment: What Citizens and Legislators Prefer," in Scheingold, *Politics, Crime Control and Culture*; Richard C. Dieter, "Sentencing for Life: Americans Embrace Alternatives to the Death Penalty," in Robert M. Bohm, ed., *The Death Penalty in America: Current Controversies* (New York: Oxford University Press, 1998): 116–34; and Frank R. Baumgartner, Suzanna L. De Boef, and Amber E. Boydstun, *The Decline of the Death Penalty and the Discovery of Innocence* (Cambridge: Cambridge University Press, 2008), 173–74.

40. *Naovarath v. State*, 105 Nev. 525, 526, 779 P.2d 944 (1989), as quoted in *Graham*, 569 U.S., slip opinion, 19.

41. See Timothy J. Flanagan, ed., *Long-Term Imprisonment: Policy, Science, and Correctional Practice* (Thousand Oaks, CA: Sage, 1995).

42. Robert Johnson and Ania Dobrzanska, "Mature Coping among Life-Sentenced Inmates: An Exploratory Study of Adjustment Dynamics," *Corrections Compendium*, Nov.–Dec. 2005, 37n. 4.

43. Ibid., 37.

44. Ibid.

45. Ibid., 8.

46. As quoted in ibid., 36.

47. Lewis E. Lawes, "Why I Changed My Mind," in Philip E. Mackey, ed., *Voices against Death: American Opposition to Capital Punishment, 1787–1975* (New York: Burt Franklin, 1976), 194.

48. Julian H. Wright, Jr., "Life without Parole: The View from Death Row," *Criminal Law Bulletin* 27 (1991), 348.

49. Lloyd Dunkelberger, "Juvenile Offenders Still Get Near-Life Terms," *Herald-Tribune*, Nov. 21, 2010, http://www.heraldtribune.com/article/20101121/ARTICLE/11211086 (accessed Mar. 28, 2011).

50. See the contributions to the special issue on imprisonment and crime in *Criminology & Public Policy* 10.1 (Feb. 2011).

51. Steven N. Durlauf and Daniel S. Nagin, "Imprisonment and Crime: Can Both Be Reduced?," *Criminology & Public Policy* 10.1 (Feb. 2011): 13–54.

52. Daniel S. Nagin, Francis T. Cullen, and Cheryl Lero Jonson, "Imprisonment and Reoffending," in Michael Tonry, ed., *Crime and Justice: A Review of Research* 38 (Chicago: University of Chicago Press, 2009): 115–200.

53. There is one important caveat here. Although gun-use laws have increased the length of sentences on the books, they appear not to have increased the actual lengths of the sentences meted out. Durlauf and Nagin, "Imprisonment and Crime," 28.

54. John H. Laub and Robert J. Sampson, *Shared Beginnings, Divergent Lives: Delinquent Boys to Age 70* (Cambridge: Harvard University Press, 2003).

55. Mauer, King, and Young, "The Meaning of 'Life,'" 24.

56. Ibid.

57. Advisory Committee on Geriatric and Seriously Ill Inmates, "Report of the Advisory Committee on Geriatric and Seriously Ill Inmates" (Harrisburg, PA: Joint State Government Commission, General Assembly of the Commonwealth of Pennsylvania, 2005), 77.

58. "Low Recidivism Rate Reported for Paroled NY Murderers," *Crime Report*, Jan. 7, 2011, http://www.thecrimereport.org/archive/low-recidivism-rate-reported-for-paroled-ny-murderers/ (accessed Mar. 28, 2011).

59. For a summary of these research findings, see James W. Marquart and Jonathan R. Sorensen, "A National Study of the *Furman*-Commuted Inmates: Assessing the Threat to Society from Capital Offenders," *Loyola of Los Angeles Law Review* 23 (1989): 9–10. See also *Prison Statistics for England and Wales 1999* (London: Home Office, 2000), 100n. 43, cited in Andrew Coyle, "Replacing the Death Penalty: The Vexed Issue of Alterative Sanctions," in Peter Hodgkinson and William A. Schabas, eds., *Capital Punishment: Strategies for Abolition* (Cambridge: Cambridge University Press, 2004), 107; and Mark D. Cunningham, Thomas J. Reidy, and Jon R. Sorensen, "Is Death Row Obsolete? A Decade of Mainstreaming Death-Sentenced Inmates in Missouri," *Behavioral Sciences and the Law* 23 (2005): 307–20.

60. Hugo Adam Bedau, "Recidivism, Parole, and Deterrence," in Hugo Adam Bedau, ed., *The Death Penalty in America*, 3rd ed. (New York: Oxford University Press, 1982), 179, as cited in Marquart and Sorensen, "A National Study of the *Furman*-Commuted Inmates," 24.

61. Vera Institute of Justice, "It's about Time: Aging Prisoners, Increasing Costs, and Geriatric Release" (New York: Vera Institute of Justice, 2010).

62. The typical prison sentence for robbery in the United States is 97 months, of which the typical time served is 60 months (including the pretrial time spent in jail), at a cost of approximately $113,000. The median loss associated with a robbery reported to the police is $100. James Austin, "Reducing America's Correctional Populations: A Strategic Plan," *Justice Research and Policy* 12.1 (2010), 21. A Bureau of Justice Statistics study of comparative sentencing found that people in the United States sentenced to prison for burglary generally served much longer sentences than those sentenced for the same crime in several European countries. See David P. Farrington, Patrick A. Langan, and Michael Tonry, eds., "Cross-National Studies in Crime and Justice" (Washington, DC: U.S. Department of Justice, Office of Justice Programs, Bureau of Justice Statistics, Sept. 2004), x.

63. For a recent analysis of mass incarceration that puts much of the blame on the war on drugs, see Michelle Alexander, *The New Jim Crow: Mass Incarceration in the Age of Colorblindness* (New York: New Press, 2010).

64. Franklin E. Zimring, "Imprisonment Rates and the New Politics of Criminal Punishment," *Punishment & Society* 3.1 (2001): 161–66.

65. Franklin E. Zimring and Gordon Hawkins, *Incapacitation: Penal Confinement and the Restraint of Crime* (New York: Oxford University Press, 1995), chap. 5.

66. Zimring, "Imprisonment Rates," 162.

67. Calculated from William J. Sabol, "Implications of Criminal Justice System Adaptation for Prison Population Growth and Corrections Policy," paper presented at "Symposium on Crime and Justice: The Past and Future of Empirical Sentencing Research," SUNY at Albany, Sept. 23–24, 2010, table 1.

68. Calculated from ibid.

69. Mark Kleiman, *When Brute Force Fails: How to Have Less Crime and Less Punishment* (Princeton: Princeton University Press, 2009), 15.

70. Porter, "The State of Sentencing 2010," 5.

71. Judith Greene and Marc Mauer, "Downscaling Prisons: Lessons from Four States" (Washington, DC: Sentencing Project, 2010); and Bert Useem, "Right-Sizing Corrections in New York," *Justice Research and Policy* 12.1 (2010): 89–112.

72. David F. Weiman and Christopher Weiss, "The Origins of Mass Incarceration in New York State: The Rockefeller Drug Laws and the Local War on Drugs," in Steven Raphael and Michael A. Stoll, eds., *Do Prisons Make Us Safer? The Benefits and Costs of the Prison Boom* (New York: Russell Sage Foundation, 2009): 73–116.

73. Greene and Mauer, "Downscaling Prisons," 22.

74. Nicholas Confessore, "Litmus Test in Primaries: Overhauled Drug Laws," *New York Times*, June 20, 2010.

75. New York State Commission on Sentencing Reform, "The Future of Sentencing in New York State: Recommendations for Reform," Jan. 30, 2009, 163–66.

76. Michigan Families Against Mandatory Minimums, "Michigan Enacts Reform of '650-Lifer' Law," *News Briefs*, July–Aug. 1998, http://www.ndsn.org/julaug98/sent.html (accessed Jan. 26, 2011).

77. Drug Policy Alliance, "Louisiana Passes Sweeping Drug Law Reform," press release, June 18, 2001, http://www.drugpolicy.org/news/pressroom/pressrelease/pr_june18_01.cfm

(accessed Jan. 26, 2011); and Larry Sharp, "Coming Full Circle," *Angolite*, Sept.–Oct. 2009, 25.

78. William Stuntz, "Unequal Justice," *Harvard Law Review* 121.8 (June 2010), 2022. See also Tracey L. Meares, Neal Katyal, and Dan M. Kahan, "Updating the Study of Punishment," *Stanford Law Review* 56.5 (2004): 1178.

79. Marc Mauer, "The Causes and Consequences of Prison Growth in the United States," *Punishment & Society* 3.1 (2001), 17. Italics in the original.

80. David M. Reutter, "Political Uproar Follows NC Court Ruling That Life Sentence Is 80 Years," *Prison Legal News*, May 2010, 34–35.

81. Associated Press, "Rapists and Murderers Going Free under Old Law," MSNBC. com, Oct. 16, 2009, http://www.msnbc.msn.com/id/33340592/ (accessed Sept. 24, 2010).

82. WSCOTV, "Victims, Families Outraged by N.C. Inmates' Release," Oct. 20, 2009, http://www.wsoctv.com/news/21350656/detail.html (accessed Sept. 24, 2010).

83. Mandy Locke, "Ruling Affirms 1970s Life Sentences," *Charlotte Observer*, Aug. 27, 2010, http://www.charlotteobserver.com/2010/08/27/1647108/nc-supreme-court-life-sentences.html (accessed Sept. 24, 2010).

84. Nelson, "A History of Penal Reform in Angola, Part 1," 19.

85. Lifers also divided over whether to keep their distance from the controversies surrounding the "Angola 3," the former Black Panthers kept for decades in solitary confinement at Angola. Lane Nelson, "A History of Penal Reform in Angola, Part 2: The Immovable Object," *Angolite*, Nov.–Dec. 2009, 32.

86. Ibid., 28.

87. Ibid., 33.

88. Ibid.

89. Adam Liptak, "Serving Life for Providing Car to Killers," *New York Times*, Dec. 4, 2007.

90. Ibid.

91. Nellis and King, "No Exit," 42; Human Rights Watch and Amnesty International, "The Rest of Their Lives: Life without Parole for Child Offenders in the United States" (New York: Human Rights Watch and Amnesty International, 2005), 5; Michelle Leighton and Connie de la Vega, "Sentencing Our Children to Die in Prison: Global Law and Practice," *University of San Francisco Law Review* 42 (Spring 2008): 990–92.

92. Leighton and de la Vega, "Sentencing Our Children to Die in Prison," 985.

93. Ibid., 989n. 19.

94. American Civil Liberties Union of Michigan, "Second Chances: Juveniles Serving Life without Parole in Michigan's Prisons," 2004, in letter from United States and International Human Rights Organizations to the Committee on the Elimination of Racial Discrimination, June 4, 2009, 3.

95. Equal Justice Initiative, "Cruel and Unusual: Sentencing 13- and 14-Year-Old Children to Die in Prison" (Montgomery, AL: Equal Justice Initiative, Nov. 2007), 14–15. On any given day, as many as 7,500 youths are incarcerated in adult prisons and jails in the United States. Campaign for Youth Justice, "National Statistics," http://www.campaignforyouthjustice.org/national-statistics.html (accessed May 25, 2011).

96. Porter, "The State of Sentencing 2010," 22.

97. Vince Beiser, "Kids Locked Up for Life," *Atlantic*, Nov. 2009; Teresa Baldas, "More States Rethinking Life Sentences for Teens," *National Law Journal*, Mar. 15, 2010.

98. "Assembly Rejects Bill to Aid Juvenile Lifers," *Capitol Alert*, Aug. 25, 2010, http://blogs.sacbee.com/capitolalertlatest/2010/08/ (accessed Jan. 27, 2011); Leland Yee, "California Assembly Failed Our Kids," press release, Aug. 30, 2010, http://disto8.casen.govoffice.com/index.asp?Type=B_PR&SEC=%7BEFA496BC-EDC8-4E38-9CC7-68D37AC03DFF%7D&DE=%7BC4416778-A9D3-4257-8659-28FC2F0767E5%7D (accessed Nov. 20, 2010).

99. Sentencing Project, "Juvenile Life without Parole," 2010, 2, http://www.sentencingproject.org/doc/publications/publications/jj_jlwopfactsheetJuly2010.pdf (accessed Jan. 31, 2011).

100. "Under current federal transfer law, an adult court judge determines on a case-by-case basis whether it is 'in the interest of justice' to charge a youth in adult court." However, under amendments pushed by Senator Jeff Sessions (R-AL) and Senator Jon Kyl (R-AZ), prosecutors, instead of judges, would decide whether to prosecute youth as adults for certain federal crimes. "JJDPA Passes through Senate Judiciary Committee," *Campaign for Youth Justice Newsletter*, Jan. 2010, http://www.campaignforyouthjustice.org/documents/Jan.2010cfyjnewsletter.pdf (accessed Jan. 31, 2011), 4.

101. Bradley Bridge, Defender Association of Philadelphia, testimony before the Pennsylvania House Judiciary Committee Hearing on HB 1999, Aug. 4, 2010, 1.

102. Ibid., 4.

103. Andrea Canning and Maggie Burbank, "Jordan Brown Murder Case Takes Emotional Toll," ABC News/Nightline, Apr. 28, 2010, http://abcnews.go.com/Nightline/jordan-brown-murder-case-12-year-adult/story?id=10288704 (accessed Nov. 4, 2010). In August 2011, the case was moved to juvenile court after a Superior Court overturned the initial decision to try him as an adult. CBS Pittsburgh, "Jordan Brown Case Moves to Juvenile Court," Aug. 23, 2011, http://pittsburgh.cbslocal.com/2011/08/23/jordan-brown-case-moves-to-juvenile-court/ (accessed Sept. 26, 2011).

104. In Pennsylvania, the JLWOP population is about 67 percent African American, 20 percent white, and 10 percent Hispanic. The lifer population as a whole in Pennsylvania is 63 percent African American. Nellis and King, "No Exit," 22, table 8, and 16, table 5.

105. Adam Liptak, "To More Inmates, Life Term Means Dying behind Bars," *New York Times*, Oct. 2, 2005.

106. Robert G. Schwartz, Juvenile Law Center, testimony before the Pennsylvania House Judiciary Committee Hearing on HB 1999, Aug. 4, 2010, 10.

107. Anita Colón, Pennsylvania Coalition for the Fair Sentencing of Youth, testimony before the Pennsylvania House Judiciary Committee Hearing on HB 1999, Aug. 4, 2010.

108. Marc Mauer, The Sentencing Project, executive director, letter to Reps. John Conyers, Jr., and Lamar Smith, May 7, 2009.

109. Pennsylvania District Attorneys Association, testimony before the Pennsylvania House Judiciary Committee Hearing on HB 1999, Aug. 4, 2010, 3–4.

110. Ibid., 3.

111. See the testimony by Dawn Romig, Larry Markel, Carol Schouwe, and Alyce C. Thompson before the Pennsylvania House Judiciary Committee Hearing on HB 1999, Aug. 4, 2010.

112. Charles D. Stimson, Heritage Foundation, testimony before the Pennsylvania House Judiciary Committee Hearing on HB 1999, Aug. 4, 2010.

113. Julia Hall, chair, Pennsylvania Prison Society Subcommittee on Juvenile Lifers, testimony before the Pennsylvania House Judiciary Committee Hearing on HB 1999, Aug. 4, 2010, 2.

114. Bobbi Jamriska, National Organization of Victims of "Juvenile Lifers," testimony before the Pennsylvania House Judiciary Committee Hearing on HB 1999, Aug. 4, 2010, n.p.

115. Solomon Moore, "Number of Life Terms Hits Record," *New York Times*, July 22, 2009.

116. Ibid.

117. Ibid.

118. Jack Leonard, "'Pizza Thief' Walks the Line," *L.A. Times*, Feb. 10, 2010, http://articles.latimes.com/2010/feb/10/local/la-me-pizzathief10-2010feb10 (accessed Nov. 22, 2010).

119. Emily Bazelon, "Arguing Three Strikes," *New York Times Magazine*, May 21, 2010.

120. Stanford Three Strikes Project, "Overview," http://www.law.stanford.edu/program/clinics/threestrikesproject/ (accessed Mar. 30, 2011).

121. Samara Marion, "Justice by Geography? A Study of San Diego County's Three Strikes Sentencing Practices from July–Dec. 1996," *Stanford Law and Policy Review* 11.1 (1999–2000): 29–57; and Franklin E. Zimring, Gordon Hawkins, and Sam Kamin, *Punishment and Democracy: Three Strikes and You're Out in California* (New York: Oxford University Press, 2001).

122. California State Auditor, "California Department of Corrections and Rehabilitation: Inmates Sentenced under the Three Strikes Law and a Small Number of Inmates Receiving Specialty Health Care Represent Significant Costs," report 2009.107.2 (Sacramento: California State Auditor, Bureau of State Audits, May 2010), 1.

123. California State Auditor, "California Department of Corrections and Rehabilitation: It Fails to Track and Use Data That Would Allow It to More Effectively Monitor and Manage Its Operations," report 2009.107.1 (Sacramento: California State Auditor, Bureau of State Audits, Sept. 2009), 2.

124. California State Auditor, report 2009.107.2, 2.

125. California State Auditor, report 2009 107.2, 23, table 2.

126. This account of the defeat of Proposition 66 is largely based on Joshua Page, *The Toughest Beat: Politics, Punishment, and the Prison Officers Union in California* (New York: Oxford University Press, 2011), 121–32.

127. Joshua Page, "Fear of Change: Prisoner Officer Unions and the Perpetuation of the Penal Status Quo," *Criminology & Public Policy* 10.3 (August 2011), 747.

128. Ibid., 748.

129. *People v. Williams*, 17 Cal. 4th 148, 161 (1998), as quoted in Rebecca Gross, "The 'Spirit' of Three Strikes Law: From the *Romero* Myth to the Hopeful Implications of *Andrade*," *Golden Gate University Law Review* 32.2 (2002), 179.

130. Among other claims, the Stanford Project has successfully argued that its clients were denied effective legal representation and that their sentences constitute cruel and unusual punishment. Stanford Three Strikes Project, "Three Strikes Basics," http://www.law.stanford.edu/program/clinics/threestrikesproject/ (accessed Mar. 30, 2011).

131. Bazelon, "Arguing Three Strikes."

132. Sasha Abramsky, "The War against the 'War on Drugs,'" *Nation*, June 17, 2009.

133. California State Auditor, report 2009-107.1, 7; and Ruth Wilson Gilmore, *Golden Gulag: Prisons, Surplus, Crisis, and Opposition in Globalizing California* (Berkeley: University of California Press, 2007), 8.

134. "Billionaire-Funded California Initiative Triples Lifer Parole Denial Intervals, Imposes Restrictions on Parole Violators," *Prison Legal News*, May 2009, 12–13.

135. Legislative Analyst's Office, "Proposition 5: Nonviolent Drug Offenses, Sentencing, Parole, and Rehabilitation Initiative Statute" (Sacramento, CA: Legislative Analyst's Office, Sept. 28, 2008).

136. In a thoroughly mixed result, voters also overwhelmingly rejected Proposition 6, which would have increased spending on law enforcement, ratcheted up the penalties for "gang-related" activities, and toughened up the criminal justice system in dozens of other ways. "Fiscal Disaster in California," editorial, New York Times, Oct. 10, 2008, A32.

137. Michael Rothfeld, "After Delay, Assembly to Take Up Prison Measure," L.A. Times, Sept. 1, 2009, http://articles.latimes.com/2009/sep/01/local/me-prisons1 (accessed Jan. 31, 2011).

138. Solomon Moore, "California State Assembly Approves Prison Legislation," New York Times, Sept. 1, 2009; Page, The Toughest Beat.

139. Solomon Moore, "California Passes Bill Addressing Prisons," New York Times, Sept. 13, 2009.

140. Rebecca Cathcart, "3-Strikes Challenger Is Charged with 4 Murders," New York Times, Dec. 1, 2010.

141. Graham, 569 U.S., slip opinion, 20.

142. Appleton and Grøver, "The Pros and Cons of Life without Parole," 608.

143. In 1972, California's state prison population was 19,773. As of June 30, 2009, it was 168,000. Rosemary Gartner, Anthony Doob, and Franklin E. Zimring, "The Past as Prologue? Decarceration in California Then and Now," Criminology & Public Policy 10.2 (2011): 291–325; and California State Auditor, report 2009-107.1, 7.

144. Dan Markel, "State, Be Not Proud: A Retributivist Defense of the Commutation of Death Row and the Abolition of the Death Penalty," Harvard Civil Rights–Civil Liberties Law Review 40 (2005), 407.

145. Appleton and Grøver, "The Pros and Cons of Life without Parole," 606.

146. Frieder Dünkel and Ineke Pruin, "Germany," in Nicola Padfield, Dirk van Zyl Smit, and Frieder Dünkel, eds., Release from Prison: European Policy and Practice (Portland, OR: Willan, 2010), 193–94.

147. Dünkel and Pruin, "Germany," 193.

148. Mauer, King, and Young, "The Meaning of 'Life,'" 32.

149. Nellis and King, "No Exit," 41.

150. Personal e-mail communication to author, Jan. 26, 2011.

151. Hugo Adam Bedau, "Imprisonment vs. Death: Does Avoiding Schwarzchild's Paradox Lead to Sheleff's Dilemma?," Albany Law Review 54 (1989–90): 495.

152. One prosecutor who did support her release was Vincent Bugliosi, who prosecuted Atkins and other members of the Manson Family. He said he supported her release, if only to save the state the extraordinary cost of her health care. "Ailing Manson Follower Denied Release from Prison," CNN, July 15, 2008, http://articles.cnn.com/2008-07-15/justice/release.denied_1_charles-manson-follower-compassionate-release-terminally-ill-inmates/2?_s=sPM:CRIME (accessed Oct. 4, 2010).

153. Ibid.

154. James Q. Whitman, Harsh Justice: Criminal Punishment and the Widening Divide between America and Europe (New York: Oxford University Press, 2003).

155. Ibid.; Christen Jensen, The Pardoning Power in the American States (Chicago: University of Chicago Press, 1922).

156. David M. Oshinsky, *"Worse Than Slavery": Parchman Farm and the Ordeal of Jim Crow Justice* (New York: Free Press, 1996), 67–69.

157. Ibid., 196–200.

158. In 1971, Pennsylvania's lifer population was 390; 20 years later, it had increased over 500 percent to 2,139. In 2008, it was 4,349. Mark Rowan and Brian S. Kane, "Life Means Life, Maybe? An Analysis of Pennsylvania's Policy toward Lifers," *Duquesne Law Review* 30 (1992): 662; and Nellis and King, "No Exit," 9, table 2.

159. Robert Moran, "Rendell to Commute Life Sentences for Three," *Philadelphia Inquirer*, Dec. 30, 2010, http://articles.philly.com/2010-12-30/news/26356500_1_pardons-board-rendell-clemency (accessed Jan. 27, 2011).

160. Advisory Committee on Geriatric and Seriously Ill Inmates, "Report of the Advisory Committee on Geriatric and Seriously Ill Inmates," 78.

161. Michael Rubinkam, "Pa. Lifers Seeking Clemency in Wake of U.S. Ruling," Associated Press, Sept. 3, 2009.

162. P. S. Ruckman, "Executive Clemency in the United States: Origins, Development, and Analysis (1900–93)," *Presidential Studies Quarterly* 27 (1997): 261, table 1.

163. Smart on Crime Coalition, "Smart on Crime: Recommendations for the Administration and Congress" (Washington, DC: Constitution Project, 2011), 175.

164. "Public Tired of Willie Horton? Whither 21st Century Clemency?," *Grits for Breakfast* (blog), Jan. 10, 2010, http://gritsforbreakfast.blogspot.com/2010/01/public-tired-of-willlie-horton-whither.html (accessed Apr. 17, 2010). Technically, that is no longer true. At the end of Obama's second year in office, he finally got around to issuing his first pardons. The nine pardons were characterized as "stingy" and "lackluster." Six of them "were for offenses so minor that they did not warrant time behind bars; six offenses were committed three decades ago." Editorial, "Mr. Obama's Lackluster Pardons," *Washington Post*, Dec. 30, 2010.

165. Stu Whitney, "Prison Time Cuts Lead U.S.," *Sioux Falls–Argus Leader*, Jun. 29, 2003, cited in Daniel T. Kobil, "Should Mercy Have a Place in Clemency Decisions?," in Austin Sarat and Nasser Hussain, eds., *Forgiveness, Mercy, and Clemency* (Stanford: Stanford University Press, 2007), 37n. 11.

166. American Bar Association, Justice Kennedy Commission, "Reports with Recommendations to the ABA House of Delegates" (Chicago: ABA, Aug. 2004), 67.

167. Ibid., 64.

168. Marquart and Sorensen, "A National Study of the *Furman*-Commuted Inmates," 21.

169. Ibid., 23, 26.

170. Ibid., 22, 28.

171. Joan M. Cheever, *Back from the Dead: One Woman's Search for the Men Who Walked Off Death Row* (New York: Wiley, 2006), 4, 36, and 206.

172. Bedau, "Recidivism, Parole, and Deterrence," 175–80, as quoted in Marquart and Sorensen, "A National Study of the *Furman*-Commuted Inmates," 25.

173. Bob Brenzing, "179 Commutations and Counting: Granholm Exits as Most Merciful Michigan Governor in Decades," *Detroit Free Press*, Dec. 20, 2010 http://www.wzzm13.com/news/news_story.aspx?storyid=145281 (accessed Jan. 27, 2011).

174. "By the Numbers: Huckabee's Clemency Record," KFSM News, July 28, 2004, cited in Austin Sarat, *Mercy on Trial: What It Means to Stop an Execution* (Princeton: Princeton University Press, 2005), 33.

175. Michael Levenson, "Patrick Names Four Nominees for State Parole Board," *Boston Globe*, Mar. 4, 2011; Ben Storrow, "Legislators See Merit in Reforming Parole Laws," *Daily Hampshire Gazette*, Feb. 16, 2011, http://www.gazettenet.com/2011/02/16/legislators-see-merit-reforming-parole-laws?SESSf05297705985580b55f7534e48eb6854=gsearch (accessed Mar. 28, 2011).

176. Bob Egelko, "Brown Paroles More Lifers Than Did Predecessors," SFGate.com, April 29, 2011, http://www.sfgate.com/cgi-bin/article.cgi?f=/c/a/2011/04/28/MNUA1J991B. DTL (accessed May 9, 2011).

177. Charlotte A. Price, "Aging Inmate Population Study," North Carolina Department of Correction, Division of Prisons, May 2006.

178. Vera Institute of Justice, "It's about Time," 2.

179. Ibid.

180. Joan Petersilia, *When Prisoners Come Home: Parole and Prisoner Reentry* (New York: Oxford University Press), 191.

181. Ibid.

182. Hamilton Project, "From Prison to Work: Overcoming Barriers to Reentry" (Washington DC: Brookings Institution, Dec. 5, 2008), 15, http://www.brookings.edu/~/media/Files/events/2008/1205_prison/20081205_prison_to_work.pdf (accessed Oct. 8, 2010).

183. Ibid., 31.

184. Sarat, *Mercy on Trial*; Kobil, "Should Mercy Have a Place in Clemency Decisions?"; and Elizabeth Rapaport, "Retribution and Redemption in the Operation of Executive Clemency," *Chicago-Kent Law Review* 74.4 (2000): 1501–35.

185. *Herrera v. Collins*, 506 U.S. 390, 412 (1993), quoted in Sarat, *Mercy on Trial*, 107.

186. Kobil, "Should Mercy Have a Place in Clemency Decisions?," 37.

187. Sarat, *Mercy on Trial*, 139.

188. P. S. Ruckman, "The Pardoning Power: The *Other* Civics Lesson" (paper presented at the annual meeting of the Southern Political Science Association, Atlanta, Georgia, Nov. 7–10, 2001), 8.

189. Sarat, *Mercy on Trial*, 37–66.

190. Kobil, "Should Mercy Have a Place in Clemency Decisions?," 37.

191. Sarat, *Mercy on Trial*, 28.

192. Ibid., 10.

193. Anthony M. Kennedy, "Speech at the American Bar Association Annual Meeting," American Bar Association, press release, Aug. 9, 2003, http://www.abanet.org/leadership/initiative/kennedyspeech.pdf (accessed Jan. 31, 2010), 5.

194. Baumgartner, De Boef, and Boydstun, *The Decline of the Death Penalty*.

195. Ibid., 173.

196. David Feige, "The Dark Side of Innocence," *New York Times Magazine*, June 15, 2003, 15. The 1 percent figure comes from David R. Dow, "The Problem of 'Innocence,'" in David R. Dow and Mark Dow, eds., *Machinery of Death: The Reality of America's Death Penalty Regime* (New York: Routledge, 2002), 5. For higher estimates, see Gordon P. Waldo and Raymond Paternoster, "Tinkering with the Machinery of Death: The Failure of a Social Experiment," in Thomas G. Blomberg and Stanley Cohen, eds., *Punishment and Social Control*, 2nd ed. (New York: Aldine de Gruyter, 2003), 312.

197. For a succinct overview of key European Court of Human Rights decisions regarding life-sentenced prisoners, see Dirk van Zyl Smit and John R. Spencer, "The European

Dimension to the Release of Sentenced Prisoners," in Padfield, van Zyl Smit, and Dünkel, *Release from Prison*, 18–21.

198. Penal Reform International, "Alternatives to the Death Penalty."

199. See Barkow, "Life without Parole," 000.

200. For a development of these points, see Marie Gottschalk, *The Prison and the Gallows: The Politics of Mass Incarceration in America* (New York: Cambridge University Press), chaps. 8–9.

201. Derral Cheatwood, "The-Life-without-Parole Sanction: Its Current Status and a Research Agenda," *Crime & Delinquency* 34 (1988): 49.

202. Susan E. Martin, "Commutation of Prison Sentences: Practice, Promise, and Limitation," *Crime & Delinquency* 29 (1983): 594.

203. Death Penalty Information Center, "Year That States Adopted Life without Parole (LWOP) Sentencing," http://www.deathpenaltyinfo.org/year-states-adopted-life-without-parole-lwop-sentencing (accessed Jan. 14, 2011).

204. For example, in Louisiana punitive and progressive impulses collided to produce more draconian life sentences and penal policies. In the early 1970s, the state's director of corrections called for the repeal of the 10/6 law because in her view it gave too much discretion to wardens to decide which lifers deserved to be released. Coming at about the same time, the *Furman* decision strengthened the push for repeal from an opposite direction as fears grew that many prisoners then on death row would be released under the state's 10/6 law. Nelson, "A History of Penal Reform in Angola, Part I," 17.

205. See, for example, the discussion of the Alabama case in Jim Stewart and Paul Lieberman, "What Is This New Sentence That Takes away Parole?," *Student Lawyer* 11 (1982–83): 14–16.

206. See, for example, the discussion of the Georgia case in ibid., 16–17.

207. Mona Lynch, "Mass Incarceration, Legal Change, and Locale: Understanding and Remediating American Penal Overindulgence," *Criminology & Public Policy* 10.3 (August 2011): 688.

208. Bedau, "Imprisonment vs. Death," 495.

209. Herbert H. Haines, *Against Capital Punishment: The Anti–Death Penalty Movement in America, 1972–1994* (New York: Oxford University Press, 1996), 140, 180; Wright, "Life-without-Parole," 566; Raymond Paternoster, *Capital Punishment in America* (New York: Lexington Books, 1991), 287; and Scott Turow, "To Kill or Not to Kill: Coming to Terms with Capital Punishment," *New Yorker*, Jan. 6, 2003, 47.

210. "A Matter of Life and Death," 1839.

211. Haines, *Against Capital Punishment*, 179.

212. Steven Brill, "Throw Away the Key," *American Lawyer*, July–Aug. 1987, 3. See also Steven Brill, "Trantino: Long Locked Up, Now Throw Away the Key," *New Jersey Law Journal* 126 (July 26, 1990): 9, 36–37.

213. Mary E. Medland and Craig Fischer, "Life without Parole Offered as Alternative to Death Penalty," *Criminal Justice Newsletter*, Jan. 16, 1990, 4.

214. Stewart and Lieberman, "What Is This New Sentence?," 17.

215. Medland and Fischer, "Life without Parole Offered," 4.

216. "A Matter of Life and Death," 1847.

217. Ibid., 1829.

218. Mauer, King, and Young, "The Meaning of 'Life,'" 12.

219. "A Matter of Life and Death," 1838.

220. William W. Hood III, "Note: The Meaning of 'Life' for Virginia Jurors and Its Effect on Reliability in Capital Sentencing," *Virginia Law Review* 75 (1989): 1605, 1624–25, cited in "A Matter of Life and Death," 1838.

221. "A Matter of Life and Death," 1844.

222. Danya W. Blair, "A Matter of Life and Death: Why Life without Parole Should Be a Sentencing Option in Texas," *American Journal of Criminal Law* (1994–95): 191–214.

223. "A Matter of Life and Death," *Harvard Law Review*, 1843.

224. Ibid.

225. "Symbolic Justice: LWOP for Serial Rapists Creates More Problems Than It Solves," *Grits for Breakfast* (blog), May 7, 2011, http://gritsforbreakfast.blogspot.com/2011/05/symbolic-justice-lwop-for-serial.html (accessed May 25, 2011).

226. See Human Rights Watch and Amnesty International, "The Rest of Their Lives."

227. Amnesty International, "Review of AI Work against the Death Penalty—Original Discussion Paper" (ACT 51/003/2002) and Full Draft Report (ACT 50.008/2002), quoted in Peter Hodgkinson, "Replacing Capital Punishment: An Effective Penal Policy Approach," University of Westminster, Centre for Capital Punishment Studies, Occasional Paper Series—Special Edition, vol. 3, "Managing Effective Alternatives to Capital Punishment: Conference Papers," June 24, 2005, n.p.

228. National Coalition Against the Death Penalty, "Death Penalty Overview: Ten Reasons Why Capital Punishment Is Flawed Public Policy," http://www.ncadp.org/index.cfm?content=5 (accessed Mar. 31, 2011).

229. "NewsNight with Aaron Brown: Interview with Innocence Project Cofounder Barry Scheck," CNN, Dec. 10, 2004, cited in "A Matter of Life and Death," 1838n. 2.

230. See, for example, the testimony of Larry Peterson, Gerald L. Zelizer, Kate Hill Germond, Jack Johnson, Richard C. Dieter, Edith Frank, and Sandra K. Manning before the New Jersey Death Penalty Study Commission, Trenton, New Jersey, July 19, 2010.

231. Somerset County Chapter, ACLU-NJ, written testimony for the New Jersey Death Penalty Study Commission, Trenton, New Jersey, July 19, 2006, 331x; and "At Death's Door: Interview by David Cook," *Sun*, Aug. 2010, as excerpted in *Utne Reader*, Nov.–Dec. 2010, http://www.utne.com/Politics/At-Deaths-Door-Sister-Helen-Prejean-Death-Penalty.aspx (accessed Jan. 31, 2011).

232. Robert Johnson, testimony before the New Jersey Death Penalty Study Commission, Trenton, New Jersey, July 19, 2006, 58.

233. Under the commission's proposal to abolish the death penalty, judges would be required to impose LWOP in all first-degree murder cases if the jury found that the crime fit any of a dozen categories of "aggravated" murder. Jurors would no longer weigh mitigating circumstances, as they did in capital cases.

234. "The Other Death Penalty Project Announces Letter-Writing Campaign to Anti–Death Penalty Groups," news release, Feb. 22, 2010, http://www.prnewswire.com/news-releases/the-other-death-penalty-project-announces-letter-writing-campaign-to-anti-death-penalty-groups-84945657.html (accessed Nov. 22, 2010); and Gordon Haas and Lloyd Fillion, "Life without Parole: A Reconsideration" (Jamaica Plain, MA: Criminal Justice Policy Coalition, Nov. 30, 2010).

235. Kenneth Hartman, "The Other Death Penalty," Other Death Penalty Project, Feb. 22, 2010, http://www.theotherdeathpenalty.org/foundingdocument.htm (accessed Oct. 20, 2010).

236. Marlene Martin, "National Initiatives and Resolution," *New Abolitionist*, Jan. 2009, http://www.nodeathpenalty.org/new_abolitionist/Jan.-2009-issue-47/national-initiatives-and-resolution (accessed Jan. 27, 2011).

237. For an overview of these cases, see Gottschalk, *The Prison and the Gallows*, 207–8.

238. Jack Greenberg, *Cases and Materials on Judicial Process and Social Change: Constitutional Litigation* (St. Paul, MN: West, 1977), 431.

239. David M. Oshinsky, *Capital Punishment on Trial:* Furman v. Georgia *and the Death Penalty in Modern America* (Lawrence: University Press of Kansas, 2010), 61.

240. Ibid., 95–107.

241. For an excellent critical overview of the Supreme Court's record on race and criminal justice in noncapital cases, see Alexander, *The New Jim Crow*, chap. 3.

242. Nellis and King, "No Exit," 11.

243. African Americans make up 35 percent of second-strikers in California and 45 percent of third-strikers, even though they constitute barely 6 percent of the state's adult population. Elsa Y. Chen, "The Liberation Hypothesis and Racial and Ethnic Disparities in the Application of California's Three Strikes Law," *Journal of Ethnicity in Criminal Justice* 6.2 (2008): 83, 85.

244. Nellis and King, "No Exit," 11.

245. Ibid., 13.

246. Ibid., 23.

247. Ibid., 20 and also 21–22, table 8.

248. Vera Institute of Justice, "It's about Time," 4.

249. B. Jayne Anno et al., "Correctional Health Care: Addressing the Needs of the Elderly, Chronically Ill, and Terminally Ill Inmates" (Washington, DC: U.S. Department of Justice, National Institute of Corrections, 2004), cited in Vera Institute of Justice, "It's about Time," 5.

250. For a somewhat skeptical view of the likelihood that the economic crisis means the beginning of the end of mass incarceration in the United States, see Marie Gottschalk, "The Great Recession and the Great Confinement: The Economic Crisis and the Future of Penal Reform," in Richard Rosenfeld, Kenna Quinet, and Crystal Garcia, eds., *Contemporary Issues in Criminological Theory and Research: The Role of Social Institutions* (Belmont, CA: Wadsworth, 2010), 343–70.

251. For example, in July 2009, when California's inmate population topped 170,000, the state had only 11,000 substance-abuse treatment slots in its prisons and just 200 slots for anger-management programs. The state had no sex-offender treatment programs even though 9 percent of California's prisoners are currently serving a term for a sex-crime conviction. Prison Census Data, "Characteristics of Inmate Population" (California Department of Corrections, Aug. 2009), http://www.cdcr.ca.gov/Reports_Research/Offender_Information_Services_Branch/Offender_Information_Reports.html, cited in Robert Weisberg and Joan Petersilia, "The Dangers of Pyrrhic Victories against Mass Incarceration," *Daedalus*, Summer 2010, 130. Just two days after this report was released, the California legislature approved budget cuts that slashed spending on prisoner-educa-

tion, drug-treatment, and job-training programs. Weisberg and Petersilia, "The Dangers of Pyrrhic Victories," 131.

252. When asked why lifers were increasingly denied access to prison employment, higher education, and other programs and activities in Pennsylvania's prisons, then secretary of corrections James Beard "stated that he had to [use] his limited resources to prepare those who would return to the streets," according to Julia Hall, a board member of the Pennsylvania Prison Society and chair of Pennsylvania's Coalition for the Fair Sentencing of Youth. Julia Hall, personal e-mail communication, Feb. 6, 2011.

253. Kenneth E. Hartman, "The Other Death Penalty," quoted in James Ridgeway and Jean Casella, "Voices from Solitary: Kenneth E. Hartman on 'The Other Death Penalty,'" Solitary Watch, May 19, 2010, http://solitarywatch.com/2010/05/19/voices-from-solitary-kenneth-e-hartman-on-the-other-death-penalty/ (accessed Nov. 22, 2010).

8

Dignity and Risk

The Long Road from Graham v. Florida to Abolition of Life without Parole

JONATHAN SIMON

America at the start of the 21st century stands out as a nation that embraces harsh and degrading punishments. This goes beyond our quantitative penchant for locking up a far higher portion of our citizens than any other country, to the qualitative way we punish.[1] Evidence for this qualitative distinction abounds. The US remains one of a very few wealthy democracies that retains capital punishment.[2] Security imperatives in American prisons, especially our unique "supermax" prisons, impose restrictions on the physical movements and human contacts of prisoners that stand out as harsh and severe.[3] American discourse about punishment, from both ordinary citizens and politicians, includes rhetoric that appears to normalize and approve prison rape and other acts of violence against prisoners. But nothing today epitomizes this harshness as much as the life-without-parole (LWOP) sentence, which saw dramatic growth in the US beginning in the 1980s and 1990s.[4] LWOP is a punishment that offers no promise of letup, regardless of how much the prisoner repents or is rehabilitated. In this regard, far more than capital punishment, which at its post-*Furman* zenith was still a tiny practice within the vast Leviathan of US criminal justice, LWOP defines the logic of contemporary penality more generally in its embrace of a totalizing promise of prison incapacitation extended to the very limits of life, and unmediated by any further consideration of the prisoner as a distinct human being. While less severe, contemporary prison sentences in many states appear to be cheaper versions of LWOP, designed to provide a less comprehensive promise of security through physically removing the prisoner from access to the community. By defining the desirable limits of penal incapacitation only in fiscal terms, LWOP helps to sustain the larger structure of mass incarceration which today threatens our democracy and our economic future.[5]

In this chapter I argue that we not wait for the death penalty to expire completely to begin what promises to be a protracted struggle to abolish LWOP in the name of restoring the legitimacy of our legal system in the eyes of the world, and creating a penal system that is socially and economically sustainable. Toward that end the chapter develops a diagnosis for America's embrace of harsh and degrading punishments such as LWOP that combines the presence of an extreme risk rationality about crime with the absence historically of a strong conception of dignity in our public law. The second task of the chapter is to suggest several sectors outside the penal field in which we can see successful efforts to rebalance issues of risk and dignity in ways that offer promising strategies for what is likely to be a prolonged legal struggle over LWOP and other forms of degrading punishment.

One such area, of great importance to our aging society, is the field of patients' rights in, and through, the provision of end-of-life medical care. End-of-life dignity is a strong example of dignity as a value independent of equality, liberty, or even the pursuit of happiness, since the dying subject is often beyond all three. A second area involves the rights of the severely mentally ill to resist compulsion by either state or family to accept medication. Mental illness challenges the very concept of dignity, and either defending the right of persons with mental illness to be left free of treatment or forcing treatment on them can seem to be both a compelling and a perverse way to defend dignity. A third area is the field of domestic relations, where the movement to incorporate same-sex couples into the states' definition and regulation of marriage has achieved some striking legal and political successes (and major losses as well) by emphasizing the idea of dignity. Especially as against "domestic partnership" laws in some states that have assured same-sex couples virtually identical legal standing to "married" cross-sex couples, dignity has emerged as a key to substantive equality.

Risk and Dignity

What explains the US embrace of degrading punishments such as LWOP? Today, almost no other wealthy democracies embrace LWOP on the broad scale that we do; some have explicitly banned it.[6] Sociologists of punishment have treated American penal exceptionalism since the late 20th century as best explained by an extreme construction of risk as "crime risk," one largely shaped by political leaders seeking to govern around the fragmented politics of race in American society.[7] In contrast, historian James Whitman contends that the primary factor that accounts for the harshness of American punishments is the absence of a constraining value of "dignity" within the US legal history or principles.[8] In contrast, Europe, where the prolonged struggle to create a legally egalitarian society against well-established status hierarchies favoring people with noble birth created a robust norm of dignity peculiarly associated with the state's power to punish, has developed a contemporary legal framework that rejects degradation and resists harsh punishments.

Whitman's account is persuasive in suggesting that dignity is often invisible in American public law and discourse and that were it present, dignity as a value would pose a significant base for resistance to LWOP and other degrading punishments, but his account does not explain the positive demand for these punishments and the rise of an extreme, fear-based version of incapacitation as a penal rationale.[9] This extreme version of the historical logic of prevention in the criminal law, which I call "total" incapacitation, has its origins in a historically specific way of imagining the problem of violent crime anchored in the alarming events and distinctive economic and geographic contexts of the 1970s (especially in the Sunbelt states such as California that led the turn toward harsher punishments) but has been generalized through the politics and policies of mass incarceration.

Treated as alternative explanations, risk versus dignity, anomalies emerge for both accounts. The risk explanation, with its emphasis on change since the 1960s, ignores the unmediated penal harshness that the US criminal justice system consistently meted out to African Americans, Asians, and Latinos, reflecting the status hierarchy long associated with the white/nonwhite divide. The dignity explanation, with its emphasis on American democracy in the 18th and early 19th centuries, ignores that during the much of the 20th century, the US led the world in the development and adoption of progressive penal techniques such as parole, probation, and juvenile justice. Understanding penal severity in the US, especially the growth of LWOP, requires taking both factors into account. Despite the absence of a strong dignity tradition in American law, no substantial political demand for LWOP sentences emerged before the 1980s and 1990s, when American penal policy came to be shaped by a strong version of general incapacitation as the primary purpose of punishment. The emergence of an extreme risk rationality around crime, "total incapacitation" as a penal rationale, and the Supreme Court's deference to state choices regarding the rationale of punishment have combined to diminish the role that proportionality played earlier in the 20th century in checking harsh and degrading punishments.

Europe, Whitman's comparative case, provides a similar combination of dignity and risk. The European Court of Human Rights, whose jurisprudence has been deeply influenced by the value of dignity expressed in the growing body of European Community principles and policies, has gone much further than the US Supreme Court in holding harsh punishments in violation of the Charter of Rights, including imprisonment to LWOP sentences at least for juveniles.[10] A number of European states do currently have an LWOP sentence, for example, the "whole-life tariff" in which an English judge may sentence a person for life and set no minimum sentence after which the parole authorities would normally be able to release the prisoner on "license" to be supervised by the probation service with the possibility of recall. However, even these sentences are subject to mechanisms of executive pardon that offer a real opportunity for eventual release and thus do not appear to be as harsh as US LWOP sentences, which are almost never modified by executive clemency.[11] At the same time, the absence of an extreme risk rationality in European penality has also played a key role in preventing European legal systems from confronting the kind of demand for degrading punishments that has shaped American politics in recent decades. However there are clear signs of such demand developing with Europe, for the example, Britain's three-strikes-like "imprisoned for public protection" sentence.[12] Currently public pressure for protection from violent offenders is carefully controlled by penal systems with a strong centralized managerialism and is insulated by the relative absence of party competition on crime risk. Were those conditions to change and European states to legislate harsh punishments including LWOP, it is not clear that the European Court of Human Rights would stop them. Thus, while developing a body of law and policy around dignity in the US is a high priority for those of us who would like to see an end to degrading punishments, combating total incapacitation and the extreme risk rationality behind it are equally so. Indeed, I want to suggest that these are not two distinct battles but in important respects one. The courts in the US are not likely to order an end to degrading punishments directly, and their willingness to burden the states administering those punishments with costs that might compel moderation will depend a lot on the ability of criminal justice officials, criminologists, and lawyers to promote a commitment to dignity within penalty itself.

The way dignity and risk combine to shape the prospects for abolishing LWOP and other degrading punishments is suggested by the US Supreme Court's recent decision in *Graham v. Florida* (2010),[13] holding LWOP for juveniles involved in nonhomicide crimes to violate the proportionality principle of the Eighth Amendment. The ruling suggests that help may be on the way. For those who are looking for a turn toward dignity as a value in our public law, the decision offered some promising hints. Without using the term "dignity," Justice Kennedy's majority opinion characterized the special harm of LWOP in ways quite consistent with the dignity tradition. Specifically, Justice Kennedy characterized LWOP as cruel because it deprives the prisoner of any hope: "It deprives the convict of the most basic liberties without giving hope of restoration, except perhaps by executive clemency—the remote possibility of which does not mitigate the harshness of the sentence."[14]

Moreover, in holding that LWOP in such circumstances could not be rationally justified in terms of any of the established penal rationales, including deterrence and incapacitation, Justice Kennedy seemed to invite lower courts to begin considering whether particular LWOP sentences constitute "cruel and unusual" punishment even for juveniles convicted of homicide crimes or, indeed, for nonjuveniles regardless of what crime they may have been convicted of.[15] But if degrading punishments such as LWOP are a product of the absence of dignity and the presence of an extreme version of "total" incapacitation as a penal rationale, as I have asserted here, the road from *Graham* to any eventual abolition of LWOP may be a long one indeed. The course of that road, however, may be altered by the strength of dignity as a value around which a broad array of controversies in US law and society are being reframed; and it may perhaps be shortened if advocates for long-term prisoners can take advantage of some of the doctrinal creativity shown in these others fields.

The Dignity Difference

Historian and legal scholar James Whitman's 2005 book *Harsh Justice: Criminal Punishment and the Widening Divide between America and Europe* helped move the discussion of mass incarceration and America's punitive turn from its focus on incarceration rates. To Whitman, the US was diverging from its peers not just in the proportion of its residents being held in prison but in the qualitative severity of punishment. American prisoners faced not just many years in prison but a regime in prison harsh in the degree of control and in a degree of continuous status degradation not unlike that once faced by African Americans under slavery and its aftermath. In the name of control, American prisons may maintain prisoners in conditions just short of severe enough to cause psychotic symptoms, even without finding the prisoner guilty of any new crimes or disciplinary violations.[16] The contrast Whitman drew was with Europe, at least the core of European countries (especially Germany and France) that made up the original European Union.

Prisons in these countries might be physically dilapidated due to state frugality, but overall the system enforces a degree of respect for the prisoner as a rights-bearing citizen different from others only in the loss of the right to liberty and those other impositions necessary to effectuate the loss of liberty. Prisoners, even those sentenced to high-security facilities for serious crimes, could expect regular visits with family (conjugal in some countries), full social rights in terms of labor in prison, and most political rights, as well as access to rehabilitative programming.

For Whitman, this striking qualitative difference is best accounted for by the prominence of the role of dignity in European public law and policy and its equally prominent absence for the US. Dignity, which now functions as a master concept in human rights law, is hard to define, but its core includes a notion of respect and solicitude toward subjects, whether owed simply to their status as human beings or through other achieved or ascribed statuses. Nora Jacobson, in her useful overview of the concept of dignity,[17] distinguishes between the history, meaning, and usage of dignity. Historically, we have inherited one strand of dignity from the Abrahamic religious traditions, in which all human beings are seen as special among all the members of creation because they were created in the divine image. A second strand, from the Greek and Roman side of antiquity, treats dignity as a function of social rank with a hierarchy. Since the Enlightenment, we also have a philosophical tradition of dignity, most influentially developed by Kant and since by many others, which to some extent draws on both ancient strands and recasts them in terms of rationality and moral freedom.

The historical legacy of dignity translates into two broad meanings. "Human" dignity, which is inherent or ontological and applicable to all of humanity (whether or not anchored in a notion of an association of divine creation), and social dignity, which arises from the status of particular social roles (whether the historical status associated with aristocratic birth or that associated with achieved social position).[18]

These historical ambiguities of meaning have passed through into the usage to which in the contemporary age dignity is put, most prominently in human rights, law, and increasingly medicine (in both its clinical and research applications). They are particularly important in the field of punishment because convicted criminal offenders have generally been rightly deprived of their liberties and may find themselves in an equality of perfect misery. What they have left is a right to dignity, which requires some consideration of their individual circumstances and fate. As legal philosopher David Luban puts it, "Human dignity is in some sense a generalization from the egocentric predicament: human beings have ontological heft because each of us is an 'I,' and I have ontological heft. For others to treat me as though I have none fundamentally denigrates my status in the world. It amounts to a form of humiliation that violates my human dignity."[19]

Whitman's account helps us understand why, despite the fact that both the US and the members of the European Community are signatories to dignity-based human rights treaties, European law has been so much more receptive to development with dignity as a central value in its penal system. The synthesis of dignity as the inalienable right belonging to even the weakest and most vulnerable with the dignity accorded to powerful people of great rank or achievement is one fought out very directly within European law during the long process of assimilating the status of noble families into the broader status of citizenship within a sovereign and ultimately democratic nation-state. Without having digested the aristocratic side of dignity, Americans do not easily recognize or accept the emotional and sympathetic regard that people of merely common rank in society were expected to show toward members of noble families and that came to be translated into the solidarity for all members of the nation-state (and ultimately the European Community as a whole).

As Whitman shows to great effect,[20] the cultural work to define and refine this status hierarchy was concentrated in the penal field. How one was punished, executed, or later imprisoned was as dramatic and important a status difference as might be found. Nobleman sentenced to die generally faced a different execution mechanism than commoners did, beheading rather than hanging or breaking. When imprisonment began to emerge as the predominant punishment, it was marked by a different prison regime for the high status, one without forced labor or deprivations of physical comfort.[21] Rather than being abandoned, this high-status model of imprisonment was retained and extended to new categories of higher-status prisoners who won recognition as different from the ordinary criminal, including political prisoners. According to Whitman, with some variation in each country, the noble grade of punishment was gradually extended to all categories of prisoners, reaching its apotheosis in contemporary Europe under the European Convention on Human Rights.

In America, by contrast, there never was a recognized aristocracy in the colonies, and "titles of nobility" were explicitly prohibited under the Constitution. The only significant statuses of distinction recognized in society and the legal system were the racial status of slavery and the gendered status of the law of family and property. In fact, both gender and race involved legal distinctions in the harshness of punishment, with African American men in particular targeted for harsh and degrading punishments, first on the plantation as a matter of private discipline and, after the Civil War, in state penal custody, where exclusively black prisoners, often prosecuted for acts that would not even be considered crimes for whites to engage in, were rented out to white businesses for a fee.[22]

Infamously, when slavery was abolished after the Civil War, the slavery of prisoners was exempted from the Thirteenth Amendment's ban on involuntary servitude. During the 1960s and 1970s, when a measure of equal protection and due process of the laws was applied to criminal procedures and corrections, the form of imprisonment that emerged was more rational and bureaucratic but retained a propensity toward degradation of the sort once attached to African American prisoners, now extended to all. While the expansion of equality in Europe has gone along with an upgrade to the status of prisoner regardless of background, the extension of equality in America since the civil rights movement, has mainly come as a downgrade, as whites who might have previously found some leeway are subjected to the now even harsher norm, while African Americans remain just as harshly punished as they were traditionally (and even more harshly when you consider the elimination of the discount for "black on black" crime that seems to have prevailed in many state systems through the middle of the 20th century at least).[23]

From Whitman's perspective, the reason America lacks dignitarian values in its legal system is largely an accident of its historical circumstances. The early absence of colonial aristocracy and the prolonged existence of a sub-citizen slave population produced a double whammy. The US never entertained the lengthy cultural struggles and negotiations to extend aristocratic status on a formal level to all citizens. The delayed and incomplete removal of slavery meant the persistence of a tolerance for degradation in US (especially southern) social relations, with a particular concentration in US penal practices. In short, democracy came too soon, and slavery lingered too long.

Whitman deserves great thanks for confronting law and punishment scholars with the qualitative difference (easily lost by criminologists in the study of abstract "incarceration rates") and for highlighting the dignity difference. The absence of dignity as a strong legal value seems to have had significant impact on our contemporary legal system, especially our punishment system. Thus, however ambiguous in meaning, dignity-based law for Europe has become one of the primary registers in which penal policies must be justified.[24] This means that the death penalty is unavailable as a penal option and that imprisonment throughout Europe must be implemented, as to virtually all prisoners, with a clear purpose of facilitating the reintegration of the offender back into the community. While life without parole for adults has not yet directly been tested by the European Court of Human Rights, the current case law suggests that broad generic LWOP laws that were not at the very least closely individualized to the particularities of both the crime the offender and that did build in possibilities for review (through clemency or pardon powers) would be found to violate the European Charter of Human Rights.[25] Such sentences are in actuality extremely rare, and current practices of clemency and compassionate release remain far more meaningful avenues of relief than in the United States.[26] For those of us primarily interested in loosening America's commitment to degrading punishments such as LWOP, Whitman's account is both too pessimistic and too optimistic. It is too pessimistic because the absence of dignity values in express form in our public law belies the significant deposits of dignity values produced by American social movements and incompletely integrated into US law. These movements have been driven by forces in US society that do not get much accounting in Whitman's history, which privileges the Federalist-era founding of the American republic and the largely Scotch-Irish citizenry which dominated the US through much of the 19th century (and whose fierce libertarian values are still powerful influences in American politics, witness the Tea Party). But American political culture has not been static. The African American population, brought here in slavery but whose political presence has been more powerfully felt in the 20th century, produced its own political values in the long struggle to survive slavery and fierce discrimination. These values, embedded in the black church, as well as in the self-improvement movements associated with figures as diverse as George Washington Carver and Marcus Garvey, give dignity a substantial role. The modern civil rights movement, led by African American clergy such as Martin Luther King, Jr., made dignity a central feature of its struggle for social and political equality. While these values have remained largely implicit in the legal revolution that followed, both the epic *Brown v. Board of Education* decision[27] and the Civil Rights Act of 1964[28] include powerful themes of dignity that have yet to be fully developed by subsequent lawmaking but remain a potentially powerful counterweight to the libertarian values of the Federalist Constitution. Likewise, the 20th-century labor-rights movement, led by Catholic and Jewish immigrants whose numbers swelled the nation's large cities at the end of the 19th century, was in many respects a movement for dignity as much as economic gain.[29] While these movement-led dignity values remain weakly reflected in public law, they represent a potent strain in our legal culture that can shape public law in the future.

However, Whitman's account may also be overly optimistic because it is not the absence of dignity alone that has promoted degrading punishments such as LWOP in the United States, nor should we expect a rapid weakening of support for degrading punishments simply because dignity begins to become more visible as a value in public law. Our history suggests that other conditions are necessary for the proliferation of degrading punishments, for otherwise we could not account for the rapid growth of such punishments just in the past couple of decades. The intense politicization of crime in the late 20th century has reshaped many aspects of our penal system and produced a form of mass incarceration unknown to earlier and no-less-undignified eras of US history.[30] Suspicion of the police remains quite robust,[31] but the prisons (and their officials) have largely succeeded in evading American cultural concerns about strong state power, at least so long as it is concentrated on individual offenders (and disreputable classes). More recent scholarship suggests that we need to look more closely at different patterns within the United States and that the role of particular agencies and actors within the states fully explains the extreme turn that (some) American punishment takes.[32]

This is important not just for historical purposes but also for considering how legal change might come to LWOP and other degrading punishments in the US. Even the European Court of Human Rights has been very cautious in intervening in the penal policy choices of member states. Much of the work that dignity does in Europe it does through the values and purposes it infuses through European penal administrations through the networks of European prison law and policy, such as the Council of Europe's Committee of Ministers on the Treatment of Long Term Prisoners.[33] In a similar way, the expansion of the 8th Amendment to address prison conditions and regimes by federal judges in the 1970s and 1980s built on the influence of rehabilitation and bureaucratic modernization on American corrections through the organized correctional profession and the Federal Bureau of Prisons.[34] Currently, however, the collapse of rehabilitation as a form of public policy in many states, and the gigantic scaling up of the prison population into an enduring crisis of management, has limited the ability of federal courts to set limits on the penal populism that has made punishments more degrading.

Total Incapacitation

Today any effort to roll back LWOP through the courts will confront the entrenched resistance of a very different body of law and policy than Europe's dignity-based human rights law, law shaped by 30 years of war on crime. No less than human rights law, what we might call "war-on-crime" law is also based on a powerful if problematic value. Rather than dignity, the master value of war-on-crime law is the victims, or rather protecting/honoring/recognizing the victim.[35] This varies greatly from state to state, and it is possible that courts will be able to accomplish more in those states where penal law remains shaped by 20th-century penal modernism (including New York, Michigan, and Illinois, among others). In California, and many other Sunbelt states,[36] the legal struggle against LWOP will confront a body of penal law and policy shaped around the victim. Contrary to common belief, this does not translate predominantly as vengeance, although that is there as well, but in a logic of security which I call "total" incapacitation, to differentiate it from the broader penal rationale of incapacitation or prevention which has long been a feature of modern penology.[37]

Incapacitation emerged as an explicit penal rationale with the rise of positivist criminology in the late 19th century. Initially the primary focus was on the institutionalized population (both prisons and asylum). Whatever other effects it might have on the general deterrence of crime or on provoking penitence in the punished, imprisonment after the rise of the penitentiary-style prison reliably provided the isolation of the prisoner from the community. This isolation is presumed to relieve the community of at least some of the pressure of criminal behavior. In the first half of the 20th century this was also assumed to produce eugenic benefits, reducing the reproductive pressure of people with criminal propensities on the broader gene pool. But beyond the total institutions of confinement, incapacitation or prevention also applied to new measures, both therapeutic and penal, designed to reduce the personal risk posed by the individuals released from the prison or the asylum, in the form of parole or probation, juvenile probation, social work, and various forms of medication designed to control everything from psychotic symptoms to male sexual drive.

Until the end of the 20th century, incapacitation mainly functioned as the dark and presumptively minor side of the dominant rehabilitative penology (in the sense that most prisoners were presumed capable of rehabilitation). In particular, the indeterminate sentence promised to efficiently move out of prison those who could be effectively and safely reformed while in the community but to hold on indefinitely to those who remained dangerous. At the end of the 20th century, with rehabilitation in retreat in most of the United States and legal elites divided about deterrence and retribution as penal purposes, incapacitation emerged as a penal rationale in its own right and as closely fitting the rise of risk management as the primary narrative of criminal justice.[38]

The degree of commitment to incapacitation or, perhaps more accurately, the degree of exclusion of other penal purposes varies across the US states, but everywhere, it clearly functions as one of the dominant rationales for prisons generally and especially as the primary justification for penal expansion. California provides an example of a US jurisdiction that has embraced incapacitation virtually to the exclusion of other penal rationales and has embraced such an extreme version of incapacitation that it deserves its own term, one which I call "total" incapacitation to express its distinctions from the broader tradition. If incapacitation generally is the idea that the distribution and length of imprisonment should represent, at least in part, the degree of risk that the particular offender or class of offenders pose to the community, total incapacitation could be defined as the idea that imprisonment is appropriate whenever an offender poses any degree of risk to the community.[39]

California penal law, policy, and practice express this commitment to total incapacitation in a variety of ways. The distribution of imprisonment, which until recently saw increases across virtually all categories of crime, reflects an imperative that for virtually all felony offenders more imprisonment means more community safety. California's legal structure allows prosecutors to exercise substantial control through their charging decisions. This varies from county to county in degree, and it is encouraged by the perverse incentive that state prison costs are borne solely by the state of California, whereas probation is largely paid for on a county basis.[40] Parole practice also expresses an extreme degree of incapacitation. The vast majority of California prisoners are released not by parole but by expiration of their determinate sentence less good-time credits, but almost all (until recently) were placed on parole supervision for three further years, when they have faced an extremely high likelihood of being returned to prison, even if they avoid arrest for a new crime.[41] Parole release, which applies only to lifers (mostly committed for murder or a felony with a third strike) has been applied extremely cautiously by historical and comparative standards and has become a growing issue for the courts that are being asked to order parole dates to be set for many California lifers who could not create stronger profiles for release but who are routinely rejected by the board of prison terms (and in the case of those on a murder commitment, the governor).[42]

In policy and practice, California is also wed to an extreme version of incapacitation through its administration of penal custody. California prisons have been designed primarily with the aim of holding as many people as inexpensively as possible, with little consideration given to programming of any kind or even to provision of adequate medical care. The only dimension on which prisoners are given deeper scrutiny is their estimated risk. All California prisoners are given a security rating of 1–4 and incarcerated in facilities designed with appropriate security features (and little else). Most experts agree that the system has far too many inmates defined as requiring level 4 custody. Beyond 4, California also assigns prisoners it considers high risk to two very large security housing unit prisons (SHUs), which are "supermax"-style prisons that operate on a total lockdown basis.[43] Due to overcrowding, many of its level 4 ordinary prisons also operate on an intermittent lockdown basis.

On the level of law, California evidences an extreme commitment to incapacitation through the combination of the extensive use of life imprisonment and the withering of parole release. California's death penalty, in both law and practice, are part of this complex as well. Those who are charged with capital ("special circumstance") murder who do not face a sentence of death are automatically sentenced to LWOP. These LWOP prisoners, along with thousands of lifers with the theoretical possibility but unlikelihood of parole form a large and growing block of indigestible harsh punishment in the very core of California's vast correctional system. Since relatively few executions are carried out in California, the more than 700 persons on death row are also effectively part of this permanent imprisonment. California adds to this already distended lifer category through its numerous sentence-enhancement laws, particularly the three-strikes law adopted by constitutional amendment through a voter initiative in 1994.[44] While states have long had special sentence laws aimed at recidivists, California's three-strikes law is by far the most far reaching in history. Under its provisions, a person who is once convicted of a violent or serious felony (the latter category includes a growing and broad list of crimes) has special penalties apply for any subsequent felony and ultimately a sentence of 25 years to life for any felony after two previous violent or serious felonies.

How did California become committed to such an extreme version of incapacitation? The success of incapacitation cannot be explained primarily by the strategic behavior of penal elites or by displaced racism. Few politicians in the 1970s saw incapacitation as a productive penal logic to promote. The appeal of getting "tough" on crime was readily apparent as early as 1968 and continued to expand throughout this period, but for most politicians this was expressed primarily through the traditional penal logics of deterrence and just punishment. Violent crime should be punished with much longer prison sentences to deter others and to reflect society's outrage at the violation of the victim's rights. Few if any politicians in this era saw the long prison sentence as a way to contain the dangerous on a long-term or permanent basis.

Rather, most politicians came to incapacitation late, after recognizing a new consensus emerging from middle-class homeowners, law enforcement officers, and the media that the new risks of a hyperviolent criminal class required a new and uncompromising commitment to prison as a permanent barrier between potential victims and the dangerous. Racism and the conflicted sentiments of white voters over the dismantling of legal privileges for whites may have been disguised through calls for harsher punishment, but the idea of general incapacitation—that is, long prison sentences to avoid crime that are based on the crime of conviction rather than on the individualized assessment of risk—owed as least as much to civil rights concerns about the discriminatory use of discretion in the legal system.

California's commitment to total incapacitation was forged in the 1970s by two important developments. First, the prison officers became committed to an extremely warlike vision of their own relationship with prisoners during the peak of convict political activism in California in the early 1970s, when violence against prison officers by revolutionary convicts combined with some significant public support for prisoners and denouncing of prison officers as racist.[45] Although the revolutionary moment in prisons was relatively brief and mostly ended with the violent repression of revolutionary inmates including prisoner leader George Jackson at San Quentin in August 1971 and, a few weeks later, of the Attica prison uprising, it motivated prison officers to organize around a common bond of victimization with the public against a common enemy. The prison officers in California were unionized by a faction devoted to organizing around these themes and became the most powerful public employee union in the state. By the end of the 1980s, the prison officers' union, the California Professional Peace Officers Association, through its broad alliance with other California law enforcement lobbies, especially the prosecutors association, had emerged as the most important force shaping the penal field.[46]

The effectiveness of the prison officers was based in large part on their early strategic awareness of a shift among California's suburban middle-class voters toward a strong preoccupation with the threat of violent crime and, in particular, home-invasion-style burglaries aimed at murder, rape, or theft. A wave of highly publicized incidents of serial killing or extreme killing swept California in the decade of the 1970s (with even more in the 1980s).[47] These crimes were noteworthy as much for their concentration among white middle- and upper-class suburban communities as for the extremity of their violence. Magnified by California's concentration of media outlets and industries and by the rapid expansion of homeownership, the serial killers helped erase any sense of geographic security to California's suburban middle class and consolidated bipartisan support for a no-holds-barred culture of control.[48]

The Supreme Court recognized California's distinctive choice in favor of incapacitation as a penal rationale in the three-strike cases[49] and adopted a highly deferential approach to reviewing the rationality of state choices in penological policy, both of which led them to largely dismiss one of the few grounds for questioning the harshness of prison sentences, one with a strong connection to dignity: that of the proportionality between the crime and the punishment. Given the extremity of total incapacitation as a penal ideology and the Supreme Court's deference to it, there appears to be a long road ahead for those who are hoping for a judicial overturning of LWOP.

But if the absence of dignity as a central legal value is both implicated and reinforced by an extreme version of incapacitation as a penal rationale, it will take more than a strengthening of dignity within the law to overcome degrading punishments such as LWOP. This is not an argument for abandoning court challenges to LWOP, three strikes, and other extreme sentences. Indeed, the availability and likely expansion of judicial forums to hear these claims is one of the best opportunities at present to wage a broader cultural struggle against total incapacitation. Such challenges enable a rare break in the public presentation of incapacitation as sanitary and effective, and provide a unique space in which to reintroduce a discourse of morality and justice into talk about punishment. But they will have their greatest effect when they can draw parallels with developments in our social and legal culture in which risk and dignity are being reconfigured to place fear under a stronger value of dignity. It is the growing strength of several such areas which provides me optimism that the road to a legal end of LWOP need not be a lifetime away.

Dignity in End-of-Life Care

In a review of the literature on "health and dignity," Nora Jacobson finds that "attention to dignity is thriving in health research and advocacy."[50] The link between health, health care, and dignity is one that has received express recognition from the United Nations, which has defined health as a "prerequisite to living life in dignity"[51] and has encouraged a growing global discussion on the right to health care. Dignity in a somewhat different, more religious sense has also emerged as an issue in debates over health-related research, including exploitation of stem cell lines for research purposes and cloning. In the same respect, the growing concern with environmental justice and racially discriminatory patterns of exposure to health-damaging chemicals and lack of access to adequate health care facilities invokes a notion of human dignity.

The medical care and nursing of people at the very end of life has generated a particularly deep engagement with dignity as a redefining principle. Dignity was first invoked by both advocates and (shortly thereafter) opponents of a "right to die" and euthanasia.[52] More recently it has become a major focus of internal efforts at practice reform among doctors and nurses, including the development of outcome assessment surveys with dignity as a key scored variable and the development of strategies to enhance dignity (or conserve it) based on empirical studies of patients.[53]

The leading dignity conservation approach identifies three areas of focus.[54] The first is excellent pain- and symptom-management care. Since pain and discomforting symptoms rapidly erode the capacity of a patient to engage in the other kinds of dignity-conserving moves that research has recommended, excellent management of symptoms opens up other possibilities. The second area involves what researchers have aptly called a "dignity-conserving repertoire," i.e., the roles, activities, and achievements that an individual takes pride in and sees as his or her way of leaving a mark on the world—one that is not undone by disease. Finally, each patient can be evaluated in terms of a "social dignity inventory," of experiences and relationships in the palliative care context that can enhance or erode dignity, including respect for privacy and support from close family and friends.

In some respects the world of end-of-life-stage palliative care seems especially far away from the world of LWOP. Terminally ill patients are among the most sympathetic figures of our time, while persons who commit the violent crimes generally necessary to earn LWOP are among the most loathed. In other respects they are not so different. In both prison and end-of-life care, there are inevitably degrading elements (relying on a bed pan, being locked in a cell), and yet the practice can turn itself to the problem of how to conserve dignity. If respect for dignity seems a very distant priority for American prisons today, it is also the case that it was only a short time ago that the priority of extending life through complete medical control was viewed as relegating dignity to the periphery of medicine. Indeed palliative care, which is in many respects defined by the priority given to dignity, was recognized first by being excluded from the medical field, as patients wishing to utilize dedicated palliative care regimes such as hospice had to be foreswear medical hope. Today that boundary is fast eroding, as publications on dignity in journals such as the *Journal of the American Medical Association* and the *Lancet* suggest.

It may be that with LWOP and other degrading punishments, just as with medicine, we will witness two tracks that never intersect and yet influence each other. One is a battle about rights, which is taking place primarily in the courts and legislatures and which pits the human rights of life-sentenced prisoners to some margin of hope against the human rights of crime victims to the smallest possible margin of risk. The other is an effort to remake the practice of imprisonment (at least long-term imprisonment) around the goal of conserving dignity. For prisons to embrace this goal it is necessary to make explicit and reject the view of prison as aimed at degrading the dignity of the individual, a view which clearly many Americans hold but which actually finds little if any support in any of the established rationales of punishment, including incapacitation.

Once we cross that threshold it is possible to imagine countless reforms to the actual practice of long-term imprisonment that would be based on the goal of conserving dignity through the punishment process, much as medical practice now seeks to conserve it during the dying process. In Europe, this kind of emphasis has already emerged through organs of the Council of Europe such as the Committee for the Prevention of Torture and the Committee of Ministers on the Treatment of Long Term Prisoners. These organs have established a strong presumption that all prisoners should be prepared for reintegration and that where states have chosen to hold prisoners for long terms (defined as over five years), the regime should specifically seek to compensate for the desocializing effects of such sentences through application of the principles of "individualization, non-segregation, and progression."[55] This may begin to engage the very meaning of LWOP itself. For example, compassionate release principles could become an important relief mechanism for LWOP.[56]

Dignity in Involuntary Treatment

California led the nation for most of the 20th century in the proportion of persons preventively detained in asylums and mental hospitals.[57] In the decade immediately prior to the turn to total incapacitation in California penal logic, the state led the nation in a dramatic shift in the framing of state power to control persons with mental illness through long-term confinement. Historically, almost anyone could be hospitalized on the petition of family members or the police, if the person was suffering from a mental illness and if medical professionals indicated that the person could benefit from coerced treatment. This was jointly based on the state's *parens patrie* power to look after dependent populations but also on the police power of protecting citizens.[58]

In the 1950s and 1960s a nationwide movement against long-term custodial warehousing of people with mental illness (and developmental disabilities) coalesced, especially in California.[59] Asylum commitment rates began dropping in the 1960s, and in California a new law adopted in 1969, the Lanterman-Petris-Short Act, created strong legal barriers to warehousing by requiring the state to show that a person was not only mentally ill but posed an imminent threat of death or great bodily harm or was unable to maintain life-sustaining activities, in order to continue holding the person after an initial 72-hour evaluation and for each extension of custody approved.

While no one defends the indiscriminate long-term custody practices of the 1950s and earlier, many people today, especially family members of persons with untreated mental illness, bemoan the highly libertarian standard set by the law at the end of the 1960s. (Even though not all states are as libertarian in this regard as California, all of them make it much harder to confine anyone than was true in the past.) According to critics, the present law leaves many people with severe mental illness—who because of their symptoms do not recognize their own degree of illness—vulnerable to violence, incarceration, and irremediable degeneration in their mental condition as a result of being untreated.[60] Some of these untreated people are also responsible for frightening acts of random violence generated by their psychotic symptoms. Critics suggest that a substantial portion of homicides every year might be avoided by allowing authorities greater leeway to compel treatment.[61]

Consumers' rights advocates and attorneys have bitterly opposed new enhancements to state authority to intervene as an effort to roll back liberty and equality gains of the 1960s. High levels of incarceration and homelessness reflect general problems of the urban poor and not a distinct problem of persons with mental illness. According to these groups, most of the problems just outlined could be solved by creating access to voluntary treatment and support services. As a result of intense disagreement, most reforms have been marginal. California, for example, authorized a version of New York's involuntary outpatient treatment law but left each county to decide whether to fund such activities, a step that so far only a few counties with low burdens and high resources have taken.[62]

Dignity is emerging in this debate as an important resource to reconstruct the law of involuntary mental health treatment. What people with mental illness who are untreated and largely unsupported by social institutions risk, more immediately than incarceration or death, is a loss of dignity that comes from losing access to what the medical literature refers to as the repertoire of dignity-conserving methods, ranging from having a recognized role in the world to even very simple things such as having grooming opportunities, belongings, and privacy. At the same time, there is little more direct assault that can be made on a person's dignity than to subject him or her to involuntary custody and treatment. As with the situation of end-stage medical care, these contradictions in dignity point the way to reform by suggesting that dignity conservation become the major objective of redesigned procedures.

A growing literature in psychology and therapeutic jurisprudence suggests that well-designed court procedures can close the dignity gap by attending to how court procedures are presented, by ensuring participation by the person subject to proceedings, and by making sure that the person is kept informed.[63] As to the form of justice, the large literature on procedural justice points to three key factors that determine whether participants feel positively about proceedings (a finding that is said to be robust to winning and losing and to be applicable to persons with serious mental illness as well): whether the decision-maker appears to be neutral, whether the person had a real opportunity to explain his or her situation, and whether the decision-maker ultimately comports him- or herself toward the person as if he or she is in fact a person worthy of respect.[64] These matters of appearance (or even artifice) may be particularly crucial to persons with mental illness, whose sense of dignity has often been eroded by the visible lack of respect that others accord to their presence and statements.

Participation is a part of procedural formality, but it also offers a substantive tool for reframing the law of civil commitment. Empirical experimentation shows that people in legal proceedings care a lot about whether they are actually heard from. This seems to hold even when people do not expect what they say to the judge to make a difference in the outcome of the case.

Mental health experts have generally been concerned that participating in adversary proceedings may actually exacerbate the mental state of persons experiencing psychotic ideation by aggravating a sense of persecution. But experimentation in criminal courts, inspired by the therapeutic jurisprudence movement, has developed models that work well to create meaningful and dignity-enhancing participation while building in informality and collaborative features. Judges, with their strong cultural meaning, seem to be particularly key to creating participation that heals rather than harms. In the Behavioral and Mental Health Court model, like many drug courts, the judge engages directly with persons subject to the proceedings, giving them an opportunity to express their concerns to the judge and often giving the judge the opportunity in return to express praise for their positive progress and concern for their past troubles. For persons with serious mental illness, the cultural authority of judges makes engagement with them both fraught and potentially powerfully therapeutic.

Information control, as in other forms of the health experience, is crucial to allowing involuntary mental health treatment to do as much good as possible and as little harm to the person's dignity. Even if a person opposes the state's effort to hold and treat him or her, having a judge explain exactly what is going to happen, why he or she has decided to allow the state to proceed with treatment, and what the goals of that treatment will be produces both a greater sense of respect from the process and possibly better therapeutic outcomes as well.

Compared to my other examples, the legal framework for involuntary treatment of persons with serious mental illness is a bit closer to the situation facing LWOP prisoners, but only a little. Like LWOP prisoners, subjects of civil commitment carry the burden of public fear and possibly disgust and are viewed through the lens of future dangerousness. Unlike long-term prisoners, they are not subject to legal condemnation and punishment. The problem of future dangerousness is neatly separated from that of culpability and guilty. Still, the rise of dignity as a resource for reframing the law of civil commitment can offer some suggestions.

Perhaps the most important is that a revitalized civil approach toward incapacitating and treating the dangerous would take some of the pressure off the criminal system to operate as society's primary response to interpersonal threat. While the violently psychotic make up only a tiny fraction of all persons with serious mental illnesses,[65] they make up a larger portion of the crimes, including mass murders and child-victim murders, that generate the greatest fear among the general public. The approach toward incapacitation in the civil commitment system, even if broadened from its currently extremely libertarian standards, would demand a high level of evidence based on individual assessment that the incapacitated individual remains a threat and is receiving treatment designed to reduce the threat as much as is possible—neither of which conditions is required of penal incapacitation.

One would hope over time for the analogy between incapacitation in the two spheres to soften the harsher elements of the penal approach. Life prisoners should become more like civil commitment subjects in the mature phase of their imprisonment, when long years of incarceration have addressed what most people would consider the retributive dimension of their punishment.[66] If after this point we are really holding a person primarily for reasons of incapacitation, for protecting the public, should the person not be subject to something more like a civil commitment standard, so that the state must convince a decision-maker that at least some substantial reasons persist for considering the person a danger to the public?

Another consideration is the importance of judges as decision-makers whose cultural authority may have real value beyond whatever analytic benefits they bring to decision-making. Given that support for LWOP reflects in part a strong history of public mistrust for administrative parole boards, which tend to operate without much public scrutiny or much in the way of adversary proceedings, it may make sense to involve judges in reviewing the imprisonment of long-held prisoners.[67]

Dignity in the Regulation of Marriage

The California Supreme Court's decision in In re Marriage Cases (2008)[68] represents one of the most striking examples of a court drawing on dignity to significantly expand existing constitutional protections of liberty and equality. California became the second state, following Massachusetts, to have its high court find the limitation of marriage to opposite-sex couples unconstitutional. Because California already had domestic-partnership laws protecting many of the specific rights and duties created by marriage, the California court saw the primary import of the existing legal arrangement to be its withholding from same-sex couples of the distinct honor accorded to the concept of marriage. In its key holding, the California court placed dignity at the very center of its reasoning on marriage/domestic-partnership distinction:[69]

One of the core elements of the right to establish an officially recognized family that is embodied in the California constitutional right to marry is a couple's right to have their family relationship accorded dignity and respect equal to that accorded other officially recognized families, and assigning a different designation for the family relationship of same-sex couples while reserving the historic designation of "marriage" exclusively for opposite-sex couples poses at least a serious risk of denying the family relationship of same-sex couples such equal dignity and respect. We therefore conclude that although the provisions of the current domestic partnership legislation afford same-sex couples most of the substantive elements embodied in the constitutional right to marry, the current California statutes nonetheless must be viewed as potentially impinging upon a same-sex couple's constitutional right to marry under the California Constitution.[70]

Marriage is, of course, like medicine, quite distant from the topical issue of LWOP and other degrading punishments.[71] Perhaps the most striking impression a comparison of these two fields in California law suggests is the tremendous disparity between the California Supreme Court's willingness to limit legislative and popular lawmaking power, whereas in criminal matters, especially questions involving the law of murder, capital punishment, and life imprisonment, the Court has twisted precedent and sometimes logic to avoid placing any limits on the states power to punish.

Common to both areas, however, is a relationship between dignity and fear. The law against same-sex marriage was promoted as a way to protect traditional marriages (the same reasoning was made explicit in the campaign for Proposition 8 and was at the center of the recent federal district court ruling finding the proposition lacks a rational basis). In *In re Marriage Cases*, the California Supreme Court had no hesitancy in evaluating the underlying risk analysis that protection of traditional marriage required the exclusion of same-sex marriage.

First, the exclusion of same-sex couples from the designation of marriage clearly is not necessary in order to afford full protection of all the rights and benefits that currently are enjoyed by married opposite-sex couples; permitting same-sex couples access to the designation of marriage will not deprive opposite-sex couples of any rights and will not alter the legal framework of the institution of marriage, because same-sex couples who choose to marry will be subject to the same obligations and duties that currently are imposed on married opposite-sex couples.[72]

Of course, the situation of same-sex couples is most inapposite to that of people facing LWOP sentences for violent crime (even though gays and lesbians have faced a good deal of stigma and at times the direct threat of criminalization). What is possible to think about across the two fields is the willingness of courts to assess populist risk judgments that mask a will to degrade. LWOP and other degrading punishments are based on a judgment about the unchanging nature of the risk posed by persons who commit violent crimes, a judgment that does not hold up to a demand for evidence. Even if criminal conviction justifies a state in disregarding the right to equal dignity of the convicted person for some period of time, that period is not consistent necessarily with the length of time demanded by incapacitative punishments, let alone LWOP.

Conclusion

America at the beginning of the 21st century has a problem with punishment. We not only punish too many people, too much; we also embrace degrading punishments that permanently damage or destroy the subject while delivering little justice or social advantage. The LWOP sentence, which has grown enormously in its frequency of use over the past couple of decades, is a case in point. It removes all hope for the future from the prisoner, who may be quite young at the outset of the punishment. The gain in crimes prevented becomes vanishingly small after the first 10 or 20 years of incapacitation, and any sense of justice in the whole-life term, as opposed to some lesser number of years, is one largely of metaphor.[73]

Our propensity as a society for degrading punishments, including LWOP, may, as James Whitman has persuasively argued, have its roots in the relative absence of a strong legal conception of dignity in US law and society, of the sort that Europe developed through its long struggle to assimilate the status hierarchy associated with aristocratic honors to the modern demands of equality and meritocracy. In this chapter I have argued that our embrace of degrading punishments is equally a product of our commitment to an extreme variant of incapacitation as a penal rationale. "Total" incapacitation goes beyond exploiting the crime-prevention capacity of imprisonment to a notion of contamination, one anchored in the distinctive historical patterns of the 1970s and the fear of violent crime in the new suburbs, especially in the newly dominant Sunbelt states such as California. Translated into politics, policy, and law by the politicians and moral entrepreneurs of the 1980s and 1990s and locked into place as mass incarceration, total incapacitation continues to shape penal policy in many states. The absence of dignity and the logic of total incapacitation play into each other. There has proved little in our penal traditions to resist the total submission of the prisoner to the ideal of public security, and the state of being afraid of violent intrusion into the family home is not one likely to conserve a sense of dignity in anyone.

The signs that dignity, or something very much like it, may be gaining new force in the Supreme Court's Eighth Amendment jurisprudence, as suggested by Justice Kennedy's majority opinion in *Graham v. Florida*, is a positive sign in this regard. But when we think about dignity and total incapacitation together, it suggests a long road between *Graham* and any judicial overturning of LWOP for ordinary adults with violent crime on their record. The Court shows no signs of retreating from the strongly deferential posture it struck toward states' penological value choices.[74] At least where state policy continues to embrace total incapacitation, it is unlikely we will see this Supreme Court compel the release of long-held prisoners. More recently, in *Brown v. Plata*, a case dealing directly with the humanitarian consequences of mass incarceration in California, dignity received explicit and important emphasis. Justice Kennedy, again writing for a 5–4 majority, wrote, "Prisoners retain the essence of human dignity inherent in all persons. Respect for that dignity animates the Eighth Amendment prohibition against cruel and unusual punishment."[75]

The strengthening of dignity as a value within the Eighth Amendment may, however, be greatly aided (and the road from *Graham* to LWOP abolition shortened) by the emergence of dignity in a wide array of legal changes going on in the United States. This chapter focuses on three examples: end-of-life medical care, involuntary treatment of people with serious mental illness, and same-sex marriage.[76] Of course there are great differences between the situation and the public perception of LWOP prisoners, on the one hand, and the subjects involved in all three of my examples, on the other. I recognize that for many people, the serious crimes such prisoners have committed separate them from the sympathy that arises for subjects in the other settings. But the most important analogies might be drawn not between the subjects but in the recognition of practical and situational similarities. Those of us struggling to confront degrading punishments in courts and legislatures might benefit from drawing very specific analogies that elide the obvious differences in subject positionality and stigma.

From the dying, we might borrow the notion that long-term imprisonment is itself an unavoidable challenge to dignity. The way our prisons administer that challenge must itself become the subject of litigation and may in time become a defining value for long-term imprisonment itself. From those who suffer from grave symptoms of mental illness confronted with coerced treatment, we might borrow the idea of procedural rights to respect and participation that cannot be diminished by the subjective conditions of the subject. In this respect courts might offer a promising alternative mechanism of release to the administrative parole systems that have historically been almost equally hated by the public and prisoners.[77] From same-sex couples, we might borrow the notion that courts have a role to play in questioning the risk assessment embedded in law. Deference to the policy choices inherent in any choice-of-risks problem in legislation does not require courts to accept as risk judgments what are, in fact, sectarian judgments of "contamination."

None of these other examples lies particularly close in a policy sense to punishment (let alone LWOP), but all of them suggest ways to reconstruct penal practices toward the end of conserving dignity. More importantly, they remind us that, like death and marriage, prisons (and asylums) are institutions with a unique power to strip human beings of dignity. For the most part these examples are not meant to suggest an alternative to a long-grinding battle in the courts on behalf of prisoners with LWOP and other life-trashing sentences. Instead, they are directions that such litigation (as well as appropriate legislative and policy strategies) may draw from as it seeks to reduce and abolish the use of America's most important degrading punishment.

NOTES

1. Émile Durkheim "Two Laws of Penal Evolution," translated by T. Anthony Jones and Andrew Scull, *Economy and Society* 2(3) (1973): 285–308.

2. Franklin E. Zimring, *The Contradictions of American Capital Punishment* (New York: Oxford University Press, 2003).

3. Sharon Shalev, *Supermax: Controlling Risk through Solitary Confinement* (London: Willan, 2009).

4. Michael O'Hear, "The Beginning of the End for Life without Parole," *Federal Sentencing Reporter* 23(1) (2010): 1.

5. See, generally, Jonathan Simon, *Governing through Crime: How the War on Crime Transformed American Democracy and Created a Culture of Fear* (New York: Oxford University Press, 2007).

6. Dirk Van Zyl Smit, "Outlawing Irreducible Life Sentences: Europe on the Brink?," *Federal Sentencing Reporter* 23 (2010): 39–48.

7. Stuart Scheingold, *The Politics of Street Crime* (Madison: University of Wisconsin Press, 1991); Franklin E. Zimring, Gordon Hawkins, and Sam Kamin, *Punishment and Democracy: California's Three Strikes Law* (New York: Oxford University Press, 2001); David Garland, *The Culture of Control: Crime and Social Order in Late Modern Society* (Chicago: University of Chicago Press, 2001); Simon, *Governing through Crime*; Loïc Wacquant, *Punishing the Poor: The Neoliberal Governance of Insecurity* (London: Polity, 2009).

8. James Whitman, *Harsh Justice: Criminal Punishment and the Widening Divide between America and Europe* (New York: Oxford University Press, 2005).

9. Franklin E. Zimring and Gordon Hawkins, *Incapacitation* (New York: Oxford University Press, 1995).

10. See van Zyl Smit, "Outlawing Irreducible Life Sentences," 41. The German Federal Constitutional Court has found a whole-life sentence, even for adults, incompatible with the principle of human dignity. Ibid.

11. Ibid., 39.

12. Criminal Justice Act of 2003, Chapter 5, Section 225, allowing a court to sentence a person convicted of a serious offense with a maximum sentence of 10 years or more to an indeterminate life sentence. As of 2008, 4,170 persons were imprisoned in England and Wales under this section. See HMS Prison Service, "Advice and Support, Life Sentenced Prisoners," http://www.hmprisonservice.gov.uk/adviceandsupport/prison_life/lifesentencedprisoners/. As of late 2010 at least 6,000 such sentences have been handed down since the law went into effect, of which fewer than 100 people have been released out of nearly 2,500 who have reached their point of eligibility. See Sophie Radice, "Why Was My Friend Peter Sent to Jail with No Time Set for His Release?," *Observer*, October 31, 2010, 35, http://www.guardian.co.uk/commentisfree/2010/oct/31/sophie-radice-indeterminate-sentences-injustice.

13. *Graham v. Florida*, 560 U.S. ___ (2010).

14. *Graham*, No. 08-7412, slip op. at 19 (May 17, 2010).

15. Of course major hurdles would be posed to such litigation by *Graham*'s definition as a case about juveniles convicted of nonhomicide crimes (see O'Hear, "The Beginning of the End").

16. *Madrid v. Gomez*, 889 F. Supp. 1146 (N.D. Cal. 1995).

17. Nora Jacobson, "Dignity and Health: A Review," *Social Science & Medicine* 64 (2007): 292.

18. Ibid., 294–95. Yet a third notion of dignity is associated with particularly virtuous conduct once associated with elevated social status but is also applicable to virtuous conduct more generally, as when a person is said to bear hardship with dignity. Deryck Beyleveld and Roger Brownsword, "Human Dignity, Human Rights and Human Genetics," *Modern Law Review* 61(5) (1998): 666–67.

19. David Luban, *Legal Ethics and Human Dignity* (Cambridge: Cambridge University Press, 2007), 71.

20. Whitman, *Harsh Justice*, 105–30.

21. There was an old tradition of fortress confinement for nobles, often complete with access to servants and retainers.

22. See Alex Lichtenstein, *Twice the Work of Free Labor: The Political Economy of Convict Labor in the New South* (London: Verso, 1996).

23. The severity of punishment, at least in some states, may be somewhat mitigated by the improved physical conditions in American prisons produced by the intervention of federal courts at the end of the last century—see Malcolm Feeley and Edward Rubin, *Judicial Policy Making and the Modern State: How the Courts Reformed America's Prisons* (New York: Cambridge University Press, 1998)—and the construction of many new prisons in the 1980s and 1990s, often replacing century-old facilities.

24. Dirk van Zyl Smit and Sonja Snacken, *Principles of European Prison Law and Policy* (Oxford: Oxford University Press, 2009).

25. Indeed, while some nations, including the Netherlands and the United Kingdom, provide for whole-life sentences, each has about 40 prisoners in that status. France also has a life term, with a 30-year minimum sentence for the murder of a child under 15 with rape and torture, but only three prisoners are under this sentence. Van Zyl Smit, "Outlawing Irreducible Life Sentences," 41.

26. See Gregory O'Meara, "Compassion and the Public Interest: Wisconsin's New Compassionate Release Legislation," *Federal Sentencing Reporter* 23(1) (2010): 33–38.

27. 347 U.S. 483 (1954).

28. Pub. L. 88-352, 78 Stat. 241, enacted July 2, 1964.

29. Jim Auerbach, "Organized Labor: Towards a New Dignity in the Workplace," *Journal of Career Development* 15(1) (1988): 65.

30. Garland, *Culture of Control*; Simon, *Governing through Crime*; Marie Gottschalk, *The Prison and the Gallows: The Politics of Mass Incarceration in America* (Cambridge: Cambridge University Press, 2006).

31. Whitman argues that US criminal procedure protections have more to do with historical suspicions of the state than with a concept of dignity. See James Q. Whitman, "The Two Western Cultures of Privacy: Dignity versus Liberty," Research Paper 64, Public Law & Legal Theory Research Paper Series, Yale Law School, 12.

32. Mona Lynch, *Sunbelt Justice: Arizona and the Transformation of American Punishment* (Stanford: Stanford University Press, 2009); Joshua Page, *The Toughest Beat: Politics, Punishment and the Prison Guards Union in California* (New York: Oxford University Press, 2011).

33. See van Zyl Smit, "Outlawing Irreducible Life Sentences," 42; van Zyl Smit and Snacken, *Principles of European Prison Law and Policy*, 34.

34. Feeley and Rubin, *Judicial Policy Making and the Modern State*.

35. Garland, *Culture of Control*, 11; Simon, *Governing through Crime*, chap. 3.

36. Lynch, *Sunbelt Justice*.

37. Zimring and Hawkins, *Incapacitation*.

38. Malcolm Feeley and Jonathan Simon, "The New Penology: Notes on the Emerging Strategy of Corrections and Its Implications," *Criminology* 30(4) (November 1992): 449–74.

39. It could also be defined as the view that only imprisonment can provide reliable incapacitation (as against community supervision and legal qualifications on freedom that limit the access of an offender to particular victims, occupations, or associates).

40. Franklin Zimring, "Incarceration Patterns," *University of Chicago Law School Roundtable: A Journal of Interdisciplinary Studies* 7 (2000): 104–7.

41. Joan Petersilia, *When Prisoners Come Home: Parole and Prisoner Reentry* (New York: Oxford University Press, 2003); Jonathan Simon, *Poor Discipline: Parole and the Social Underclass, 1890–1990* (Chicago: University of Chicago Press, 1993).

42. John Irwin, *Lifers: Seeking Redemption in Prison* (New York: Routledge, 2009).

43. Shalev, *Supermax*.

44. Zimring, Hawkins, and Kamin, *Punishment and Democracy*.

45. Eric Cummins, *Rise and Fall of California's Radical Prison Movement* (Stanford: Stanford University Press, 1994).

46. Page, *Toughest Beat.*

47. James Alan Fox and Jack Levin, *Extreme Killing: Understanding Serial and Mass Murder* (London: Sage, 2005).

48. See Jonathan Simon, "Consuming Obsessions: Housing, Homicide and Mass Incarceration since 1950," *University of Chicago Legal Forum*, October 2010, 141–180; Jonathan Simon, "Capital Punishment as Homeowners Insurance: The Rise of the Homeowner Citizen and the Fate of Ultimate Sanctions in Europe and the United States," in *Is the Death Penalty Dying? European and American Perspectives*, ed. Austin Sarat and Jürgen Martschukat (Cambridge: Cambridge University Press, 2011).

49. *Ewing v. California*, 538 U.S. 11 (2003); and *Lockyer v. Andrade* 538 U.S. 63 (2003).

50. Jacobson, *Dignity and Health*, 2.

51. "General Comment No. 14: The Right to the Highest Attainable Standard of Health" (Article 12 of the International Covenant on Economic, Social and Cultural Rights on May 11, 2000).

52. Jacobson, *Dignity and Health*, 298.

53. Max H. Chochinov et al., "Dignity in the Terminally Ill: A Cross-Sectional, Cohort Study," *Lancet* 360 (December 21–28, 2002): 2026–30; Max H. Chochinov, "Dignity-Conserving Care—A New Model for Palliative Care: Helping the Patient Feel Valued," *Journal of the American Medical Association* 287 (17) (2002): 2253–60.

54. Chochinov, "Dignity-Conserving Care."

55. Van Zyl Smit and Snacken, "Principles of European Prison Law and Policy," 182. "Individualization" is meant as a bar against applying a uniform control regime to all long-term prisoners without regard to their individual characteristics and risk. "Non-segregation" follows from the individualization and bars a practice of routinely segregating such prisoners from the general prison population on presumption that they are uniformly dangerous. "Progression" means that the regime offers opportunities for the prisoner to earn improved circumstances over time, some horizon of hope for the future. See ibid.

56. O'Meara, "Compassion and the Public Interest."

57. See Joan Didion, *Where I Was From* (New York: Knopf, 2003).

58. See Paul Appelbaum, "A History of Civil Commitment and Related Reform: Lessons for Today," *Developments in Mental Health Law* 25(1) (2006): 13.

59. Paul Appelbaum, *Almost a Revolution: Mental Health Law and the Limits of Change* (New York: Oxford University Press, 1994).

60. E. Fuller Torrey, *The Insanity Offense: How America's Failure to Treat the Seriously Mentally Ill Endangers Its Citizens* (New York: Norton, 2008).

61. In a pattern familiar from the broader war on crime, a New York reform law authorizing courts to order medication on an outpatient basis is named Jenna's Law, after a woman who was pushed to her death in the New York subway system by a man with violent psychotic ideation who had refused family pleas to resume taking medication.

62. Miles Palley, Stephen Rosenbaum, and Jonathan Simon, "Beyond Deinstitutionalization and the Asylum: Reforming the Regulation of Madness" (MS, University of California, Berkeley, 2011).

63. Bruce Winick, *Civil Commitment: A Therapeutic Jurisprudence Model* (Durham, NC: Carolina Academic Press, 2005).

64. Tom Tyler, "Psychological Consequences of Judicial Proceedings: Implications for Civil Commitment Hearings," *Southern Methodist University Law Review* 46(2) (1992): 437.

65. According to Fuller-Torrey, only about 10 percent of the four million people with serious mental illness pose a threat of violence. See Fuller-Torrey, *Insanity Offense*, 6.

66. Some people may consider a whole-life term a just retributive response to at least some aggravated murders. But in comparison with international norms, after 20 or 25 years of imprisonment, a prisoner might be said to have fulfilled the retributive demand of his or her conviction.

67. Cecelia Klingele has recently pointed to judicial reconsideration of sentences as a long-used but little-known method of addressing overincarceration. See "Changing the Sentence without Hiding the Truth: Judicial Sentence Modification as a Promising Method of Early Release," *William & Mary Law Review* 52 (2010): 465–536.

68. 43 Cal. 4th 757 [76 Cal. Rptr. 3d 683, 183 P.3d 384].

69. The adoption by voters of Proposition 8 in November 2008 had the effect of reestablishing a constitutional distinction between same-sex and opposite-sex couples for the purpose of marriage but did not overturn the California high court's constitutional reasoning.

70. In re Marriage Cases, 43 Cal. 4th at 782–83.

71. Although, as my colleague Melissa Murray points out, there is a long connection between the marital field and the penal field, one which courts have at times drawn on expressly, as for instance in the use of marriage as a resolution of criminal charges of sex with a female under the age of statutory consent. See Melissa Murray, "Marriage as Punishment" (paper presented at the annual meeting of the Law and Society Association, Chicago, May 27, 2010).

72. In re Marriage Cases, 43 Cal. 4th at 784.

73. Robert Blecker, "Less Than We Might: Meditation on Life without Parole," *Federal Sentencing. Reporter* 23(1) (2010): 10–20.

74. Indeed Justice Kennedy himself struck this deferential posture in *Harmelin v. Michigan*, 501 U.S. 957 (1991), reaffirmed in the three-strikes case, *Ewing v. California*, 538 U.S. 11 (2003).

75. *Brown v. Plata*, No. 09-1233, slip opinion at 18.

76. I am not arguing that these are the most important or interesting such examples out there; indeed other, better ones may yield more useful comparative insights.

77. Courts may not be able to do a better job assessing risk (although there is little reason to think they would be worse than current parole boards), but there is evidence they could do a better job conserving the dignity of the long-term prisoners and the trust of the public.

About the Contributors

Rachel E. Barkow is Professor of Law at NYU School of Law and coeditor (with Anthony S. Barkow) of *Prosecutors in the Boardroom: Using Criminal Law to Regulate Corporate Conduct* (NYU Press).

Josh Bowers is Associate Professor of Law at University of Virginia School of Law.

I. Bennett Capers is Associate Professor of Law and Associate Dean for Intellectual Life at Hofstra Law School.

Sharon Dolovich is Professor of Law at University of California, Los Angeles.

Marie Gottschalk is Professor of Political Science at University of Pennsylvania. Her books include *The Prison and the Gallows: The Politics of Mass Incarceration in America.*

Jessica S. Henry is Assistant Professor of Legal Studies at Montclair State University.

Charles J. Ogletree, Jr., is Jesse Climenko Professor of Law at Harvard Law School and Executive Director of the Charles Hamilton Houston Institute for Race and Justice. His many books include *The Road to Abolition? The Future of Capital Punishment in the United States* (coedited with Austin Sarat; NYU Press).

Paul H. Robinson is Colin S. Diver Professor of Law at University of Pennsylvania Law School. He is coauthor of *Law without Justice: Why Criminal Law Doesn't Give People What They Deserve* (with Michael Cahill).

Austin Sarat is William Nelson Cromwell Professor of Jurisprudence and Political Science at Amherst College and Justice Hugo L. Black Visiting

Senior Scholar at the University of Alabama School of Law. He is the editor or author of numerous books, including *Mercy on Trial: What It Means to Stop an Execution.*

Jonathan Simon is Adrian A. Kragen Professor of Law at University of California, Berkeley, and author of *Governing through Crime: How the War on Crime Transformed American Democracy and Created a Culture of Fear.*

Index

Aristotle, 40, 65n195

Arizona: LWOP reform, 202; penal practices, 100; rehabilitation, 101, 128n22, 128n30

Arkansas, 95n112, 253, 256, 258

Arroyo, Randy, 75

Ashcroft, John, 168

Asian Americans, 284

Assistant U.S. Attorneys (AUSAs), 124

Atkins, Susan, 253, 275n152

Atkins v. Virginia, 232

Attica prison (New York State), 75, 295

Austria, 78, 79, 196

"bare life," 100, 109, 123

Barkow, Rachel: collateral consequences of noncapital sentences, 182; death penalty abolitionists as obstacles to LWOP reform, 259–260; LWOP and abolition of the death penalty, 169; LWOP justification, 88; morally salient differences in cases, 43; procedural protections in LWOP cases, 16–17; Supreme Court and death-in-prison (DIP) sentences, 87; Supreme Court's death penalty jurisprudence, 231–232; "two tracks" of constitutional sentencing law, 56n69

basketball sentences, 228

Baze v. Rees, 181, 208

Beard, James (Pennsylvania secretary of corrections), 281n252

Beccaria, Cesare, 73, 235

Beckett, Katherine, 99, 117, 118, 135n150

Bedau, Hugo Adam, 236, 252, 261

Behavioral and Mental Health Court model, 301

Belgium, 78, 196

Bennett, Thomas, 114–115, 125

Berg, Nicholas, 173

Berman, Doug, 186n52

bifurcated trial structure in death penalty cases, 11, 25, 31, 81

Black, Conrad, 98

"black-letter law," 187n72

Blackmun, Harry, 45, 180–181, 215n27, 232

Blackstone, William, 40

Blair, Danya, 138

Blecker, Robert, 1, 5

Bloody Code, 26–35; capital punishment, contemporary, 29–32; death penalty, 11; enforcement of, 26, 27, 29, 41; equitable discretion, 26; errors of severity, 32; harsh punishment, 50n7; LWOP statutes, 11; mandatory LWOP sentences, 26–29, 32–35

Blume, John, 5–6

Bordenkircher v. Hayes, 37, 57n83

Boston, 118

Bowden, Bobby (prisoner), 114. See also *State v. Bowden*

Bowers, Josh, 10–11, 207, 210, 231

Brazil, 79

Brennen, William, 215n27

Bright, Stephen, 232

Brill, Steven, 261

Britain, 196

Briton v. Rogers, 23n42

"broken windows" approach to policing, 135n150

Brown, Jerry, 247, 249, 250, 256

Brown, John, 173

Brown, Jordan, 244

Brown v. Board of Education, 181–182, 290

Brown v. Mississippi, 178–179

Brown v. Plata, 305

Bugliosi, Vincent, 275n152

Bulgaria, 106

Bundy, Ted, 250

Burger, Warren E., 81–82

Bush, George H. W., 69, 112, 254

California, 246–251, 293–296; asylum and mental hospital commitments, 299–300; commutations, 255, 256; death penalty, support for, 3; fiscal/social disaster, 248–250; harsh punishment, 284; incapacitation, commitment to, 19, 293–296; indeterminate sentencing, 101; JLWOP, 220n89; juvenile lifers, 243; Lanterman-Petris-Short Act (1969), 299; life sentences, 138, 246; Los Angeles, 118; LWOP reform, 267; LWOP sentences,

Cuomo, Mario, 261
Cyprus, 196
Czech Republic, 196

Dahmer, Jeffrey, 250
Dallas Morning News (newspaper), 171
dangerousness: chronic spouse abuser,
    161n26; criminal records as proxy for,
    142–144; error rates in estimating future
    dangerousness, 201; habitual criminal
    statues, 143; incapacitation, 293; lengthy
    prison terms, 295; of offenders, 14; pedo-
    philes, 162n30; requirement to inform
    jury of LWOP when raising future
    dangerousness, 262
Darley, John, 40
Dauzart, Noel, 85–86
Davis, Gray, 69, 192
death: American obsession/fascination
    with, 15–16, 173–174; lifers' preference for
    death over life, 44, 75, 176; Stewart on,
    Potter, 1
"death is different" jurisprudence: finality,
    43–44; Graham v. Florida, 231; LWOP
    sentences, 15; myth of death's difference,
    42–45; prosecutors, 169; Thomas on,
    Clarence, 10; U. S. Supreme Court, 43,
    191, 194, 209–210, 231–232
death penalty: advocacy against, 186n52;
    Bloody Code, 11; California, support for
    in, 3; categories unfit for, 212; deterrence,
    217n43; Europe, 289–290; exclusion/
    containment, permanent, 16, 122; fair-
    ness in, 180–181; finality, 43–44; juvenile
    offenders, 208; LWOP sentences as
    alternative to, 2–5, 15–16, 32, 46, 66, 173,
    259, 263; LWOP statutes, 11; mandatory
    LWOP sentences, 10; moratorium on,
    44, 170; "new death penalty," 71, 125, 190;
    as "new 'peculiar institution'", 180; pro-
    portionality review, 11; public support
    for, 74; reinstatement of, 232; reinvigora-
    tion of, 16; retribution, 197–198; severity,
    44; temporal implications, 122
death penalty abolitionists: blacks, ban-
    ishment of, 180; Capers on, I. Bennett,

15; capital punishment, 173; death,
    fascination with, 173–174; the innocent,
    focus on, 259; LWOP reform, obstacle
    to, 16, 18, 191, 259–260; LWOP sen-
    tences, advocacy of, 2–3, 5–7, 15, 66, 74,
    169, 197–198, 208, 229–230; prisoners'
    response to, 263–264; Ryan, George,
    174; slavery abolitionists, 180; successes,
    174, 195; tough-on-crime politicians,
    66, 182
death penalty cases: bifurcated trial struc-
    ture, 11, 25, 31, 81; "death penalty mode,"
    124, 167–169; morally salient differences,
    43; procedural protections, 122–123,
    167–169; racial discrimination, 168, 173,
    178; rape cases, 178; staffing, 168
Death Penalty Evaluation form, 167
death penalty sentences. See also death
    sentences: drop in, 3, 6; Furman v.
    Georgia, 169–170; juries, 31; justification,
    139; legislatively enumerated aggravating
    factors, 31, 54n44; LWOP sentences, 21;
    retributivism, 139
death penalty statute, Georgia's, 186n40
death row inmates: appeals dropped by, 75;
    North Carolina, 174–175; number of, 87;
    population growth, 6
"death row volunteers," 44
death sentences. See also death penalty
    sentences; death-in-prison (DIP)
    sentences: administration of, 25–26;
    availability of, 208; commutation of, 9;
    death-in-prison (DIP) sentences, 12;
    dehumanization, 124; discretionary,
    25; discretionary jury sentencing, 52n,
    52n23; drop in, 74; equitable discre-
    tion, 25; following Gregg v. Georgia, 179;
    juries, 184n18; LWOP sentences, 3, 83;
    mandatory, 52n23, 82; particularized
    sentencing, 11
death-in-prison (DIP) cases: capital cases,
    68; capital punishment, 72–80; imposi-
    tion of, commonplace, 68; irrevocabil-
    ity, 72, 76–77; procedural protections,
    80–87; redemption, possibility for, 72;
    standards for, 68

death-in-prison (DIP) sentences, 66–95; academic studies of, 67; arbitrariness in, 12; capital punishment, 67–68; capital-style jury sentencing for, 46–47; death sentences, 12; definitions, 68–71; dignity, 68, 72, 75–76, 78; exclusion/containment, permanent, 76; human rights, 12, 68, 78; implications, practical and theoretical, 87–89; imposition of, arbitrary, 67, 83–87; international opposition to, 67, 78–79; LWOP sentences, 66–67; noncapital sentences, 66; for nonviolent drug offenses, 85; number serving, 66, 67, 87; release, possibility of, 12; repeal efforts, 88; review of, 89, 91n22; scrutiny of, 12; severity, 66–67, 72, 73–75; tough-on-crime politicians, 73

dehumanization, LWOP sentences and, 16

deontological desert, 145–146, 148

desert or justice principles. See also rehabilitation: central demand, 156; crime-control potential, 145; criminal law's moral credibility, 149; deontological desert, 145–146, 148; empirical desert, 15, 145–146, 148; justice, inherent value of, 145; LWOP reform, 202–203; LWOP sentences, 138–139, 140, 145–157, 202–203; Model Penal Code, 139, 151–152; moral blameworthiness, differences in, 139, 146, 156; ordinal ranking demands, 146–148; parole boards, 144; shared intuitions of the community, 148–151; utility of desert, 148–152

determinate sentencing: American penal system, 101, 103–104; contemporary, 29–30; equitable discretion, 49; individualized capital sentencing, 30–31; law-and-order conservatives, 30; left-liberals, 30; legislators, 30; mandatory sentencing, 47; mandatory-minimum statues, 29–30; sentencing guidelines, 29–30; unconcern with particularities of individual cases, 120; U. S. Supreme Court, 30–31; war on drugs, 30; Wilson's "wicked people" argument, James Q., 103–104

deterrence: American penal system, 119; cost vs. benefits, 141; death penalty, 217n43; effectiveness, 140, 151, 156; efficiency, 140; exclusion/containment, permanent, 119; LWOP sentences, 14, 120, 138–139, 139–142, 159n5, 197; offender's awareness of deterrence-based rule, 140; perceptions of, 141–142; punishment, 14; punishment, certainty vs. severity of, 235; punishment rates, 141; recidivism, 172; release presumed at some point, 159n5; three-strike laws, 141

Dieter, Richard, 208

dignity, 282–310; Abrahamic traditions, 287; African Americans, 290; capital punishment, 78; death-in-prison (DIP) sentences, 68, 72, 75–76, 78; the dignity difference, 286–291; Eighth Amendment, 305; end-of-life care, 19–20, 297–298, 305; Europe, 12, 19, 284–285, 287, 288, 289–290; fear and, 303; *Graham v. Florida*, 285–286; history of the concept, 287–289; as inalienable right, 288; libertarian values, 290; LWOP reform, 19–20, 284, 286; LWOP sentences, 12, 286; mental health treatment, involuntary, 299–302, 305–306, 309n61; mental illness, 19–20; mercy, 35; punishment process, 298; reintegration, 290, 298; risk and, 283–286; same-sex marriage, 19–20, 302–304, 306; total incapacitation, 292–296, 304–305; United States, 19, 289, 290–291; Whitman, James, 19

DIP. See death-in-prison (DIP) sentences

disadvantaged background, culpability and, 54n41

disproportionate sentencing, 210–213, 230–233; drug offenders, 211; Eighth Amendment, 123, 191, 205–206, 210–211; life sentences, 147–148; LWOP reform, 191, 210–211, 212–213, 230–233; LWOP sentences, 16, 17, 212–213; mandatory LWOP sentences, 210; mandatory minimums, 210; noncapital cases, 123; noncapital sentences, 211; U. S. Constitution, 213; U. S. Supreme Court, 230–233 distributive principles. See desert or justice principles; deterrence; incapacitation

District of Columbia, 71, 256–257

DNA, 56n69, 174

Dolovich, Sharon, 12–13, 89, 234

Dominican Republic, 168

Donaghey, George, 253, 258

Douglass, Frederick, 173

Dow, David, 56n69

"Drop the Rock" campaign, 238–239

drug offenders: arrest of, 160n16; disproportionate sentencing, 211; federal defendants sentenced to whole-life sentences, 33; LWOP sentences, 204

Drug Policy Alliance, 237–238

Dukakis, Michael, 69–70, 112, 201

Duncan v. Louisiana, 39

Dünkel, Frieder, 252

Duval, Patrick, 256

Eighth Amendment: all sentences, applicability to, 194, 211; cruel and unusual punishment, 146–147, 172; dignity, 305; disproportionate sentencing, 123, 191, 205–206, 210–211; *Furman v. Georgia*, 30; *Government of the Virgin Islands v. Gereau*, 9; *Graham v. Florida*, 177, 285; JLWOP, 79; LWOP reform, 194; noncapital cases, 177; noncapital offenses, 32–33; prison conditions, 291; *Schick v. Reed*, 9; U. S. Supreme Court jurisprudence, 181, 194, 209–210, 305

Eisenhower, Dwight David, 9

El Salvador, 79

empirical desert, 15, 145–146, 148

end-of-life care and dignity, 19–20, 297–298, 305

England: 17th to 19th century criminal justice system, 11; Bloody Code (see Bloody Code); Criminal Justice Act (2003), 307n12; early juries, 51n13; executions during Henry VIII's reign, 27; felony murder, 242; life imprisonment, 78; life sentences, 197, 251; "whole life tariff," 285

Enlightenment, 287

equitable discretion, 25–65; abuse of, risk of, 35; Bloody Code, 26; capital cases, 49; capital sentencing, 42; conviction/guilt phase, 25, 49; criminal justice system, contemporary, 26; death sentences, 25; determinate sentencing, 49; equitable perspective, 36; juries, 39–41, 47; juries, modern, 34; juries, premodern, 27–28, 33–35; lay sentencing discretion, advantage of, 39–41; legal and administrative discretion, 36; LWOP cases, 10–11, 47; LWOP reform, incorporation in, 45–49; mala prohibita conduct, 43; mandatory LWOP sentences, 25–26, 32–33; mandatory sentencing, 26; mercy, 31, 65n195; noncapital cases, 43; prosecutorial discretion, 35–38; prosecutors, 26, 34, 36–37; punishment decisions, 45–46; sentencing discretion, allocating, 41–42; sentencing/penalty phase, 25, 49; U. S. Supreme Court, 42–43

Erbo, Jose ("Pinquita"), 168

Europe: capital punishment, 78; death penalty, 289–290; dignity, 12, 19, 284–285, 287, 288, 289–290; executive clemency, 285; harsh punishment, 285; lengthy prison terms, 79; life imprisonment, 79; life sentences, 197, 251–252, 308n25; LWOP sentences, 12, 78, 285; punishment regime, 19; reintegration, 290, 298; retribution, 251–252

European Convention on Human Rights, 196, 288

European Court of Human Rights, 79, 284–285, 290, 291

European Union, 78, 286–287

"evolving standards of decency," 232–233

Ewing, Gary, 82, 84, 172

Ewing v. California, 9, 172, 230

exclusion/containment, permanent: American penal system, 8, 13, 96–105, 110, 121; "broken windows" approach to policing, 135n150; collateral consequences, 115–118; death penalty, 16, 122; death-in-prison (DIP) sentences, 76; deterrence, 119; exclusionary authority, 118; LWOP sentences, 8, 13, 16, 96–105, 110, 121–122, 179–180; moral division between respectable and non-so-respectable, 135n151; "no-go" orders, 118; "off-limits" orders, 117; prisoners, irredeemability of, 13, 17, 122; punishment, 119; reintegration, 110, 122; retribution, 119; trespass laws, 117–118; "zones of exclusion," 117

ex-convicts: "bare life" of, 100, 109; legal disabilities placed on, 115–116, 136n153; obstacles to successful reentry, 115–116; social marginalization of, 99–100, 108

executive clemency, 255–259; atrophy of, 229, 255; Europe, 285; frequency of, 193; *Graham v. Florida*, 192, 193; LWOP reform, 192–193; LWOP sentences, 68; mercy, 258; noncapital cases, 77; parole, 193; penal reform, 255–259; prison population, 253; rarity of, 90n15; retributive theory of clemency, 257–258; U. S. Supreme Court, 77, 192; use of, drop in, 253

Federal Bureau of Prisons, 291
Federal Death Penalty Act (FDPA, 1994), 167, 169
federal government, 5, 68
Feld, Barry, 22n32
felony convictions: collateral consequences, 99, 119; drug violations, 141; legal disabilities following, 116, 121, 136n153; number (2006), 96; "states of exception," 127n17
finality, 43–44, 122
Florida, 68, 83, 84, 118, 234
Fort Lauderdale, Florida, 118
Fourteenth Amendment, 9
France, 78, 197, 286, 308n25
Frase, Richard, 203
French Revolution, 173
Frontline (television series), 155–156
Furman v. Georgia: backlash after, 260–261; capital punishment, 184n12; capital sentencing, 30; commutations resulting from, 255–256; cruel and unusual punishment, 184n12; death penalty

sentences, 169–170; decision, basis of, 184n12; Eighth Amendment, 30; Louisiana's 10/6 law, 278n204; LWOP sentences, 16, 169–170; LWOP statutes, 260–261; mandatory LWOP sentences, 30; racial discrimination, 264; reliability in capital sentencing, 6; states' response to, 208

Garrido, Phillip, 250
Garvey, Marcus, 290
Gawande, Atul, 176
general incapacitation, 295
Georgia: capital cases, 225n131; death penalty statutes, 186n40; mandatory LWOP for habitual offenders, 83; prisoners over fifty, 7; racial discrimination, 186n40, 215n27, 265; three-strike law requiring mandatory LWOP sentences, 4
Georgia Board of Pardons and Paroles, 193
Georgia State Board of Pardons and Parole, 69
Germany, 78, 196, 251–252, 286
Goldberg, Arthur, 264
good-time credit: indeterminate sentencing, 101; lengthy prison terms, 71; North Carolina, 113–114; Sentencing Reform Act (1984), 157
Gottschalk, Marie, 17–19, 95n113, 169, 195
Government of the Virgin Islands v. Gereau, 9
Graham, Terrance, 79, 265
Graham v. Florida, 192–195, 203–205; adolescent brain development, research in, 243; categorical challenges to sentences, 206, 210; cruel and unusual punishment, 177, 190; "death is different" jurisprudence, 231; dignity, 285–286; Eighth Amendment, 177, 285; executive clemency, 192, 193; hope, denial of, 233–234; JLWOP unconstitutional for nonhomicide cases, 9–10, 17, 48–49, 79–80, 177, 192, 212, 217n46, 233–234, 285–286; Kennedy, Anthony, 204, 251, 305; LWOP reform, 190, 229, 243; LWOP's unique severity, 12, 68, 72, 79–80, 177; offenders

human rights: capital punishment, 12, 78; Charter of the Fundamental Rights of the European Union, 290; death-in-prison (DIP) sentences, 12, 68, 78; European Convention on Human Rights, 196, 288; European Court of Human Rights, 79, 284–285, 290, 291

Hungary, 106

Hutto v. Davis, 82

Illinois: JLWOP, 220n89; life sentences, 233; moratorium on capital punishment, 44, 174, 180–181; parole, elimination of, 68; penal modernism, 292; Pew Center partnership, 95n112

Illinois Prisoner Review Board, 220n89

imprisonment. See also life imprisonment: antisocial tendencies, exacerbation of, 97, 99; cannabis offenders, 237; communities, effect on, 8; cost of housing prisoners age forty to seventy, 7; exclusion/containment, permanent, 8, 13, 96–105; high-status model of, 288; incarceration rate, 228; LWOP sentences, 12–13; mass incarceration, 18–19; percent federal lifers convicted of drug offenses, 85; power and function of, 12–13; racial control, 98–99, 127n11; "reintegrationist" attitude toward, 13; robbery, typical sentence for, 271n62; solitary confinement, 176

In re Marriage Cases, 302

incapacitation, 142–145, 292–296. See also exclusion/containment, permanent; American penal system, 109, 119, 284; California's commitment to, 19, 293–296; civil rights concerns, 295; dangerousness, 293; effectiveness, 142, 143, 151–152, 156; efficiency, 142; emergence as penal rationale, 292; general incapacitation, 295; LWOP sentences, 14, 22n28, 120, 138–139, 142–145, 197; nondangerous offenders, 144; preventive detention, 13, 142, 144–145; prior criminal records as proxy for dangerousness, 142–144; prison officers, 295–296; public safety, 302; punishment, 14; recidivism, 172;

rehabilitation, 292–293; total incapacitation, 109, 292–296, 304–305; wastage of resources, 144

incarceration rate, 227, 228

indeterminate sentencing: 1970s, 29; American penal system, 101, 203; California, 101; disillusionment with, 266; good-time credit, 101; liberals, 198; parole, 101; rehabilitation, 198; rejection of, 198

Indiana, 4, 95n112

"individualization, non-segregation, and progression" principles, 298, 309n53

Inman, Amelia, 22n28

inmates. See also death row inmates; LWOP inmates: older prisoners, 95n113, 133n115, 255–257, 265–266; respect among, 136n152; subhumanity of, perceived, 115

Innocence Project, 18, 175

International Criminal Court, 196, 251

International Criminal Tribunal for Rwanda, 196

International Criminal Tribunal for the former Yugoslavia, 196

Iowa, 68, 233

isolation, punitive. See also exclusion/containment, permanent: American penal system, 106; incapacitation, 292; paranoid psychosis, 176; slowing of brain waves, 176

Italy, 78, 196

Jackson, George, 295

Jacobson, Nora, 287

Jamriska, Bobbi, 246

Jenna's law, 309n61

Jim Crow, 264

JLWOP (life imprisonment of juveniles without possibility of parole), 243–246; African Americans, 22n32, 203; Amnesty International, 263; California, 220n89; cruel and unusual punishment, 79; Eighth Amendment, 79; Florida, 234; *Graham v. Florida,* 9–10, 17, 48–49, 79–80, 177, 192, 212, 217n46, 233–234,

noncapital sentences: collateral consequences, 182; death-in-prison (DIP) sentences, 66; disproportionate sentencing, 211; invalidation of, 82; number serving, 186; unconstitutional, 206

"non-segregation" principle, 298, 309n53

nonviolent offenses and parole reform, 91n22

North Carolina: commutations, 256; death row inmates, 174–175; good-time credit, 113–114; lengthy prison terms, 113–115; life sentences, 240; penal reform, 95n112; racial discrimination, 174–175; three-strike law requiring mandatory LWOP sentences, 4

North Carolina Department of Corrections, 240

North Carolina Fraternal Order of Police, 114

North Carolina Supreme Court, 133n117, 240

North Carolina Victims Assistance Network, 114

Norway, 78

NOVJL (National Organization of Victims of "Juvenile Lifers"), 246

Nussbaum, Martha, 31, 35, 65n195

Obama, Barack, 254, 276n164

O'Connor, Sandra Day, 172

"off limits" orders, 117

Ogletree, Charles, 182–183

Ohio, 2, 95n112, 255, 257

Oklahoma, 258

Oklahoma State Penitentiary, 75

Oshinsky, David, 264

Other Death Penalty Project, 263–264

Padilla, Eladio ("Caco"), 168

Parchman Farm prison (Mississippi), 253–254

pardons: atrophy of, 255; Kennedy, Anthony, 258–259; mercy, 258; Obama, Barack, 276n164; political risks, 255; presidential, 254; Ryan, George, 258

parole, 109–115; abolition of, 68; in California, possibility of, 13; disappearance of, 13, 68, 109–115; eligibility for (see parole eligibility); executive clemency, 193; fate of, 198; fear of being "Willie Horton-ed," 112; in federal life cases, 56n72; *Graham v. Florida*, 193; high-profile mistake, 201–202; indeterminate sentencing, 101; life imprisonment, 68–70; life sentences, 111; life with the possibility of parole in capital sentencing, 46; lifers, 170; LWOP reform, 17, 198; LWOP sentences, 193; premature parole of violent felons, worries about, 5–6; recidivism rate, 7; reintegrationist systems, 97; release, average time served before, 69; release, correctional supervision following, 166n66; release, fallibility of, 256–257; release, fraction of parole applications resulting in, 69; release, geriatric, 256–257; release, meaningful opportunity to obtain, 193–194; release, political resistance to, 111–112; release, possibility of, 12, 43, 68, 99, 104, 110–111, 184n18, 233, 293–294; release, predictors of success following, 105; release, right to, 214n21, 214n23; release, systematic denial of, 119–120; release at some point, presumption of, 159n5; release of nonviolent offenders, 173

parole boards: composition, recommended, 257; desert or justice principles, 144; qualification for membership, 257

parole eligibility: African Americans, 8; California, 111, 113; LWOP inmates, 22n28; "Marsy's Law," 113; minimum time served before, 71; Texas, 101

parole reform, 91n22

parole reviews, 119–120

Parsons, Joseph, 75

Patterson, David, 238

Pearl, Daniel, 173

Pelican Bay prison (California), 106

penal modernism, 292

penal populism, 291

penal reform, 227–281. See also LWOP reform; Alabama, 95n112; below-the-radar efforts, concentration on, 248;

proportionality review: appellate level, 49; capital punishment, 30–31; categorical disproportion, 32; death penalty, 11; *Graham v. Florida*, 48–49, 205, 206, 210–211; *Harmelin v. Michigan*, 82, 205–206; LWOP sentences, 9, 32; noncapital cases, 82–83; U. S. Supreme Court, 32–33, 48–49, 81, 82–83, 210–211, 230–231, 284

proportionate punishment, 120

Proposition 5 (California), 250

Proposition 8 (California), 303

Proposition 9 (California), 249–250

Proposition 66 (California), 247–248

prosecutorial discretion: legal and administrative discretion, 36, 57n83; mandatory LWOP sentences, 35–38

prosecutors: bargaining power, 26, 34, 37–38; capital sentencing, 42; "death is different" jurisprudence, 169; discretionary power, 40; equitable discretion, 26, 34, 36–37; habitual criminal statues, use of, 37; LWOP sentences, 26, 34, 170; LWOP statutes, 262; plea bargaining, 26, 36–37, 53n34; requirement to inform jury of LWOP when raising future dangerousness, 262; transfer of policymaking authority from legislators to, 37; win-at-all-costs mentality, 36

"protective pairing," 108

Pruin, Ineke, 252

public safety: incapacitation, 302; lengthy prison terms, 236; life sentences, 236; LWOP sentences, 7

punishment. See also disproportionate sentencing; exclusion/containment, permanent: America's problem with, 304; certainty vs. severity, 235; deterrence, 14; dignity in the process, 298; equitable discretion, 45–46; Europe, 19; exclusion/containment, permanent, 119; imagination, 176; incapacitation, 14; justifications of, penological practices and, 136n157; legitimacy of, 121; ordinal ranking of, 146; proportionate punishment, 120; purpose of, 14–15; "results matter" criterion, 162n39; retribution, 14, 88–89,

197, 251; traditional rationales, 182; United States, 19, 20; Wilson's "wicked people" argument, James Q., 103–104

punishment rates, 141

racial control, 98–99, 127n11

racial discrimination: in capital charging and sentencing, 45; capital punishment, 177–178, 264–265; *Coker v. Georgia*, 178–179, 182; death penalty cases, 168, 173, 178; *Furman v. Georgia*, 264; Georgia, 186n40, 215n27, 265; *Graham v. Florida*, 265; *Gregg v. Georgia*, 264; JLWOP, 22n32, 203, 265; life sentences, 177; LWOP sentences, 7–8, 22n32, 179; *McCleskey v. Kemp*, 173, 178, 179, 215n27, 265; North Carolina, 174–175; three-strike laws, 179; U. S. Supreme Court death penalty jurisprudence, 178–179, 264–265

Racial Justice Act (North Carolina, 2009), 174–175

Ramsey, Millard, 22n28

Rapaport, Elizabeth, 257

rape cases: capital punishment, 264–265; death penalty cases, 178; LWOP sentences, 23n42; for rape of black women, 178

Rathbun, Mark, 71

Reagan era, 104

recidivism: age, 235–236; deterrence, 172; incapacitation, 172; juvenile offenders, 199; lifers, 112, 133n115, 235–236; older offenders, 95n113, 133n115, 255–257; parolees, 7; rehabilitation, 198–200; released murderers, 236

Reconstruction Amendments, 178

redemption, 72, 258

reentry: LWOP reform, 266; obstacles to successful, 115–116

rehabilitation: abandonment of, 101; aim of, 101–103; American penal system, 13, 100, 101–104; Arizona, 128n22, 128n30; community-based programs, 102; conservatives, 198; current state, 201; disillusionment with, 266; high-profile mistake, 201–202; incapacitation, 292–293; indeterminate sentencing, 198; juvenile offenders, 199, 203; LWOP reform, 198–203; LWOP sentences, 159n5; recidivism, 198–200; rehabilitation of, 17; reintegration, 102–103; rejection of, 198; release presumed at some point, 159n5; rise of, 200–201

Rehnquist, William, 39, 101, 257–258

reintegration: American penal system, 97, 102–103, 104, 110; definition, 97; dignity, 290, 298; Europe, 290, 298; exclusion/containment, permanent, 110, 122; rehabilitation, 102–103

Rendell, Ed, 254

retribution: American penal system, 119, 197–198, 252–253; death penalty, 197–198; empirical desert, 15; Europe, 251–252; exclusion/containment, permanent, 119; *Graham v. Florida*, 251; international law, 310n66; Kennedy, Anthony, 25 1; LWOP sentences, 14–15; moral-desert concept, 14–15; penal reform, 251; popularity of, 18; punishment, 14, 88–89, 197, 251

retributive theory of clemency, 257–258

retributivists, strict: LWOP sentences, 3–4

reversal rate: capital cases, 77; noncapital cases, 77

Rhodes v. Chapman, 106

Richardson, Bill, 73

Richmond, Virginia, 118

Richter, Curt, 157

right to counsel, 47

risk and dignity, 283–286

robbery, median loss associated with, 271n62

Roberts, John, 80

Robinson, Paul: desert or justice principles, 202; fine-grained analyses by juries, 46; LWOP and community's view of justice, 40; LWOP justification, 88, 94n109; punishment, purpose of, 14–15; traditional rationales for punishment, 182

Rockefeller, Winthrop, 258

Rockefeller drug laws, 238–239

Romania, 196

Romano, Michael, 248

Roosevelt, Franklin Delano, 254

Roper v. Simmons: adolescent brain development, research in, 243; death penalty for juvenile offenders, 208; juvenile offenders, 203, 217n46, 232; LWOP, rethinking/banning of, 243; Texas, effect on, 171, 262; victims' rights advocates, 245

Rudolph v. Alabama, 264

Rummel, William James, 146–147

Rummel v. Estelle, 82, 152, 154

Russia, 106

Ryan, George: death penalty abolitionists, 174; moratorium on capital punishment, 44, 174, 180–181; pardons, 186n47, 258

Sabol, William, 237

same-sex marriage and dignity, 19–20, 302–304, 306

San Quentin prison (California), 295

Sarat, Austin, 182–183, 257

Scandinavian countries, 228

Scheck, Barry, 263

Schick v. Reed, 9, 230

Schmidt, Norman, 71

Schwartz, Robert G., 244

Schwarzenegger, Arnold, 69, 247–248, 249, 253

Scottsboro Boys case, 178

Seattle, Washington, 117–118

Sebelius, Kathleen, 7

security housing unit prisons (SHUs), 294

Sentencing Commission, 161n28

sentencing discretion, 41–42

sentencing guidelines, 29–30, 56n69

"sentencing math," 29

Sentencing Project: cost of housing prisoners age forty to seventy, 7; life imprisonment, 83; life sentences, reports on, 252; number serving life sentences, 110; recidivism rate of lifers, 236; release, average time served before, 69

Sentencing Reform Act (1984), 157, 161n28

severity. *See also* harsh punishment: death penalty, 44; death-in-prison (DIP) sentences, 66–67, 72, 73–75; lengthy prison terms, 71; life imprisonment, 75; LWOP sentences, 12, 44, 66–67, 68, 79–80, 177

Sex Offender Treatment & Evaluation Project (SOTEP), 200

"sexual slavery," 108

Shafer, Raymond, 254

Shapp, Milton, 254

Sheleff, Leon, 9, 72

Simmons v. South Carolina, 262

Simon, Jonathan, 19–20, 109, 115, 185n36

Sing Sing prison (New York State), 234

Singel, Mark, 70

Sirhan, Sirhan, 251

slavery: abolitionists, 180; American toleration for degradation, 19; harsh punishment, 289; "sexual slavery," 108

Slovakia, 106

Soales, David, 238

Social Security benefits, 265–266

Socrates, 73

Solem v. Helm, 48, 82–83

solitary confinement and slowing of brain waves, 176

SOTEP (Sex Offender Treatment & Evaluation Project), 200

South Carolina, 4, 83, 84, 238

South Dakota, 68, 233

Spain, 78

Sparf v. United States, 52n19

Stanford Three Strikes Project, 248

State v. Bowden (North Carolina), 114, 125, 133n117

"states of exception," 109, 123, 125, 127n17

Steiker, Carol and Jordan, 175, 186n45, 186n52, 208

Stephen, James Fitzjames, 28, 51n11

Stevens, John Paul, 181, 208

Stewart, Martha, 98

Stewart, Potter, 1

Stimson, Charles D., 245

Stowe, Harriet Beecher, 173

Stuntz, William, 37, 40, 240

Sullivan, Joe, 265

Sunbelt Justice (Lynch), 128n22, 128n30

supermax prisons, 106, 176

Swarthout v. Cooke, 214n23

Sweden, 196, 228

Switzerland, 78, 197

Tacoma, Washington, 256

Tate-LaBianca murders, 253

Tea Party, 290

Tennessee, 4, 69, 74

Tenth Circuit Court of Appeals, 9

Texas: commutations, 255; JLWOP, 243; "life row," 262; LWOP statutes, 170–171, 208, 262; parole eligibility, 101; penal reform, 95n112; prisons, 128n22; *Roper v. Simmons,* effect of, 171, 262

Third Circuit Court of Appeals, 9

Thirteenth Amendment, 289

Thomas, Clarence, 10

three-strike laws, 4–5, 246–250; African Americans, 179; California, 82, 84, 88, 94n111, 172, 179, 204, 242, 246–250, 294; CCPOA (California Correctional Peace Officers Association), 247–248, 249, 250; deterrence, 141; *Ewing v. California,* 172; federal government, 5; felonies covered, 4–5; Georgia, 4; habitual criminal statues, 2; Indiana, 4; *Lockyer v. Andrade,* 172; Louisiana, 4, 84; LWOP sentences, 2; mandatory LWOP sentences, states with, 4–5; Maryland, 4; Montana, 4; New Jersey, 4; North Carolina, 4; number sentenced, 4–5; racial discrimination, 179; South Carolina, 4; Stanford Three Strikes Project, 248; Tennessee, 4; Utah, 4; Virginia, 5; Washington, 5; Wisconsin, 5

total incapacitation, 109, 292–296, 304–305

tough-on-crime politicians: death penalty abolitionists, 66, 182; death-in-prison (DIP) sentences, 73; LWOP sentences, 2–3, 5, 66

trespass laws, 117–118

tricoteuses, 173, 175

Truman, Harry S., 254

"truth in sentencing," 161n28

Turkey, 106